TRANSFORMATIONS OF MIND

Transformations of Mind deals with issues that cut across the disciplines of philosophy, theology, religious studies, and Buddhist studies, and moves between moral philosophy, philosophy of religion, and aesthetics. Written by a philosopher, it is also a work of self-inquiry. The fragments of autobiography it contains reflect the kinds of perplexity that have traditionally led people towards philosophy as a way of making sense of their lives. Unfortunately, many of those who have approached contemporary philosophy in this spirit have been alienated, not by its difficulty, but by its disconnection from life and its suffocating refusal of subjectivity.

The autobiography also charts a progress from an ancestral version of Christianity towards non-theistic, Buddhist forms of spiritual exploration.

The book offers, then, a conception of philosophy as an activity that begins already before reflection, in silence and meditation, which are conceived as conditions for the emergence and cessation of contending states of mind that influence perception and action. The philosopher thus becomes a kind of cartographer of a shifting interior landscape.

Michael McGhee draws on both the Greek and Buddhist traditions, recognising that it is time for Western thinkers to acknowledge and respond to an intercultural canon. His aim is to integrate ethics and a non-theistic philosophy of religion through the medium of aesthetics, mapping Buddhist 'mindfulness' and the Greek virtues and vices of temperance and licentiousness, continence and incontinence, onto an account of the development of the moral sentiments and their relation to practical judgment in the context of oppressive political and social realities.

MICHAEL McGHEE is Lecturer in Philosophy at the University of Liverpool. He was founder of the *Convivium* series of meetings between British and Indian philosophers, and is editor of *Philosophy, Religion and the Spiritual Life* (Cambridge, 1992).

TRANSFORMATIONS OF MIND

Philosophy as Spiritual Practice

MICHAEL McGHEE

University of Liverpool

CAMBRIDGE UNIVERSITY PRESS

PUBLISHED BY THE PRESS SYNDICATE OF THE UNIVERSITY OF CAMBRIDGE
The Pitt Building, Trumpington Street, Cambridge, United Kingdom

CAMBRIDGE UNIVERSITY PRESS
The Edinburgh Building, Cambridge CB2 2RU, UK http://www.cup.cam.ac.uk
40 West 20th Street, New York, NY 10011-4211, USA http://www.cup.org
10 Stamford Road, Oakleigh, Melbourne 3166, Australia

First published 2000

Printed in the United Kingdom at the University Press, Cambridge

Typeset in Monotype Baskerville 11/12¼ pt. [SE]

A catalogue record for this book is available from the British Library

Library of Congress cataloguing in publication data
McGhee, Michael.
Transformations of mind: philosophy as spiritual practice /
Michael McGhee.
p. cm.
ISBN 0 521 77169 2 (paperback) – ISBN 0 521 77753 4 (hardback)
1. Philosophy. 2. Buddhism and philosophy. I. Title.
B72.M39 2000 100–dc21 99-34667 CIP

ISBN 0 521 77169 2 hardback
ISBN 0 521 77753 4 paperback

Phoebus is dead, ephebe. But Phoebus was
A name for something that never could be named.

Contents

Acknowledgements

Earlier versions of much of the material I have worked on and used in this book appeared originally as follows: 'In Praise of Mindfulness' in *Religious Studies*, 24, 1988, 65–89; 'Temperance' in *Philosophical Investigations*, 12, 1989, 193–216; 'Notes on a Great Erotic' in *Philosophical Investigations*, 13, 1990, 258–72; 'A Fat Worm of Error?' in *British Journal of Aesthetics*, 31, 1991, 222–9; 'Facing Truths: Ethics and the Spiritual Life' in *Philosophy, Religion and the Spiritual Life*, ed. McGhee, Cambridge 1992 and in *Journal of the Indian Council for Philosophical Research*; 'Chastity and the (Male) Philosophers' in *Journal of Applied Philosophy*, 10, 1993, 45–58; 'Individual Buddhists' in *Religious Studies*, 29, 1993, 443–52; 'Another Part of the Wood: Reflections on Recent Indian Philosophy' in *Journal of Applied Philosophy*, 11.1, 1994, 113–16; 'The Turn Towards Buddhism' in *Religious Studies*, 31, 1995, 69–87; 'Drugs, Ghosts and Self-Knowledge' in *Journal of Applied Philosophy*, 12, 1995; 'The Locations of the Soul' in *Religious Studies*, 32, 1996, 205–21; 'After *Dover Beach*: Arnold's Recast Religion' in *The Edinburgh Review of Theology and Religion*, 4, 1998, 84–106; 'Moral Sentiments, Social Exclusion, Aesthetic Education' in *Philosophy*, 74, 1999, 85–103; 'Drawing from Life: Representing a Spiritual Tradition' in *The Edinburgh Review of Theology and Religion*, 5, 1999.

Introduction

Listen, wisdom is something dared, and what matters beyond all else in philosophy, which is the love of wisdom, is a spirit of inwardness, which you have to cultivate for yourself, a practice of inner silence, even before reflection, which philosophy is thought to start with. Inwardness lets in another possibility, a new position from which what had seemed the very terms of reflection can come to be reflected upon. It is a moment of philosophy, therefore, before analysis, which it then inspires, but if it is absent analysis is sterile.

Philosophy is also a conversation, and what matters beyond all else here is demeanour, how we listen, how we speak or write, not seeking dominance, not indifferent to the well-being of the other, but encouraging inwardness, a friendly, even an 'erotic' spirit, and we have to learn when thinking can be shared, when its communication can only be indirect, and when we have to stay silent.

This is a record of conversation and self-inquiry, conversation with teachers and friends, and between a younger and an older self, in which my past has corrected my present, I hope, as much as my present has my past. One may be ashamed of a younger self, but also be shamed by it. I began this piece of writing in 1982, in the midst of a period of personal disarray and a few months before the Falklands/Malvinas conflict. Some may be disconcerted by sudden shifts of temporal location, but I do not apologise for the way in which ideas assert and reassert themselves over long periods of time and in different contexts. The readers I have addressed, sometimes half-consciously, reflect a progress, strangers who have looked at me askance and disapproving, or companions, travelling mostly at night, when there is more to see, when the presence or absence of clouds matters and is not conformable to the will, or so it seems, until the will alters or subsides, and there everything is, quite visible, then disappears again. I have revealed more of myself than is usual in British books of philosophy, books in which the person of the author is often not there, at least not consciously, as what must also be shown. The intrusion, as it may appear, of the states of my own subjectivity, will be judged a lapse of taste by some, and they may be right, though I believe that these 'contrary states' set limits on what I can do as a philosopher. But in treating of yourself, 'how can you generalise the one case so irresponsibly'? Well, one has to gamble that 'the one case' turns out representative, take the same risks as the poet. It will be found so, or not.

Philosophy, the love of wisdom, but what does that cant, that pious, phrase mean? Love of something we know? And if not, how can we love what we do not know? We have to define it by contrast, by the *endurance* of non-wisdom, as it were, the palpable sense of ignorance and delusion, sudden sense but mostly darkness, and perhaps something answers to a longing and perhaps not. My late teacher, Peter Winch, wrote a book called *Trying to Make Sense* (1987), a pregnant title, poignantly illustrated on its cover by Magritte's *Les Amants*, trying to say to another what one can hardly say to oneself: in making sense one emerges as a person into the world, though it takes another to receive it: 'are even lovers powerless to reveal / To one another what indeed they feel?' And it suggests a perplexity, a trying to *understand* that there is genuinely something there, not yet available to our condition, and an attempt at *making*, at *poiesis*, language something that we build out of the right silence, sense something we make, – *jäher Sinn*, a sudden sense – as we come to a new understanding of things, formerly concealed, an understanding that coheres at the point of expression only, after enduring *aporia*, living with no sense of a road ahead, and then there it is again, the sign of a path. My talisman is Keats's *Negative Capability*, defined in a letter to his brothers in 1817 as 'when man is capable of being in uncertainties, Mysteries, doubts, without any irritable reaching after fact and reason'. Some philosophers reach very quickly and very irritably after fact and reason, but maybe we have to learn from the poets, if we are to *make* sense. Winch is associated with Wittgenstein and Simone Weil, and I have learnt a great deal from, come on, I have been *formed* by, the work of all three of them. But what you learn or need to learn depends on where you started, and though this is a book of philosophy it also (it *thereby*) reflects a laborious, slow progress, a day-labouring sometimes, Wirral, the Mersey and Liverpool, the Dee, the Welsh hills in the distance, hares started in the fields below Storeton Woods, the fifties, a grim, penitential and authoritarian Catholicism, seminary, philosophy and the loss of faith and years of teaching, a slow transition, to Buddhist practitioner, not 'believer', for my emphasis is on the interior conditions of action rather than on *belief* or, worse, 'conviction'. But the introduction of Buddhism renders transcultural the canon of reference and possible inspiration, and is a sign of the times, as we enter an Interculture, the only help against the destructive values that have accompanied the global market. So I have been addressing 'thinkers', philosophers, theologians and Buddhist scholars, specifically perhaps those concerned to make sense, if not of religion then of spirituality. I have tried to make sense of an alien but compelling Buddhism in terms of western thought, and to look again at western thought in terms of Buddhism, in terms, that is, of a Buddhist *naturalism*. I have followed the trail of those who have returned to the Greeks, in my case to Plato, finding a troubled, human philosopher. My understanding of Plato, such as it is, has developed in response to Nietzsche. I have felt forced to move backwards and forwards between them, impressed by both, trying to adjudicate, trying to reconcile. The form of my personal life, which I so irresponsibly generalise, has forced me at the same time towards reflection on the relations between reason, feeling and sensuality, and on the Greek virtue of *enkrateia* or self-control and the vice of *akrasia* or lack of control, in a way which I hope brings the two sets of themes into convergence. Thus I have also discovered meaning in the virtue of *sophrosune*, which seems to be like self-control, which is in fact its imitation and beginnings. *Sophrosune* has been translated sometimes *as* 'self control', which is unfortunate, but more often as 'temperance'. I have tried to connect it with, to illuminate it by, the Buddhist virtue of mindfulness (*smrti samprajanya*) since it seems to me that 'temperance', as a relaxed relation to desire and appetite, is rather a concomitant of *sophrosune* than the thing itself. Aristotle offers an etymology and tells us that it 'protects wisdom' (meaning 'practical wisdom', the capacity for undistorted judgement and unimpeded right action, *phronesis*) and so I have associated it with the practice of meditation and the virtue of mindfulness, both of which have an outcome for the *body*, its states of energy, our relation to it. Meditation or *dhyana* has an effect on the body as well as upon the mind, upon the one being, and that has led me to think in terms of a 'dhyanic' or a 'dhyanised' body. So, I have approached 'the spiritual life' non-theistically, beginning from a position, which I share with others, of post-Christianity. But that is where I came to and then moved on from. My Christianity dissolved, at length, but it was a degenerate form, from another time than this one, and I remain in sympathy with certain profound theologians and thinkers who remain still within a still forming Church. I have been addressing them, quite sure that I can learn from them and from the Christian tradition, but sure also that Christianity needs to understand more than it now does about world spiritual traditions, not to mention spiritual practice, e.g., *meditation*, which is not a practice for an elite, but appropriate and possible for most people. And that is another theme of this book, another range of possible readers. We westerners can hardly now do philosophy as though there were no Asian or East Asian traditions from which we can learn, especially given the early examples of Schopenhauer and Heidegger, though by that token, Asian thinkers may also be able to learn from the west, an ironic thought, because they have often been forced to, in a way in which we have never had to know about them, and that is an embarrassing imbalance which makes both for resentment and conceit. I have tried, I am bold to boast, to do philosophy of religion in a new way, a way that has moved on from a western preoccupation with the issues of natural theology, though those issues still have a place and cannot be ignored. There are philosophers I respect who are theists, 'Platonic theists'. Philosophy is a strange game, given to fashion, a most unphilosophical tendency, since philosophy must constantly look to its own assumptions, to what it had not noticed it had taken for granted, which is why it needs to start in silence. There are philosophers too clever and quick, too clear about what they think, too assured about their command of good sense, to give close attention to their own premises, and they are just the ones most likely to deride the theists . . . if they are not theists themselves, the comedy of opposite views and equal conviction. I hope I do not deride them myself. But I do disagree with them. Or rather, their arguments seem only to articulate what would be the case if they were right, they express their *belief*. But so do their opponents. So I disagree with both, theists and atheists alike, with a proper agnosticism. But disagreeing here gives one work to do, and what I have attempted is a description of a non-theistic spirituality. I have friends enough who have struggled with religion, who have struggled in particular with *belief*, seeing it as the gateway to religion. If only I could believe . . . is what they say. I have attempted a philosophy of religion into which I have sought to integrate both aesthetics and moral philosophy, to make them all one single, integrated thing. Though I also disclose the secret ambition of all aestheticians, to show that aesthetics is the *sine qua non* of philosophy. To be more specific, the concept of the 'aesthetic idea', and its connection with the free play of imagination and understanding, developed in Kant's third Critique, the

Critique of Judgment, provides, I think, a wonderful description of one of the fruits of inwardness. It describes the conditions for a shift in sensibility, and has a more powerful role, since it illuminates the structure of sense. Kierkegaard tells us that subjective thinking requires 'indirect communication', which is essentially 'artistic'. Such communication, I suggest, is a matter of introducing an *image*, the evocative image that constitutes Kant's aesthetic idea: under the condition of receptivity that poetry or art can itself engender, conception occurs. There is a quickening around the image of its field of connections. To put it more Platonically, the image *begets its kind* in the mind of the other. It is a form of what Diotima is made to call 'procreation in beauty', one which produces the spiritual progeny of wisdom and virtue, perhaps. So the task of the philosopher is to capture the structured movements of mind and action, coiled up unseen in particular thoughts and particular actions, but unfolding and flickeringly displayed by the power of the imagination in aesthetic experience. Philosophy is also reflection on experience, then, but reflection on a particular *kind* of experience, that of the *sense* of mind and action: philosophy must wait upon art and beauty.

At the heart of my account is the idea of *Besinnung* and *Besonnenheit*, a certain quality of attention, and a self-possession that is an *outcome*, not a principle, the development of both of which is a condition of revelation . . . perhaps. But the most significant revelation that has come to me, and I owe it to Tanabe Hajime, the Japanese philosopher, and to Simon Tugwell, is that human imperfection, properly understood, is a main route to knowledge. Once we start to talk of human imperfection we have to get the tone right. I do not know whether I have. But there is anyway a stiff and mainly male resistance to tones of voice associated with the acknowledgment of human failure, one which has its own tone of voice, strangely, of moral reproof, the unconscious disguise of resentful embarrassment, and the issue is how we are to do philosophy at all. I have gone for explorations of human subjectivity and what it might reveal about the world that remains undisclosed to one who does not follow that path. But that doesn't absolve me from objectivity about just those matters. It is all to do with what one thinks one should be objective *about*. My turning to Buddhism was a matter of my *imagination* being seized by the metaphors of awakening and the mental poisons and release. Unlike that of the existence of God we here have questions which seem in principle determinable, though I think theological language, in spiritual *situ*, may be a plumbline, into the depths, but V. S. Pritchett's character in *Our Wife* might be right when she opines that it is only a theory that plumblines go down straight. I believe I have developed a plausible kind of ethical naturalism in which so-called 'moral language' is reinterpreted and grounded in a well or badly informed responsiveness to others, an *appreciation* of them that motivates action and restraint. The point about the Greek virtues that I have mentioned is that I try to show them to represent stages in the development of this responsiveness, in the development of a sensibility which may give rise to imperatives, but is not founded on any such, a sensibility which can be strengthened and widened in its scope, under the pressure of historically determined conditions. But this responsiveness to others still has to contend with issues about what constitutes well-being and harm. There is a temptation, not wholly to be resisted, which makes us rest in an ultimate pluralism about conceptions of well-being and human flourishing. However I have sought to temper the diversity of ultimate ends with the thought that human beings live either in the light of knowledge and understanding, or in the false light of delusion, or the darkness of ignorance.

I have learnt from many teachers and colleagues, some of whom will look askance at what I seem to have taken from our conversations. Ah, yes, conversations, with philosophers, and academic colleagues from other disciplines . . . and with students. I must not be nostalgic about those days before the cuts, before the new social controls depressed and undermined the university community, alienated its members from one another and from their students. Now it is a hurried word, a snatched, a compressed exchange, in for teaching, away again for 'research', to publish the demanded pound of under-considered flesh. I doubt whether I could have written what lies ahead if I were starting out now, in the present atmosphere of institutional neurosis, in which the 'research assessment exercise' penalises long-term projects, so that someone who has not published within the period is counted as 'not research active', and 'pulls down' their department. I was given space to develop as a philosopher in the time that it takes, never forced to seek to put into print what I was not ready to put my name to. So I remember with gratitude the serious philosophical culture sustained by the East Anglia philosophers, until they were forced to shake the dust from their heels. I owe much to Martin Scott-Taggart and the late Martin Hollis, to early conversations with David Corker. More recently I have been sustained by the friendly scepticism of my colleagues at Liverpool, and by the culture established there by Stephen Clark, in which I felt free to think as I needed to. Terry Diffey and Timothy Sprigge were enormously encouraging when I needed encouragement most, and I was glad of the shrewd comments by David Bastow on a pretty formless draft of this book. Over the years my greatest debt has been to Michael Weston, Anthony Gash, David Cockburn, Robert Morrison, Prabodh Parikh and Probal Dasgupta, for their friendship, conversation and conviviality, though I cannot say what would have become of me without the subtle *kalyanamitrata* of Sangharakshita or the generosity of members of the Order he founded.

CHAPTER ONE

'A philosophy that is not a philosophy'

I

I had thought to say that philosophers need to remember that they are also human, but how does that make them different from anyone else? And yet, thinkers, philosophers, stand in a particular relation to their own humanity because they offer representations of our human relation to reality, and their vocation rides upon an interior acknowledgment of human *weakness*. If humankind cannot bear very much reality, then what philosophers cannot bear cannot be disclosed or represented by them either, our experience will be too narrow, our discernment too weak, and so our philosophy fail through the failure of our humanity. So we fail if we are too weak, but one of the conditions of success is a due recognition of weakness . . .

. . . It depends on our response to our limitations and the manner in which we discover them. But it has been an abiding fear of mine, that the state of my own humanity, the way I think and feel, the way I *act*, or fail to act (soured by my deeds) may also affect, adversely, my philosophy, my capacity to see, to see error, to see ordinary truths. (And is the nature of that fear that I shall be *found out*? There are surely other reasons, of a more pressing kind, to take care of the self – for the sake of others, for instance, who are harmed in proportion to our not taking that care.)

But one thing at a time. It is frightening, that the way I am, the way we are, may distort perception, perhaps deeply distort it, and we not know it, be quite blind. And there is nothing more chilling than to hear the deluded speak, with complete confidence in themselves. Maybe the distinction between appearance and reality, in its human applications, is grasped in an overcoming of delusion that depends upon interior conditions, upon upheaval and radical change . . .

One problem is that philosophy is so *contested*. It is not that contest, or *agon*, is bad in itself, *au contraire*. But there are different conceptions of what it is to do philosophy at all, and there are these *guardians* of particular conceptions of philosophy, who are not prepared to recognise anything that falls outside the terms of the conception they guard, in a tense conceit of selfhood. Certainly there are many activities embraced within the field of philosophy, all of which have their place; the difficulty comes when people identify philosophy itself with one particular set of activities. For example, I can imagine a familiar kind of philosopher who would honestly not see what the fuss I am making about interior conditions and human frailty was all about. Surely, they would say, philosophical questioning is straightforward enough once you get the hang of it. There are questions about the nature of mind, about the logical relations between statements, the structure of our concepts, that can be dealt with quite 'objectively', without all this reference to the moral virtue of the philosopher. Well the claim was not so much about virtue as about its absence, but essentially they are *right* about what they specify. The mistake is to *reduce* philosophy to this particular set of activities, often premised upon assumptions about how the world really is that *may* after all derive from a too 'narrow body of accepted consciousness'. In any event, maybe philosophy depends upon an *awakening*. I thus make a Buddhist connection, but also allude to Heidegger's treatment of truth as *aleitheia* – the truth is something that had escaped one's notice and is now apparent, something you awaken to, a sudden sense of the before unapprehended relations of things. You are not looking in philosophy for correct but unrevealing definitions, but for illuminations of the field of sense, increase in understanding, the sight of what was formerly concealed from view. The shape of an expression's magnetic field shines for a few moments, then disappears again. The task of the philosopher is to trace the pattern that reveals itself only for moments and then slips from sight. This, I ought to say, brings Heidegger close to Wittgenstein's notion of grammar and perspicuous representation, a connection caught, perhaps, by Gottfried Benn's (1963, 99) '*Ein Wort, ein Satz-: Aus Chiffren steigen / erkanntes Leben, jäher Sinn*': 'A word, a phrase – out of ciphers rises recognised life, sudden sense'. It also brings Heidegger and Wittgenstein very close to the Kantian concept of an aesthetic idea, but that is for later.

I am not opposed to conceptual analysis, to the analytic tradition, far from it, the world needs it. The mistake is to suppose that you can go on in headlong and start analysing concepts and their logical relations, *before* you realise the form of your own subjectivity. Something prior is required, an *ascesis*, that is not easy to describe, but its spirit can be evoked. An attitude of humility does not catch it, the term has been too much abused, it is a certain quality of receptive attention that needs to be cultivated first. Inwardness or interiority are the conditions upon which philosophy depends: analyse, if you like, what then swims into view, and certainly do not dissect your impressions until they have worked on your soul.

I am telling a very old story, to which it is so hard to *listen*, even though listening is the very theme. Matthew Arnold sees it clearly, this inwardness of spirit, which is in peril from our mechanical and material civilisation, and now from our electronic compulsions, but is the condition of the imagination, in free play, the condition of culture, an inward operation, from which we are ruthlessly distracted. Thus Arnold, but it is Kant he is following.

2

The Japanese philosopher, Tanabe Hajime (1986), wrote a book first published in 1946, which he called *Philosophy as Metanoetics*.[1] It has a startling thesis, announced with humility in his moving Preface. Language is such a delicate instrument, is it not, and words can so easily be misunderstood, especially those which we know by rote and have no profound relation to. The startling thesis is that if you want to be a philosopher you need to confess your sins and repent.

This is profound as well as startling, since it more or less gives us everything. Why do we have to confess our sins and repent in order to do philosophy? Well, the claim is that it is already a part of philosophy. The condition of self is a crux. Repentance and transformation already invoke essential polarities, that there are states of the self in which it is submerged in ignorance and delusion and strikes out wildly, and a state of being awake, and the painful transition, from a scattering of distracted and dissipated energies to some kind of unity, from a state in which one is incapable of acting well to one in which one sometimes finds oneself doing what is needed without, it seems, any effort of one's own.

---

[1] The title alludes to the New Testament notion of *metanoia*, which has the sense of a profound change of mind, a conversion suggesting repentance for the past.

That way of putting things, stressing repentance, has a context, the situation of the Japanese at the end of the last war, and the notion of 'repentance' was a political theme, not always sincere. Tanabe describes his feelings as the war finally turned against Japan, the moral dilemma about whether or not to speak out against the government's public evasiveness, its inability to reform, its suppression of criticism, all freedom of thought, its secrecy; but it also seemed traitorous to express ideas that might 'end up causing further divisions and conflicts among our people that would only further expose them to their enemies' (*l*). Tanabe tells us he was tormented by his own indecision, and wondered whether he should go on teaching philosophy or give it up 'since I had no adequate solution to a dilemma that philosophically did not appear all that difficult'. He spent his days wrestling with his doubts, driven to the point of exhaustion, and in his despair concluded that 'he was not fit to engage in the sublime task of philosophy':

At that moment something astonishing happened. In the midst of my distress I let go and surrendered myself humbly to my own inability. I was suddenly brought to new insight! My penitent confession – metanoiesis (*zange*) – unexpectedly threw me back on my own interiority and away from things external. There was no longer any question of my teaching and correcting others under the circumstances – I who could not deliver myself to do the correct thing. (*ibid.*)

'I was suddenly brought to new insight.' The dilemma was resolved, it became clear what he should do. Presumably the resolution *came* to him. It was not so much that he *decided* that he should do the one thing or the other: the point is that he no longer had to make a decision. We are dealing with the interior conditions upon which doing philosophy may turn out to depend – if philosophy articulates truths whose disclosure depends upon just those conditions. And notice the lack of choice implied in that forceful metaphor of being thrown back:

The decision was reached, as I have said, through metanoia, or the way of *zange*, and led to *a philosophy that is not a philosophy*: philosophy seen as the self-realisation of *metanoetic consciousness*. It is no longer I who pursue philosophy, but rather *zange* that thinks through me. In my practice of metanoesis, it is metanoesis itself that is seeking its own realisation. Such is the non-philosophical philosophy that is reborn out of the denial of philosophy as I had previously understood it. I call it a philosophy that is not a philosophy because, on the one hand, it has arisen from the vestiges of a philosophy I had cast away in despair, and on the other, it maintains the purpose of functioning as a reflection on what is ultimate and as a radical self-awareness, which are the goals proper to philosophy. (*ibid.*)

Tanabe is drawing on New Testament turns of phrase, specifically the Pauline, 'It is not I who live but Christ who lives in me.' He is also drawing on the New Testament notion of *metanoia* and relating it to the Japanese term *zange*. We are going to need to relate the idea of being thrown back upon one's own interiority to that of a radical transformation, or at least a shift of perspective, of the kind referred to by Tanabe in a way which connects it to penitence and confession. (*Zange-do* is a *practice* of penitence and confession, an integral part of a Buddhist life, for Tanabe, a thought we need to dwell on, openly making amends for wrong-doing, as he does in his own text, not being ashamed of the limitations of his humanity, but seeing them as a condition of transformation and movement.) There is a more immediately problematic issue. Tanabe says that 'it is *zange* that speaks through me', that 'it is metanoesis itself that is seeking its own realisation'. The suggestion seems to be that an awakening consciousness is working its way through the philosophy, that the consciousness to be achieved is already active, bringing itself to awareness, and that it is triggered by the recognition of failure and human limitation. In other words, the consciousness is already an ethical one, and it is intimated in the midst of action by the experience of remorse. It suggests at least that our doing philosophy will alter as this consciousness advances, showing things to be described we would not otherwise have seen. The process of awakening is an awakening to what is the case, particularly, perhaps, to what you have *done*, or what the community you are a part of or are associated with has done, which becomes part of your own past. You realise the damage you have done, with a vivid awareness, perhaps, that you cannot repair it. (Remorse tells you something about what you have done or failed to do, but is at the same time an introduction to yourself.)

Tanabe spells his thought out in more detail, in terms that derive from the tradition of Pure Land Buddhism. Specifically, his experience of exhaustion and despair leads him to the distinction between 'self-power' (*jiriki*) and 'other-power' (*tariki*).[2] In introducing his discovered conception of 'a philosophy that is not a philosophy' Tanabe writes:

To be sure, this is not a philosophy to be undertaken on my own power (*jiriki*). That power has already been abandoned in despair. It is rather a philosophy to be practised by Other-power (*tariki*), which has turned me in a completely new direction through metanoesis, and has induced me to make a fresh start from

---

[2] In the context of devotion to Amida Buddha, the contrast is between what depends upon one's own efforts and what depends upon the compassionate help of Amida himself.

the realisation of my utter helplessness . . . This Other-power brings about a conversion in me that heads me in a new direction along a path hitherto unknown to me . . . This is what I am calling 'metanoetics', the philosophy of Other-power. I have died to philosophy and been resurrected by *zange*. It is not a question of simply carrying on the same philosophy I had abandoned in my despair, as if resuming a journey after a temporary interruption. It cannot be a mere repetition without negation and change. In the life of the spirit, 'repetition' must mean self-transcendence; 'resurrection' must mean regeneration to a new life. (*li*)

The New Testament allusions are clear here too, but the ideas are transposed into the context of Pure Land Buddhism, in which faith in the saving power of Amitabha is paramount. Such faith must give us pause in the context of philosophical reflection. We need to dwell on the nature of such faith and raise serious sceptical questions. More immediately we should note the metaphors of path and journey, the distinction between a well-trodden path and a familiar destination on the one hand, and the idea of a new direction and an unfamiliar path on the other. Sometimes it is not clear that what lies ahead is genuinely a path, and nor are you sure where you are supposed to be going, or even whether there is anywhere to go, but you are lost and cannot follow the old way. The Buddhist concept of *sraddha* or 'faith' is traditionally construed as an increasing confidence in a path, one moves forward hesitantly, without certainty, with misgiving, and then the path becomes more definite, broader, clearer.

In fact Tanabe does not make it very clear how the vision of philosophy as metanoetics really arose in his own case. It seems from what he has written that in a despair that followed a serious struggle with his moral dilemma, he experiences an unexpected shift of perspective, in which the dilemma resolves itself, and in which he suddenly *sees* that the goals of philosophy, understood by him as 'reflection on what is ultimate and as a radical self-awareness' depend on the sort of interior change and awakening he has undergone: for one thing, it brings home to him the need to distinguish between 'self-power' and 'Other-power'. The felt need to make sense of the experience of *tariki*, I suggest, forces him to see how the interior state of the inquirer determines the capacity to see. He cannot continue to do philosophy, if I may gloss it thus, simply as an objective investigation into conceptual relations, because he has realised that perception of the truth depends upon a shift in the interior conditions of inquiry, conditions that become manifest even in the midst of thoroughly acknowledged human failure.

There is a surely pressing question for a philosopher already apparent. Tanabe invokes the concept of *tariki*, but how are we to assess the corresponding notion of an invisible higher being, Amitabha the Compassionate One, who comes to his assistance and in doing so shows him the limitations of *jiriki*? Moreover, it might be said that Tanabe sounds like a Christian, and perhaps deliberately so, with a particular audience in mind: we could as well be invoking the Compassion of Christ as that of Amitabha. Christ and Amida are in the same case, it would seem. 'It is no longer I who live, but Christ lives in me.' If philosophical scepticism is the virtue of epistemological vigilance, as I think it is, we need to look carefully at the conditions of these invocations.

The question can be sharpened up further by looking at an example with some points of comparison, in which the question turns not on the figures of Amida and Christ but on God. However, before doing that there is a further point. Our assessment of what Tanabe, or a similarly disposed Christian, has to say, depends very much on the *application* of the key terms they are using. We cannot just take it for granted that we know what this is. When people start talking about repentance and confession of sins we need to be sure about what they are *calling* 'sin' in the first place, and what they count as 'repentance', before we make our excuses and run. There is a remark in Kierkegaard's *Concluding Unscientific Postscript* that one man may agree with another word for word and both be guilty of the grossest possible kind of misunderstanding. They might both agree about the connections between sin, repentance and confession, for instance, but be radically apart in the phenomena they call by these names . . . and not notice until it is too late. (So we do not grasp the *sense* of such expressions independently of the kind of reference.)

3

Tanabe's moving account of his exhausted despair recalls the condition of Tolstoy (1987) as he describes it in his *Confession*, though perhaps Tolstoy was in a worse case:

over the course of a whole year, almost every minute I asked myself whether I had not better kill myself with a rope or a bullet. And at the same time as I was experiencing the thoughts and observations I have described, my heart was agonized by a tormenting feeling. I can only describe this feeling as a quest for God. I say that this quest for God was not a debate but an emotion because it did not arise from my stream of thoughts – it was in fact quite contrary to them – but from my heart . . . (63)

Pace Tolstoy, there need be no antithesis between 'a debate' and 'an emotion'. The emotional insistence which went against his 'stream of thoughts' was in fact also a process of thought, towards the idea of God as a cause, the cause of his own being. Tolstoy could well be brought into play in a discussion of the efficacy of the traditional proofs, which have sometimes been represented as merely intellectual and remote from religion. Tolstoy's emotion has the *form* of a cosmological argument. His official position is that Kant and Hume have disposed of the proofs, but his heart forces him to ask questions about his origins. That does not make the argument 'valid', of course. But this is a *maternal* cause he is talking about: 'I cannot hide myself from the fact that someone who loved me gave birth to me. Who is this someone? Again, God.'

Even though he was convinced that Kant had shown that the existence of God was indemonstrable, Tolstoy was drawn to think in those terms and his thinking thus, under the conditions of stress that he described, had an outcome:

'He knows and He sees my search, my struggle and my grief. He does exist', I told myself. And I had only to recognise this for an instant and life would rise up within me and I would feel the possibility and joy of living.

Not two or three, but tens of hundreds of times, my mood suddenly changed from joy and animation to despair and a consciousness of the impossibility of living.

It is clear that I do not live when I lose belief in God's existence, and I should have killed myself long ago, were it not for a dim hope of finding him. I live truly only when I am conscious of him and seek him. What then is it you are seeking? a voice exclaimed inside me. There he is! He, without whom it is impossible to live. To know God and to live are one and the same thing. God is life. (64)

Life rising up within him seems also to be both a visitation and the form of an interior, responsive change: 'to know God and to live are one and the same thing. God is life.' Some might take Tolstoy to be implying here that the expression 'knowing God' just *means* 'living', in some presumably exalted sense of that term. But the traditional theological understanding of a phrase like 'God is life' is that it implies that God lives in a higher way than we can understand and is the source and giver of a life we can come to share. So a person knows God to the extent that they enter into, participate in, the life of which he is the source. 'Knowing God' is thus also a state of the person. An essential qualification takes us to the Johannine thought that a person who does not *love* does not know God, so there is an implied connection between love and this entry into life, and a corresponding contrast, easily overlooked, between these positive human phenomena and those more negative, unregenerate ones which mark their absence. The life thus determined is thought to be independent of the vicissitudes of worldly success and failure. So knowing God is certainly not to be *reduced* to any kind of *conviction* of what is the case, though clearly someone who 'knows God' in the sense that their interior disposition and way of life fulfil the criteria is likely to have the corresponding conviction. On the other hand, they needn't. Someone may satisfy the criteria and never give a thought to 'the existence of God', or even think theistically at all.

Our account of the use of theological discourse should not be allowed to founder on the assumption that there is something that counts as *the* use of such language. We have to take account of differences manifested in *lives*, especially since *life* is such a crucial spiritual category, take account of the ways in which the meaning of words is 'printed in the subtle fibres of our nerves'. Or better, we need recourse to different lives in order to show the differences in use. But particular lives may not be accessible to us: as G. H. Lewes said, in a sentence whose meaning it takes a *Daniel Deronda* to spell out: 'We only see what interests us, and we have only insight in proportion to our sympathy.' The extent to which the use of religious language can be described or illustrated is itself limited by our own experience. Who knows, for instance, the realities to which Hopkins gives expression when he says 'we hear our hearts grate on themselves . . .' Not everyone can say without foreboding that they comprehend the realities to which he thus refers. Not everyone will know at all what he refers to, what he expresses an attitude *towards*. Similarly, when Tolstoy refers to entering into 'life' we need to be cautious about assuming that we know what he is referring to. Tolstoy is interesting because we cannot really be sure what is going on with him and we must beware of making assumptions about what *must* be going on. A Freudian might be right to pinpoint certain remarks, for instance his description of himself as a 'fledgling': 'if I lie on my back crying in the tall grass, like a fledgling, it is because I know that my mother brought me into the world, kept me warm, fed me and loved me. But where is she, that mother?' In finding God, he has, in reality, the Freudian might say, found the comfort of the mother after the experience of abandonment. The trouble with this though is that while it may in fact be accurate about Tolstoy, there is a danger of a premature closure on the recognition of other possibilities. We may not know what is going on, and it may be that Tolstoy is taking the first steps into forms of life that are currently inaccessible to us as particular individuals, but marked and flagged in various traditions, and there may in consequence be problems about our capacity to show the use of the language he draws on. This scepticism is not grounded in the thought that Tolstoy's experience is essentially private. On the contrary, I am cautioning against the assumption that we are all already familiar with the conditions upon which particular experiences depend. Tolstoy clearly draws on the language of the New Testament and the idea of having life 'more abundantly'. The problem for the philosopher is to give an account of what constitutes this more abundant life: what are the phenomena here referred to, the experience of which is counted as 'knowing God'?

But all this begs the question, someone will say, of how we can be sure that anyone *genuinely* or *really* 'knows God', let alone, to return to Tanabe, genuinely or really knows that Amida or Christ has intervened in their lives. Do we not have to establish first that there really is a God to know, or that it is at least rational to believe that there is? and so forth?

William James (1929, 187) has commented on the Tolstoy passage along with one from Bunyan:

The fact of interest for us is that as a matter of fact they could and did find *something* welling up in the inner reaches of their consciousness, by which such extreme sadness could be overcome. Tolstoy does well to talk of it as *that by which men live*; for that is exactly what it is, a stimulus, an excitement, a faith, a force that re-infuses the positive willingness to live, even in full presence of the evil perceptions that erewhile made life seem unbearable.

James seems accurately to describe the situation both of Tolstoy and Tanabe in his remark that 'they could and did find *something* welling up in the inner reaches of their consciousness' – by which such extreme sadness could be overcome. James's breakthrough seemed to be to offer just this sort of at least quasi-empirical account of what is going on, leaving on one side questions of theological implication. Nevertheless, the question of what 'we' are to make of all this depends very much upon who 'we' are and upon our life experience. The realities of failure, despair, etc., may be alien to us and we may falsely project an accommodating and complacent reading of their situation that satisfies us prematurely.

George Eliot's remark about how we learn words by rote but that their meaning must be paid for with our life-blood, and printed in the subtle fibres of our nerves, can be connected with Kierkegaard's distinction between subjective and objective thinking. And *that* may help us explore further how, for instance, the sense of the distinction between *jiriki* and *tariki* has to be lived through, how *metanoia* or repentance may be the form of a lived reality that changes how we do philosophy. The point is that there is a certain kind of thinking that remains closed to us until we are ourselves thrown back into inwardness, or our own interiority, as Tanabe puts it.

4

In the *Concluding Unscientific Postscript* Kierkegaard establishes a connection between the idea of 'the subjective thinker' and that of 'the existing individual' thus:

While objective thought is indifferent to the thinking subject and his existence, the subjective thinker is as an existing individual essentially interested in his own thinking, existing as he does in his thought. (67)

In a note about this passage, after going on to discuss very suggestively the nature of the communication that is appropriate to these different modes of thought, objective and subjective, Kierkegaard twice makes the point that the existing individual (here the 'religious individual') is in 'constant process of becoming' ('inwardly' or 'in inwardness'). It is clear that these two ideas, 'existing in thought', and being in constant process of becoming, are connected. The contexts to which Kierkegaard appeals at this point are the 'erotic relationship' and the 'God-relationship'. Furthermore, the two references I have just made to different forms of *communication* and to different forms of *relationship* make it quite clear that despite the apparent idealist bias of his focus on *thinking*, and the apparent self-absorption of his preoccupation with *inwardness*, Kierkegaard is quite emphatic that the true individual exists *in relationship*, the form of which changes with, because it *expresses*, changes in the form of inwardness.[3]

Kierkegaard conceives the 'subjective thinker' as 'essentially interested in his own thinking, existing as he does in his thought'. I take the expression, 'existing as he does in his thought', to be an attempt to capture the idea that human energies are constructed around those forms of thought which motivate a person to action, so that they exist and move within horizons of thought which focus their energies and determine their reasons for action. I make the connection with *action* in

---

[3] Cf., what Kierkegaard says about the 'loving maiden' in the note referred to above.

an attempt to alleviate the residual Cartesianism of Kierkegaard's thinking, which sits ill with his emphasis on *relationship*. However, the subjective thinker is *essentially interested* in this thinking, interested, that is to say, in the terms in which their life is led. Here is our key thought again. Strangely, to be interested in one's own thinking requires one to stand outside it, in a condition of *suspension*:

und ganz in der verschweigung
ging neuer Anfang, Wink und Wandlung vor.[4]

'enclosed within this silence/ stirred new beginnings and the sense of change'.

Despite the connotations that an expression like 'subjective thinker' is now likely to have, it seems to me that its sense in Kierkegaard is something like 'the self-aware or self-conscious thinker', so long as we make clear that what we are conscious of as a Kierkegaardian 'existing individual' is the form of our present or habitual thinking. This is an important qualification, since it implies a particular form of self-consciousness, one about which I have already been emphatic. I can be aware of what I am doing, be aware of a particular desire or impulse to action, and be aware of it in terms that reflect my established way of thinking (in the light of which an impulse or desire may appear acceptable or unacceptable, for example). However, to become aware precisely of *my thinking* is to gain a purchase on its totality. This is not an immediately clear notion, but it may be clarified by saying that sometimes a person can develop a distaste or dissatisfaction with the general way in which they interact with others, say, the way they think about others, or themselves, the way they speak about others or themselves, and this unease, if it is *attended* to by one who is 'essentially interested in (their) own thinking', can develop without their always being able to conceptualise the reasons for that pre-reflective unease. Perhaps we could call it a 'pre-reflective *dukkha*', upon which they are now precisely to reflect, allow it space to emerge. In other words, it is possible to develop an attitudinal awareness of my established thinking, but this only makes sense if we can acknowledge, not only that my established ways of thinking can *change*, in a way that determines the form of my own becoming, but also that the submerged terms of that change are already available within the *emergent attitudes* implicit in the new form of self-consciousness. I said at the beginning that what matters beyond all else in philosophy is a spirit of inwardness, and I distinguished

---

[4] (From Rilke's first sonnet to Orpheus.)

this from a merely reflective turn of mind. Perhaps the reason for this may now become clearer. Reflection reflects . . . a pattern of thought. We need to learn how to *suspend* thought, and then to see what emerges out of this silence. Spiritual traditions claim that new possibilities of thinking emerge, ways of thinking that may now provide a point of view upon the thinking that preceded them. This gives a certain sense to Kierkegaard's talk of a *double* reflection: not only must we learn how to reflect, we must learn the means of reflecting upon the forms of our own reflection, learn to be attentive to them. If we were to reflect on our unease, or seek to trace it back to its source, we may well find ourselves in a different space, in which the unease has clarified itself into a conscious attitude to a determinate object, giving form to a self of larger scope, to an enlargement of being which may also at first present itself in the form of an Other-power that stands over against what one had taken to be one's very self.

Kierkegaard contrasts the subjective thinker, the existing individual, who is essentially interested in his own thinking, existing as he does in his thought, with someone who, in a religious or ethical context, *merely* thinks 'in an objective manner'. The latter, remember, is 'indifferent to the thinking subject and his existence', and Kierkegaard implies a corresponding indifference on the part of the thinking subject to the form and content of their own thought. The subjective thinker is contrasted with someone, that is to say, in whom there does not occur what Kierkegaard claims is essential to religious thinking, viz., the subjective appropriation in inwardness of that which is thought, a process in which the individual is transformed *pari passu* with the development of their thought, the thought in which they exist, the thought by which, I suppose, they are worlded. Indeed, the trajectory of the 'constant process of becoming' to which Kierkegaard refers may be said to be traceable *along the path* of what constitutes the *appropriation* of the existing individual's thought. Thus coming to 'know God' in Tolstoy's example, is a process of subjective appropriation, a matter of an internal change to be understood in terms of an access to 'life' through 'love'. None of this occurs in the 'objective thinker's appropriation' of religion. Of course the objective thinker also undergoes change, but whereas the process of attention and inwardness characteristic of the subjective thinker gives space for the formation of emergent possibilities, to an awakening, the fate of the objective thinker is to lose awareness and unknowingly submit to a diminishment of the power of perception and action.

The point we can retrieve from Kierkegaard about 'subjective think-ing' is that it is an activity of thought which, so far from being *external* to the formation of the individual thus engaged, is just what *forms* them as a person. It seems to me that we can connect that point with Tanabe's sense of his being thought rather than thinking – 'it is no longer I who pursue philosophy, but rather *zange* that thinks through me'. What we get is the sense of an emergent consciousness or being in the world, a self of larger scope that seems at least initially to be set over against one's very self, something that comes to one, but prompted by an attentive inward-ness, a waiting on what waits.

This is important: such claims, and I include those of Tanabe, are pre-sumably made on the basis of a *tradition* of accumulated experience of determinate changes in determinate circumstances. *That such changes occur* is the *empirical* ground of Kierkegaard's enterprise, and is the condi-tion of his sensitivity to the difficulties of communication between persons established at different points along the line of transformation, a line of transformation which (if it exists, and we can hardly be neutral here) determines for us the criteria for what it is to be a person in the first place.

It is not that the 'objective thinker' does not 'reflect' upon their life or has no self-awareness. *The terms* in which they reflect upon their life simply *reduplicate* the established way of thinking; *that* is what they fail to reflect upon, the totality of the established way of thinking itself, of which they thus become merely the creature. They do not pay attention to their own impulses of thought, to doubts or contradictions, they do not *listen* to themselves, their own thoughts or their own actions, the margins of consciousness, the snatches of new thoughts and feelings. And this is the essential point: if they did reflect upon their established way of thinking it would have to be 'in terms', though, of course, in *other* terms than those available in the established way of thinking; it would have to be from a point of view, which we should have to understand as an *emergent* point of view, so that the moment of (attitudinal) self-consciousness of the totality of one's way of thinking is also a moment of *revelation*. One way of making sense of what Kierkegaard is trying to say about 'inwardness' and 'subjective appropriation' is to think of certain beliefs or thoughts or facts as having, under relevant conditions, a known *motivational efficacy*, and as having this precisely because such beliefs or thoughts or facts represent the *intentional objects* of an emergent sensibility or form of inwardness. To think such thoughts 'subjectively' is to allow their content to affect one's inwardness, and is to have regard to the form of their impact. The criteria of identity for the thought include the form of that inwardness. To put it in Wittgensteinian terms, the form of one's inwardness represents the *grammar* of one's 'thought' in the sense that one's inwardness is constituted by the constellation of conceptually related other thoughts, images, impulses, etc., which give one's 'thought' its specific identity within a set of relations as the thought that it is. When such a 'thought' is thought 'in an objective manner', on the other hand, *there is no such hinterland*. This is not to say that there is *no* hinterland in the objective thinker: it will simply not be that which belongs to the grammar of the unappropriated thought. It will be the usual preoccupations of the conscious mind.

Kierkegaard talks of the existing individual as in a constant process of becoming, and it is clear that the direction of that becoming is determined by the subtle movements and intimations of the forms of energy that we call *thought*. But it is just here that we can recall the problem of whether indeed we have a genuine path before us or a real direction to go in. The situation is an interior one: essentially, we find ourselves in a position in which there is no well-established and clearly marked path for us to follow after the pronouncement that God is dead, no clear lines of formation left by which we can construct ourselves. All that is left to us is what can be yielded by *attention* and listening: it is just here, in the processes of thought and possible becoming that we can summon the image of hazarding ourselves along what may or may not be a path, what may or may not lead to *aporia*, a 'no through path'. However, it seems to me that as far as Kierkegaard is concerned that is the situation *anyway*, whatever we may think about the death of God: the idea of a well-marked path precisely gives too much room to the objective thinker. They can learn by rote the terms of traditional *Bildung* and not know its always unfamiliar realities. Kierkegaard's remarks about the existing individual being in constant process of becoming allows us to think of ourselves as *constituted* by a series of transformations, regenerate or unregenerate, allows us to think of ourselves, indeed, as radically subject to the process of dependent origination. The forms of consciousness arise in dependence upon conditions, and among those conditions is a certain 'double reflection' or attentive self-awareness upon which there seems to depend the emergence or awakening of attitudes and states of mind that are already a protesting critique of our unregenerate actions, the established impulses, if you like, of the State of Nature, for which we feel a remorse that seems to be working its way within us towards expression.

5

I remarked earlier that there was some unclarity in Tolstoy's account. Does he imply, for instance, that 'knowing God' just *means* living a certain sort of (interior) 'life'? If he does imply that, someone may say, then he is a kind of reductionist or non-realist about theological language, even a crypto-Buddhist without realising it, believing that references to God can be translated into references to a certain way of life, a certain experience of life. This is something to return to, but in understanding the position we need to remember that everything turns on the profundity or otherwise of that 'experience of life'. There can, in other words, be spiritually significant forms of reductionism, as well as trivialising ones. It depends upon the depths swirling below those 'inner reaches of consciousness' mentioned by James. I would say that the investigation of those depths is the real task of the philosophy of religion, and that it has to be a kind of spiritual exercise.

I am inclined, though, to doubt that this is Tolstoy's position. It is true that he was dismayed by the religious attitudes of his own class and the official Church. Lives did not seem to be in any way affected by the faith that they professed, in that sense he was surrounded by people who professed to 'know God' but whose lives showed that by the traditional criteria they did not. It was the poor and uneducated who lived their religion, he thought. Tolstoy came to realise, as he saw it, that knowledge of God depended upon interior change of the kind he sought to describe, upon the reaching of certain human limits. There is no reason to doubt that he was realist about God, in an entirely classical way: knowledge of God in his essence is a gift of grace, Aquinas tells us, and belongs only to the good. It is clear that Tolstoy found *something* welling up, etc., *and* that for him the test or the justifying condition of the claim that someone 'knows God' is whether they 'love', live a certain sort of life. However, a person's entry into this, as it may be, quite real *life*, does not entail that they 'know God', unless we simply stipulate that the former is all we are referring to when we talk of knowing God, and thus become crypto-Buddhist again. To put it another way, what *establishes*, in a certain tradition, the truth of the claim that a person knows God, is their access to this new 'life', but it is not what *makes* it true under that description. Some philosophers may be inclined to say at this point that it is indeed a further question whether Tolstoy knows God. The *criterion* by means of which we are supposed to judge that someone knows God is not identical with the truth condition, and can indeed be described without reference to that truth condition: we can describe the phenomena as they manifest themselves to us without making any reference to theological language, even if it were to turn out to be the case (and how would we find it out?) that to leave out that reference was finally an error.

One way of responding to this on the part of theologians is to invoke *faith* at a crucial point in the proceedings, to say that indeed there is no identity between the assertion condition and the truth condition and that there is no independent means by which we can show that there is a God for Tolstoy to know (e.g. natural theology does not deliver any such knowledge or rational belief). Someone who said that might emphasise that this is just our human condition, our predicament is the predicament of *faith*. There is no means of reassuring ourselves that we are right to believe that living this special life is a criterion of knowing God. It is not just that we are disposed to call such a life 'knowing God': it is our *faith*. The problem with this position, though, is why anyone should be talking about *God* in the first place, as opposed to the human phenomena that Tanabe and Tolstoy describe. Human beings sit round their camp fires . . . the Archbishop reassures us that God loves us as a father loves his children . . . 'this is our *faith*', you may say. A further problem is whether this is the right place to *locate* faith. Isn't it the case that the context of Tolstoy's deliverance is a Christian, theological one, into which language life is breathed by his experience? We *start* with the interior turning about. That is our *given*, whether we are Christians, Buddhists or what it might be. We need to be very cautious indeed, either about minimising its significance or about building up a superstructure of dogmatic *Aberglaube*.[5] Tanabe's account, I suggest, now becomes germane. The phenomenology of his experience forces him into seeing point in a distinction between self-power and Other-power. It is *as though* help comes from outside us at the extreme point where self-power can no longer prevail. This is a crucial human experience, but one has to ask the question whether the distinction is not a perspectival illusion necessary, or at least unavoidable, at a critical stage, but then to be overcome. St Paul asks, 'who can deliver me from the body of this death?' The idea of an outside intervention seems to depend upon an unavoidable identification with a particular sensibility, which you take to be your very self, in such a way that the emergence of one that is more expansive

---

[5] Literally *Aberglaube* means 'superstition', but Matthew Arnold used it as a general term to refer to the structure of dogma that begins with belief in a personal first cause. (See his 1873 *Literature and Dogma*.)

appears a grace from outside. Exhausted by efforts constrained by a particular self-view, we experience an expansion that seems at least a grace of nature. Theologies are built on this. As for philosophy as metanoetics, we learn the subjective conditions of inquiry and knowledge. At the least we discover ourselves, though that 'at least' surely signals ignorance of what such discovery may amount to. Tanabe's philosophy as metanoetics depended upon a particular experience of being thrown back, as he put it, upon his own interiority. It was a shift of consciousness from which emerged 'a philosophy which is not a philosophy'. But Tanabe was modest as well as humble, perhaps too modest. His philosophy that is not a philosophy is so described because he gives some recognition still to what it is not. I suspect his real point is that what it is not is not really philosophy at all. But irony doesn't always catch the attention of a self-confident audience.

CHAPTER TWO

Contrary states

I

But what is the sense of the question, *how should we live?* – where am I supposed to place the emphasis, find the intonation which reveals the fragments of the conversation? The only echo I can find: 'then how *should* we live?' But where does it come from? What has already been said or argued? 'If we shouldn't live like *this*, then *how?*' The question arises out of *conflict*: how *should* we live? how *should* we live? – Not out of serene reflection on the good life, but out of a *frustration* with our own conduct that gives us reason to *explore*, to explore what? – the sources of the frustration. How can we live so that we no longer go on doing *this* or *this?* (And how am I going to fill in these markers?) But it is also a challenge, come on, then, so what's the *answer?* What do you *really* know? Who are you?

We bring about unsatisfactory states of affairs which, under other circumstances, present themselves as the objects of dismay or sympathy, the causes of which we might otherwise seek to remove: but we were the cause . . . and sins of omission . . . we do not will the good with the energy that the good requires. Leave aside, what is the good? Even by our own lights. Energy and unsatisfactoriness, *virya* and *dukkha*, an adjustment between insight and response. We have to realise how *terrible* it all is without being overwhelmed by it.

We should not live like *this*, incapable, unable to possess ourselves of the energy that the good requires. We are sleepwalkers. The real centre of feeling is that events should *force us to conceive strategies*, even if, lamentably, it is only the need to look through the keyhole, which is also a reality, not to look elsewhere. We are creatures working out our lives in ignorance (*avidya*, confident that we *know*), victims of cravings and aversions which mop up our energies and distract our attention from the realities that surround us on every side, not knowing our alienation from the *beings* also there whom we may well conceive as *surrounding* us. Once we recognise the antecedents of the question we can move towards its answer. We already make judgments about what we *ought* to have done, about what we ought not to have done. But what are we *saying?* Let the sounds echo in your mind, until you hear the charge, the resonance, the stress . . .

The resonances are multiple, but for many they are overlain by one awful oppressive sense of guilt and anxiety, the unrelenting bare 'ought' or 'ought not', like the 'thou shalt not' writ over the door. But you can be relieved of the ancestral anxiety, fear of punishment, rescued from the faces of the unsmiling generations. There is no bare, no final 'ought', it is an illusion. You may be so oppressed by the sound of its angry, fearful ultimacy, that you hear nothing else. But the *anger* is worth listening to, and the *fear, they* underlie it. Listening to the sounds of 'ought' and 'ought not' reveals the voices of many emotions and *they* are interesting. There is no such thing as 'the moral ought' except as a symptom of a negative sensibility (Nietzsche). On the other hand, 'ought' may have an entirely different use as the means of unlocking the doors of feeling.

. . . the charge, the resonance, the stress. All right, *remorse* . . . and that is quite different from guilt. But what else? How else can it be said, how else would you stress it? What is the tone of your voice? Might it not be – *bewilderment?* And why should it be that? You saw the point of doing it but failed, you saw why you shouldn't have done it, but you were unable to restrain yourself: and you are *bewildered*: how can that be, that I should fail to do what I intended to do? You have made the old discovery. I ought to have done it . . . here implies the belief that there was reason to think that I *would* have done it. You are saying, perhaps, I *would* have done, I would have not done it, had I been *capable*. You did not have the energy that the good requires. 'We ought not to be like *this*' implies the belief that we are incomplete. We cannot bring to act what we ourselves conceived. 'I ought to have done that' *implies*: I would have done that, had I not been infirm of purpose, because it is just what I conceived of doing. Or I conceived the need for restraint. The initial conditions are absent for being ourselves.

A skinny old woman with thick, long, white hair is sprawled out on her back in sleep on the pavement, part of her blouse has ridden up and a withered breast is there for all to see who pick their way past her. Earlier she had sat on the other side of the traffic barrier, bent over her leg, her hair cascading down, her drawn mouth set in absorption, picking at dirty shreds of bandage stuck along her shin. She is small,

worn out, incontinent, decayed. Someone must be giving her food: she
eats out of two old milk powder tins that she keeps by her, and one of
them has lain at her side with yellow rice spilling out onto the pavement
while she slept. She is by herself, but she is absorbed in herself and mad,
and does not beg, or notice passers-by.

All right, so I will get emotional, we need a little anger to speed our
pulses until our power of action is beyond the need of such injections,
he has realised that he shares the wickedness of the present age, and has
learnt the name of the dark clouds that hang without a wind above the
earth, so that there is nowhere any fresh air to breathe: we do not will
the good. That is all. We do not will the good. That is the word. And
wouldn't any one of us, if it were our own mother, have taken her gently
into our arms, have washed and fed her, given her clean clothes, poor
old *ajee*. And might it not be our own mother, what difference does it
make whose mother it is you shed tears over to be in such a state. It is
not that we want that this should happen, that is not the charge, that we
are devils, the charge is one for human beings: *it is not the case that we do
not want it*. That is the nature of our shame, the minstrel boy to the wars
is gone, in the ranks of death you will find him, oh would that you would,
but our minds are elsewhere, we scarcely notice what it is we begin to
feel as we step over her and slightly frown as though, perhaps, the
thought had been, the street cleaners have been careless here. We do not
want it, no, but nor do we want it not, we do not will the good.

How does 'ought' unlock the doors of feeling? The sense of 'ought'
and 'ought not' is to anticipate, to point towards *reasons* and reasons
reveal the forms of *feeling*. Sometimes it is straightforward and quite conscious. At other times, it is devastating and exciting, since the judgments
express an unease not yet *expressed*, still inarticulate, unrevealed. And
then reasons form themselves and sensibility *shifts*.

In many practical contexts 'ought' is a modal auxiliary whose logical
role is to imply the desirability of (an) action: in other words, it implies
that there is a reason for doing something. A 'desirability-feature' I would
call it, if I was a 'proper' philosopher. You are dead, now, and I think of
you fondly. You were the first one to let me know that I wasn't as 'proper'
as I sought to appear, also to myself. And what after all are 'values'? We
use the term and give no account of our use. I shall say that our values
are not merely reflected in our reasons for action, but are reducible to
such reasons, are a summary reference to the *kind of reason that motivates
us*. (Though we shall have to see what we are calling reasons in the first
place before we can see the significance of *that* claim, shan't we?)

But don't we fail to live up to our own values? Yes. In that case, don't you have to say that our values are not the reasons we act on, but something like, the reasons we *ought* to act on, and that doesn't get us too far, does it? Again, yes. But how should we construe the 'ought'? We should read it as follows: our values reduce to the reasons we act on, or *would* act on, if we were not incapable in some way, would act on *if we could get our act together*.

In other words there is no moral, only a practical and an epistemic ought: the latter a use of 'ought' which implies a reason for belief rather than for action.

You might say that a person's values represent their *horizon of thought*, the horizon of the thoughts that move them. And I say that because I want to find an application for Blake's *Reason is the bound or outer circumference of energy*. I do not mean to include anything that could be called, for example, 'a moral thought' (where its being 'moral' is a function of its form), but simple propositions about what is the case: the case in which living, personal beings stand, especially. It is perceptions and representations of what is or might be the case, that lead to action. More precisely, we are moved to act, and this is not yet to be moved to particular actions, since the latter may be strategies which have to be *conceived*, an intervention of imagination.

So I have to say more about reasons for action. There is a subtle relationship between the practical and the epistemic or inductive use of 'ought'. I am in a position to draw your attention to a reason for action (by the use of a practical ought) because I already recognise (epistemic ought) that just this kind of consideration tends to motivate (you). I found it plausible to say that a statement like 'you ought to give up smoking' does not *state* but rather *implies* a reason for giving up smoking: 'it will ruin your health', perhaps. But a reason is just a thought or perception that moves or engages us. Or, better, in the face of 'considerations', we *move* or seek to act. The judgment implies the belief that some unspoken thought, some unspoken consideration, will make you move. It does not 'offer' you a reason for acting. It just implies something like; you *would* give up smoking if you realised that it will ruin your health; and the statement is intended to *make* you realise (that some such motivation is in the offing). On the other hand, 'you *know* you shouldn't smoke', implies the belief that you *are* motivated by the 'consideration', *but not sufficiently*. That is the heart of the matter. We are moved to action or restraint, but we cannot get it together. You are moved by the relevant thought or scene and if you were moved sufficiently you would not as a matter of fact be doing this. Derelict action or inaction simply implies an (epistemic) deficiency of action, a breakdown between motive and action. A motive is precisely a motive to action, and the impetus needs to be sustained if it is to issue in action. It is this relation that provides the ground of judgments about *how we ought to be*.

But there are two ways in which 'practical ought-judgments' can break down, have to be withdrawn, be *wrong*. It may turn out that the empirical causal connection expressed in the reason – say, 'it will ruin your health', 'make you less attractive' – is false. Or it may turn out that the person you are talking to doesn't *mind* if their health is ruined, if they become less attractive: these may even be things that they want to bring about. Someone may want to live dangerously, go out in a cloud of glory and cigarette smoke, or be indifferent to the consequence. So there is an unspoken assumption here about what the agent *wants* or *would be moved by* (and these are not necessarily the same thing): related to the fact that your ought requires you to enunciate and which they are logically entitled to hear. You can't just say, well, you just shouldn't . . . except that perceptive people cannot always articulate their insights and sometimes a dumb 'you just shouldn't' may be worth listening to.

There is a subtle shift of focus in moral argument or persuasion, from assertions about what you think someone ought to *do*, to assertions about how they ought to *be*, about what *attitudes* they ought to have, for instance. Another way of putting this: when we talk about what you ought to *do*, we refer you to reasons, when we talk about how you ought to *be*, we refer you to your *relation* to reasons. This is very interesting. You are saying, 'well, you *ought* to care', but not on the grounds that there are reasons for caring, as though one were giving someone a reason to *do* something, but rather, the implication is: there is reason to think that you *would* care, you *would* have that attitude, if . . . what? If you were in your right mind? If you were in touch with your feelings? In possession of your own humanity? A substantive claim about what a 'well-constituted' human being is *like*? Attend to the resonances. It may be simple incomprehension or incredulity, you shouldn't be like *that*. In Beirut the other day, soldiers were seen beating up a young woman *who was holding a young baby in her arms*. They ought not to be like that . . . meaning . . . how can it be true that they *are* . . . what is the *explanation*? Then you think you are merely naive. You know well enough the nature of the conditions under which cruelty flourishes, it is, after all, our original condition. And yet still, they ought not to be like that . . . meaning . . . they wouldn't be, if the 'proper' conditions obtained, if they were in their right minds, in possession of their feelings . . . ? The discussion lurches between . . . 'such considerations *ought* to motivate you, i.e., *would* motivate you, if you were capable of action, if you could get your act together, *that* is the direction in which you would move' . . . and . . . 'you *ought* to be obedient to, under the sway of, determined by, such considerations, i.e., you *would* be, if you were in contact with your feelings, your humanity, your "deepest motives"'. Naturally, this posits some 'deepest motives', some account of 'humanity', 'feeling', and isn't that absolutely the crunch? A further determination of subjectivity is required. That then is our task.

We are rendered incapable by many things, slavery to appetite, attachment, inertia, demoralisation, lassitude, the waste of spirit, all the several infirmities of purpose. There is reason for the belief that I would have done it, would have not done it, had I been *capable* of action or restraint. In the face of the refuser's denial, however, the critic's judgment that they ought to care implies, in certain contexts, the belief that the absence of the relevant attitude, or its dormancy, is *anomalous*. However the critic is also expressing an *attitude* to that absence; the tone of the judgement *may* express the very attitude whose absence in the moral refuser is deplored, and whose presence in the critic is no doubt the ground for the judgment that there is reason to believe it will be present in the refuser ('ought to be'). This is not mere presumption. The issue of presumption, or ignorance, comes when we start to discuss the *content* of the attitude.

Reasons for action; we are actually talking, then, about the 'bound or outward circumference' of energy, the conceptual horizon of motive, the determination of which reveals the profile of the species in its present condition, boundaries which are given expression in the language. They are what motivate us or what *ought* to motivate us (in the relevant sense, i.e., *would*, if we could get it together). They are how we *conceive* the alternatives, and such conceptions determine the limits of what is an alternative (for us). But we are members of a linguistic community in which the options that have been conceived and found favour are available in received patterns of thought and practice, patterns into which, of course, we all receive our initiation, but also from which we are all *capable of distance*: by bracketing and negating: so we are able to represent to ourselves the form of alternatives even when we cannot conceive them as real. What I am calling 'reasons for action' are the intentional objects of emotions or motivations, as I shall try to explain. Emotions are just a special case of what I call 'motivations', we notice them because they involve a change in our energy state, of enhancement or diminishment. But first let us trace the contours of feeling. 'Feeling' is ambiguous between sensation and emotion, and the two are not to be

confused. The way in which their difference is traditionally spelt out is
by saying that 'emotions are directed towards an object', (which is what
I referred to when I said that reasons are the intentional objects of emotions). What this means is that your emotions have to be *intelligible*. You
cannot just be proud, or embarrassed or afraid or envious or sympathetic
(though you *can* just be happy or unhappy. Joy and Sorrow are the
general forms of feeling within which specific emotions arise). There has
to be an intelligible story available which shows what you are proud *of*,
embarrassed *by*, and so on. To put it another way, an emotion is directed
at an object as it is perceived *under a certain description*. But the implication
of this is that our emotions are already available to *rational scrutiny*
because the descriptions which attract our emotions are true or false,
grounded or ungrounded. Certain emotions, indeed, have a strength of
their own and come with their own package of systematic misrepresentation. We could say that our 'world' is constituted by the foci of our
emotional lives. It is particular states of affairs, particular facts, that are
the objects of our emotions. But now more needs to be said. Many
people are happy enough to acknowledge that the emotions have intentional objects and that this is how they are to be distinguished from sensations. But they may still see emotions as private stirrings within the
breast, the butterflies, the tightness in the stomach, the knife in the base
of the spine. Now many such sensations form a part of our experience
of the emotions, but they are *not* the emotion itself. In order properly to
understand the emotions we need to see how they are related to *action*.
Properly understood, they are a *strategic orientation* towards the world as
we take it to be. Sartre was right to say that my jealousy just is the need
to look through the keyhole. An emotion is a matter of being moved to
conceive strategies in the face of the way we take things to be, to restore
things, to remedy, to compensate in some way. That is why I said that the
emotions are just a special case of motivation, the being moved to act by
our sense of how things are ('impressions move the soul'). But we notice
them because they involve a change of pace, a change of pulse, and we
notice often the presence of the sensations that accompany them in
advance of their structural relation to action. The conceiving of strategies may remain internal, it may be an oppressive visitation of images
and attempts at compensation. People are also ready to agree with that,
but refuse a further aspect of the emotions, which is that they are not a
part merely of a private inner space of conflict or rejoicing. They are
written in our faces and our bodies, in the totality of our bodily gestures.
That is one aspect of their relation to action. People can act or pretend

because there are characteristic demeanours and states of energy. Now return to the idea that reasons for action are the intentional objects of emotions or motivations. We are moved by *facts* or what we take to be facts, the perception of a certain fact will make us act, will *cause* us to act, or cause dismay, the loss of the power of action. But these facts, as we take them to be, are our *reasons* for action, the facts that move us are our reasons for action. We can draw attention to them, and we scour the landscape for their possibility. I can state a fact which I expect to cause you to act. But they are also the forms of justification for what we have done. We explain *and* justify by referring to the states of affairs that prompted us to act. These are the 'reasons' or 'considerations' which make us act. But there is a further point, that we have to *conceive* the particular action to take. That is an exercise of imagination, not of 'instrumental rationality'.

There is still something else. In order to render a person's action intelligible we have to relate it to the world as they see it, we have to *represent the object* in a relevant way, which shows it to be an appropriate object of that emotion. But that is not enough. We also have to *represent the subject* (the person) in a way that renders it intelligible that *they* should be moved in that way by their perceiving things thus and so: not only the state of the world, but the state of the subject (Alfred Lorenzer). Philosophers distinguish between the object of the emotion and the cause. Among the causes of my being moved in this way is some state of my being. And the states of my being are capable of transformation.

Showing the intelligibility of an emotion is not the same thing as showing it to be 'rational': you have not shown that the emotion is 'rational' or 'rationally warranted' or 'rationally justified' by showing that it is *intelligible*. They are 'rational' by default if they are not irrational in the sense that they depend upon misrepresentation, but that is all. Another way of saying this is that though there are proper or appropriate objects of emotion (objects which belong to particular emotions) it is *not* the case that there are appropriate emotions, just the ones we know about, and those we don't (yet).

One could have a go at describing the 'world' of those soldiers in Beirut, their actual conditions, how they conceive them, how their mentalities are formed by those conditions without their knowledge; at talking about their values, nothing that they have chosen or decided upon, because they are the backing, the determinants of what they do decide or choose, about what they count as a reason at all. And the question is, what is *submerged* by this appetite for violence? What a person acts on, without reflection, is by no means the limit of the range of considerations that they think, on reflection, as counting in the case. But what *some* people take as counting, even on reflection, remains pretty chilling. Some of them might later feel remorse, perhaps regularly, revisiting the scene with different eyes, with opened eyes? Well, we know, do we, the range of human responses. Reflection, after all, is not enough. There's a passage from one state to another, but there isn't an external criterion by means of which we can check the 'rationality' or 'correctness' of our own progress, from taking pleasure in brutality to doing one's utmost to prevent it happening. (Though the two are not incompatible: one would have to stop *indulging* one's pleasure in brutality in order to gather sufficient energy to manifest a decent application of the phrase 'doing one's utmost to prevent': not only in definition, but also, queer as this may sound, in judgments.) We are talking about a transformation of perceptions whose husks lie scattered about in the evaluations of the language, evaluations which give us our first access to our own souls. We can see the possibility of an inner transition reflected in the arcs of possible speech. Embedded in speech and action reside reasons which may not be presently available to us because they express states to which we do not yet have access, states in which we are yet to be, and, unless merely imitatively, we shall not come to use such language, appeal to such reasons, except as the product of some interior turning around and change of perception, so that suddenly the incident with the young woman with the baby in her arms sickens us.

Of course, some of them were sickened already, but acted with enthusiasm for fear of those whose enthusiasm or indifference seemed absolutely real.

2

I went on a winter retreat with the Buddhists about eight years ago, in the late seventies. It was bitterly cold and, like several others, I caught a chill. There was a lot of meditation, in an overcrowded shrine room, warm and full of incense, about twenty men sitting still, blankets around their shoulders, and in the silence I seemed to venture towards the edge of a deep pool, was caught with awe into its depth. But after a few days, with the toll of the chill, the pull of that feeling, I went into a sort of shock, could only stare out of the window, an hour at a time, or retreat to my mattress and lie there helpless. But as the hours passed, and I started to grow desperate with my own paralysis, I realised that I had been singing insistently to myself snatches of Ariel's songs, again and again, *into something rich and strange, . . . merrily, merrily, shall I live now, Under the blossom that hangs on the bough . . .*

In meditation you should sit still and straight, but not stiffly, not to lose yourself again in the circles of your own habitual thoughts, merely intensifying them, but to grow aware of your own body, your own spirit, starting to realise the mistake in centring on thoughts which are the precipitate of the self-enclosure out of which you now slowly start to move. It is a waste of time, the 'most rarefied form of self-abuse'(Graves), if it does not release imagination into life. A telephone rings a long time somewhere far away, the sound is drowned by that of a passing car, and then returns, endlessly ringing, and then is disturbed by another car. A lorry moves along the approach road towards the Porters' Lodge, two birds are singing and a man on a racing bike moves smoothly up the hill, the telephone rings still footsteps go past the door, I see the hair and freckles on my forearm as I write, the faded blue of the tee shirt, on the table a pair of scissors at right angles to the edge, a scattering of pens, scraps of paper, a mug. My own landscape, my own horizon, is like a stage set: I have no thoughts about a world outside teeming all over the globe. There might be an abyss on the far side of the furthest trees I can see, the perforated edge, the dotted line, of the horizon keeps me from the world. I describe the landscape within the dotted line of my horizon.

In meditation one's attention is really at first to one's states, not just of 'mind', the recurring danger of *vipassana*, but of body as well, and such attention *becomes* a changing awareness of interior changes that occur spontaneously under these conditions. The resident danger of a diet of *vipassana* meditation alone (without the balance of *samatha* practice, I mean) is a tense awareness of tense mental states in a tense body, which *causes* a nested set of super-ego responses to pile up one on top of the other. So first the body has to relax and become dhyanised by slow degrees.

I am immersed in my thoughts, my stride has their rhythm, and in a shop window, clearly and precisely, I see the face and figure of one who is suffering and at once the suffering is no longer there caught in the window but the look of one moved by kindness looks back at me.

Beauty is only a problem when it brings one to life. To meet beauty you must be alive already. One believes such a quickening is conditional upon the presence of the *eromenos*, the loved one, and so one cannot bear to lose them, seeking to cage them, by which you lose them anyway. Or is it like this? The sight of beauty is like a sudden shaft of sunlight that pierces and dilates, and one cannot bear it for long and must look away, a dog-rose branching up into the hedgerow wet after rain, a pink, unopened rose caught in the light with drops of sparkling water on the leaves below, motionless because our time is too quick to see the pulses of its energy: its vibrations are too much for me and I cannot stay to look for long, it dilates perception and I cannot bear it. Beauty is only beginning of terror if you think that such a hard to dilate self cannot burst or expand.

When people begin to meditate, they become strongly aware of emotions and thoughts that had previously been repressed . . . in my own case I distinctly remember that I would rise from my meditation mat choking in a heaviness, a thickness of atmosphere that made me stumble almost unconscious to my bed to allow blackness to descend and reveal itself in the images and thoughts that slowly formed themselves then in my mind. Nothing alarming, in the event, but what one might expect, self-hatred, fear, sadness, they came out, I had not to be lost in them but to see, come down to aggressive infancy again and unrestrained desire, the rages of jealousy, the vigorous sucking at the breast, sucking the pillow and jerking off in a frenzy of body and mind . . . I went on a long retreat, for three weeks, where I woke up, where I danced for joy, through perception cleansed the landscape sparkled with life and light. I sat so deep and opened my eyes as a bell rang to come away from the centre of the earth, the earth a jewel, out from a jewelled life into the glory of its creation, from original unity into differences. I did not cry to sleep again, not that, I saw the world revealed with gladness, was there in the presence of my brothers and sisters . . . and then I felt again the weight, the burden, the darkness of my hatred, not revealed in its objects but in its intolerable presence. I felt the presence of sorrow, and not joy, all the weight of the feeling, and I had to stumble away, with this dead weight on my back, the old man of the sea, the old man whose weight weakened my limbs till they trembled, but I drew away to a dense, dark wood, a dead wood, of brown, stunted trunks, brittle branches, dead, dead, dead, I crawled in through the wire, ducked beneath snapping twigs and lay inert, and there an invisible bile rose in my gorge, forcing my body to its contractions and coming through me in waves, the spew of hatred, towards myself I felt it, let it come, against my dearest friends, I let it come, presented to it the faces of my loved ones and watched its flow. It came, and then went. And so I crawled out of the dead wood again and walked back to my companions, walked towards them with no strength, weak, as it were, from some great exertion. But the increase in awareness can be described in more specific terms. So, one becomes aware of, there expands and unfolds before one's gaze, a particular *world*, constituted by a particular self and the forms of contact available to it, which has, whether it is aware of it or not, a particular *presence* in the world. One's own house or hovel is it of being, the dwelling that one has been forced into constructing: one will not like what one sees. The main thing, in my case, then, was various forms of weakness of response. This is not surprising if one takes seriously the idea of a divided and dead-locked individual. I'm sorry if you think this is all too . . . *personal*. At the moment it has to be, otherwise philosophy is merely the temptation to dissociate yourself from your actual self as though it had nothing to do with you. I am describing myself and the people I know, God love them, and I don't think that philosophy is finally a temptation, but a way of life, a way of conducting and becoming aware of one's life, not merely carried on with eyes to the front, never looking back over one's shoulder, at the unconscious squandering of energy even for *doing* philosophy. I cannot see how someone could 'spend their whole time doing philoso-phy', though they do, they do, writing about conceptual puzzles unre-lated to the conceptual difficulties that have knotted up our lives. I cannot understand how someone could have an *interest* in philosophy. One thinks then of the Jungian shadow. Enervation is the obvious outcome of division. One thinks then of Nietzsche's description of the *values* of such an individual. You find that you are, in certain respects, and certain areas, a weak person. Contempt, of course, is not the only response to weakness, though it is the fear of contempt that persuades us to keep our so visible weaknesses to ourselves, to hide them, even from ourselves, in case we become the victim of our own contempt. Weaknesses, as is well known, require defensive systems. The lack of strength shows itself in fearfulness, in resentment, in hatred, in spite, in a series of strategies of avoidance and evasion, in a particular kind of persona, hiding behind which, etc., . . . an unloved, unlovely, despised little being, who now, looked on with kindness, greeted with friendliness, sees at last that it may begin to flourish, given the right nourishment, flourish and grow strong, and jettison the defences, because less threat-ened, less vulnerable, less aggressive and reactive, more vigorous, able to 'face all things', ah, the darling man begins to emerge now, shyly steps out into the sunlight, does he?

If our perceptions are expressed in the language, then so is our failure of perception. Language is thus potentially always another cramp. But it is hardly just 'in the language'. The notions of *presence* and *atmosphere* are crucial and neglected. By presence I simply refer to the presence of *persons*, the way in which someone is *there* (Simone Weil). The atmosphere that is generated by the presence of certain persons, by certain states of the persons concerned, is, I'm afraid, inimical to certain 'expressions' or 'manifestations' of being, inimical to the possibility of other presences. Atmosphere is the product of presence, and can then determine presence. Certain presences cancel each other out. Some die in the cold air. Some expressions need an appreciative medium if they are to flourish, if their presence is to be brought forth. So the spiritual aspirant needs a *sangha*, a community of fellow seekers. So does the philosopher, or at least this one, but they are hard to find. On the other hand such communities are hardly immune from corruption. Perhaps the point is that the *sangha*, the university, the church, are occasional forms of relationship, there and then gone, evanescent. Atmosphere and presence are palpable, like a smoke-filled room or the sound of laughter. I recognise the difficulties of women among certain groups of men. It is not just that a certain sort of presence is not *permitted*, but that it is the victim of distorted perception. I find that I have become a caricature of myself, that I am acting out . . . what? their perception of me, of what I seek to express. The impossibility of being more than a caricature of oneself, of your femininity, for instance, in the presence of certain 'other minds', *shows* how one-sidedness works, both internally and externally. What exists outside the general structure of a person's perceptions is not, after all, 'less even than a dream', but, on the contrary, given a precise, distorting definition: and you feel it, you feel yourself somehow embodying it, you realise that that was what you were doing. 'I was just being what he wanted me to be', or what he was only able to see me as. I just became it, inexplicably. You do it instinctively, until you become aware of what is going on, when silence and self-restraint become options. *Sub specie aeternitatis* has got to be a felt perception, a subtle reordering of priorities that creeps upon one, or else it is simple compensatory fantasy. One sees people pursuing and planning their career with vigour, speaking out of the confidence that has been lent them by their position, their education, their class, self-assured, without hesitation, knowing what they think, never giving voice to doubts. And I have had only small confidence in my 'views', and, expressing them with diffidence, have found my audience not hear my views but only the diffidence.

CHAPTER THREE

'. . . you hear the grating roar'

I

Matthew Arnold's now neglected *Literature and Dogma* of 1873 was a sensitive, intelligent response to the new spirit of positivism and the growing acknowledgement of the Death of God. He manages at once to embrace the positivist critique of *theology* and to illuminate *religion* by means of its experimental method. We can see in the progress of his poetry and his theological writing the felt processes of the loss of faith and the spirituality of his response to it.

What emerges from his reflections is the experiential notion of a *revelatory life* freed from the traditional dogma he had come to reject. I want to explore the gradual formation of this notion, with the aid of some key Buddhist concepts that help, I think, to highlight Arnold's essentially non-theistic thinking, the development of which bears comparison with Tanabe's 'metanoetics'. We start with the bleakness of *Dover Beach*, which is where most religious commentators remain, but then move by degrees into mature religious writing in which something like a phenomenology of *jiriki* and *tariki* emerges. We start in fact with a cultural disappointment and sense of nihilism, the Death of God, the painful dismantling of traditional dogmatic structures which were perceived at least to be entirely discredited by serious and honest thinkers. It is an historic moment in which the most strenuous efforts of *jiriki* leave us desolate. The self-power I refer to here is the intellectual effort of traditional metaphysics and natural theology, as well as their critical subversion. It is this whole dialectic that Tanabe presumably has in mind as the contrast when he refers to his 'philosophy that is not a philosophy'.

The neglect of Arnold does not extend to *Dover Beach*. The theologian Don Cupitt refers to it in the Introduction to his book, *The Sea of Faith* (Cupitt, 1984, 18), whose title is drawn from the poem, and it is a phrase that is now well-known as the name of a movement of 'non-realist' spiritual renewal inspired by Cupitt's work. However, I do not think that the use he makes of it entirely fits the spirit of *Dover Beach*. Cupitt writes:

The sea of faith in Matthew Arnold's great metaphor, flows as well as ebbs; but the tide that returns is not quite the same as the tide that went out. It will rise equally high; and there is continuity.

But in Arnold's 'great metaphor' the sea of faith does *not* flow as well as ebb: it simply ebbs, and it is in the poetic suspension of the space between the high tide and the low that Arnold focuses his thinking. When he refers in *Dover Beach*[1] to the 'Sea of Faith', it is to declare that he only hears its melancholy, long, withdrawing roar. Although the movement of the *tides* is regular and predictable, we cannot be as confident as Cupitt about the possible future forms of 'faith'. Nor is it clear that Arnold himself would *welcome* the Sea of Faith's being once again at the full, for the ebbing tide has uncovered what the full sea concealed. At least, we would need a *different* metaphor for what replaced it. But in any event there is reason to think that Arnold would not be impressed with Cupitt's own suggestion, of a voluntarist commitment that rescues us from futility. Arnold's biblically derived notion of 'Life', by contrast, allows our concept of nature to alter with our shifting conception of the possibilities of conditionality as they make themselves manifest to a self-in-transformation.

Listening and hearing are images of inwardness and aesthetic experience. You listen for a sound you thought you heard, and sometimes, hearing a sound, you are compelled to listen to it. Art is a form which compels the attention in this way. Rilke's first sonnet to Orpheus has the wild animals fall silent under the spell of the god's singing, they hear it, fall silent and listen, compelled, under enchantment. It is in this 'Verschweigung', this keeping silent, that the conditions are met for beginnings, indications, transformation. That just about suggests that one also has to come out of the enchantment one needed to enter in order to hear and listen (a feature of meditation also). In *Dover Beach* the process is painful and the outcome hardly seems so assured, no sense of enlargement, or of a temple within the power of hearing. But the sense of hearing provides more veridical perceptions than that of sight in this poem. The visual is comforting and deceptive, whereas what is heard disturbs us with the truth. We hear the grating roar of pebbles under the action of the waves bring in 'the eternal note of sadness'. Why is it *grating*?

---

[1] I have used the Allott edition of Arnold's poetry, London, Longman, 1979.

and how is it heard to bring the note of sadness in? The physical sound brings in *thoughts* whether we like it or not, as do other physical features of the landscape. These 'natural correspondences'[2] force themselves upon us and are not, at least initially, a matter of convention or artifice.

The sound of the pebbles grates because it disturbs an enchantment. I wonder whether in Arnold's personal case it isn't the realities of life that finally disturb the enchantment of poetry, the poetry he was finally unable to write under the pressure of what life brought him. Enchantment was necessary, but only as a condition or preparation. The opening lines of the poem enchant us and provide the image for the enchantment not just of poetry but also of the Faith:

> The sea is calm tonight.
> The tide is full, the moon lies fair
> Upon the straits; – on the French coast the light
> Gleams and is gone; the cliffs of England stand,
> Glimmering and vast, out in the tranquil bay.

The *calm* sea and the full tide, *moonlight* on the straits, the *gleam of lights*, the cliffs *reflected glimmering* (an *illusion* of stability) out in the *tranquil* bay, these are images of enchantment and illusion, to be contrasted starkly with the bleak final lines. But the opening has another role, it seems to me, in tension with what I have just said, as an objective correlative for the joy, love, light, etc., that Arnold is about to realise cannot be secured or sustained by the traditional Faith. There is a grating interplay between the enchantment they draw us in to and the image they provide of positive human states. The ambivalence comes because we are still under the illusion that the latter can only be secured by the former.

The next lines decisively alter the so-far merely visual experience; other senses are brought into play, and they mark a shift:

> Come to the window, sweet is the night-air!

The window perhaps is already open or is opened now, and then, with the brilliant 'Only', something *disturbing* is acknowledged, a qualm or hesitancy is voiced, whose cause is not perceptible till one approaches the window, till the *beloved* approaches the window, and is addressed again:

> Only, from the long line of spray . . .
> Listen! you hear the grating roar . . .

---

[2] Cf. Richard Wollheim's classic essay, 'Expression' in his *Art and the Mind*, London, Allen Lane, 1973.

It is not difficult here to *look*, so there is no achievement in *seeing*, where seeing is connected with illusion and deception, but *listening*, the image of inwardness, forces us to hear sounds that prompt and focus thoughts, not of our choosing, truths that one does not want to hear because they are grating but which have to be acknowledged, since they force themselves upon the attention, or at least on that of the poet. The poet is found to be in the act of acknowledging them, giving expression to his recognition, but also attempting to bring the same knowledge to the beloved, by drawing her attention to what has prompted him, for he is still addressing her as he addresses us, as though in need that she should understand what he is coming to understand, because if she doesn't, if we don't, then distance falls between them as lovers. But he makes a mistake in the presumption that what prompts him will evoke the same in her, or us. The sound of the grating roar of pebbles as they are dragged and sifted by the waves also shifts the sense and security of the visual experience: the land becomes 'moon-blanched', he is now describing it to *her* as moon-blanched, as drained of its natural colour, as really more sinister than the enchantment allows us to see. What we hear *may* cause us to think in a certain way; it is not that something we have already thought is secured by a convenient image. Such images only become convenient later because they have already generated the thoughts they then remind us of. Arnold is seeking to *beget* the thoughts and images that have already been conceived in himself, but sometimes he forgets this and presumes that conception has already taken place.

The grating roar of the pebbles is heard to bring in the eternal note of sadness, and it becomes clear that the beloved who listens is also presumed to hear it. Sophocles had heard the sound on the Aegean 'and it brought/ Into his mind the turbid ebb and flow/ Of human misery'. So the turbid movements of human misery stand in grating interplay with the gleaming images of enchantment and illusion, sustained while the window remains closed, or the sounds without unattended to. Arnold hears the same sound. Or rather, he poignantly suggests to the beloved that '*we/* Find also in the sound a thought', an assumption of unity and agreement not present a few lines later, when he moves to the first person singular, 'But now I only hear', ambiguous between 'but now I hear only . . .' and 'but now only I hear . . .'. as though he recognises that he is alone in this and cannot after all assume a common understanding, since what he comes to see is seen alone and like a prophet he is isolated by his knowledge, which he desires nevertheless to share. And as a poet all he can do to achieve this is bring images to the mind that they might

beget their kind. Indeed he has realised that what Kierkegaard calls subjective knowledge can only be communicated indirectly, and we make a
serious and common error if we suppose that the assent of another
entails a shared understanding. The thought that he says 'we' find in the
sound is actually at one remove from the sound itself, because it is
prompted by that of Sophocles. It is that the Sea of Faith was once too
at the full, as at Dover:

> . . . and round earth's shore
> Lay like the folds of a bright girdle furled.

When this girdle is removed, the shore round which it lay is left exposed
and naked. As Kenneth Allott remarks, the context is one for feelings of
loss, exposure and dismay. Perhaps it is also a sexual image, and a sexual
anxiety and dismay, the enchantment of dress removed, the genitals
exposed, an ambivalence, a slight recoil, that leads him to think 'I' for a
moment rather than think 'we'. When the Sea of Faith recedes it leaves
exposed the vast edges drear and naked shingles of the world, that had
lain concealed from view, as had the realities of human misery, by the
calm, full tide, with the moon lying fair upon the strait. The Sea of Faith
conceals the truth, and generates illusion. There is no allusion to the
sense of smell here, but the smell of the shingle at low tide is not sweet
as the night air is . . .

An impulsive and passionate response or counter-thought to this dis-
maying recognition of false appearance, and of the reality it conceals, is
caught in the next line, which offers the hope of a saving contrast to
falsity and enchantment, and the correction of the physical recoil by a
saving impulse of tenderness, if we dwell in the pause of the caesura:
'Ah, love, let us be true . . .' Perhaps the emphasis might fall on the *us*, as
it does, I suggest, in the thought: 'let *us* be true', since truth is not where
we had relied on it to be, or what we had been brought to expect, or not
where Arnold had, but is outside Eden, outside enchantment. Then,
splendidly turning the sense of 'true', the 'to one another' opens us to
the moral possibilities of relationship in the scene of human misery. It is
important that the turn is an instinctive one, not a matter of a considered selection within a range of prior choices available to a self-confident
ego. It is where he *finds* himself turning in thought in the crisis of his loss
of faith. At the bleakest moment a possibility presents itself to his consciousness as the direction to follow, the image of a path and destination,
but it needs precisely to be *followed*, to be attended to. The two things I
have sought to stress come together here – out of endured dismay

something *comes* to him, the image of a possibility, that cannot be traced to his own choice or decision (*tariki*), and its coming depends also on a stance of attentiveness to just the conditions of his dismay and melancholy. But he is turning in appeal to another person, as a necessary condition of salvation, so that the latter resides in some form of relationship.

Moreover, we are offered a reason, or rather the beloved is, for *our* being true/ To one another. As we look out to the tranquil bay towards the French coast in the moonlight, we see the world as it appears at the high tide of the Sea of Faith, a land of dreams. But despite this appearance the world

> hath really neither joy, nor love, nor light,
> Nor certitude, nor peace, nor help for pain.

And nor, after all, it seems, does the flesh. The philosopher Anthony Kenny (1988, 160) has remarked, mistakenly in my view, that Arnold at this point 'offers human love as the only consolation', and comments that it is an inconsistent consolation: 'if there is no love and no certitude in the real world, how can one rely on the truth of the beloved?' But Arnold is not at all offering 'human love as the only consolation'. He has seen the need to transcend consolation. It is true that one cannot *rely* 'on the truth of the beloved'. Arnold was clear enough about the limitations of 'human love', it is even there in that desperate move from 'we' to 'I' and back to 'we' again, in the need to find common understanding, so precarious a possibility when understanding is so grave. In *The Buried Life*, for instance, he asks:

> Are even lovers powerless to reveal
> To one another what indeed they feel?

So maybe it is a mistake to suppose that Arnold is offering consolation.[3] His thought turns to, and then he offers, a beckoning and difficult *standard* by which 'human love' might be measured, a standard he cannot live without because it is internal to what he has understood, and appeals to the beloved, to share the attempt to realise it.[4] And there is no

---

[3] Aelred Squire (1973, 3) makes the same mistake, commenting that many of us have 'gone far beyond Arnold's provisional answer to this terrible absence; human love often proves little more than a makeshift barrier against the blind forces of a world 'where ignorant armies clash by night'.

[4] 'Conduct', of course, becomes the lodestar of his thinking in *Literature and Dogma* (1873). In *East London* the poet encounters an 'ill and o'erworked' preacher, who is cheered by 'thoughts of Christ' (italics mine):

> O human soul! as long as thou canst so
> *Set up a mark of everlasting light,*
> Above the howling senses' ebb and flow,
> . . .
> Not with lost toil thou labourest through the night!

inconsistency if we stress the biblical resonance of the word 'world'. Joy, love, light, etc., are not to be found 'in the world', nor in the urgent but disappointing flesh, perhaps. They are to be found only if we are not *of* the world, even though we are *in* it, *here* as on a darkling plain, where ignorant armies clash by night.[5] Arnold implies that in the real world, as opposed to 'the land of dreams', the only *possible* place in which to find joy, love, light, etc., is within and between human beings, but only in a relationship of 'truth'. He is thrown back, to echo Tanabe's phrase, on his own interiority, or better, on an interiority that needs to connect with another. There is some complexity in the lines, because they appear to express two propositions at once. The first denies that the desired states are to be found in the world such as '*seems* to lie before us like a land of dreams'. In other words it is an illusion to suppose that joy, love light, etc., come to us through Faith and a relationship with God (or through the enchantment of the flesh). The second denies that they are to be found in the world as it *really* is, a place in which ignorant armies clash by night.[6] The implication is that we have to withdraw from *both* these worlds and together found another, or help to give it birth, one which, indeed, in *Dover Beach*, Arnold can scarcely *conceive* except in that fleeting notion of truth to one another. The extreme difficulty of that enterprise comes out in *Stanzas from the Grande Chartreuse*, also composed in the early eighteen fifties, and also reflecting the honeymoon tour. In that poem the world of 'faith' is already 'dead'. The poet talks of wandering between 'two worlds, one dead, the other powerless to be born'. So what are the conditions under which it may be brought to birth, the conditions of gestation, what can we do or undergo of a kind that would count as gestation, and what kind of world might it be? The point is that there is no way back for Arnold, and no clear sense of what would count as a way forward. This is the condition we need to dwell on and return to, and maybe doing that is the condition that has to be met. The direction in which Arnold in fact turns for 'consolation' (let *us* be true / To one another) might appear more revelatory than consolatory if we think of it as a prompted, prompting thought that gradually shows him the unrealised object of his *melancholy*. The pressure of the dismay or melancholy when it is dwelt upon can force its object into consciousness, can force

---

[5] Compare *Stanzas from the Grande Chartreuse* (italics mine):
> As if *the world* had ever had
> A faith, or sciolists been sad!

[6] Nor, *pace* Kenny, does Arnold say that the beauty of the world is a dream: the beauty of the world is the *image* of a dream: the dream of faith.

into consciousness the form of a world, the sense of a universe, in Valéry's phrase. It is as though to bring this world to birth we need to know what the processes of gestation are in order to endure them. The poet is impelled towards a perception or intimation of the real site of joy, love, light, etc., in the *possibilities* of human relationship, in a world where its present *realities* show us to be 'here'

> . . . as on a darkling plain
> Swept with confused alarms of struggle and flight,
> Where ignorant armies clash by night.

But the world that is powerless to be born can only come to birth through *action* and ethical connection. We cannot rest with enchantment or with poetry, finally, and this is what Arnold begins to see.

Roger Scruton (1990, 8) has written that Arnold 'foresaw' on that 'darkling plain' the threat posed to the 'impulse of piety, upon which community and morality are founded' by naturalistic explanations of religion. Arnold, though, is not *foreseeing* a threat to 'the impulse of piety' on the darkling plain, but telling us that the full tide of the Sea of Faith has concealed from us, and its going out reveals, that we already are and have been, '*here* as on a darkling plain'. (*Here* is where we are, whether or not we are believers.) The forces of positivism against religion are merely the latest version of an old story. As far as 'piety' and 'morality' are concerned, Arnold's thought is going to focus with greater and greater concentration upon the primacy of the impulse to 'morality', and he is not going to found it on 'piety'.

2

I heard the trains differently this evening, caught their note at last, the before-bare blasts had swept through me, sound only. This evening I heard their energy and power. Even the fire crackers had a different sound. Then I make the essential qualifications, recall *goondas* and corrupt politicians, but the squalor does not cancel the vibrant note . . .

. . .the vibrant last note of the organ piece, held unendurably long, to the point of pain, in Oxford, in Christ Church, in the twilight, together for one day, before I leave. We sat in stalls, in a transept, the dim light made the stained glass glow, lit the faces of others who sat across from us, a few paces away, absorbed, facing different ways, silent figures in the semi-darkness, between the pillars, I remembered her body, quiet here.

And so the time was up and we walked together through the streets to the station, to the last train, to say goodbye. The train arrived, she boarded it, I took her hand and held it as we waited. We looked each other in the eye, held the look steady through the deficiency of speech. There was no help so we kissed and the train parted us . . .

. . . *Die Sonne sinkt*: it is behind cloud so that the rays fan out wide: kites wheel and turn, a strong wind blows across the verandah, a train hisses towards the Junction. I can stand unseen in the warm air, looking over the decay of a formal garden below me, look towards the distant hill at Ganeshkhind. The stone balustrade is reflected in the moonlight onto the marble floor, where a young woman danced naked for her companion, who sits cross-legged on a cushion, in the same moonlight, the silence of their desire, retained in the air, in their bodies, not consummated, even now as she sinks upon him, they settle and are still. I think of them, of the stillness in the air, and a band of energy flows along the channels of my body and seems to sustain it, as though my body could go and the energy still be there.

Sometimes, in the late evening at Grove Park, I would walk by myself in the darkness along the quiet paths near the house, paths overhung by trees, praying quietly, afraid of the silence around me but pressing on, and stand by a gate looking into a field towards trees and the light along the line of the horizon, and felt happy in the presence of God, which was all around me, relieved by my new chastity of the affliction of guilt. Once, during the day, as I walked, recollected, near the house, the rays of the sun caught the brown bark of the pine tree, and a thrush sang out loud, and I could not for a moment catch my breath for the joy of it. I remember now the innocence of what I wrote before I started to do philosophy, before I subjected myself to its disciplines. I wrote poetry, delighted in the word, the right, effortless word, the poetry writing itself. It has been like that again, now, after so long. The poetry gradually stopped, and I lay in bed at night with the thought that the cold hand of philosophy had frozen all my lyricism.

One day a girl came to the seminary with her father, who was there on some business with the Rector. She stood by the open door of the car, talking to some of the other seminarians. She was about twenty and pretty, graceful body, amused, intelligent face, and I was standing in my cassock about fifteen yards away, in my cassock, aged eighteen. Suddenly the sight of her was quite unbearable and I was compelled to rush away to my room where I lay on my bed in agony, and could face no one until well after I knew she was gone.

But this does not capture the sense of the *physical power* of the feeling. I said that I was unable to face anyone, but there wasn't any strength in my limbs, to proceed was against the force of gravity. When I met my Buddhist teacher for the first time I had to walk through the physical aspect of my fear as though through a swamp to approach him. I feel in my body all the time the release and the inhibition of energy, the ebb and the flow of energy. When my energies are low so are my spirits as I drag my body around a dreary campus that, outside the limits of my oppressed perceptions, may be sparkling in the brightest light, as I have also sometimes seen it. And writing all this doesn't release me from being either at the mercy of these modalities of energy, or in command of them. I do not even know whether that is how to conceive the alternatives: in command of them?

I had wanted to connect the idea of energy with that of emotion and reasons for action: reason is the bound or outer circumference of energy – it would be good to be Blake's philosopher, in mental fight – it is also its *eye*: the thoughts that move us, the perceptions, are the intelligence and the focus of our energies, of our constant motion, of *eros*, where mind and matter fuse, intelligent energy, *thumos*, spirit, essentially always informed and directed. That is why 'aesthetic perception' is important for my thinking, since it is the locus of realising what is the case, it is the exemplary *seeing something* and how it affects us. The image of the girl gave rise to pain I made no sense of. And she was not the topic of sexual fantasy at all, I was too much disturbed for that. This strong physical dimension to emotion tends to be neglected in contemporary philosophy because we have discovered the importance of the intentionality thesis. Nevertheless what we feel in *our bodies* is, primarily, not so much sensation, but the course of *energy*, and that has a precisely intentional aspect; an aspect which gives the energy *form*.

Jealousy, for instance, a good example in philosophy, everyone becomes a little more alert in class: it is not the name of a single 'feeling', but a complex of possible feelings whose appearance depends upon events: hope and fear, despair, relief, suspicion, hatred, revenge, rage – the events that surround sexual relations: the felt need to look through the key-hole, to take steps, lay traps, conceive strategies. What one feels in one's body is the ebb and flow of energies which take directions.

It depends upon the state of affairs, the course of events, it arises in dependence on conditions, in strong reaction, say, to the image of them lying together, perhaps weeks after the event, physically tossed about by thoughts of her *stupidity*, even though you knew she had acted for the best, opposing thoughts in violent contention, the names, these thoughts, of opposing *energies*, you at their mercy wondering what will happen next, astonished at the swiftness and the directions of your own thoughts and the physicalness of their pain. When you ask yourself why you should fall into such a rage, it is not to ask for a description of the state of affairs upon which it was focused, but to seek the *cause*. What brings it about that this chain of events should bring about this turmoil? And what would have to have been the case for you to have smiled and wished them well, doing so without pretence, not through gritted teeth? What kind of stupidity? What kind of *intelligence*? Spinoza says that the jealous lover is forced to contemplate, and recoils from, the image of his beloved (it is a male subject here) combined with that of the genitals and seminal fluid of his rival: his semen springing, mingling with the flood of her mucus. And he writes about the woman 'prostituting herself' to another man, a man's description this, which carries the distorting perception of the one who is jealous, incapable of a more favourable, not to say accurate, assessment of her motives. The battle is between truth and falsehood too. Spinoza adds another touch: 'we must add that a jealous man is not greeted by his beloved with the same joyful countenance as before, and this also gives him pain as a lover'. This does not say that the man who has *reason* to be jealous is no longer greeted with a joyful countenance, but simply the man who is jealous. His state of jealousy itself, and this may slip below the level of the consciousness of either of them, may be what checks the joyful countenance: *he* doesn't greet *her* as he had before, and her feeling of joy as she approaches him meets resistance, and its sudden dissipation brings her up short, and in confusion. I know this from life. There have been times . . . when I was unable not to repel affection. Büchner has Woyzeck murder Maria as a *punishment* for her *sin*. That description *allows* his violence. To say that someone has a reason to be jealous is to say no more than that the situation is of the sort that *arouses* jealousy in *those within whom certain conditions are met*. But now, if you do not think that these conditions are capable of being changed, if you think they are the universal and unalterable lot of human kind, or if you do not notice such causality at all, then you will be tempted to think that your fear, or your jealousy, is rationally warranted simply because it has an intelligible object. Instead of simply looking at the objects of emotion, at the objective correlative, we need to look at their subjects, and subjectivity here is not to be found simply in the presence of the feelings themselves, but in the subjective conditions under which they arise.

3

You may say that I have reduced values to responses to facts. It is true that I do sometimes talk like that. But it may look different if I qualify it. It isn't so much that we respond to *facts*, which, of course, we do, it is the context in which we do so. Primarily, we respond to each other, to animals and plants, to the presences of beings, to beings in their presence, to the landscape, the circular horizon of the sea, to rocks and cliffs. The world is the totality of things, not facts, says Strawson against Wittgenstein. But the totality includes beings as well as things and the 'world' is constituted by their relations and connections. I do respond to facts, but only in the sense that I respond to the fact that you . . . And really I respond to *you*: it is attraction and repulsion, care and indifference.

I talked about *bewilderment*, remember, about how 'you *ought* to care' expresses such a response. The logic is familiar enough from other contexts. 'Well, that ought to get you there now', the mechanic says, implying he has reason to think that it *will*, and then he's called out again a few miles up the road, and as he scratches his head he nevertheless says, 'well, it ought to have got you there', implying a disappointed rational expectation, he had good reason to suppose that it would. The implication is that he must have been wrong in his diagnosis. We could follow up these resonances. *There is a context of innocence and a context of experience.* First, the naive response, which is very common, not so naive: someone is refusing the terms of your moral appeal, they do not care about such things, they are unmoved and, of course, to that extent they are *dangerous*. 'But you *ought* to care', the Judgement of Innocence, is an expression of *incredulity*, an expression of a disappointed rational expectation in a case that *matters*, you are saying, but people *do* care about these things, you are *weird*. It is an expression of incredulity in the face of recalcitrant experience. The sheltered background belief is that people as a matter of fact respond in particular, predictable ways, and here is someone who doesn't, someone anomalous or weird. The utterance may carry all the weight of fear and loathing that the context may elicit. Disappointed rational expectations cause dismay because they make a difference. That is one reason people may believe there is a special 'moral ought': but it is the context that gives it its special emphasis. Its logic is neutral. But though I think it is plausible to claim that many people do in fact respond in this way to the moral derelict, it is clear that the response itself is inadequate. The background belief is manifestly false. The more brutal the environment the innocent find themselves in the less likely are they to retain that belief. On the contrary, it is all too likely that brutality becomes precisely what they expect, and they come to look askance at its absence rather than its presence: a kind act then becomes weird.

Certain thoughts and actions are available only at a particular 'level' of energy . . . when one's energies are diminished then certain perceptions of what is the case, upon which action depends, are just beyond one's scope. These thoughts and actions themselves provide the criteria for measuring the level of energy at which one is living, they are the outer criteria in which certain inner processes stand in need. If one's energies are diminished then certain thoughts are beyond one, certain actions impossible. Other thoughts, other actions, older routes, assert themselves. As new energies increase, and one is more creative in one's life, then the channels along which older energies had flowed, are flooded by the larger stream. But until the older channels are finally washed away the depletion of energy means that what is left must take its former course. This is a corollary of what I have been trying to say. If our thoughts are the horizon within which we act, if our thoughts move us to act, nevertheless the state of our energies determines what thoughts we can act on, determines the thoughts that are going to strike us or hold our attention.

Akrasia is sometimes translated as 'weakness of will', sometimes as 'incontinence', contrasted with the virtue of continence or *enkrateia*, sometimes, and perhaps, better, translated as 'self-control'. The *enkrates* is literally someone in control or command of their own impulses (an 'en-crat'). *Enkrateia* is the virtue of control . . . over unruly desires that threaten our ability to act well, to do the right thing. The 'a-crat' or *akrates* lacks that control and is consequently unable to act well. Our normal state, perhaps, is to shift uneasily between precarious control and lack of it, though excessive control is a familiar enough and debilitating state. 'He's a very controlled person.'

However, there is a related and much more significant Greek virtue, that of *sophrosune*, that belongs to the *sophron*. It is often translated as 'self-control' too (in a way that fails to distinguish it from *enkrateia*). It is better translated as 'temperance', though I am inclined to think that temperance is an *outcome* of this virtue rather than the thing itself, which as I said earlier, I would prefer to render as 'mindfulness' since that captures something of Aristotle's etymology, 'protecting wisdom' (*Nicomachean Ethics*, 1140b11). Whatever we think of Aristotle's etymologising, it gives us a clue to his understanding, which connects it with *phronesis* or practical wisdom, a capacity for right judgment and right action, not blinded by desire, a keeping safe of a mind unclouded by desire, a natural state of relaxed frugality. In that case, then, perhaps it is better to think of *sophrosune* not as 'temperance' but as a state of mindfulness or *smrti samprajanya*, and of temperance as the natural frugality (Krishnamurti) of the *dhyanic* body, an outcome of the virtue, not the virtue itself. Perhaps they arrive together, the one reinforcing the other. Someone who has this virtue is able to act well when the occasion demands, not because they have the power to keep unruly desires at bay, but because their desires are not unruly, and simply recede. Aristotle contrasts the 'temperate man' with the 'licentious' (*akolastos*, literally 'unchastised')[7] and remarks that while the licentious man is 'unduly distressed at missing what is pleasant . . . the temperate man is so-called for not being distressed by the absence of what is pleasant, or by abstinence from it' (*Nicomachean Ethics*, 1119a20). So there are clearly two distinct though connected phases here, obscured by translating *sophrosune* as 'temperance', the soundness of mind and the natural frugality that goes with it.

But it is worth recalling Tanabe. We could say that *enkrateia* or 'control' is a virtue of *jiriki* or 'self-power'. If we want to look for the corresponding virtue of 'Other-power' we may turn to *sophrosune* or 'mindfulness', when action comes but does not seem to depend upon our effort: the grace of effortless action.

We philosophers . . . almost universally assume that the main obstacle to stable ethical action is *akrasia*, weakness of will or incontinence or lack of control . . . 'that which I would not . . .'. . . . *'video meliora . . .'* . . .

. . . But I want to bring to the centre the idea of an 'ethical sensibility' and to show on the way that the familiar struggle between continence and incontinence, control or lack of control, is simply a stage in the development of our affective lives, so that *akrasia* is a *secondary* defect, not the root, not the main hurdle in the way of performing ethical actions. It is a secondary defect whose possibility depends on a prior infirmity, or lack of development, of *sensibility*. And the Greek virtue to associate with this flourishing sensibility is *sophrosune*. *Enkrateia* is a virtue which records one state of *thumos*, one state of the energies of a human being, *sophrosune* a virtue which records another, they are both stations on a progress towards a developed sensibility. It is only when we are

[7] I am grateful to Mr David Bates for his patient explanations of various Greek terms, and I apologise to him if I have failed to learn.

'temperate' that 'nothing prevents' (not because we are 'cool': temperance is an outcome of the flourishing sensibility not, as I once thought, its condition). When we are continent the things that prevent action are held in check. Our temperance is an expression of the state in which action is without the effort of resisting impediments. Again Tanabe comes to my rescue, because all this can sound like a kind of *hubris*. The point is that this kind of effortless action comes to us as a gift: we *find* it so, a given, a grace, an aspect of the 'Other-power' that is in reality an awakening of mind.

I want in some way to connect the idea of treating persons as 'ends' (persons-in-their-humanity rather than the Kantian respect for an apparently abstract humanity-in-persons) with the idea of an appreciation of them in relation to their (possible) beauty, beauty understood in a Platonic sense, as the object of *eros*. But that is going to take some explaining. Nevertheless it will go to the heart of an ethics analysed in terms of *sensibility*. But the idea of such an *appreciation of persons* will be the ground out of which there springs a concern for their well-being, the willing no one harm. So *they* are not the ground of ethics, and we shall be accused of offering the 'ethics of old women' until we make good and harm dependent on an adequately robust conception of what it is to be a person at all. Appreciation is not the object of any kind of 'moral imperative', either, though it *will* give rise to a sense of necessities that could easily look like imperatives. Imperatives are for the enkratic and akratic, that is, for most of us most of the time. Our radical egocentrism, our even older communalism are among the impediments to appreciation, among the forces that obscure our capacity to see.

4

I didn't expect to play the *eromenos* to your *erastes*, in fact I have never really been able to see myself in that role at all – shining youth leaning mischievous against the doorway, naked, erect, smiling. Oh no, but I was no shining youth myself, so many years of physical self-disgust. In one way I regret that I couldn't, wouldn't, didn't allow it to happen. I really was Sartre's woman in bad faith when you put your hand over mine in the car and I was too frozen to respond, it was too far from my experience, though my attitudes were all 'correct', and too far from my imagination. You called my bluff. Afterwards I wanted to come to your room, but I couldn't bring myself. And yes, at least and probably only in imagination, I should like to have been taken by an older man, looking down at me with kind, intelligent eyes, raising my pleasure at his own pace, wanted to hold some Socrates, whose conversation would have started me into philosophy. But it is an image which gives *form* to the rising pleasure, and direction, the eyes have to be intelligent and wise . . . It's all an *image* of friendship, and its reality *may* stand in the way of what it is an image of, though perhaps men need more friendship between older and younger, so that they can learn to be receptive and vulnerable. Having been a good *eromenos* may make you a more intelligent *erastes*, and in any case it may be better for such erotic relationships not to be sexual. We rush to sex and it triggers all our unresolved, unconscious feelings which then destroy our joy. Maybe there is chastity after the resolution, but the quality of sexual experience must surely depend upon the general state of our emotional lives, already in place, so not a cure, then. No, the emotions have to be fixed first.

I remember smells, of my grandfather, stale pipe tobacco on his clothes, not identified in words, but breathing in the air's familiar qualities and as well the rough trousers, his knees and lap, sweat, breath, prickly chin, hairs in his nostrils, caves inches away, pores. I climb over him, hesitate, and kiss shyly his face, his cheek. One moved familiarly within the element of smells, those that surrounded my grandmother and the rest of my mother's family, and their house, and the different rooms, sour bedding, roasting meat, boiling vegetables. Sweat and the stale morning breath of my mother whom we try to wake, she hugging we tugging her sheets. Sweat and cigarette, different unnamed qualities of sweat inspired with the air, cold urine on the sheet, cries and calls, abruptly and silently except for bronchitic breathing stripped from the bed in the night, dropped to the floor, kicked to one side, the sweet smell of clean linen, of a new baby at my mother's breast, privileged and uneasy seeing it bare, the great brown wet nipple in and out of the baby's mouth, its gasps and sighs, the smell of the milk, the welcoming, proud circle of beaming children watching and she beautiful, still, smiling, black-haired. It is evening, the curtains are drawn, the fire is hot, the taxi which brought her back has driven away. In the morning in the street the breadman's horse steams and snorts and stamps its legs, and with the intervals of a pulse its droppings land and rise to a mound, that topples, their smell in the steam. The children shout and laugh, point and stare. Heaved out of the bath we shuddered violently, overwhelmed by tremors, carted through to the fire, roughly dried by my father, cheerful, energetic, strong, catching the rhythm of our shivers and slowly calming us down, a warm vest from off the fire guard. I did not *believe* that my grandfather was angry. I saw his anger flare up through his body, flush his face, twist his posture, raise his voice, charge the room with tension, knife the base of my spine. I witnessed and remember events beyond my comprehension in the interstices of my forgotten routines. We watched in silence as he carved the meat, frowning face, eyes peering over glasses, light snorts through his nostrils laced with hairs. There was the ebb and flow of some altercation that cut through my body as the waves passed between them, him and my uncle, whose face grew red in an angry exchange, a gesture of contempt in the movement of the old man's arm. The sound of their voices was always severe, it was the way children were addressed, and the tone of voice works on a child. My grandfather's voice was rough and his face stern as I slowly approached in fear, and relief as he suddenly softened and gave me a wink. I watched them with my mother bent over me, whispering in my ear, comforting me leaning back against her body, rocking myself between her legs as she sat on the chair and we watched, afraid of the angry voices. I remember all the eyes being turned on me in expectation after some mock interrogation, many interrogations throughout my childhood. I came downstairs from bed and opened the door into the kitchen. My father turned and looked at me without speaking. I ran to the opposite armchair and buried my face in the cushion in order to hide. Silence and dark and heat from the fire. When I looked up he had not disappeared but watched me still.

The gang emerged bare-back from the dense woods and fanned out into a harvested field of wonderful gold, stooks of corn leaning together all around, they were *dens*, and we eagerly split up and wriggled into them. He was thirteen and I was ten, we lay there grinning, then all at once he pulled his trousers down to show his erection, and looked at my astonished face with benign interest. At last . . . I touched it, as he seemed to want . . . and held it for a few moments in a gingerly way, moving it on his belly, repelled by the mottle of the stretched skin, which made me think of chicken. Then I took my hand away. He seemed to indicate that I should open my trousers and his hand strayed towards me, but I shook my head emphatically, shocked, and also sensible that I had nothing to compare, and we withdrew from the den, no words spoken. But I remember his expression, benign, complacent, interested, then we were kicking through the stubble in the sunlight, moving back towards the woods.

I had obviously woken up in the middle of it, I must have been thirteen, it was clutched stiff in my palm, a spread of pleasure, a rising and receding in my body. When the sweet little ejaculation came I thought that this hot fluid must be urine and was afraid that I had wet my bed, and what would they say, how could I tell them *that* now? But the moisture was too oily between my fingers. They had told me nothing. Then a dreadful thought came with a measured slowness and sureness to the centre of my mind, as I wondered what was going on: this must be what they mean when they say, *thou shalt not commit adultery*. I had committed adultery, I was an adulterer, I had committed a mortal sin, a sin that kills the soul, and I had done it. In the confessional in the singular Catholic terror I blurted something about impurity, father; 'by touching?' yes; 'alone?' (*what?*) yes . . . pardon? '*pollution?*' . . . . . . yes, do they call it that? . . . a confession then to be made a thousand times. Once, in the same confessional, in the wearisome regular round, the Irish priest had hissed that if I did not stop *now* (it was like smoking or drinking) *I would be fiddling with myself on my deathbed*.

5

It is early days since I came out of the ivory tower to see how the world lives . . . On the other hand, I have seen it all before. I know these people very well, I was brought up with their kind, we had fights in the streets as children and went round in gangs. My own father would know them at once. He was a child in Merseyside in the twenties. When I see the ordinary poverty of the working people in the urban areas, the state of their clothes, the expression in their eyes, I am reminded of what my father and his sisters have told me about the old days, when they had no shoes, drank their tea from a jam jar, went without food for a day or so or ate badly. A boy in his class had got no shoes, a teacher bought him some, the next day he still had no shoes, his mother had sold them. But when you find yourself in a strange land, and this one is very strange, you find that your mind spontaneously provides you with models and analogues. Staying in an Indian city for a year has unexpectedly activated childhood memories, my parents' stories, the sense of oneself as the product of a very specific folk-culture. Startled by so much difference, you are surprised by recognition. 'The common behaviour of mankind is the system of reference by means of which we interpret an unknown language.' You see those young men walking down the street, four or five abreast, with clean pressed shirts and trousers with knife-edged creases, they will have emerged from their dwelling of a few square feet shared by too many others, I know their walk, the swagger of precarious self-respect, have seen it before, in the Teddy Boys walking down our street, the same look, the same walk: and they impressed us. The clothing is very cheap, but it is as smart as you could want. You may be poor but your children are always well turned out. But let us jump several classes – and castes – to the respectable, lace-curtained minds of the long-nosed middle class and their conventional piety and prudishness. Oh, I've seen their sort before, too. They seem to have spread all over the world. I have a picture of Catholic Ireland in the fifties. In Pune, at least if you're a man, you're pretty safe on the streets at night, you are not likely to get mugged. But look at that animated group of young men striding down the street, thin young men with sharp faces, whose response to a passing 'foreign' is mild derision, nothing happens in Pune – or relatively little. But you can see how it might in a moment. Young men – that's what it's all about, and always has been: cannon or trench fodder in their time, they have also been storm troopers, they have raped and pillaged. They could get together and *skin you alive*, under certain conditions, hang you from a lamp-post and cheer on and dance to the rhythm of your last ejaculation, drench you in kerosene and roast you in the street.

Unexpectedly, continence is itself a physical pleasure and eroticises the landscape. Sexual feeling spreads out through the body beneath the surface of the skin, electrifies touch. I do not feel the sudden shock of attraction, the sudden arousal that then subsides unsatisfied, since sexual feeling is already present and simply increases and intensifies, not suddenly present and suddenly absent. It makes me feel freer because I already enjoy what otherwise I try to extract from others, dependent for it upon them and wanting to make them captive. Couples walk along together hand in hand, one another's captive. It has been raining heavily and I've been unable to work. The sky is still dark and there's more rain to come, but there was a lull and I went out for a walk down to the Broad and through the meadows into the woodland. Everything was damp and green and the bluebells were out, dripping water. Philosophical difficulties crowd in too thickly and I wonder whether I shall ever sort them out or get them said, as thoughts pass quickly through my mind and out again. I clumped along in my boots with my hands in my pockets and a phrase from Mozart's *E Flat Divertimento*, the theme of the *andante*, insistently repeated itself as I walked.

6

We got out at Malavli station and walked up through Bhaja village into a three-sided valley. The valley floor was about three quarters of a mile wide and perhaps the same distance deep, the horse-shoe shape facing, like a magnet, the long, straight unbroken line of the much steeper ghats behind us, two miles away, their tops in and out of low monsoon cloud, their sides lit up light green against grey by the broken rays of the sun. Along the plain beneath them ran the Bombay–Pune road and the railway from which we had come. I had been reminded of the Welsh hills on the train, and had realised that British soldiers would have passed the same scene, generations of them. The bare hill sides. But though the ghat behind us was bare, the ridge that faced us as we made our way barefooted along the valley floor, was dark green with the foliage of shrubs and small trees, a brilliant green broken by bare volcanic rock from which the soil had been washed by the flow of rainy season streams. In the rock of the ridge to the east, and our left as we walked, we saw the Buddhist caves, the arched entrance to the chaitya hall, the rows of narrow chambers or cells. To one side of the caves water splashed onto rocks. The sides of the ridge were veined with long silver lines everywhere of falling water, splashing down into brooks, diverted thence by human hand to the sodden rice paddies, along the narrow, raised edges of which we now made our way, our shoes and socks absurdly in our hands, our bare feet squelching through puddles of brown water or slippery oozing mud, warm, yielding, moist, small land crabs escaping down holes or into pools we were about to cross. The floor of the valley had not been long cultivated, I was told, before it had been jungle, now, in the monsoon, a fertile valley, along which once, however, there must have travelled troops of other soldiers, earlier than the British, because in the heights above us, in the bend of the ridge, the highest points were broken and separated, forming a pass through the hills, the two sides of which, from where we were precipitously high, were guarded by two great forts, Lohagad and Visapur, veiled by dark sweeps of cloud and mist.

You looked down the valley and saw the Bombay train a mile away, the unshadowed slopes of the opposite ghats weakly but luminously green as pale rays of sun slide through the grey mist from breaks in the heavy cloud above the ridge to the left. Behind the Centre, to the left as you faced north, more paddy was fed by a stream which runs from a small fall, which, if you climbed up through it, over the slippery wet boulders, brought you into a meadow of pale grass, of cactus, orange flowering shrubs and exposed rock. I had climbed it the first morning, felt danger, like a boy alone in the woods, but wanting to venture. There had once been tigers. Beyond the small meadow the hill became steep.

I climbed back down through the water, cautious, careful, slow, white bare legs, so pale.

It had grown dark by seven thirty, but we can see the lights of the villages in the distance at the foot of both ends of the magnet, lights clustered, fields of force, the lights of a passing train attempting to connect them, the sound of Hindi songs in the wind blowing up from Bhaja. It is still pleasant to be out on the terrace. There is a breeze, we hear it through the leaves of the mango tree, see its effect, as it grows, in the large clouds that loom and swirl above us, that billow like the sea, the close sky contained by the frame of high ridges. But here there is no washing sound of the sea: instead the shrill electric rattle of crickets charges the air, the considered castanets of frogs break in down by the waterfall, and a stray bird calls. I see fireflies, which dance and dart like butterflies. As we talk we notice that all the lights have gone out, the music stopped: a power-cut. We sit in silence for a while, resume the talk. The lights come on again, not all at once, but a string of lights in rapid sequence, east to west. After a pause, the Hindi songs are also switched back on.

My two friends had been at medical school together. They talked of old times. I listened from the bed. On the floor was a mattress and some foam matting. Time passed with old stories and travellers' tales. It was time to sleep. Someone closes the shutters, which dampens the sound of the crickets, the paraffin lamp goes out. I close my eyes to florid images and the echoes of sensation, across the fields with naked feet, the green rice, warm clay between my toes, balancing unsteadily on the slippery earth, the scuttling crabs, the gurgling water, my wary eyes sweeping ahead for snakes and scorpions, uneasily giving my feet into opaque brown puddles. I linger sweetly in half unconsciousness, and there, in the narrow space between wake and dreaming, I am suspended above a rank shoreline, whether of sea or lake, and partly in and partly out of the water, which washes a little forwards and recedes, there lie, with their equipment, the dead and half-dismembered bodies perhaps of soldiers, half-formed before me, decomposed and water-logged, blown half-floating in the tide. The scene is then replaced, there are people making their way up a broad hill side, working their way up the slope, but, as I hover above it, watching, the hill, and the people walking up it, change, for a few moments, into the strong, sloping neck of a great, powerful bull, and then change back, the hill and the people, and then the living bull. I fell asleep and dreamt I was walking through sand hills. I enjoy leaping out and falling into the soft sand below, but in the dream these were

Indian sand hills, and they were impossibly steep and high, too steep for one to be saved by the softness of a levelling slope, but sand hills were for jumping from and I leapt into the abyss.

Today there was more rain, and we walked with our trousers rolled up to our knees, wearing shoes, sodden and slimy with mud, through flurries of rain and bursts of sunshine, donning and doffing rain gear as it got too wet or too hot. We might have been in the Lake District as we slithered through the mud, waded through the streams, except that the wet was so warm and there was no chill in the strong breeze. But at times the shrubs that bordered the narrow paths that twisted upwards gave me the illusion that I was climbing the steep wooded banks of an exuberant Cornish garden: the shrubs bore purple flowers, their paler buds papery and thick, long as ripe loganberries. I wanted the company of a botanist to give me names, though I should have been as inarticulate in a Norfolk lane. The steep paths, as on any hill, were simply grooves or channels furrowed into the earth by many feet, but now become the course of muddy little streams, and from time to time they brought us up on to some level ground, a meadow of grass and rock, a corner cultivated with rice. There were no buildings to be seen yet, though we were close to a village: the fortified ridge towered the more precipitously the closer we moved in, craning our necks to look. Part of it was still in mist in a lowering sky, the dark grey of the high rock and the perilous battlements in black silhouette against the turbulent dark clouds that swirled above and the dripping vegetation promiscuous on the green slopes below. The whole plateau, the table top of the ridge, was fortified, looking across at Visapur, its twin. A king had a rope stretched across the ravine from one fort to the other and had promised half his kingdom to anyone who crossed it. At last a girl from the circus caste took up the challenge, and had almost reached the further side in safety when the king's men severed the rope and she plunged to her death. We had walked round the bottom of a knoll which had obscured sight of the path, but could see it clearly now, could see how such a story might be told, see where someone might have fallen. There was even a cairn of stones there on the floor of the pass. We were still clambering like schoolboys, moving upwards in a zig-zag, using all our limbs, through water, stones and mud. There were cacti, long tubular structures, an angular, fleshy meccano of parts, indefinitely extendable, it seemed, upwards or outwards, sometimes a hundred square feet of cactus that might grow eighteen inches on a window ledge, with thick ear lobes of leaf to embroider the edges. A small-leafed shrub with orange flowers grew everywhere, the serrated leaves sparse on long climbers, the blossoms suspended in the air on invisible stems, little concentrations of pinched orange squares, a millimetre across. We turned a corner and fifty yards ahead against the sky stood the figure of a little human being, bare, spindly legs, a stick to lean on, upper body in a rough cowl of sacking over the head. As we approached the little old herdsman turned and peered at us, forehead daubed red, toothless, grinning, greeting us in country style with 'Ram Ram' as we passed him.

We are below the immense tower built on a precipice, it is surely unscalable, it is flush with the vertical ridge. But there is a story of a mother who worked in the fort, locked in one night by mistake; she needs to go home to feed her child; but the guards will not open the gates for her; she is desperate; at night, it is said, she climbs down the impossible abyss and hurries to her child in the village, returns the next morning as normal through the open gates, but the guards seize her and roughly question her, how did she get out, they do not believe her answer, they threaten torture, bring her to the king and she falls at his feet, begs his mercy, tells her tale. The king rewards her for her maternal care, for revealing the gap in their defences which must be made good. But now I am walking incredulously up wide flights of perfect, black stone steps, through pointed arches, the steps wet and treacherous in the rain, especially where they have crumbled, the course of little streams. The Moguls and then Shivaji, his sharp, bearded face, warrior on a rearing black horse. We climbed and turned, higher and higher, the hurrying steps of running soldiers echo the other way, swords and armour, death and wounding, screams of pain and shock, below the ramparts the same village huts, the loaded carts, the bullocks straining and expressionless. We came out onto the plateau, the flat top of the ridge. Thirty yards away there is a small square tower with a dome, built in black stone: within it lay a tomb, you could climb through the entrance and then turn, and look back upon, in silence, a deserted fort.

Thirty or so yards further on, I am walking towards it with curiosity, there is a rectangle of black stone, six feet by three by four, the side that faces me open. I peer inside and brush with my head a pair of small brass bells on a string, but I see with a shock that below me on the sunken floor there protrudes from a decorated paving, a small, round, polished lingam, a rounded glans without a foreskin, pushed up, engorged. I have stepped away in wonder, I stumble on a boulder, it is not a boulder but a carved stone, I make out the features of a bull.

We came round the far side of the ridge, returning to the Retreat Centre from behind. We passed some tribal people gathering wood, and, in a flat, rocky landscape halfway down, gently sloping with a stream bubbling between boulders, we saw some of them washing clothes. Others were already ahead of us as the descent suddenly got steep again, young women, straight, steady, a stick in one hand, the other sometimes raised to balance the load of firewood on their heads. They were moving down the steep, slippery slope, how I wanted to see them closer, by the side of a stream, between flowering shrubs, disappeared round a corner, while we merely slithered and slid behind. But when we turned the corner we came upon a little scene. One of them was only a girl, of twelve or thirteen, having trouble with her burden. They were standing around her, she giggled nervously, a darling child, a little sister. An old, white-bearded man was putting her load back on her head: she stooped her slim body to receive it, her eyeballs cautiously raised as she got it balanced. The others stood and watched, their firewood on their heads, made friendly comments. When the little girl saw us she stood sturdy again like the others, they began to look solemn, but started to grin as our arms and legs shot out on all sides as we careered madly towards them down the steep slope. As I came level with the old man I almost fell flat on my back: he exclaimed aloud, and his eyes went to his stick, which lay on the ground: he looked back at me and pointed towards it. I was to take it. I had no further trouble. They were beautiful young women, fine in their ragged clothes, the girl such a lovely long-legged colt. We went on ahead, my friend still slithered and dug at the earth with a half-open umbrella, arousing giggles behind us, as they stepped like princesses, with perfect poise, six kilos of illicit firewood on their heads, in stately procession down the same impossible steep slope. I left the stick at the bottom of the hill. In the evening it was my turn for the foam-matting on the floor: the tiles seemed to rise and fall as though quietly breathing, and when I closed my eyes I was swept up over green hills, to swoop down over the tops of trees and up again, with enormous faces forming and unforming below out of the animated earth.

CHAPTER FOUR

The energy for war

I

There was this little incident, I was nine or so, I was trailing home one afternoon, tired, dreamy, across New Ferry Park, at the edge of which along my tedious route there were some allotments on the other side of iron railings, and along these railings I was running my stick, whose bark I had peeled off, when I thought I heard groans coming from the other side, from a little green tool shed, with nettles growing round it. I say I thought I had heard groans, but in fact I was *sure*, I mean there was no doubt, that I heard groans, moans, coming from the little shed, though quietly. But I refused to believe that I could hear groans, so help me, at nine I could lodge a doubt against the evidence of my senses. I had thought I should have to tell someone, go back to New Ferry, to the police station. But I felt too frightened to tell them in case I was wrong and they shouted at me. And so it was impossible that someone could be lying in that little hut, groaning. I was fearful, too, that it might be someone lying in wait, so I wouldn't investigate by climbing the railings, which was anyway not allowed and someone might see and shout and tell the police. So I just hurried home, sped by bad faith.

Is there much *will* for a diplomatic settlement? Leave aside the more important question whether that is the right way to proceed in the circumstances. The media present the crisis with barely concealed *excitement*, and it is horribly clear that the excitement is not restricted to them. It arouses the more strongly, and reinforces, an excitement I find within myself, about patriotism and, of all things, military glory. They obviously laid the channels early, no doubt it is in the genes. I have to fight it out of my body. In that state of mind, with the imagination working all in one direction, there is no space for reflection . . . for *us*, and I don't include the calculators in power . . . upon the fact that young men will be smashed to pieces or burnt alive, that wives will be laid low with grief, children lose their fathers, parents their child, we shall have the rituals of loss later. Such thoughts lack presence in a mind in such a state, lack substance, do not capture the imagination, which is wholly engaged in another enterprise which would be subverted and lose impetus if such reflections had any energy behind them. To a warlike mind the will to peace becomes an emasculation of the spirit. There may be, there *are*, circumstances in which it is. But I am talking about our circumstances. What we have to deal with is the basic reality that even when the case is just . . . not everyone goes to war with a heavy heart, with an adequate representation of its reality contained within them, an adequate representation adequately contemplated.

They say they don't want lives to be lost, but they think that the stakes are sufficiently high. I am faintly susceptible to the propaganda, I can feel the ebb and flow of its movements, the usual demeaning language to diminish our sense of their humanity as they sink ridiculously beneath the waves. It is an interesting reflex of the media that, as though it were a necessity of thought, if a certain kind of action is to be envisaged, our ordinary perceptions have to be stifled, anaesthetised, because otherwise they would have too much contrary power. But maybe the situation is worse than this. It is not that our ordinary perceptions have to be anaesthetised, but that they have to be roused from sleep, our dormant xenophobia, activated by the presentation of its objects, in the absence of which we deem ourselves free of such passions, a precarious self-knowledge, as though we could know what passions we are prey to before we catch sight of the things that arouse them ('I don't believe in jealousy'). It follows that I should think that in the world of political calculation, all this is there, if left unspoken, since how otherwise could they be prepared to kill, *in circumstances such as these*? What I am susceptible to, or what I become aware of, sweeping (faintly?) through my mind with pleasure, is the sheer energy we have available for this kind of confrontation and activity. It is not just a reluctantly adopted last resort. The sheer energy is focused upon, depends upon the exclusive presence of, an inadequate representation of the reality, not the reality in all its aspects, aspects which engage, if we are lively enough, quite other motivations, motivations that would impede our warlike progress. There is tremendous energy available within our systems for this kind of enterprise, energy that has a life of its own, its own inventiveness for finding ways and means to further its goals. That is why trust can be put in the soldier on the ground, or the pilot in the air: the best is the one who has the imagination to see what needs doing and is able to carry it out. But the excitement, the intense interest, is coursing through the bodies of the politicians too, though I do not say that it is governing their actions, the imagination caught up with fascination in the bombing raids, the sinking of ships, the shooting down of aircraft. This is the form in which our energy is available to us, the form in which it is most readily tapped and exploited, it comes, to martial music in antique packages, tied around with its own limits of pride and shame, its own conceptual apparatus. It is not a matter of emasculation for peace, but of finding new channels for these tremendous energies, new directions determined by intelligence and creativity. Our energy needs somewhere to go, needs forms, needs the imagination. We live totally within the reaches of the imagination. It is a mistake to think that it works only within the private inner world of a few artists. The very shape of human life, as it contends against its material conditions, is the product of *imaginative enterprise*. We are all enchanted by the pictures of our own imaginations, and the potent imagery of our still forming culture, to release ourselves from discredited forms, to engage with new ones. The imagination spills out into the world of action, which is its natural domain, where it is achieved and brought to act. It is already at work, not just for conceiving means, but for conceiving *ends* in the world as it presents it to us. The individual imagination, though, begins to atrophy if the work is already done for it, stifled when action is always merely habitual, following stereotypes of the culture. But war also rescues us from tedium, take these soccer hooligans, move from the Falklands in 1982 to the World Cup in 1998. Isn't it obvious that some people are only really *alive* when they can be berserk, where else can such vital energies course through them? They have to plan it all in advance, deliberately bring it about that they can have pitched battles. Football doesn't arouse these passions, it already to some extent contains and sublimates them. There needs to be excitement and arousal, exciting life, and it will be found in atavistic forms, in ignorant armies, unless the imagination can be charmed and significant life created.

As I write I get the sense of a breakthrough just beyond my grasp, just beyond the horizon, but it dissolves again. One thing, though. I feel that I can now write what I like, that I have established a form for myself, in which what I want to say and how I want to say it are central, not just apologetic intimations in an academic essay where it does not really belong. But thought is sequential, and at other times the thoughts about the deaths of the young men and the grief of their women and children have a stronger presence: the facts of human misery force themselves upon the imagination, and this also generates an energy for action, for protest against this careless war and destruction. This is a different state of mind, and represents a different state of society. And one may still be under the necessity of declaring war, even in the face of that fuller knowledge, fuller representation. One does not talk about 'war in general'. Why should anyone care about the death or maiming of a young man or the harrowing of his family? Why should anyone care about that, any more than that someone should enthuse instead about military exploits? What are the scales in which these things are balanced: or is it scales from the eyes?

I am depressed and ashamed because I do not *know* whether or not the Task Force should have been sent. There is no question, in some people's minds, or there seems to be none, whether they believe the one thing or the other. Drive them back into the sea is the ancient advice of our ancestors, whose spirit still powerfully moves us. And where are we if there is no conviction, or if all conviction belongs to a warlike spirit. So many minds are untroubled by doubts in all this, they are in a position to take some sort of action, they have a picture of what they want and how it is to be achieved. I do not think it is a virtue to be troubled by doubt, nor necessarily a vice. But here to be troubled by doubt is to be found wanting, and I am troubled by doubts, and am thus overtaken by events. But even so I can still say this, that the possibilities of non-violence (*ahimsa*) are scarcely explored, because there is too little will for it and too little imagination.

I have been writing about the experience of weakness. As Spinoza writes: 'the greater the pain, the greater the power of activity employed to remove it'. This is the actual condition of one moment of egocentrism, which is not a vice but an initial condition. The energies of such a person are already diminished, and they may be exhausted still further by this kind of endeavour and perspective – 'contemplation through a crack in the door' – which limits and directs perception and behaviour. One genuinely has little strength for anything else, no wonder Arnold writes 'powerless to be born'. One needs a period of convalescence. There are flashes of perception of another kind, but there isn't the energy to sustain them and they are lost to view as more pressing concerns reassert themselves. That is why they are still the subject-matter of art. But another moment of egocentrism is easily confused with some kind of liberation. 'Between the emotion / And the response / Falls the shadow' – as though all would be well if only the gap between conception and execution could be bridged. It all depends on what you are going to do! The weak have their partners in the dance, the strong. Sometimes it's turn and turn about. But there are also those who have always felt the full and undisturbed pleasure of their own power of activity within a particular sphere of being (Simone Weil). Indeed it is one of the conditions of such power that they are surrounded and sustained by the presence of the weak. I do not come into daily contact with these people, who have never met any resistance, whose strength is assumed and reinforced from the very beginning. But I suppose I still try to avoid people with a certain kind of social strength and power, and feel ill at ease in their company. I don't have any breeding and don't know their ways, so I don't know how to behave. I cannot strike the right note. I feel the echo of my own hesitancy, and where I am in my element, like a dolphin in the waves, a child on a swing beneath a great green oak, none of it exists for them, it is less even than a dream. And the way that people commonly talk about egocentrism merely serves to reinforce it. Leavis talks about ego-centric self-enclosure, discussing Blake, in opposition to what he calls 'identity'. Nevertheless there is the smell of self-contempt in the surroundings of that description. Iris Murdoch once used the phrase 'the fat relentless ego'. But I can hear hatred in that phrase: thyself thy foe, to thy sweet self too cruel. It may be true that purity of heart is to will one thing, but a person can follow evil without deflection as well as good . . . or can they? With their whole being? And who is the one who determines what is to count as 'with one's whole being'? Willing the good is not simply a matter of eliminating doublemindedness, though it is bound to include that. *We need a separate account of the good.* It is still a further question, in which direction one's energies may go. No, I am thinking of energies again in merely quantitative terms. The energy for the good comes from a different state of the person. I still do not know how to talk about 'energy', even though it is *the main thing.* Anyway, it is not that for some people there is no interval between the intention and the act – that does not carry the weight of the analysis. What matters is the nature of the act, and the nature of the thought that lodges, as Simone Weil puts it, *in* that interval.

2

In Buddhism one of the 'mental poisons', 'conceit', is described as dependence upon comparison: thinking that you are superior to others, that you are inferior to others, that you are equal to others. This is another moment of egocentrism. The truth value of such judgments is not at issue. It is the preoccupation with comparison itself, as an habitual pattern of thought. It reminds me of Lawrence's (1950) comment in his essay *On Democracy*, that one man is neither equal nor unequal to another man. Perhaps what I am talking about is envy – comparison become invidious, a form of enmity. But why is one *affected* by comparison? Why do I make comparisons, form them in my mind, to my relief or alarm, what is the origin of the pleasure and the pain? The answer is not that we are social beings, which simply begs the question about the possible forms of society. Redundancy may cause you to lose your self-respect, but only because you are one kind of agent in one kind of society. Why should I be disabled by some comparison? It is easy to say that we live in these comparisons, that we form our identity around, not particular comparisons, for that is always changing, but around a favourable place in some available hierarchy. There you have it, an historical determinism that continues to oppress us.

Why do I need to maintain a favourable profile within the society, the society as it is presently constituted, using that to determine, or allowing that to determine, my actions, arousing fear at my own contrary inclinations or desires, or maintain a favourable self-image, repressing unruly thoughts and desires. What does all this protect us from? is it because once there were kings and barons and their descendants rule us still? the internal resonances of the state of the power relations. More to the point, here are the forms of thought that possess us until they can be suspended and something else make itself heard. The general forms of unregenerate thought.

I felt the rise of disappointment when I heard that hopes were growing of a UN solution. So there won't be a landing, then . . . But I am a very mild sort of chap, softly spoken, reticent, though it is true that I shout at my children sometimes. Indeed I am least inhibited when I shout at them, poor mites. Otherwise my anger is of the cold, remote sort. Many people are like that. They do not raise their voices. I can't bear to hear the raw, ugly sound of anger coming from myself. It is unaesthetic. Except, as I said, I can get enraged with my children when they don't go to sleep when I want them to. I don't want to, and can see ways of avoiding it, but they require more effort than I have been prepared to expend. I don't want them to have to shrink from me. So already the chips were down. But if I feel this disappointment (look, I don't want to exaggerate, all I said was that I could *feel* it), I am sure that I am not alone. It is terrible that we have got this warlike spirit in our veins, not the energy but the *direction*. Functional once, no doubt, and still, but *here*? How can we wrench it from the one object to another? Not by wrenching. And the quality of the energy seems to depend upon the direction it is going in.

What is the relationship in which I stand to my own thoughts? As I have been writing I have noticed how I have described their progress along their own paths, their ancient cultural paths, automatically, as though I were tuned to a radio frequency. I become aware of my own thoughts, feelings of pleasure, alarm, jealousy, as though I were merely a witness, thoughts which are either at the centre of my attention or at the periphery. Except that there is a point where I am *thinking* these thoughts and another where I am merely observing them taking their course, their natural course, in the direction of action. What is the difference between their being peripheral enough for me to be aware of them, distant from them, watching the clouds drift across the sky, and becoming engaged by them, their becoming not an object but a *form* of attention, as though they arise and their pattern possesses me and I am in their grip and then that is just what I am thinking and imagining and what I am intending and what I am doing . . .

3

I didn't expect to be writing about this and I wish that I wasn't. My reluctance is partly due to my having to drag myself away from the pull of the things that do hold my interest. So it presents itself as a chore, as an irritant distracting me from the real task, as though this were not itself the real task, behind which my energies should gather themselves. The strange thing is that I feel that I should be able to relax if I could only as it were 'give in' and say to myself, yes, the Task Force should be sent and the attrition continue, relax in the current and be carried along, get a weight off my mind. But fortunately that thought is one of the sources of the resistance I feel to giving my assent. It has been hot and airless. Last night there was thunder and again, this afternoon, I heard thunder in the distance. Then it was overhead. Now the birds are singing, but the sky is overcast. I've been down to the coffee bar for some tea. It is pleasant to live in an erotic haze, but I don't want to live in that medium, involved in a permanent sexual chase and unable to remove myself, my mind, my thoughts, my actions, from it and from self-preoccupation. On the other hand, a person needs to be concerned with themselves (*le souci de soi*), to repair the damage while they have the chance, while they have time, for when the chips are down . . . one's actions will already be determined. One is not free any longer at *that* point. The death squads and the torture chambers, the electric shocks and the beatings, and the screams. I do not want to imagine it but I can. They do it, for the sake of 'duty' or out of 'inclination', to extract information, to silence, to destroy resistance. People disappear, in their thousands, without discrimination, but often efficiently: men, on the whole, proud of their skill and their status. A man could get used to it – so could our sisters, I make no distinction on that score – like someone gets used to handling corpses, temporarily still alive, get bored and irritated or giggle at the predictable conduct of their victims, familiar with their thresholds, the subject of stories later, their sobs and shrieks, their sexual parts. Some he would admire, others he would despise. Other men will do it with despatch and distaste, try not to prolong the agony. These are effective means, and what is against them, what is to stop them from doing it, from applying the electrodes and switching on the current, loyal officers who love their children, who are moved to tenderness, perhaps, in the soft arms of their lovers (though we do not expect this), who play football with their friends, but ruthless at their work in sound-proofed rooms with the doors wide open on account of the faulty ventilation. A man does it, believes that it needs to be done, and there are no limits to the means available for achieving the relevant ends, the mind, the imagination, is fertile in conceiving means, and there is no interval between conception and execution where everything is allowed, where everyone is the owner, collectively, of Gyges' Ring, no shadow there where everything is in darkness. There is nothing to stop them from doing it, and there is zeal to spare, for men are frightened not to be seen hard at work by their superiors. People club bullocks in slaughterhouses. It's a monotonous job, they slay millions of absurdly gobbling turkeys every year: it's distasteful to the refined taste, but people want the meat, and someone has to do it. If it gives some men and women pleasure, and they are inventive, then maybe they will be more efficient and effective. And what does it matter, either, if a few hundred men get killed in the present war, for are they not men after all, even the conscripts who will be slaughtered like lambs because they have no sinews to stiffen, blood to summon up. Why should people get impassioned, what is there against it? Many of the soldiers are engaged by it, they live in that dimension, this justifies them and they can feel alive in the tension and the excitement and the danger of daring operations, all concentration and awareness, and, in extremities, when death is inevitable, then they are perfectly fearless and terrible in battle, because they do not go, like weaker men, in fear of their lives. And after all that, when the fighting is over, there is nothing but vacancy and with-drawal and the memory of a time, the only time, that they felt themselves alive. Women grieve and children suffer, but this is how it always was. There is *nothing* against it, *nothing*, to have people in your power, for torment and abuse, to see them afraid, to have their person at your dis-posal, as a matter of course, to finger them, to hurt them, to disgust them, to be able slowly to unbuckle your belt, make them do what you want, discard them like a plastic cup you crumple in your hand, destroy their looks, pull out their hair, knock out their teeth. There is nothing against it, there is pleasure in cruelty, the imagination is at work here too, creative also of cruelty. *There is nothing against it but the mind that recoils.* Duty and obligation and right are its garbled echo heard from a long way off.

CHAPTER FIVE

The division of the soul

I

It is interesting, is it not, that when Plato introduces 'spirit' or *thumos* in the *Republic*, as he arrives through reflection at the division of the soul into Reason, Spirit and Appetite, that it is manifested as an indignation directed to *oneself*: it is Kant's Imperative, there from the start, our first felt moral task. Nevertheless, it is only a phase of the moral life.

Self-possession or *Besonnenheit* . . . the expression is ambiguous, between the edgy uncertainty of *enkrateia*, and the relaxed fullness of *sophrosune*, between the joyful, effortless action celebrated by such thinkers as Schiller, Nietzsche and Blake ('virtues of delight') and the effortful, necessitated product of moral struggle. Passage from the one to the other is obscured from view unless we see moral struggle as a *phase* or *modality* of ethical sensibility and not as an inescapable and permanent aspect of the ethical.

The trouble with a *life* of *enkrateia*, a virtue that can be too successful, is that a person undergoes transformations they are not even aware of: 'that pale religious lechery, that wishes but acts not', for instance. If you toss out nature with a pitchfork, it will still in the end return.

So what is an 'ethical sensibility' you may well ask. Just as I want to map the movement from *akolasia*, through *enkrateia* to *sophrosune* onto the stages of the development of a moral sensibility, I want to understand the latter in terms of a movement of *eros*, from physical beauty to beauty of soul.

The inner state that manifests itself in *sophrosune* is well understood in the Buddhist tradition, in descriptions even of the first or lowest of the *dhyanas* or states of consciousness arising from the practice of meditation. Thus the practitioner suffuses, pervades, fills and permeates his body with the pleasure and joy arising from concentration, and there is nothing in all his body untouched by the pleasure and joy arising from concentration.

But for all that I cannot pretend that you are not beautiful, that your bearing does not arouse such tenderness and desire within me . . . meeting mortal beauty . . . and why do I have to remind myself that it is mortal? and what kind of threat is it? the threat of infatuation, never to look away again, no longer self-possessed . . . your beauty comes between us, I just want to look at you, hardly listening to what you say, in a state of wonder I want to stare, please go on talking so that I can helplessly listen. I have to rise to such heights of energy from here if I am not to be afflicted, if I am to join in the dance, be able at last to play. Here it is all too earnest, it is merely earnest as Schiller says, and me too gross and heavy to enter such a dance of naked bodies as has its outcome in freedom. Not to be afflicted by arousal, but to change my whole picture of what it is. That state of intensity, awed by beauty, completely held, that has to be a *clue*. And sometimes I can be awake enough to absorb rather than sexually respond, my whole body fill with a lovely energy that seems sexual no longer but an access to an unknown world, not just a change in my inner state, but also a threshold. And I *know* that I cannot say that it *is* this, it is too fugitive, it is the sense of a possibility, and maybe I am completely deluded. I can tell you, I am very weary of 'seems'.

2

In *Twilight of the Idols* Nietzsche claims that Socrates makes a 'tyrant' of reason. The idea that it at least should *rule* is presented explicitly by Plato's Socrates in the *Republic*, as part of his account of 'harmony of soul'. Rule does not imply tyranny, so we need to be clear whether the complaint is about the claim to rule itself, or about an oppressive form of it. It seems to be the latter.

Nietzsche's claim connects with the conditions of the formation of the very distinction between *enkrateia* and *sophrosune*, for Plato hovers in his account of *sophrosune* between what is recognisably the self-control associated with *enkrateia*, and what is recognisably 'temperance'. Thus the *Symposium* attempts to represent Socrates as an *embodiment* of a certain state of the soul, the description and the image of which sits uneasily with the description of harmony of soul in the *Republic*. Briefly, what Plato describes in the *Republic* as 'harmony of soul' is really a description of *en-*

krateia, whereas what he describes in the *Symposium* is *sophrosune*, and this latter virtue is a state of *eros, and* its object. I think that Nietzsche is right to insist that Socrates is 'a great erotic' who 'exercises fascination'. But he is an 'erotic' I believe just to the extent that he is possessed of *sophrosune*.

There is a moment of arousal, hardly arousal at all, which is just a quiet pleasure or satisfaction in the presence of an object of desire, as one might feel, say, seeing the naked body of a young man or woman, the strange lightness of movement, the sense of the body's balanced forces. And thus in the ugly, Silenus figure of Socrates, also an object of *eros*, a pleasure in the presence of someone beautiful, radiating beauty. Alcibiades talks of an arousal at the pitch of religious excitement at the mysteries. This is necessary, since if we follow it we gain a quite differ-ent picture of the moral life, different from that picture of internal divi-sion that Nietzsche sees in Kant and thinks he sees in Socrates. You see, what this book is really about is a tracing of the consequences of the pause, the suspension of activity, including mental activity, with which philosophy has to begin. In that interlude possibilities present themselves at the very same time as a felt unsatisfactoriness, a new sensibility emerges, in conflict with the old. And so for a long time we can have nothing but struggle, so that many people think that there can *only* be struggle. And yet the idea of another state is present, precariously, in Plato's account of *sophrosune*, which we translate as 'temperance', a kind of effortlessness of action that hardly belongs to us and yet can come to constitute us.

Part of the brilliance of the *Symposium* lies in its attempt to represent the *demeanour* of Socrates. We hear it described by Alcibiades in the latter parts of the dialogue, a demeanour of chastity and 'self-control' (but is it *enkrateia* or *sophrosune?*) significantly different from the description of his sexual excitement in the gymnasium at the sight of young Charmides' body in the earlier dialogue. The joke of *Charmides* is that Socrates manages to detain the youth for a discussion of the 'self-control' (*enkra-teia?*) his physical presence is severely testing. The irony is that Socrates is deadly serious, and that talking here, really about the conditions for the possibility of that very conversation, is an intense, unstable pleasure which would be destroyed by an attempt at seduction (a theme pursued in *Phaedrus*, in his distinction between the chaste and the 'honourable' pair of lovers). There is an issue, too, about the relation between lived experience and what one might take the reality of the virtue to be, another ironical difference, as the youth struggles to define what is actu-ally though precariously present in front of him, and which he has scarcely had to contend with himself. So who knows what the difference is between *sophrosune* and *enkrateia*, at what point in one's life does one realise that there *is* a difference?

On both occasions Plato shows that it is vital to imagine the *presence* of someone who has the virtue,[1] as well as that of someone who hasn't, if we are to find plausible a key claim made in the *Republic* (402), that an 'educated person' is 'not attracted to' a physically beautiful person who lacks beauty of soul. But I know too . . . that Nietzsche's confrontation with Socrates is also a confrontation with *me*, a male philosopher, and what is at stake, among many other things, is the intelligence of my own strategies, their rightness or wrongness, in the face of sexual desire. But Nietzsche is a philosopher, also male, and what we have to look at are competing descriptions of what it is to be a human being at all. And maybe neither men nor women can offer that account alone, or understand one another's emphases. It is possibly too easy to think to find the feminine or the masculine within oneself androgynously when difference partly consists in embodied life experience. Perhaps the whole account of the 'tyranny of reason' is an account of a possible formation of *men*. I am critical, as a philosopher, of the terms of that formation, and I have tended to suppose that the criticism opens up a common conception of humanity. But maybe it opens up rather, an alternative formation of maleness. We are concerned, partly, with strategies in the face of sexual desire, the discoveries of ways to free oneself from sexual *passion*, to live in and to surf *eros* without being oppressed by it. But we are talking about a male experience of desire, of the possible range of such experience. Perhaps in the end we neither of us, men nor women, can do more than describe a possible body of experience and its relations. One speaks out of the heart, and the words remain after speech, and spoken again they touch hearts, which open to them like flowers in the sun, and open also to the touch.

3

In order to characterise the idea of 'value' I have used the metaphor of 'horizons of (motivating) thought'. One advantage of 'horizons' is that they recede as we move through the landscape, and their movement

---

[1] Apropos of this exercise of imagination it is perhaps worth looking at how R. L. Stevenson imagines the presence of Mr Hyde: he refers to the instinctive revulsion of those who set eyes upon him.

reflects ours. Profiles of humanity emerge out of the contours of such thoughts, such 'considerations' as move us to action, as quicken us or *animate*. So the presence and demeanour of Socrates is determined by the spirit that animates him, the energy that resides in his body and radiates outwards.

These motivating thoughts do not contain unacknowledged evaluations, remember. They are empirical propositions, whose contents express such facts as represent the intentional objects of our emotions. They are thus *reasons for acting*. If our reasons are opaque, we can sometimes clarify them by further descriptions of their object. Such further descriptions (or further reasons) are the source of the charge upon the key words, the evaluative terms by means of which we express our attitude to the facts. The facts and our primitive response to them ground the charge. Such further descriptions lie beneath the surface of our evaluative language, embedded in the history of a community, its collective memory, what it has learned and what it has forgotten. Take the case of enmity, for instance. Sometimes enmity is unavoidable, but why should anyone seek to avert its arrival? To explain this is a matter of showing what enmity is *like* (precisely to offer further descriptions). We may come to realise the reasons for avoiding enmity (reasons already staring us in the face out of our own tradition) when we bring it upon ourselves and experience it, including the loss of what it brings to an end, the return of which is the sweeter for its absence. Do you know the *bitterness* of enmity? You need to be familiar with friendship too in order to *appreciate* that bitterness, and with that bitterness to appreciate friendship. 'Behold how good and pleasant it is for brethren to dwell together in unity! It is like the precious ointment upon the head, that ran down the beard' etc. But that is not said, or understood, in the absence of a terrible other experience. Consent depends upon knowledge of the alternatives. It is a communal assent of this sort that gives us the language we inherit and need to (re)appropriate. At the point where reasons come to an end poetry begins. This is not to say that enemies are not useful, they are the ones most likely to tell us the truth, I am thinking more of a state of war. And it is true that hooligans search enemies out and really *live* in a state of battle. But that depends on how much *agon* they undergo, and what it costs them. Nevertheless, the idea of there being something that it is like to be in a state of enmity is underdetermined. What it is like depends on a sense of the available contrasts, on what you lose by it, and to lose something you need to have had it.

Why should Kant's grocer avoid doing something that would be dishonest? Let us have him say that he is not prepared to do it because to do so would be *dishonest*. But isn't that merely superstition? Why should that concern him? What does that matter, can nothing more be said? There must be some, what shall we say, some *rationale* for offering that as a reason. The point is that it is not a reason at all, but a summary reference to the phenomena and the way they affect us. We have, in a way, to resort to *taste*, to the taste of 'good and 'evil', what they are like. We have to refer to the *difference* that honesty and dishonesty makes. You cannot understand what is 'wrong' with being dishonest except through experience of the relevant phenomena, whether at the receiving or the criminal end: the taste of ashes in your mouth. It is *easier* to see what is 'wrong' with it if you are at the receiving end, though someone who has been there may well change places if they get the chance: now it's my turn. You do not need to have become entangled in the alienating effects of dishonesty, for example, to see what is 'wrong' with it. It may be brought home in other ways, in works of fiction or history. Or you might just find yourself a long way down a well-used road. Thus one spells out the detail of dishonesty which constitutes the reason against. That doesn't mean there aren't people who are indifferent to the recitation of such detail. Of course there is already an evaluative charge on the descriptions of what makes it 'wrong', but they only reflect the response to what it is like, to the facts of the case. To describe what dishonesty is like, in terms of the breakdown of trust, etc., of course includes references to what we might call consequences, the consequences of specific actions. But that doesn't mean that it's not true that dishonesty is *intrinsically* wrong. There is a confusion about the nature of consequentialism. What is intrinsically wrong, i.e., what is wrong, independently of any references to its consequences, is *a particular package of actions and their consequences*! Actions and particular consequences are already built into the description of the action as 'dishonest'. If the consequentialist *then* says that it is by reference to its consequences that an action is wrong, and applies this to an action under a description which already includes a kind of consequence, *then* they are being perverse.

'All warfare is based on deception. Therefore, when capable of attacking feign incapacity; when active in moving troops, feign inactivity. When near the enemy, make it seem that you are far away; when far away, make it seem that you are near . . .' (Sun Tzu). That is to say that *waging* war depends upon deception. But doesn't deception, doesn't lying, entail a *state* of war? Which is part of what is against lying.

Truthfulness is then a product of peace, a condition in which one is not impelled to lie. And self-deception evinces a state of war within the psyche.

It may be true that I am 'privileging' a particular sensibility, but, in a strange way, it already speaks through me, speaks for itself, a sensibility that is *emerging in the species*. How close I see now I came to Tanabe in that formulation, of metanoesis working through him. Well, there's some sense in this. We *start* with dirty hands, we inherit the law of the strongest and its values, it's where we start from: we don't have a *choice* of two directions to go in, we are already deep in a particular territory, and are becoming sensitive to voices from elsewhere. That we are already constituted by *aidos* and *dike*, shame and justice, shows the direction of the trajectory, between the two contrary states of the human soul.

A person possessed of *sophrosune* is, we might say, erotically charged, manifests a state of *eros*, and it is easy to forget this unless we keep our imagination *vivid* even when, *especially* when, we are trying to do philosophy. That is why Socrates was a great erotic, and attractive. But this notion has to be explained, by the idea that temperance is an *outcome* of a certain flourishing sensibility, the product of a transition, from the love of physical beauty to the love of beauty of soul, which brings about a certain *state* of the body: not simply the state of enjoyment or pleasure without excess, but also the *coursing of energy* through the body that is also an aspect of a flourishing sensibility. It is because of that *coursing* that contrary impulses recede, but it is what makes Socrates a figure who attracts.

The resilience and function of fantasy, my mind strays to thoughts of a woman, her image occupies a compensatory role in my mental and emotional economy, her image just arrives, it does not need to be summoned. But the need is already weakening if all this remains without repression merely at the periphery; because basically I do not want to follow the impulse, I do not want the reality of entanglement. In the refectory queue in front of me a closely entangled couple arouse my prurience, but the sight also suffocates me. On the way from the station this afternoon a half-tight skinhead approaches a girl, lurches towards her, big boots, tight jeans, bottle in hand, and she hurries away, visibly frightened, and after her he hurls abuse. There is a state of mind in which one does not form relations with women as individuals, but makes demands upon the gender as such, unable to differentiate, as though any woman owes it to you. I understand it, it's there in myself, we've a long way to go.

What I have said about the erotic charge of Socrates, a product of the state of *sophrosune*, shows how important it is to *represent* him, to show the embodiment of his state, the body of his consciousness. I had thought there was a sexual interest in him, but now I am not so sure. On the other hand, maybe Plato sensed a necessity for Alcibiades to slip under the blanket with Socrates, even though he sharply admonishes him for thus seeking to offer dross in exchange for gold, and it is against the tenor of his conscious thought. Perhaps, as Lacan puts it, he needs to see 'Socrates' prick', to grasp it, for *his*, not Socrates', satisfaction. A confusion in the body of image and reality. Perhaps it would not be clear what the cause of the attraction was. We are supposed to think that Socrates is an embodiment of beauty of soul. I am trying to express why that might attract, and strongly. Even in a sexual case it is a person in their *energy* that attracts and not merely their form, which may indeed be an expression of it under certain conditions. My own Socrates has not repressed his energies, as Nietzsche suspects him of doing. Nor are they sublimated if sublimation implies an *unconscious* process. The figure of Socrates represents the *presence* of someone possessed of beauty of soul, represents a human perfection which becomes thus a measure of comparison and judgment. But there is more. He also represents, he is the figure, of *one who knows* (Lacan). To that extent Socrates is what a man would become, a male exemplar of a human perfection the admirer also desires. He is the figure of what we would have, but in order to get it we have to renounce the getting and become. The difficulty, and this is part of Diotima's teaching, and the lesson of Alcibiades, is to understand the conditions under which such perfection, such wisdom and virtue, may be realised. The further difficulty is to be clear about the fault lines in the conception. Nietzsche's suspicion of Socrates is one of his great contributions, for 'Socrates' summarises a major Western strategy in the face of the male and the human predicament. This means we have to sort out the source of the *attraction* from the faulty *conception*.

I said, innocently enough, that perhaps Plato sensed a need for *Alcibiades* to slip under the blanket with Socrates. But maybe it was his own necessity and Alcibiades was his substitute. And the only acceptable way of representing this to himself was by means of Socrates' rejection, his not supplying the goods. It would have been difficult to represent to himself the idea of Alcibiades as *erastes*, an active younger partner, even though he implicitly accepts the irony that he *is* the *erastes* to Socrates' *eromenos* qua bearer of beauty of soul. His attraction to Socrates takes a confused sexual form, but the only way he can see himself as Socrates'

lover is by seeing the truth. What I mean is, it is true that he is attracted
to Socrates' beauty of soul, but that also provides him with the means
by which he can *admit* that he is the lover of Socrates, even though the
fact that he has a sexual attachment, which he cannot admit, is in reality
a confused recognition of what he really desires.

Socrates is also an image of *harmony of soul*. But it is one thing to
present an *image* of harmony of soul, which I connect with *sophrosune*,
and quite another to get the *description* right. Plato's own difficulties seem
to me to be just those of someone who is struggling, aren't we all, with
the transition from the state of *enkrateia* to the state of *sophrosune*. Our
states are contrary, Socrates represents us. The imaginative figure of
Socrates transcends the Platonic account of him.

4

There is a connection between what one attends to and the state of one's
desires, the *sanskharas*: everything else, from the point of view of the
attention, is 'less even than a dream'. Here is where mindfulness begins,
at an already determined ethical point, with the faintest intimations at
the edges of desire. And so, to become aware of such things, there has
to be a *suspension of activity*, and in the suspension *geht neuer Anfang, Wink
und Wandlung vor*, stir new beginnings and a sense of change.

The *sanskharas*. By focusing on motivation I echo a central element of
the traditional Buddhist analysis of the human person in terms of the
five *skandhas*, the so-called five 'heaps' or 'aggregates' or 'constituents', of
form (*rupa*), feeling (*vedana*), volition (*sanskhara*), discrimination (*sanna*) and
self-consciousness (*vinanna*). But these are not heaps all on a level as it
were. The general form of our self-consciousness (*vinanna*), what it feels
like (*vedana*), is determined by the state of our motivations (*sanskharas*)
which also determine the quality of our perceptions (*sanna*) and are the
motor of action. This is the psychological model I am using, one that
gives primacy to the notion of motivation for an understanding of action
and perception. A motivation is not a desire, but a thought or perception which rouses us, under the right conditions, over which we have
some control, to action. But for this to happen we must already be thinking, or have been aroused already to active thought, about the course of
events, for not only do we need energy to act, we need energy *actively to
think about* what we see going on around us, otherwise we do not see the
relations of cause and effect, the connections, within the succession of
events, so that 'begging', for instance, is the name of an appearance, of

an immediate set of actions only, without the sense of the totality in which it has its identity, a sense that depends upon my ability to engage in *acts of thought and imagination*. Thus the relations that we see and the motivations that we are capable of are interconnected. If our desires are relatively crude we have only a crude apprehension of the relations between things, and what lies outside our apprehensions appear merely as *discrete objects*, that is we do not see them *in their relations* (almost the exact opposite of old Schopenhauer). But the process of active thinking is also a process of *active imagination*, and the development of motivations builds up alongside *recognition* of things in their relations, just because *they* are the intentional objects of those motivations, not just the beggar, but what makes them a beggar, etc. To refer to my *motives* in giving the beggar some money is to relate the action to an end: e.g. my motive was to assuage my own discomfort or, more positively, to make sure they eat. A motiveless action (a motiveless malignity) would thus be an action that had no further end, one done perhaps for its own sake. Such actions may be *expressive* of particular states of mind, an envy or hatred of goodness, for instance. But to talk of someone's *motivation*, as I said just now, is to refer to the sort of thing that moves them to act. We generalise over cases. Someone acts 'out of embarrassment': we locate the particular incident to which I reacted in a particular way – my discomposure when we notice what my Freudian slip revealed, when I say for instance that Oedipus killed his mother and married his father – to other incidents of the same general kind. To act out of fear is similarly to act in a charac-teristic way in a characteristic situation. Or I may act out of generosity, acting out of a *lively* sense of what I can do for someone.

5

I must have been conceived about VE Day, in early May, 1945: the final surrender of the Nazis to the Allied Forces. There we were, my genera-tion, being conceived, and somewhere else they were finding the camps. So how do we justify ourselves, not having the burden of bearing witness to what escapes imagination and destroys even through the memory . . . what do *we* bear witness to, what are we able to know? And twenty million Russians dead. You cannot imagine such facts, they say. The imagination is brought to the edge of an abyss in which it fears to lose itself, and so, not thus losing itself, it is lost in small preoccupations that provide boundaries for action that are too tight for the excess of energy. There is a Kantian prescription for a certain kind of artistic endeavour, to bring the imagination to such a pitch that it begins to swoon. What you cannot imagine you can easily forget: we want images, not facts and figures, images of the two contrary states of the human soul, and we were conceived just as they were finding its extremest term: so what, if anything, are we for? A few months earlier, in the January of that year, the Austrian philosopher, Ludwig Wittgenstein, completed the Preface to his *Philosophical Investigations*, published only posthumously, in 1953. Perhaps he was writing it at more or less the same time as Tanabe was writing his:

It is not impossible that it should fall to the lot of this work, in its poverty and in the darkness of this time, to bring light into one brain or another – but, of course, it is not likely.

Now I am not so sure about the *tone*. Read it again. Perhaps he was in the grip of some depression when he wrote it, I read conceit and despair. He knew he was the best of the philosophers. He knew his vanity too, he confessed it:

I was obliged to learn that my results (which I had communicated in lectures, typescripts and discussions), variously misunderstood, more or less mangled or watered down, were in circulation. This stung my vanity and I had difficulty in quieting it.

It is relatively easy to confess to vanity when you have as it were something to be vain about. It is more difficult when you haven't, the absurdity of the vice shows up the more. But 'it is not impossible that it should fall to the lot of this work, in its poverty . . .' Why 'in' its poverty (*in ihrer Dürftigkeit*), rather than despite it, when it was also something variously misunderstood, mangled or watered down? He was the best, as he well knew, in the darkness of that time, it was the best he could achieve and yet it was *poor*, though not so poor that it could not bring *light* 'into one brain or another' (the *best* brains?) . . . 'but, of course, it is not likely'. Why 'of course'? 'Not likely' because of the poverty of the work or because of the weakness of the brains it might bring light into? For, despite its poverty, or '*in*' its poverty, do you not hear the lovingness in the use of that 'in'? it could still bring light. But take him at his word, as one always should with such a master. The work is poor, despite being the best around, and it is only *possible*, i.e., not *likely*, that it should bring light into a couple of brains: the weak flicker of a candle flame, a dim, flickering light in the darkness of that time. Take him at his word, and the time was very dark. In the pitch dark, all the wires down, the generators dead, a weak candle whose little light throws faint shadows on the wall, as someone stumbles across the room . . . let us have no illusions, the voice we hear is at the lowest ebb of its spiritual energy. When we were conceived, the war was over and the tide had turned. But there was still darkness over all the earth. And even now we only live in the eerie illusion of light, and sometimes the clouds darken further, and sometimes seem to recede, the sun also shines through, but light is also blinding and there are different forms of darkness: you can see more in the dark, you can see the heavenly bodies, the realities which sunlight excludes. The night was made for loving and for watching too. There is also light and light: the lights that guide us may be generated by our unexamined and maybe foolish ends. The day is bright, but the night is deeper, so let us not be obsessed with light, oh Bharat, upon whose shores I walk with such suspicion and excitement. Wittgenstein was like Kant, a martyr to truth, and maybe his sense of the poverty of his work derived from a measure that most of us cannot read. True philosophy is written in the language of poetry, musical as is Apollo's lute, and its hand feels cold only to the overheated brow. Wittgenstein wrote his Preface while European cities were the ruined shambles through which their populations picked their way. In the wake of the Reign of Terror, in 1795, Friedrich Schiller offered the public a book on . . . *aesthetics*. And I would emulate the intent.

6

We know what it would be like to be temperate, even though we act incontinently, since sometimes, in the repose of sense that follows the satisfaction of desire we are released at least to contemplate the intentional objects of awakened affects. There is such repose in one another's arms, the bed sometimes begets 'noble *logoi*', noble conversation. Maybe it is in bed that we first start to talk intimately about ourselves, make our confessions, reveal or express our strivings. Or so Diotima is made to say, that ethics begins in pillow talk. Maybe that is where men and women start to talk and listen. And maybe ethics begins also with babies and *Entsagung*, in the renunciation their presence demands.

The idea of the imperturbable Buddha: we can represent the negation of our own failures, embody it in an image, represent it as a possibility. The idea of an enlightened being, or a completely or fully enlightened being: we can already make a distinction, on the basis of our own experience, and from different points of view, between more or less 'enlightened' persons, but it seems that we can indefinitely carry on performing an operation of comparison, in either direction, upon either term, so that we can always think the possibility of a more enlightened state in comparison with any present state. But such an operation is idle if we cannot supply a content. It does not imply that there must be such a state: it may simply present itself as a bare possibility, and we always need reasons for starting to think that our present state may be less than satisfactory, *except* that the reasons may only emerge *after* we have dwelt with some attention on the sense of unsatisfactoriness itself. By unsatisfactoriness I mean *dukkha*. When you first start to hear these words they have no associations and so they are cold and lifeless. They have to be used.

As temperance grows, the more capable are we of focusing on and acting in the light of the directed attention of a released sensibility. The less continent we are, the less energised such perceptions become, the narrower the focus, the less vitality for ethical responses. In contrast one needs to fix an exemplifying image, of someone fully engaged in what they are doing, concentrated, undistracted, alert.

7

But isn't there a narcoticising dimension to the Kantian idea of beauty? the object preadapted to our cognitive faculties? Well, Kant lays at least as much stress on the *sublime* in nature which is, by contrast, *disruptive*, and in which the imagination feels itself at the edge of an abyss in which it fears to lose itself. Freely adapting this, the idea of an affront to the imagination allows us to think of the more disruptive aspects of art, in which the whole sense of our lives is disturbed, a disturbance of the forms of imagination that contour our horizons, the settled forms of unregenerate life.

Imagination may have a more quotidian employment in the service of one's present projects. But the set of one's purposes and desires itself forms a pattern one is afraid might be disrupted, the pattern of one's work towards finding a favourable place for oneself in a society whose values one has internalised. Fear of one's own *desires* may lead one to repress them, but then they have their revenge as one slowly changes without noticing the gradations from one state to another. Fear of one's *moral consciousness* may have as powerful an effect because that too will disrupt the pattern of one's life, the standing up to be counted, the object of resentment and hostility, rocking the boat. Perhaps this is what I fear most, to be tried and found wanting, suddenly without warning a set of conditions coalesces, a response is demanded, and you are not there, not aware, incapable of the action the situation calls for.

An ancient Buddhist practice, apparently, was to loiter in a cremation ground, through the night as well as the day, observing the corruption of the body in its progressive stages. I spend a lot of time talking and thinking about physical and natural beauty, but ugliness, squalor, corruption hardly seem to enter into my thinking at all. Does that mean that I simply avoid them, turning away, refusing to look them in the face, to assimilate them? Avoidance is a major cultural force. I wrote about the Falklands, I felt it, I was involved in it, but almost at the same time the Israelis were bombing West Beirut, and though I was briefly appalled by it, it did not really affect me, even though it is all much worse than the Falklands Crisis. All we see of the world is what our attention is focused on and, *a fortiori*, we don't see the underlying reasons for this. We take the focus of our attention to reveal the state of things, but it only reveals what it reveals, and what is outside the focus is not apparent to us, so that we don't even know what someone is talking about who points to things outside its scope. And we take our perceived world to be a ground of judgment, whereas it is only the present *scope* of our judgment, the *erkanntes Leben* that is an expression and product of our *condition*. Moreover, I talk about the fear of being found wanting, yet I also feel a kind of *envy* for those who have stood the test, like certain dissidents, for example, whose comfortable lives are over, and in imagination I cling to the bed clothes, not that, not that . . . Maybe what is running through me is the felt need to prove my valour, demonstrate my manliness, like those young men in Spanish towns who run with the bulls. To be able to say, *ich war dabei*, which is not Spanish, I know. We have to remember that the hollow men do not always assent to the proposition that they are hollow men, nor the prisoners in the cave that they are prisoners, nor fragmented human beings that they are fragmented.

8

Whatever we are calling 'moral beauty' or 'beauty of soul' is an object of *eros*, an energetic *eros*, and we have to show how it could be. Socrates, or some other exemplar, has got to be shown to exercise fascination, to draw us towards him. But first, since I have praised the image and criticised the description in Plato, what is this idea of 'harmony of soul', and what is its role?

Gyges the shepherd acquires a magic ring which renders him invisible at will. And so he seduces the queen and murders the king with her help (almost *Hamlet*), and isn't that what anyone would do if they had the chance, the wish-fulfilment fantasy, ambition, power, sex? is Glaucon's challenge to Socrates. No one is just save under compulsion. Anyone who denies they would do such things is either lying or a fool. It is a seductive story, it has to be a story, because it thus enters our imagination, and we imagine the situation, and we imagine in our intimate minds what we would do ourselves. Gyges is the figure of someone who is able to act with impunity, one for whom there are no sanctions because he can escape them all. Later writers respond by talking about inner sanctions. We can take that seriously or be cynical. Let us be cynical for a while and assert that the voice of conscience is merely the sound of other people's voices in our heads, an internalisation of the outer sanctions, superego, and suppose now that there are none, what would we do? Let us *really* think what we would like to do. Immediately, I suppose, male fantasies arise about power and seduction, the seraglio, precisely Gyges' fantasy acted out. Forget the oversimplification for a moment, forget the difference between imagination and fantasy, where fantasy does not work out the realities and imagination does. We can do what we like, and what we would do is just the sort of thing that Gyges did and, in those circumstances, he is indifferent to issues of justice, as we would be. Because questions of justice only arise as a result of some sort of agreement between people of similar mental make-up who realise that they get trampled on themselves from time to time as well as trampling over the interests of others. So they set up ground rules. This is what people are really like, say Glaucon and Adeimantus. And if you are strong enough, or invisible enough, then you do not need to worry about the ground rules which are for weaker men. And surely they are empirically right. This is what human beings are like. And women are the same: give me the daggers.

So how is Socrates to respond? In fact, he agrees that this is what human beings are like. This is what we are like as a matter of fact, it is, as Schiller would say, empirical humanity. But our behaviour reveals the state of our desires. It expresses our state. Socrates acknowledges that this is how human beings are, and then offers a diagnosis, and the behaviour thus exemplified is diagnosed as proceeding from a disordered soul, from a state of disharmony. It may be empirically the case that people in general are just only under compulsion, but it is not true that justice is merely a means to an end, it is also an end in itself and is desired for other consequences. Justice is the peculiar excellence of the mind and injustice is its defect. *Aidos* and *dike* again.

Already Socrates needs to be represented as *someone who knows something*, and *not* as someone who merely believes something: not like Faust, *Habe ... Philosophie ... durchaus studiert ... da steh ich nun, ich armer Tor / Und bin so klug, als wie zuvor ...* poor fool, I stand no wiser than I was before. Which is to the point, not only Gyges, but Faust, who gains power and wants to seduce a woman, the *formation* of his desires remains unaltered. Socrates is the figure of a transforming knowledge. And we want to know what he knows, we want him to share his wisdom, though we have to face the truth of his acid aside:

It would be very nice, Agathon, if wisdom were like water, and flowed by contact out of a person who has more into one who has less, just as water can be made to pass through a thread of wool out of the fuller of two cups into the emptier.

That is Plato's task, to make sense of Socrates, to assimilate this person who was his teacher, to work out what he knows – which surely can only come about through coming to know it oneself – and what it has made of his body and mind. Nietzsche's real complaint is with Plato, and there is justice in it, but there is something to be said on Plato's behalf.

And so we come to the idea of 'harmony of soul', not a merely abstract notion, but figured in Socrates, exemplified in a particular human being with a determinate presence and impact on others. The diagnosis of injustice is that it is a defect of the soul, and justice is its peculiar excellence. Men are as Glaucon and Adeimantus say – let us concede it, but they are so for a reason, there is an explanation. We know why they are like that – this is the 'ought-judgment of experience': they ought to care, though they don't, and we mean by this that there is reason to believe that they would care, if they were not in some way prevented, and they *are* prevented . . . by the disorder in their soul. So what constitutes this disorder, this sickness, and what constitutes the *order* that is shown in the figure of Socrates?

9

A foreigner passing through Athens who knew how to read faces told Socrates to his face . . . that he contained within him every kind of foul vice and lust. And Socrates answered merely: 'you know me, sir'. (*Twilight*, 30)

This, then, is Socrates' 'case', presented with a happy play on 'containment', that he 'contained within him every kind of foul vice and lust', and Socrates' remedy is to have found a way precisely to 'contain' them:

When that physiognomer had revealed to Socrates what he was, a cave of every evil lust, the great ironist uttered a phrase that provides the key to him. 'That is true', he said, 'but I have become master of them all'. (33)

And this is the basis of Nietzsche's verdict that Socrates makes a tyrant of reason, a verdict already there in Blake's percipient comment in the *Marriage of Heaven and Hell*:

Those who restrain desire do so only because theirs is weak enough to be restrained. And the restrainer, or reason, usurps its place, and governs the unwilling. And being restrained it by degrees becomes passive, til it is only the shadow of desire.

Thus the tyranny of reason. Socrates has made a diagnosis of injustice, and has offered a remedy. And now we have to study his remedy.

Part of the point of insisting that reason should rule and 'spirit' obey and support it, in the *Republic*, is that otherwise the physical appetites will come to dominate and so 'wreck life entirely' (*Republic*, IV, 442). Nietzsche's gloss on this insistence that reason should rule is that the hidden thought is that since the instincts want to play the tyrant, 'we must devise a counter-tyrant who is stronger':

Socrates saw *behind* his aristocratic Athenians; he grasped that *his* case . . . was no longer exceptional. The same kind of degeneration was everywhere silently preparing itself; the old Athens was coming to an end. And Socrates understood that all the world had need of him – his expedient, his cure, his personal art of self-preservation . . . Everywhere the instincts were in anarchy, everywhere people were but five steps from excess . . . 'The instincts want to play the tyrant; we must devise a *counter-tyrant* who is stronger'. (*Twilight*, 32)

Nietzsche's view is that the degeneration he refers to here is just the comparative weakness in the face of the 'instincts' that leaves people 'but five steps from excess'. He defines weakness of will as 'the inability *not* to react to a stimulus' (42). A sound or healthy human being, on the other hand, would be able to impose moderation upon the relevant desire, and would actually value this 'enemy within', as something he could struggle with and transform. However, in an environment of degeneration or *decadence*, where imposing moderation on an unruly desire is presumably not an option, the 'radical cure' is *renunciation*. I take it that the thought here is that moderation is not an option because any indulgence becomes addictive and so renunciation is the only alternative to excess. Nietzsche remarks shrewdly that hatred of sensuality reaches its height, not in those who are strong enough for successful renunciation, but in those who are too weak ('pale religious lechery'?) Needless to say, 'hatred of sensuality' does not indicate an environment in which sensuality could be transformed or 'spiritualised'. *That* depends upon accommodation and recognition. But it is reasonable to protest here that surely more strength is required to renounce sensuality completely than to impose moderation on it. I think a reasonable reply would be that 'healthy' human beings would not need to alter the form of their lives in order to impose moderation on their impulses – that is the point, perhaps, of saying that renunciation is the *radical* cure. The vital forces of the renouncer Nietzsche describes are brought to the task to an extent not necessary in the 'healthy', and the whole course of their life is changed accordingly.

Individuals are unjust because the elements of the soul do not stand in the right relationship, and the appetites are given free play. So what are the elements of the soul? The translation calls them Reason, Spirit and Appetite. What would it be like if they stood in the *right* relationship? Reason would rule, because Reason is able to judge what is best for the whole; Spirit should obey and support Reason, and both of them should control Appetite, because our physical appetites are naturally insatiable and the danger is that they will grow and take over and destroy life completely. 'Spirit' might reasonably be taken to refer to one's emotions. It should not be understood directly as referring to 'the spirit' or the 'spiritual', but as related to talk of high spirits or low, a spirited response, a spirited horse. It refers to the states of one's energies. The sort of scenario Plato offers is that in which reason judges something to be harmful towards which appetite inclines, and the role of 'spirit' is to wax indignant and bring appetite into line . . . like the auxiliaries acting on behalf of the guardians.

There is something immediately and obviously wrong about this. Anger and indignation are particular emotions legitimised here by their support of reason. So what about the range of emotions that do not immediately seem to have such a role? What constitutes a permissible expression of the human spirit?

I mentioned Plato's anxieties about the insatiability of appetite and how it needs to be kept in check – he also talks about the frenzy and agitation of sex – and criticised it as a *particular* experience of the appetites, and contrasted it to the experience of the *dhyanic* body.

But it seems to me that Plato plays a trick on himself at this point in the *Republic*. When he talks about harmony of soul he refers to it as a *harmonious agreement*, and then claims that it is constituted by the following arrangement: reason rules, spirit obeys and supports reason, and together they keep appetite in check because otherwise it will destroy life completely. But what reason are we given for supposing that appetite, that the body, should be happy with, should give its assent to, this regime in which it suffers *repression*? Isn't it the case, rather, that reason 'usurps its place and governs the unwilling'? And isn't this precisely a tyranny? Are we not in reality offered here a description of *dis*harmony, and isn't it the case that a *dis*ordered soul expresses itself in an indifference to

justice? It seems to me that Nietzsche is entirely right to see in this representation an expression of a primary fear of excess and loss of control:
precisely an unacknowledged *emotional* stance, though one which is intelligible given a certain self-understanding, which we can look at critically,
and a certain situatedness. And thus an interest protrudes itself from the
very beginning, the interest in mastery and control. Heidegger shows us
how much this master interest infects our understanding and our language. And what of those emotions which do not obey and support the
judgments of reason? And the unruly appetites, naturally insatiable. Are
we not being offered here, implicitly, a representation of *women*? The
implicit and unacknowledged *end* of mastery and control, the fears and
anxieties that feed it, in situations that demand it, becomes the criterion
for judging that certain emotions are *inappropriate*. Once no doubt this
was functional. The men are disciplined to curb what does not serve the
current demands of *reason* (emotions as well as appetites). I am not persuaded at all, though, that mastery and control are peculiarly male
desires. Men and women both seek to control their environment, their
women, their men. It is a human response to seek to bend others to one's
will, and not just selfishly, but for good functional social reasons. And an
oppressed class doesn't suddenly shine with virtue when it comes to
power at last. Nevertheless, we do seek instinctively to preserve the integrity of our own being, and it is true that in part we act according to a
conception we have of it. If reason is just a way of referring to the fact that
we do make judgments about what is best for the whole, then we have to
listen to our own judgments: but if we can listen to them, we can also
subject them to critical scrutiny. We act with integrity perhaps when we
act to preserve the totality as we judge it to be, but we act authentically
when we feel forced to act against that conception in the light of one not
yet articulate.

We need the body to be willing. It is willing if there is pleasure. So a
condition of temperance, the state of effortless ethical action, is one in
which the practitioner suffuses, pervades and permeates their body with
the pleasure and joy arising from concentration (*samadhi*).

But there is a bright side to all this, something to be retrieved. A disordered soul will manifest itself in actions which show the agent indifferent to the interests of others. Harmony expresses itself in actions that
are not thus indifferent. But we shall have to ask ourselves what the relationship is between a person's harmony of soul and their concern for the
well-being of others: *how* is justice the peculiar excellence of the soul?
Just because Plato messes up his account of harmony of soul doesn't

mean that there is no such thing as harmony of soul. And also, we have been offered in fact a criterion by which to judge what constitutes the well-being of the human person.

A person is well to the extent that the elements of their soul exist in a harmonious relationship, one does good to them to the extent that one's actions promote that possibility, evil to the extent that one's actions diminish it. A criterion, in other words, for Nietzsche's 'well-constituted human being', one, remember, who 'must' do certain actions, recoils from others . . . But we shall find that the weight of the account depends upon giving content to *what* they recoil from, *what* they must do.

When I first took up *yoga* I was astonished by the sense of physical well-being it brought about, the sense of balance and centredness. It changed the rhythms of my appetites. On the other hand, what this Platonic stuff entirely misses out, in blaming the body for the absence of virtue, is wickedness. It doesn't offer any account at all of pride or self-love, for instance.

Spinoza distinguished between affects on the basis of whether they tend to increase or diminish the power of action. But I wonder whether we can transcend even that distinction. The idea of emotions that tend to increase the power of action sounds a good thing. But maybe it reflects the contours of a present and limited experience, and it would be better still if we did not need to depend upon such occasional inputs of energy but could rely upon a constant stream, not living as we do by fits and starts. I wept for long after we finally parted, out of the pain of our separation, even though it was what I wanted. The thought was unbearable that we would not be part any more of each other's life, I couldn't imagine the future without you, which implied the absence of a future for myself, a future that we didn't share, in the same bed, at the same table. The future was a gap, a blank and unimaginable to me in that state, who needed a future to imagine, while I thought of it in those terms, terms not separable from the state because they were the painful thoughts of one in pain. But why could we not simply have parted? And why now, at another time and place, though I bear no grudge, do old feelings bestir themselves, ancient alarm bells ring, though not so strongly? Nevertheless, I have to take a breath, *contend* with them, swat at them hard. But I can still sit in meditation and be restored and brimful out of my own resources, out of resources that seem to well up within me.

CHAPTER SIX

'Wandering between two worlds . . .'

I

The movement of Arnold's thought over the twenty years that followed *Dover Beach* is from the dismay and nihilism of the loss of faith to the inner call of 'conduct' and 'righteousness', the pivotal concepts of *Literature and Dogma*, published in 1873. Their distance from clear consciousness and presumably therefore from *expression* in the earlier phase determines the famous melancholy, which I suggest is the discontented voice of their insistence. As he says in *The Buried Life*,

> Yet still, from time to time, vague and forlorn,
> From the soul's subterranean depth upborne
> As from an infinitely distant land,
> Come airs, and floating echoes, and convey
> A melancholy into all our day

This is the authentic language of an attention drowsily but desperately turning to what lies only at the periphery (or here, below the surface) of thought and volition. It is daunting, to become biographical, and sobering, that the twenty years we are talking about are the years which have been thought to have destroyed his poetry, the years as a Schools Inspector.

It is only through a long and quickened discipline of attention that what presents itself at first as 'vague and forlorn' etc., is going to enter forcefully into clear consciousness, thence through action into *life*. In *Dover Beach*, 'the *eternal* note of sadness' is not a consequence of the loss of faith: its sound is present even when the tide is full. It *may* intimate the loss of faith, but it is worth considering that the grating roar of the pebbles is a part of the *total* experience of the tranquil bay, something disturbing us *within* the enchantment and we *hear* it bring the eternal note of sadness in, and precipitate the associations which lead to the insight, not just that Faith is illusory, but that it is *irrelevant* to the one thing needful. In *Stanzas from the Grande Chartreuse*, Arnold stands in the Carthusians' 'world-famed home' of penitential cries, white uplifted faces, the knee-worn floor, the inner strife of souls, their death in life.[1] As he stands there, the whispers of his rigorous teachers pierce the gloom, teachers who had purged the faith and trimmed, (or, maybe, quenched)[2] the fire of his youth, and showed him the high, white, (or maybe the pale, cold)[3] star of truth: 'What dost *thou* in this living tomb?' (my italics). But, he assures us, he has not rejected those at whose behest he long ago so much unlearnt, so much resigned:

> Not as their friend, or child, I speak
> But as, on some far northern strand,
> Thinking of his own Gods, a Greek
> In pity and mournful awe might stand
> Before some fallen Runic stone –
> For both were faiths, and both are gone

Thus the Anglican Arnold regards a Roman Catholic monastery in the French Alps, and waits 'forlorn', with 'nowhere yet to rest his head', in a mood less spirited perhaps than Nietzsche's, but voicing a moment of historic doubt, as Eliot thought,[4] a perplexity in the face of the new positivism:

> For the world cries your faith is now
> But a dead time's exploded dream;
> My melancholy, sciolists say,
> Is a pass'd mode, an outworn theme –
> As if the world had ever had
> A faith, or sciolists been sad

There is a continued biblical resonance in these further references to 'the world'. Although the lines are weak and even petulant, Arnold holds on to his melancholy, holds on to and endures a sense of loss, allows himself to experience it despite the scoffing of the 'sciolists'. The tension that Arnold describes in this poem, in which he is *suspended*, unable to go back

---

[1] If we recall the later reflections of Heidegger upon Nietzsche's announcement of the Death of God, we might think of this Carthusian way of life as a paradigm of the *Bildung*, the form of self-development, that had become impossible for people in Arnold's intellectual position. Heidegger's alternative emphasis on *Besinnung*, though, is solipsistic by contrast with Arnold's explicit attention to the ethical relation.

[2] Kenneth Allott draws our attention to this 'more candid' version of the poem, published in *Fraser's Magazine* in 1855.   [3] See previous note.

[4] Eliot says, rather grandly, that it is a moment which has passed, 'which most of us have gone beyond in one direction or another' (quoted in Allott, 1979, p 302, from Eliot's *A Choice of Kipling's Verse*, 1941).

or imagine a way forward, is an experience of powerlessness brought about by the progressive closure of options by his 'rigorous teachers', a comprehensive *aporia* behind and indeterminacy ahead. But his holding on to the sense of his melancholy is a *condition* of the coming to birth of the world he is waiting for, when *jiriki* is rescued, as it seems, by *tariki*. Here a Buddhist would further recognise, I think, an authentic experience of *dukkha*, a sense of suffering, pain, or unsatisfactoriness which, as an emotion, must, if it is to be understood, be traced to its intentional object, so that the melancholy becomes a *clue*, not to Arnold's individual psychology merely, but to something submerged and unacknowledged or unrealised. The melancholy refers us to something missed or missing, is the insistent voice of our own unrealised possibilities, seeking expression. These possibilities are precisely conceived as ethical, a movement out of egocentric self-enclosure: 'let *us* be true . . .'

I have already suggested that in *Dover Beach* the turning to one another is not so much a consolation as a revealing of that whose absence makes us sad. The sadness is not assuaged by faith, we hear its note even where faith is present, but it becomes clear that what is absent are the conditions upon which joy, love, light, certitude, peace, and help for pain, depend. But since these had *seemed* to be secured by traditional religious faith *and*, as seemed implicit, by sexual life, and had, presumably, at least been tasted in a way that depended upon that faith and the onset of sexual joys, Arnold's self-conscious melancholy is not mere self-indulgence. It is a withdrawal from a mislocation and he needs to linger on it, to develop the tension in which it is apparent that *he* (necessarily alone at this point) has 'nowhere . . . to rest (his) head':

> Wandering between two worlds, one dead,
> The other powerless to be born,
> With nowhere yet to rest my head . . .

This New Testament reference to, and indeed identification with, the 'Son of Man', shows that Arnold makes a *spiritual* experience of the loss of faith. Faith was a kind of home, as foxes have holes and the birds of the air have nests. But as a home, Faith is no longer available to him, and he has glimpsed its irrelevance to his needs.

In *The Buried Life* the ethical theme is developed, and he explores and diagnoses our *failure* to be 'true to one another'. He discovers the name of our 'nameless sadness': which is, that 'we hardly read in each other the inmost soul, concealing our thoughts, alien to the rest of men and alien to ourselves'. Perhaps the two forms of alienation are connected, the one because of the other, so that there is a passage to self-knowledge that can only be negotiated through an interest in the welfare of others. We are, like Kierkegaard's objective thinker, out of contact with 'our hidden self', our own concealed interior, a self established in ethical connection.

To put it another way, and I have hardly made this connection forcefully enough yet, the failure of reflective attention and what it brings to birth is manifest in the presence implied by its absence, that of the world in which 'ignorant armies clash by night'. That is what stays with us, the darkling plain, if we do not in some kind of mutuality develop a spirit of inwardness. 'Alien to the rest of men and alien to ourselves' represents a living, palpable form of life.

So Arnold gives a source of our melancholy in our mutual and self-alienation. But often, he says, even in the world's most crowded streets, and in the din of strife, 'there rises an unspeakable desire/ After the knowledge of our buried life':

> A thirst to spend our fire and restless force
> In tracking out our true, original course;
> A longing to inquire
> Into the mystery of this heart which beats
> So wild, so deep in us – to know
> Whence our lives come and where they go

Again he perceives the necessity of an inward turn, but it is an inward turn that has an outward expression, a turn to the interior conditions of action and relationship. The melancholy was the key to a revelation, about the nature and demands of the ethical relation. The experience of *dukkha* led to a tension in which he glimpsed the inner necessity of our being 'true to one another'. He attends or waits on the insistence of the thought that has pressed upon him, and that attending has opened out its content. We do not know ourselves, or each other, and the possibility of overcoming this ignorance and the melancholy that attends it depends upon an escape from egocentrism, the unfolding of the ethical life. The ethical life is the place of self-knowledge, for it is only there that the self unfolds. But this seems for Arnold not just to amount to the thought that our motivation and behaviour are things we can learn and acknowledge about ourselves, but that ethical action, as he conceives it, is the condition of an awakening and coming to life that appears to bring us to the point of knowledge not otherwise available. 'We hardly read in each other the inmost soul.' In Arnold 'hardly' tends to have a double meaning, 'scarcely', but also 'only with difficulty', and no doubt the ambiguity is played on in this line. It is a sobering reflection that the so-called 'problem of other minds' is already a reflection on our moral condition. Part of our difficulty is to realise how *profoundly* unaware we are of what goes on in each other, because of our various absorptions, so that there are agonising failures to communicate grounded in ignorance. Moral truths, we shall see, are often uncomplicated, simple, and almost impossible to discern. A person, it might be me, would be horrified if they realised the extent of their own tyranny. *There* is a moral truth, this person is a tyrant, and they would be incredulous if this piece of news were announced to them. It is the sort of thing that is passed down the generations, like a stiff upper lip. This person will not acknowledge their suffering, their affliction, one doesn't complain about pain, one bears it, one does not ask for sympathy, and one passes this to one's children, who internalise an attitude that they have not the strength to support, so the parent becomes a saint and they become a sinner, and they cannot see how things could be different. So, we talk of moral autonomy, reflecting on what is right or wrong, and we do not realise that moral heteronomy already infects the very soul of the one who thus reflects. They have received without awareness a moral estimate, not their own, of intimate feelings and impulses, the implicit judgment that they are unacceptable, and they have no idea of this infection, which in their turn they pass on.

2

Arnold shows an astonishing percipience, quite early in his poetry, about the interior conditions of action and of the ethical life. His clear-sightedness is evident in his frequent references to *energy* or *virya* ('our fire and restless force') and its relation to the spiritual quest and the ethical life. It becomes clear that Arnold conceives the ethical life, and the development of its interior conditions, as capable of revealing something that we might call 'trans-human' or trans-natural, as forcing upon us a *revision* of what we take to be 'human' or 'natural'. What he develops is essentially a modest, non-theistic transcendentalism. The 'natural' has already lost its traditional contrast with the 'supernatural', but it remains an 'open' category. If we think of Arnold as tracing out the conditions of action and what they give rise to, we can see him poised at least on the edge of territory he would not want to call *either* 'supernatural' *or* 'natural'. For instance, in the late sonnet *Immortality*, Arnold reflects, in Allott's words, on the idea of 'conditional immortality', an idea he had found in Goethe, that we must already be a 'great soul' if we are to be a soul at all in a future life. He imagines first a version of the consolatory and resentful desire for life after death that has often been cited as a motivation for belief:

> Foiled by our fellow-men, depressed, outworn,
> We leave the brutal world to take its way,
> And, *Patience, in another life*, we say,
> *The world shall be thrust down, and we up-borne*

But this weary and depressive desire for a vindicated life beyond the brutal world is dealt with swiftly:

> No, no, the energy of life may be
> Kept on after the grave, but not begun;
>   –only he,
> His soul well-knit, and all his battles won,
> Mounts, and that hardly, to eternal life.

The idea of a 'soul well-knit', of concentrated vital force, is crucial to his religious thinking. He presents it as the condition of virtuous action and of spiritual discovery. 'His soul well-knit, and all his battles won' recalls the (post-mortem) picture he offers of his father, Thomas Arnold, in *Rugby Chapel*, and it really is *post-mortem*:

> O strong soul, by what shore
> Tarriest thou now? For that force,
> Surely, has not been left vain!
> . . .
> Yes, in some far-shining sphere,
> Conscious or not of the past,
> Still thou performest the word
> Of the Spirit in whom thou dost live –

The same achieved strength of soul is the condition of the possibility of the quest of the Scholar Gypsy. He is the type of the seeker after secret knowledge, which is secret because it depends upon conditions that seekers must establish within themselves. The disclosure of reality depends upon the state of the knower. And what Arnold is moving towards is the idea that *ethical life* is the condition of disclosure. The idea of a secret knowledge is not that of an inaccessible privacy, but of a form of knowledge or understanding access to which requires the password of a reconstituted self.

Arnold's sense in his poetry of the importance of concentrated action, of the gathering of a person's powers, *in the direction of* the ethical relation, of 'righteousness', stands always though in what seems an unhappy, personal contrast with the theme of distraction and the dissipation of energy: at least, his authorial voice is often on the wrong side of the contrast, and this gives an edge to a continuing melancholy which has begun to see what is needful, has clear pictures of it, and exemplars, but is unable yet to achieve it. To put it another way, what we find in Arnold is the story of *akrasia/enkrateia* and *sophrosune*. On the other hand, it is a contrast which gives point to the idea of concentration (or *samadhi*) itself, it sets out the topography which gives sense to his talk of 'whence our lives come and where they go'.[5] This contrast is in *The Scholar Gypsy*, where the theme of conditional immortality is continued. Whereas *we* tire our wits upon a thousand schemes and are . . . what we have been, the Scholar Gypsy had *one* aim, *one* business, *one* desire:

> Else wert thou long since number'd with the dead!
> Else had thou spent, like other men, thy fire!
> The generations of thy peers are fled,
> And we ourselves shall go;

This purity of heart seems to be a condition of transformation or development: the Scholar Gypsy has the further virtue of *smrti-samprajanya*, a mindfulness or recollectedness which maintains a clear and undistracted comprehension of purpose. Arnold seems highly alert to the value of this virtue through a weary familiarity with its absence. What the immortal Scholar Gypsy has that we do not have, and it is what makes *him* immortal and not us, is 'powers fresh, undiverted to the world without'; we, by contrast, 'fluctuate idly without term or scope':

> Thou waitest for the spark from heaven! and we
> Light half-believers of our casual creeds,
> Who never deeply felt, nor clearly will'd
> Whose insight never has borne fruit in deeds,
> Whose vague resolves never have been fulfill'd;
> For whom each year we see
> Breeds new beginnings, disappointments new;
> Who hesitate and falter life away,
> And lose tomorrow the ground won today –
> Ah, do not we, wanderer, await it too?

Whose insight never has borne fruit in deeds. This is the crucial moment, expression in the life or in action. We await the spark of heaven too, but

---

[5] This line recalls Socrates' ironic opening words in the *Phaedrus*: 'where have you been and where are you going?' The ability to answer the question depends upon an interior change, of just the kind Arnold seeks to describe.

forlornly, as light half-believers of our casual creeds, who never deeply felt, nor clearly will'd. That determines the nature of our 'awaiting'. It is interesting to return to Tanabe here, and to remark that the limitations of *jiriki* would have to be evinced in the person of the energetic Scholar Gypsy rather than the light half-believers of casual creeds. It is *his* human limitation that marks the limit of *jiriki*: the danger for the rest of us is that we are not attentive enough. But even though we are *all*, for Arnold, between two worlds, one dead, nevertheless he already sees here how the other world might develop the power to be born. It is a way that depends upon the gradual and progressive accumulation and gathering of our powers. In other words, he conceives a gathering of energy around the moral conduct which was the original faint intimation of *Dover Beach*, and a path begins to open.

One of Arnold's poetic achievements is that he has made conscious, and given us the sense of, what it is to feel deeply and will clearly. But it is only rare exemplars who manifest this, the Jesus of the Gospels, the Scholar Gypsy, his father. Sometimes he writes as though there were no bridge across the gulf, no clear path from the one state to the other. But he does also attempt to describe an intermediate state, between dissipation and focused concentration, in his personally painful discussion of spiritual progress, also in *Rugby Chapel*, which starts elegiacally near the chapel in autumn and ends in a straggling march through an Alpine snow storm:

> Cheerful, with friends we set forth –
> Then, on the height, comes the storm
> . . .
> Friends, who set forth at our side,
> Falter, are lost in the storm

And when we arrive at nightfall at the inn the gaunt and taciturn host asks whom we have brought, whom we have left in the snow:

> Sadly we answer: we bring
> Only ourselves! we lost
> Sight of the rest in the storm.

Arnold finds in his powerful and energetic father some of the marks of an exemplar, some embodiment, as it were, of the notion of the well-knit soul he sought to understand and articulate. His father's life and demeanour have given him the sight of a *possibility*, whatever we may think about the dynamics of their actual relationship (some of Arnold's writing suggests a kind of defeated paralysis in the face of Thomas Arnold's perceived and surely muscular exemplariness):

> And through thee I believe
> In the noble and great who are gone

pure souls honoured by former ages, who else . . .

> Seemed but a dream of the heart,
> Seemed but a cry of desire
> . . .souls tempered with fire,
> Fervent, heroic, and good,
> Helpers and friends of mankind.

The initial necessitated turn to the idea of an ethical standard by which human life might be measured has taken us unexpectedly far. For in conceiving ethical action Arnold has described a progress from scattered and ineffectual energies to the gathering of powers and concentration to be found in the demeanour of the *Bodhisattva* figures, if I may so call them, whose possibility is confirmed by the exemplary life of his father and those like him. The keeping the possibility of such an achievement steadily in view (through the virtue of mindfulness) is itself partly secured by the presence, even if only in imagination, of at least apparent exemplars, who are *recognised* as such. In the Buddhist tradition, the notion of *sraddha*, which is often translated as 'faith', is a matter of the development of *confidence* in a path or a process. This virtue is really a multiple one, of imagination, which supplies images, and of a steady gaze, which stays upon the images thus supplied. So there is an inner unity or interdependence between the Buddhist qualities of *virya, smrti samprajanya* and *sraddha*, which Arnold seems to me to have grasped. This is evident in the following comments against Newman in *Literature and Dogma*:

faith, instead of being a submission of the reason to what puzzles it, is rather a recognition of what is perfectly clear, if we will *attend* to it . . . *attention, cleaving, attaching oneself fast* to what is undeniably true, – this is what the faith of the scripture, 'in its very nature', is. (233)

Sraddha and mindfulness are manifested in the instinctive turn towards ethics, which grows under the steadfast way Arnold has kept his attention upon it. Under the pressure of his melancholy, of his experience of *dukkha*, Arnold glimpses a resolution, an impulse or movement of thought and imagination. The steady gaze opens out the scene of ethical life from the darkling plain of human misery to the driven march through the Alps of spiritual progress. These explorations have been achieved through the self-conscious dis-illusionment of Faith. There is no *welcome*, in these thoughts, for the turn of the tide.

CHAPTER SEVEN

Kant's aesthetic ideas

I

In his *Critique of Judgment* Kant makes powerful use of the notion of an 'aesthetic idea'. This notion seems to me to be instructive, not just for the discipline of aesthetics, but for the way to proceed in philosophy more generally, since it gives us a hint about how to delineate meaning, about the limits and form of any attempt to do so.

Kant's notion seeks to capture a dynamic state of mind, such as is to be found in aesthetic experience, to capture not only its form, but also, and, in a way, much more interestingly, its *dynamism*. Philosophers usually do not see that meaning is really a dynamic structure of mind, and that it is revealed in a peculiarly intense way within aesthetic experience. In my view Kant makes a unique contribution to our understanding of both through his hesitant, exploratory account of 'genius', the faculty of producing 'aesthetic ideas', and its relation to aesthetic experience. R. K. Elliott (1973) describes it as 'a state of intense psychic vitality' and talks about how Kant effectively makes poetic evocativeness a criterion of success in art. (Indeed, for Kant, the expression of aesthetic ideas is, surprisingly, a criterion of *natural* beauty as well.) Again, the notion of poetic evocativeness can instruct us in how to deal philosophically with meaning. Meaning is not to be defined but *evoked*. Elliott writes:

At some stage in the contemplation of a work, suddenly it evokes a whole world of thoughts and images. Many attain a degree of realisation, but the rapid and transient play of Imagination does not allow attention to be fixed on any of them. We seem to be aware of indefinitely many further ideas and images which are on the point of coming into being. It is a state of intense psychic vitality, the sort of ecstasy which a great work for which we feel a special affinity sometimes produces in us when we experience it in exceptionally favourable circumstances. (96).

The idea of psychic vitality needs to be kept in mind as firmly as the notion of evocativeness: Kant is concerned with the form of a possible experience. It seems to me important also that Elliott should talk in terms of a 'world' of thoughts and images, since that gives a structure to the thoughts and images that are evoked, they are not chaotic but coherent. As Kant (1952) puts it, imagination creates a second nature out of the material supplied to it by actual nature. He implies that we can thus entertain ourselves as a diversion from commonplace experience, but he also has a serious point to make, suggesting that we can remodel experience:

By this means we get a sense of our freedom from the law of association (which attaches to the empirical employment of the imagination), with the result that the material can be borrowed by us from nature in accordance with that law, but be worked up by us into something else – namely what surpasses nature. (176)

Kant has different things in mind here. The poet can, for instance, attempt by means of aesthetic ideas to interpret to sense the rational ideas of 'invisible beings, the kingdom of the blessed, hell', etc., but also

as to things of which examples occur in experience, e.g. death, envy, and all vices, as also love, fame, and the like, transgressing the limits of experience he attempts with the aid of an imagination which emulates the display of reason in the attainment of a maximum, to body them forth to sense with a completeness of which nature affords no parallel; and it is in fact precisely in the poetic art that the faculty of aesthetic ideas can show itself to full advantage. (176–7)

It is precisely poetic evocativeness that bodies forth ideas 'with a completeness of which nature affords no parallel', as we shall see in a moment. But first I want to connect this idea of a second nature, perhaps tendentiously, to Arnold's image of the poet wandering between two worlds, one dead, the other powerless to be born. A world is dead if we can no longer live within its terms. In one sense the world that has died is the world of the faith that Arnold's is the first generation to lose. But there is also a sense in which it is the world of the ignorant armies, one that we have to die to. But in any event the world that is powerless to be born is one which lacks the conception upon which birth depends. The second world has to be conceived, that is to say imagined, before it can be lived. This is an ethical task, to create a second nature which is also a second *human* nature, one that surpasses the human nature we know. This is not to deny that the primary ethical task is to *act*. What we are talking about is how to make sense of such acts, is the conceiving of a *world* in which we can live.

Kant introduces the notion of an aesthetic idea in paragraph 49 of the *Critique*:

> by an aesthetic idea I mean that representation of the imagination which induces much thought, yet without the possibility of any definite thought whatever, i.e. *concept*, being adequate to it, and which language, consequently, can never get quite on level terms with or render completely intelligible. (175–6)

And he expands it in the following way, which gives an indication of what he had in mind in saying that the poet embodies ideas 'with a completeness of which nature affords no parallel':

> If, now, we attach to a concept a representation of the imagination belonging to its presentation, but inducing solely on its own account such a wealth of thought as would never admit of comprehension in a definite concept, and, as a consequence, giving aesthetically an unbounded expansion to the concept itself, then the imagination here displays a creative activity. (177)

In other words, to use an example, an artist offers us a representation of a human face, it is a representation of a particular that falls under that concept, but the evocative power of the artist's drawing induces a stream of thought that goes well beyond the singular thought that what we are presented with here is a human face, and yet constitutes an *understanding* of the face, newly revealed or returned to consciousness. Andrew Harrison's remarks (1973, 131) about Picasso's 1937 etching of a *Weeping Woman* are germane, though he was not explicitly discussing Kant:

> The picture is a structural analogue, not merely of an appearance, but of an experience. As with all such structural analogues, it presents us with a paradigmatic possibility. It shows us the form of a possible experience, something we may not have attended to hitherto. This is a genuine shift in, or addition to, our concept of grief, but it is not an addition to any theory of grief.

I would only add that the possible experience whose form it shows oscillates between that of the grief itself and the possibilities of responsiveness to it, an oscillation, I should add, that is one of emphasis and attention, switching from one aspect to another of a single phenomenon.

Kant goes on in similar vein, as he struggles to formulate this crucial and neglected idea:

> the aesthetic idea is a representation of the imagination, annexed to a given concept, with which, in the free employment of imagination, such a multiplicity of partial representations are bound up, that no expression indicating a definite concept can be found for it – one which on that account allows a concept

to be supplemented in thought by much that is indefinable in words, and the feeling of which quickens the cognitive faculties . . . (179)

The quickening of the cognitive faculties is clearly important for Kant's whole account. The idea of 'much that is indefinable in words' refers us back to the notion that language can never get quite on level terms with or render completely intelligible the 'much thought' that the aesthetic idea expressed in the art work (or in nature) is said to induce. He also talks of a 'wealth of undeveloped thought for the understanding, to which the latter paid no regard in its concept, but which it can make use of, not so much objectively for cognition, as subjectively for quickening the cognitive faculties, and hence also indirectly for cognition' (179). As Harrison says that the *Weeping Woman* does not contribute to a theory of grief, so an aesthetic idea is not made use of 'objectively for cognition' but the understanding can make use of the ideas it evokes, presumably because it shifts the attention towards other possibilities of cognition, and in any case evokes the surroundings of cognition. Kant has already referred to the notion that the imagination can 'create . . . a second nature out of the material supplied to it by actual nature' (176), so we have the idea of a structured evocation of a world in the intense experience of a possible form of experience. Art can summon this up, and philosophy more discursively seeks to trace out the pattern. Aesthetic experience, then, is an experience, as Gottfried Benn has written, of *erkanntes Leben, jäher Sinn*, recognised life, sudden sense, as though the illumination of sense throws light on a portion of life, shows a structure normally concealed. And it is right that language can never get quite on level terms with it or render it completely intelligible, because what is quickened in the mind is the intelligible form of thought and language themselves. What are the conditions under which this can happen? Of course Kant's aesthetics was enormously influential, but since I have been discussing Matthew Arnold it is worth recalling that in *Culture and Anarchy* Arnold makes use of this idea, as a condition of the possibility of culture, that individuals need that suspension of normal activity in which the free play of imagination and understanding can occur. Education depends upon the release of imagination and understanding into a state of free play, the teacher must be able to *quicken minds*.

So, the dynamic state of mind to be found in aesthetic experience has a structure, that of a cascade of particulars intimating or showing the nature of a universal, and in so doing showing the structure of *sense*. It seems to me that Kant's reflections come close to the heart of

Heidegger's philosophical practice implicit in his interesting distinction between correctness and truth, when he dismisses the 'correct definition' in favour of 'truth' or *aleitheia* understood as a revealing or unconcealing. My impression is that Heidegger's notion of 'truth' is better understood as a notion of *sense*. A philosophical definition of technology, for instance, can be correct but unilluminating, whereas it is the task of the philosopher to bring to mind what is normally concealed from view. At least some works of art are supposed to express the truth understood in this way. Heidegger (1971) talks of a work of art expressing a thing's 'general essence', and when he offers an example, that of the peasant shoes by van Gogh, it is clear that their 'general essence' is evoked rather than defined, shown through an evocation of the kinds of relation within which the shoes have their identity. Just as Valéry talks about poetry giving us a 'sense of a universe', so Heidegger seems to be offering us the lineaments of a *world* in his account of the 'general essence' of the shoes, the world in which the shoes are located as just those shoes. The task of philosophy is to illuminate sense, lighting up, perhaps, the *field* of sense, the filaments of connection and distinction. Illumination can only be impressionistic, can only be *illustration*, it seems to me, and in this, Heidegger's practice and that of the later Wittgenstein may be seen to converge. Wittgenstein is concerned to offer perspicuous representations of sense, and this is done, again impressionistically, by a concern with concrete particulars and by grammatical comments which show the sense of an expression in contexts pertinent to particular confusions or bewilderments. But the dynamic state of mind of aesthetic experience is itself a revelation of sense in exactly the same way. If one thinks of the aesthetic idea as an image that affects the mind, brings it into a state of free play around itself, we might think of the artistic image as begetting its kind and its circle of connections and differences in the minds of its audience, in flashes of *erkanntes Leben*. An 'aesthetic idea' is a particular representation of the imagination. In other words, it is an *image*, an image with evocative power, an image which carries some of the charge of the universal even in its particularity. But *nature* can express ideas in this way, for Kant, not just works of art:

Beauty (whether it be of nature or of art) may in general be termed the *expression* of aesthetic ideas. But the proviso must be added that with beauty of art this idea must be excited through the medium of a concept of the Object, whereas with beauty of nature, the bare reflection upon a given intuition, apart from any concept of what the object is intended to be, is sufficient for awakening and communicating the idea of which that object is regarded as the *expression*. (184)

That point can hardly be neglected, for in the natural and the rural land-scape, as in the city, we constantly see what Marcuse calls 'images of lib-eration', images of what we might be liberated *for* and images of what we may be desperate to be liberated *from*. The forms of the outer world may provide us with our first access to the forms of the inner: we become fascinated by some natural scene, perhaps, without knowing yet that our connection with it is a foreknowledge of what it will reveal: 'as a dare gale skylark, scanted in a dull cage . . .' But how can we thus already know what we do not know?

This evocativeness of the individual image is a main criterion for Kant of aesthetic value. The pleasure that grounds the aesthetic judg-ment is the heightened experience of what the image thus evokes, and nature or the work of art has *Geist* or 'soul' just to the extent that it expresses ideas in this way, and lacks *Geist* (and therefore 'beauty') if it doesn't. The criterion of aesthetic value, then, is the presence or absence of aesthetic ideas, the capacity to 'induce much thought'. But the 'multi-tude of partial representations' that language can never quite get on level terms with, can at least be evoked, can find some degree of articu-lation, and is thus communicable. Kant seems to be saying as much in his concluding remarks to paragraph 49:

> genius properly consists in the happy relation . . . enabling one to find out ideas for a given concept, and, besides, to hit upon the *expression* for them – the expres-sion by means of which the subjective mental condition induced by the ideas as the concomitant of a concept may be communicated to others . . . to get an expression for what is indefinable in the mental state accompanying a particu-lar representation and to make it universally communicable . . . is a thing requir-ing a faculty for laying hold of the rapid and transient play of the imagination, and for unifying it in a concept . . . that admits of communication without any constraint of rules. (180)

What is articulated could plausibly form a reason or set of reasons for the judgment that the work is 'beautiful' or at least successful, even though the ground of the judgment is a subjective pleasure, because the pleasure is in the excitement in the mind of thoughts and images. In other words, the pleasure that is the ground for the judgment of taste has a *content* in the sense that there is a retrievable flow of thoughts and images the quickened experience of which *is* the pleasure that grounds the judgment, and this pleasure can be communicated in terms of its *content* by means of an effort at producing 'further descriptions': the judg-ment-grounding pleasure can be evinced in the form of reasons for the judgment. If we refer to the *content* of the harmonious activity of imagination and understanding, our criterion of aesthetic value will provide grounds for the *expectation that others will agree with our judgment*. Certainly the aesthetic judgment is grounded in a subjective pleasure, but since we have discovered that it is a pleasure we take in an activity of the mind whose content can in some way be reclaimed, we can say that someone can at least in principle articulate in part the *content* of their pleasure in the form of *reasons*, reasons on the basis of which the judgment turns out to have been made. Because we implicitly appeal to such reasons as the grounds of our judgment, we expect others to agree with us, that is to say, since our expectation is entirely epistemic, we think others *ought* to agree with us in the sense that we have reason to think that they *will*. But still they might not, and there the discussion ends. Someone can be told *what* pleases without thereby being pleased.

2

I think many commentators (including, e.g., Nietzsche and Adorno) who have trouble with the idea that the judgment of taste is grounded in a *disinterested* pleasure do not realise that the pleasure Kant refers to is just this 'quickening of the cognitive faculties', this heightening of consciousness, state of *activity*. The pleasures that are supposed to be 'interested', i.e., the pleasure we take in the good or the pleasure we take in the 'agreeable', are pleasures that derive from the recognition, whether conscious or not, of some relation of the object to our projects and desires. To say that the pleasure in the beautiful is dis-interested is merely to deny that it is of that kind, not a response founded on the perception of an interest. The positive claim is simply that aesthetic pleasure is constituted by the feeling of engaged activity:

> The quickening of both faculties (imagination and understanding) to an indefinite, but yet, thanks to the given representation, harmonious activity, such as belongs to cognition generally, is the *sensation* whose universal communicability is postulated by the judgment of taste. (60, my italics)

One has to admit though that Kant wavers in his view of disinterestedness. It seems to me that he has two different theses. Thus he sums up the First Moment as follows:

> TASTE is the faculty of estimating an object or a mode of representation by means of a delight or aversion *apart from any interest*. The object of such a delight is called *beautiful* (50).

But he glosses this in different ways, at one point saying:

All one wants to know is whether the mere representation of the object is to my liking, no matter how indifferent I may be to the real existence of the object of this representation. (43)

But elsewhere,

Everyone must allow that a judgment on the beautiful which is tinged with the slightest interest is very partial and not a pure judgment of taste. One must not be in the least prepossessed in favour of the real existence of the thing but must preserve complete indifference in this respect, in order to play the part of judge in matters of taste. (43)

These are two distinct claims. In the first passage he says that the delight which grounds the judgment of taste is one which does not depend upon a perception of the object's relation to an interest. But what he says in the second passage seems vulnerable to the familiar anti-Kantian criticism. What it says first is that if my delight in the object is partially determined by interest, then the subsequent judgment of taste is not 'pure'. What it goes on to offer is a *recommendation* about how to avoid this: 'one must not be in the least prepossessed . . .' etc. But this recommendation is just an overstrong version of an important tradition which recognises the necessity for Heidegger's 'eine Gelassenheit zur Dinge', a 'releasement towards things'. If you relax attachment, you may become more aware of beauty, and beauty can do its work. Otherwise, 'the tree which moves one man to tears of joy is in the eyes of another merely a green thing that stands in the way'. But you can be surprised and delighted by beauty no matter how attached you may be to the object . . . or the person. Kant thus offers us a dynamic view of aesthetic experience, which includes the insight that it can change our conception of what we thus look upon: 'a boundless expansion to the concept itself'.

So, Kant's idea is that the judgment of taste is grounded in a feeling of pleasure that is 'apart from any interest', a negative claim merely, whose positive counterpart is simply that what constitutes aesthetic pleasure is the quickening of the cognitive faculties, the free play of imagination and understanding, induced by the evocative image, the aesthetic idea, in such a way that the particular gives us the sense of the universal by evoking an array of connections and relations. The stir of partial representations, then, is not chaotic, but gives us the sense of a universe. I take it that the image begets in the mind a stream of connected images and thoughts and feelings, evoking poignant similarities and contrasts. I introduce this Platonic notion of begetting here, because it seems to me to capture something sought by Kierkegaard in his notion of indirect communication. There is a constant temptation to think that communication is always direct. I suggested that Arnold falls into that temptation in those moments of his *Dover Beach* in which he uses the first person plural, 'we / Find also in the sound . . .', a failure to recognise that one can only bring an image to a person and *hope* that it will beget its kind in their mind. Whether it does depends upon interior conditions within *them*, interior conditions for the possibility of a free play of imagination and understanding. (Free in the sense that both are relieved of their ordinary empirical employment).

3

There is, however, another way of thinking about the impact of the aesthetic idea, the play between the particular and the universal, and that is in the context in which the concrete particular becomes a concrete universal through the medium of its exemplary role. As Aristotle said, the play may be about Pericles, but it is also and at the same time about a certain sort of man in a certain sort of situation. This gives us something interesting about the combined engagement and detachment of aesthetic experience, the oscillation between the two, for we contemplate the work of art both as a representation of a particular and of what the particular exemplifies. What is wrong with the yokel who strives to save Desdemona is, of course, that he fails to see that the play is a representation. But what is that a failure to see? The representation is also representative and we see it as such and respond to it as exemplifying a kind of thing. In that sense our emotion is different when we respond to an instance of a kind of thing but not *as* an instance of a kind. In the midst of life we are not often admitted to that dual experience, but respond immediately in a way not tempered by the contemplative ability to respond reflectively to the kind of situation that confronts us. Though perhaps we are admitted to it more than I have just acknowledged. I have often been astonished by people whose emotions seem entirely immediate and strongly reactive, but who will suddenly give a reflective account of the nature of their situation with an entirely different emotional resonance, which then becomes swamped again by immediate reaction. Aesthetic emotions are contemplative in the sense that they are responsive to the representation as a kind, and they allow us to reflect upon the nature of our engagement with situations of that kind. It is the difference between the *immediacy* of just being jealous because my girl is flirting with a rival, and being able to *reflect* upon jealousy, to see it in its totality by contemplating it, in an artistic representation, or in the flesh.

But art is not the only place in which this kind of thing can happen. It can happen in the street or in the kitchen, in moments of 'aesthetic perception'. There is a certain receptivity of mind and body in which ordinary perceptual experience becomes charged with a peculiar perceptiveness. We do not have to restrict it to the beautiful in nature or to works of art . . . and nor, really, did Kant. It is the evocativeness that drives the judgment of beauty, the power to hold the attention in this particular, charged way gives content to the word. He is not offering an account of conventional beauty. A fading flower in the garden may become the focus of an intense activity of imagination and understanding. Its fading is, after all, a fate we share, we recognise the destiny, all flesh is grass. It is tempting to say that for a moment one sees impermanence itself, not just that of this flower, but a glimpse of its connections with all other things that perish, swirling into vision and away in a moment. And the swift perception is charged and heavy with the shaking and discovery of *attitudes* and responses. The particular flower concentrates the universal, is an image of our, of a general, dissolution, and the perception is also charged with *perspectives*. One does not see impermanence alone, its web, instantiated and glancing off everywhere, but one *awakens* to it, you see the vanity of human wishes, the foolishness of one's own, as you see the record of her life in the photographs: *vita brevis* stares at you from the swaddled infant clasped to the Victorian bosom, the girl with freckles in the frilly dress, the Irish colleen with her thick ginger hair . . . the mother and then at last the old lady whose end we have raced to through the pages of the album. What am I doing with my life? Of course we knew already that 'all men are mortal', but we never appreciated it, it was a truth that we did not give time to work upon us, to make its mark on our soul, to turn it around. We did not yet see with 'feeling intellect'. In aesthetic perception we know it and find an attitude to it, thought and feeling united in *insight*. The insight is a double recognition: you awaken to some reality, and you awaken in that very moment to the response which seizes just on it: the response is the *form* the awakening takes.

Even so that does not capture Kant's point that language can never quite get on level terms with it or render it completely intelligible. When the flower becomes the focus it is charged only with a *sense* of the universal, the latter only a function of the particular, the swirling thought and imagery of connections and perspective, of diverse things that are *the same*, cannot be *complete*. In any event, one does not merely see the flower. You are walking through a crowd in the city, and are alive to the faces and demeanours, the postures, the attitudes of those who come towards you and pass, and now there is a couple in their early thirties, arm in arm in love, she laughs at his aside, he smiles, but his face is apprehensive, and he waits for her kind glance, turns then not seeing as the glance stays to take his measure with dispassion – and you see at once their whole attitude to each other, their mutual personal dependence, but you see it as a concrete universal (which stays even if it is not true of *them*), a fundamental form of human relation *coheres* in your mind and you know you can be free of it. Not only do you see with perfect clarity the totality of which gesture and glance form part, but you see its universality, a *dominant* form of the sexual relation itself, the needs that give rise to it, your own past and future, their prison house, our prison house, and, most particularly, you *realise* your whole-hearted rejection of it . . . which you then forget . . .

. . . to be mindful is to not forget. How can I forget thee, O Jerusalem?

But here we need to make distinctions and establish connections. Aesthetic perception can of course just happen, though perhaps its possibility may be diminished by a too dense immediacy of mind and action – the green thing that stands in the way. Art, music, the sound of Orpheus singing, can bring about a suspension of ordinary consciousness, can bring one into a state of intense receptivity and awareness. And this is what meditation may also do, the same calm conditions of receptivity, within which there may flare up that same sense of a universe, that same discovery of emotion directed towards a world. But the vision needs to be sustained, and the virtue of mindfulness is just that virtue, of keeping the vision there, once it has engaged the mind in a new orientation. So *smrti samprajanya* is like *sophrosune* in the sense of Aristotle's 'protecting wisdom', a keeping recognition and insight safe, rather than in the sense of 'temperance'. They are the same virtue, protecting the newly formed mind, so that it may issue in action of a corresponding kind. Both mindfulness and *sophrosune* depend upon the cultivation of a tranquil recollectedness, a suspension, an interlude, away from the old unsatisfactory mind, and this can be brought about through meditation or aesthetic experience. Out of this springs a vision and an orientation, and mindfulness is needed to allow this orientation *expression*. One of the delusions of meditation is that the intensity of the vision will lead you to think that it has already been brought to act when it has not. However, *temperance* is that state in which the newly formed mind has established itself as a flourishing sensibility, when the new understanding has become the dominant form of your experience.

4

To forget oneself is to slip from the self that is being formed by the *sustained attention to particular realities*, to the particular realities of *beings* and one's connections with them. In that case mindfulness can be tied to *moral freedom*, since its activity implies the bringing of an achieved understanding to particular instances, but in such a manner that nothing within the individual *prevents* . . . ethical action or restraint. That 'nothing should prevent' is the further fruit of the virtue, since its embodiment is at the expense of impediments. The presence of the virtue develops what used to be called the 'intuitive understanding', issues in the emerging presence of a particular mind which is the ground of 'ethical' conduct. Remember, that we *begin* already with a particular kind of mind, begin in a state of self-enclosure.

You should not believe that beauty is nothing but beginning of terror. That we are still just able to bear it says something about our *present* condition. That it should be *terror* merely reveals the distance between reality and our capacity to bear it, human kind cannot bear . . . etc. But if there is terror to face we have to learn to face it, this guardian of the threshold, otherwise it becomes a force field to limit our horizon and diminish our persons, said so complacently, as though there were nothing to feel or fear. We have to open ourselves up by slow degrees, be dilated and expand . . .

And that *is* a sexual, a female, image, of receptivity, to the reality of the phallus. Receptivity is often conflated with passivity, to which it can indeed sometimes descend, but receptivity has to be a state of energy, an intense expectancy of the whole being, intensely alert and charged. As for the male, the phallus probes the reality of the woman, and we have thus two models of arousal and knowledge which need to be integrated within the individual human being, men and women both female and male, since the woman can seize, interrogate and milk the seed of the man. Otherwise we have the phallocentrism that marginalises other ways of knowing or a receptivity turned to glazed passivity. Its probes and its interrogations *know* the reality of the woman whom its probing reveals, and are *ignorant* of what is thus concealed, by the nature of its own activity. Even for the man it is not satisfactory (Heidegger's *Gestell*). The phallic probing can become mindless. Nietzsche's 'erotic whirl' is, of course, precisely *male*, sowing its seed and begetting wisdom and virtue, in a youth, not a woman. But if we are to use the image, then the soil has to be fertile and receptive, eager to receive it, knowing what it is about, certainly not merely 'passive'. What we have is a sexual image of Platonic friendship, in which, however, we drop the male/female polarity of the *image* in favour of older/ younger or *erastes/eromenos*. More to the point the implication of the Platonic image of the older 'man''s *begetting* is that we then have to think of wisdom and virtue as being conceived and gestated, we have to think of the pain of childbirth, of nurturing wisdom and virtue through infancy to maturity. And that is the role of the younger partner, one already endured by the older. On this view, both men and women have to be *female* before they can be *male*. So that men and women both (Diotima) have to be vigorously male and female in the development of their lives. Men and women have to learn to be both *erastes* and *eromenos*, begetters and bringers forth, in different phases and different aspects of their lives. As for phallic probing and interrogation, that is of course the Socratic *elenchus*, the probing and interrogating of beliefs and received opinion – by one who knows only because they have already endured what they seek to beget.

Mindfulness is not a *merely* intellectual virtue, since the raising of awareness carries the whole person: and what constitutes the 'whole person' . . . the raising of awareness will itself reveal.

There is already a reply to Rilke's comment about beauty in St Thomas, who claims that 'knowledge of God in his essence is a gift of grace and belongs only to the good'. When we ask what makes the good *good* we find that term glossed by reference to their possession of *love*. Only then, through their greater *desire*, are they open to receive reality. Without such a dilation of the soul, terror and anguish are the response to the beatific vision. The look of love, after all, is filled with fire: the fire of heaven is the fire of hell.

Less theistically, perhaps, if kin calls to kin, who knows what angels or other beings are beyond our strength to greet or contact till we make ourselves whole and live in the spirit.

> Who, if I cried . . .
> > . . . *Und dennoch, weh mir,*
> I invoke you, almost deadly birds of the soul . . .

Or must we become their peers before we meet our visitors? and is that less terrible?

Indirect communication, which Kierkegaard regarded as essentially *artistic*, is the bringing someone to the point of *aesthetic perception*. Otherwise one knows, for instance, that we all shall die, only in an 'objective manner', unaffected by what affects us, without realising the attitudes that focus on it and wait to be awakened. One goes without the 'subjective appropriation' that belongs to the dawning of insight, and is the real source, and form, of what Kierkegaard called the transformation of our whole subjectivity.

5

What one does through meditation, then, is to develop a state of energetic receptivity to ideas, and the virtue of mindfulness protects and sustains the mind which they thus inform, so that eventually they can have effective power. But it is a slow transition, from their inception to their natural expression in action. Meditation is blind if the ideas do not come, and the ideas are empty if they do not enter the mind in the form of a vision of things, in the form, indeed, of a *possible re-orientation*. Meditation is not necessarily the site to which ideas come, though it may be. *Samatha* meditation is a practice that makes the subject calm, tranquil and receptive, relaxed and alert in body and mind. *Vipassana* meditation is a practice of reflection precisely upon ideas and insight. However, it seems to me that these are merely different phases of what is in reality a single process that spills out into the day and into speech and action.

So I envisage a complex sequence, meditation or aesthetic experience, bringing about an alert attention, a suspension of normal life, followed by re-orienting ideas, then the process of protecting and sustaining this new mental formation, and then its outcome in action, fitful and in conflict at first, and finally without conflict. In fact 'temperance' names only the final outcome. *Sophrosune* is the virtue of fidelity to a vision or purpose, a steadiness of attention which genuinely 'protects wisdom' and is analogous to the Buddhist virtue of *smrti samprajanya*.

As Aristotle noticed, it is vital to realise the limits of what it is in our power to do at a particular time: to be a coward, or to act unjustly, 'is not merely to do these acts . . . but to do them from a certain state'. Indeed, *quand les jeux sont fait*, one's state reveals itself whether one likes it or not. Thus, one legitimate concern with moral integrity provides a person with a reason for bringing it about that they are capable of just acts, incapable of unjust ones. They would see the consequences of their failure in some human or other suffering. This is the real meaning, I think, of Tanabe's *zange-do*, or practice of *metanoesis* – a thinking again as one looks back with remorse at what one has done *changes* one's very person, which must then be reflected in one's philosophy because it alters what is there to be described, shifts the horizon. Such a concern derives from the presence already of an ethical attitude whose issue in action (or restraint) depends upon the removal of impediments or the gathering of energy, thus bringing about a 'certain state' which I shall call moral freedom. For one may acknowledge such reasons and lack the capacity to act accordingly. It is into this context that I should want to insert the practice of meditation, or some comparable contemplative activity, since they are a condition of the recovery of the paradigm, the exemplary grasp, in attitude, of particular realities, that yields reasons for action, and whose presence or absence determines our state. Changing one's state in such a way that the insight is effective cannot be done by self-power, by *jiriki*, because that is just what is to be changed: understanding *dawns*, it comes, as it were from outside, even though that grace depends upon sustained and vigorous effort, the effort of the attitudes working their way towards expression ('it is metanoesis itself that is seeking its own realisation'), the power that moves in us being not our own only because we are constituted by it, by what we do not yet know.

But one's dominant attitudes are already in place, maintaining the given homeostasis, as they are activated by relevant states of affairs. But they are activated only under *antecedent subjective conditions*, activated and reflected in strategic and expressive behaviour. Effective change depends upon putting a brake upon those behaviours, which are already in motion, where one sees reason to do so, reasons that reflect the ethical attitude that is seeking expression, and needs space, a space partly achieved by meditation, in which the power of disinterested attention grows. We have to bring ourselves into a state in which we are able to do just acts and not do unjust acts, a state of moral freedom. The radiant friendliness of a genuinely happy person is the image of this freedom. We thus reconnect freedom and happiness as goals of moral endeavour. A person who is morally free has the capacity for disinterested action, that is to say, action for the sake of the welfare, not of all, but of *any*, oneself included. But this is to act for the sake of *justice* to any, within the bounds of some conception of their welfare. To treat another as an end and not merely as a means is to attend to them for their own sake: such disinterested attention gives rise to determinate attitudes, the different modes of delight, compassion and solidarity. When it is returned we have the first meeting of persons, which begets the possibility of *sangha*.

CHAPTER EIGHT

. . . *And his rational ones*

I

Nietzsche's announcement of The Death of God offers cultural rather than directly metaphysical news, but it is worth taking seriously Heidegger's (1977, 61) interesting gloss:

The suprasensory world is without effective power. It bestows no life. Metaphysics, i.e., for Nietzsche Western philosophy understood as Platonism, is at an end. Nietzsche understands his own philosophy as the countermovement to metaphysics, and that means for him a movement in opposition to Platonism.

We need to be careful how we proceed here since 'Platonism' isn't all one thing, there isn't a single Platonic moment, and it is any way too easy to caricature: 'Plato thought nature but a spume that plays/ Upon a ghostly paradigm of things', which is succinct, but diminishes the reality of both the 'spume' and the 'paradigm' at the same time. Heidegger's remark seems apposite to Nietzsche's (1968, 40) 'History of an Error', to *How the 'Real World' became a Myth*, his readily received satire on the fate of Plato's supposed Two Worlds, the Real one and the Apparent one, the former our origin and goal and source of value, the latter our place of exile, our land of shadows. Once the 'real world' evaporates, once we lose our sense of its presence or lose our ever more tenuous faith in its possibility, we are left with only the devalued apparent world (not even that, since 'apparent' belongs to a distinction that has just been undermined) and terminal depression sets in (passive nihilism), unless, more actively, we can rise to a radical readjustment of our views about the nature and source of value. And, of course we are not far distant from Arnold's 'dead' world of *The Grande Chartreuse*.

Moreover, there is some irony in the claim that the 'suprasensory world is without effective power . . . bestows no life'. It is intended to imply that such a world is spent. On the other hand, however, the reason could be that the human race has become incapable of receiving it, the conditions could be absent upon which its efficacy depends. One can imagine a Kierkegaardian commentary along such lines, at best we think only 'objectively' about religion, it is not within our power to appropriate it subjectively, because the inner conditions have been lost, or we have lost the sense of their possibility. There is the hint of an admission of this in Nietzsche. The Platonic stage is characterised as follows:

(1) The real world, attainable to the wise, the pious, the virtuous man – he dwells in it, *he is it.*
    (Oldest form of the idea, relatively sensible, simple, convincing. . .)

There are two things to notice here, the first is that Nietzsche refers to the 'real world' as an 'idea', the second is that there is the implicit admission that it is *unattainable* to the non-wise, the non-pious, the non-virtuous. Whatever we may think of the idea, we are brought into territory in which it is acknowledged that the subjective condition of the agent becomes decisive. So, Kierkegaard's distinction between objective and subjective thinking is apposite here, and we can see how it works by going back to Kant, to his *Critique of Judgment*, to an aspect of his account of aesthetic ideas, viz their relation to 'ideas of reason', that I neglected earlier. In fact the third *Critique* seems to me to suggest a more subtle Kantian position than Nietzsche seems to allow, in his description of the third stage of the History:

(3) The real world, unattainable, undemonstrable, cannot be promised, but even when merely thought of a consolation, a duty, an imperative.

It is 'the same old sun, but shining through mist and scepticism; the idea grown sublime, pale, northerly, Konigsbergian'. At the fifth stage the real world is an idea no longer of any use, useless, superfluous, and thus 'refuted', and finally abolished.

The point, I suppose, is that it is certain *ideas* that have lost their potency, it is the *idea* of a suprasensory world that 'bestows no life' and 'is without effective power'. Such ideas are 'dead' when they are no longer incorporated into the 'world' in which we move and have our being. That is not to say that their process of dying isn't also a kind of mortification for us. Whether we are to blame or not we should not underestimate the extent to which we are ourselves undermined by the dismantling of a 'world'. Essentially it is a loss of bearings and identity, though for that to happen, clearly, we need to have inhabited that world, lived vitally within it.

The problem we are dealing with, I should say, is a problem between generations. Certain ruling ideas give expression to vital experience which cannot be transmitted through the language, even though the language of their expression is still transmitted, sometimes, alas, like Chinese Whispers. It no longer reflects vital movements of thought and imagination, though it may have the power to beckon people towards such experience. The ideas are *inert* if they no longer reflect vital experience, but they lie like a dead weight around the necks of those to whom they are transmitted, still with the power to strangle. And I mean 'strangle', as in strangle the life out of someone, the queer, gasping contortions of stifled life, respectable, cowed and afraid.

2

As far as Kant is concerned the suprasensory world is precisely an *idea*, an idea of reason, and is thus an indemonstrable concept, as he puts it; such a world, or such a dimension of the world, is not a possible object of knowledge, we can only think the idea. This claim is problematic. It is fairly obvious that no sensible intuition etc. will be 'adequate' to an idea of what is 'suprasensory'. But Kant has already presented us with these exclusive alternatives, knowledge or idea, by restricting the scope of the categories of the understanding and thus of 'knowledge' to the empirical world of the senses, the manifold of intuition. However, this does not rule out the possibility of forms of knowledge of a suprasensory world *not* dependent on the *five* senses (cf. Blake), but on forms of supersensible intuition, a world whose reality was insisted on by Rudolf Steiner, and described by him in worrying detail. Whatever we may think of such an idea Kant cannot formally exclude it. On the other hand, whereas it seems that for Kant the generic idea of a supersensible world is the type of the indemonstrable concept and does service for more specific ideas, such as that of God and the soul, we may do well to distinguish between those ideas which are genuinely indemonstrable, and those which are not. (It is interesting that Heidegger does the same as Kant here, treating Nietzsche's announcement of the Death of God as an announcement about the death of the metaphysical, suprasensory world in general.)

Whatever we may think of the status of individual ideas of reason, it is perhaps even more important to reflect on Kant's account of the conditions under which such ideas are *awakened*.

One of the characteristics of an *aesthetic* idea is that it is a representation of the imagination which induces much thought and to which no *concept* is adequate. As we saw earlier, it is a particular representation or image whose cognitive resonance surpasses delineation by the concept it falls under: so no concept is adequate to it, though it gives an 'unbounded expansion' to the concept, in the sense, I take it, that it augments, or at least displays, our *conception* of what it is to fall under the concept. By contrast an 'idea of reason', for Kant, is a concept to which no sensible intuition or representation of the imagination is adequate. The idea of a noumenal realm beyond phenomena, for instance, is for Kant an idea of reason, and in paragraph 49 he gives other examples, 'the rational ideas of invisible beings, the kingdom of the blessed, hell, eternity, creation, etc.' (1973, 176–7). However, ideas of reason and aesthetic ideas stand in a particular relation. The poet can interpret ideas of reason to sense through the means of aesthetic ideas, through images: they can approximate to a 'presentation' of rational concepts or intellectual ideas, 'thus giving to these concepts the semblance of an objective reality' (176) – and then degenerating, presumably, into naive theological realism, when people lose the sense of the 'semblance'. In the case of the idea of a world beyond the senses, for instance, it is the experience of, or representations of, the sublime in nature, that acts as the intuition that stands for or 'presents' the idea. The aesthetic idea is the image that *sets the mind in motion* towards the ideas that what it represents has awakened.

Some background is needed here. There are two general forms of the judgment of taste, the judgment of the beautiful and the judgment of the sublime. What we think of as the sublime in nature is again divided between the mathematically and the dynamically sublime, between magnitude and might, looming crags and mountains or torrents and waterfalls, etc. The experience of Sublimity is quite different from the harmonious experience of beauty. Kant talks about it as being 'dead earnest in the affairs of the imagination', as an 'outrage' on the imagination, which he talks of as finding itself at the edge of an abyss in which it fears to lose itself. It fears to lose itself because the task of the imagination, its quotidian empirical employment, is to 'present' to the understanding the manifold of sense in a whole of intuition. Its task is to present the manifold in a shape which can be recognised or brought under a rule or concept by the faculty of understanding (no cognition without recognition). But now, what we call the sublime in nature are phenomena which *overwhelm* the imagination in its effort to carry out this task. This very failure awakens reason. In the case of the mathematically sublime, where the size of a natural Object is such that the imagination spends its whole faculty of comprehension upon it in vain, it must carry our concept of nature to a supersensible substrate (underlying both nature and our faculty of thought) which is great beyond every standard of sense. (104)

We may well question the 'must' in this sentence. On the other hand, we do need to acknowledge the power of such experiences. They disturb our settled sense of the world, as well as our sense of a settled self, and seem to tug us beyond both, with the intimation that they are the outcome of conditions that lie beyond their settled, familiar formations: '. . . a supersensible substrate (underlying both nature and our faculty of thought)'. This comment suggests a notion that belongs to the Buddhist tradition, that of non-duality, the 'non-difference' of subject and object, but that must wait. Except that the crucial question is what we do with such experiences, and the Buddhist reference may suggest there is more than one direction to go in. In particular, the question is whether this sense of something far more deeply interfused has the power to *extend* our experience, beyond its present limits, and in what sense it might do this, in what sense, particularly, it might be 'supersensible'. (What I have in mind here is the temptation to interpret the idea of what lies beyond the senses exclusively in terms modelled upon our notions of empirical reality, when we should really be thinking, say, in terms of value, which also lies 'beyond the world'.)

Before we can begin to deal with that, however, there is something else. Kant tells us that 'The mind feels itself *set in motion* in the representation of the sublime in nature' (107). The key thought here is devastating in its simplicity and power, especially since we are dealing with ideas that include those of God and the soul, it is that of the mind being set in motion, set in motion *towards* ideas that are thus the *precipitate* of the experience of the sublime. I said just now that Kant will help us to explain Kierkegaard's distinction between subjective and objective thinking. One way of understanding the need for 'subjective appropriation' is to see that the mind must be set in motion by religious ideas, *by* them, and, more radically, *towards* them: if this dynamism is absent, then we are no longer dealing with religion, but the relevant ideas are merely incorporated into mundane thought.

Crucially, for Kant, it is the idea of something supersensible that is awakened in us by the experience of the sublime:

But this idea of the supersensible, which no doubt we cannot further determine – so that we cannot *cognise* nature as its presentation, but only *think* it as such –

is awakened in us by an object the aesthetic estimating of which strains the imagination to its utmost, whether in respect of its extension (mathematical), or of its might over the mind (dynamical) (120).

In a famous passage of the *Prelude*, the young Wordsworth strikes out into the lake at night, and suddenly

> a huge cliff,
> As if with voluntary power instinct,
> Upreared its head. I struck and struck again,
> And growing still in stature the huge cliff
> Rose up between me and the stars, and still,
> With measured motion, like a living thing,
> Strode after me . . .

Wordsworth manages to capture aspects both of magnitude and might, as well as living presence, in this description. The effect is that the boy steals back to the cavern of the willow tree, leaving his boat at the mooring-place,

> And through the meadows homeward went, with grave
> And serious thoughts; and after I had seen
> That spectacle, for many days, *my brain*
> *Worked with a dim and undetermined sense*
> *Of unknown modes of being* . . . (my italics)

There is a slight but significant difference between Kant and Wordsworth here. Whereas the poet talks explicitly of a 'sense' of *unknown* modes of being, the philosopher allows us only to 'think the idea' of *unknowable* modes of being. We have to ask which of them is the closer to lived experience. Wordsworth is strong on 'sense' and 'intimation', but maybe Kant has denied himself this possibility in advance by his prior account of the limits of knowledge.

The huge cliff is the occasion of Wordsworth's sense of unknown modes of being, it is their representative image, their 'presentation'. Representations of those objects that overwhelm imagination and carry reason beyond it stand as markers for those very ideas. But now, as Kant says, and let us follow him for a while, we cannot *cognize* nature as the 'presentation' of the supersensible, we can only *think* it as such. Later, in the 'Dialectic of Aesthetic Judgment', Kant emphasises this point. The idea of the supersensible is an indemonstrable concept, a rational idea, it is 'only an idea and affords no proper knowledge' (213), though aesthetic ideas, representations of imagination, can stand as a presentation of them:

For the sublime, in the strict sense of the word, cannot be contained in any sensuous form, but rather concerns ideas of reason, which, although no adequate presentation of them is possible, may be excited and called into the mind by that very inadequacy itself which does admit of sensuous presentation. (92)

The point of all this is that for Kant ideas not schematically employed with sensibility and imagination (the categorial concepts of the understanding) do not yield knowledge, they can only have a regulative, not a constitutive function. However, there is too much variety in his list of indemonstrable rational ideas in the third Critique for it to be entirely plausible to treat them all in the same way. We cannot pretend that reality is comprehended by our meagre powers of observation and perception, that it does not transcend the narrow focus of our human interests, and my own view is that though the concept of God is genuinely indemonstrable in Kant's sense, if we understand it in his terms, nevertheless we should at most be agnostic about whether any realities answer to the idea of a suprasensory world (or dimension of the world), and about the status of the idea of the soul or of invisible beings.

Leaving all that aside, consider the significance of Kant's thought that the mind is set in motion towards these ideas by key experiences, specifically of the sublime in nature. The context is one of strong emotion, and we do not need to restrict ourselves to nature. The point of saying that they are intellectual or rational ideas without any authentic presentation in experience, is to emphasise that there is no question of *establishing* whether or not they correspond to reality, even if they *do* (so they are essentially regulative and not constitutive ideas). There is no procedure for answering the question, are these ideas 'correct', are they 'right'? Asking these questions is a mistake, a grammatical mistake, to anticipate Wittgenstein, though we can ask about their (regulative) *function*, in the way, perhaps, that we can talk about the 'picture' of the Last Judgment, and its place in a person's life.

So I am following Wittgenstein, and the powerful philosophy of religion associated with Dewi Phillips, in insisting on the notion of a picture that has a hold on the mind, that gives shape to the mind and its energies, rather than on the idea of belief, as illuminating religious practice. I am finding an unexpected source for this position in Kantian aesthetics. Certainly many 'believers' will be unhappy with any such account of their 'beliefs'. On the other hand, we need to recognise that the self-understanding of many religious people is itself constructed out of a philosophical position. Their beliefs and convictions do not ground their religious practice, but are the product of second-order reflection upon it, a second-order picture often more intimately known than Christianity itself (ah, and what is *that?*). *Pace* Nietzsche, it seems to me that his announcement of the Death of God is really about the death of this picture. It seems to me that 'believers' do not so much 'believe that there is a God' as think God. Their minds are God-shaped or 'dei-form' in the sense that their thinking is determined by theistic categories. It really is a basic part of their 'noetic structure', as Plantinga asserts, though I disagree with him that as such it is something they are 'committed to'. These concepts govern their thinking, they just find themselves thinking in terms of God and an after-life, for instance. The Death of God is the decline of this kind of thinking. *These pictures no longer hold us captive.* Of course, it is true that this 'us' refers to a Northern European culture, and it is proper to point to the flourishing of versions of Christianity elsewhere in the world. However, Nietzsche's real claim is about the believability of Christianity, or, as I would prefer, a particular picture of it. His claim is that Christianity has been discredited and seen through and the implication is that it can therefore always be seen through, no matter how long it takes.

In any event it seems to me that 'believing in God' is properly construed as confidence in his Word, something internal to religion, and that 'believing in the existence of God' is a philosopher's construct, as Malcolm and Phillips have both emphasised. Someone may say, but you distort what I believe. I really believe that there is a God. In what way, though, is that different from saying that you really think in terms of God's activity, etc. If you say, well, it's not that I really believe there is a God, but that I believe there really is a God, then we have to ask whether you are treating yourself to an adjudication on these matters that is not genuinely available to you. There is nothing that counts as assuring yourself that you are right to believe there is a God. However, realising that there is no determining procedure can lead you in more than one direction. You may conclude that there is no reason to 'believe' and abandon religion; or you may continue to believe, passionately, in the knowledge that there is no *reason* to believe; you may conclude that the absence of a procedure is itself evidence that raising the question of whether there is a God is some kind of a mistake, even if the absence of a procedure does not *entail* that there is no God, and hold that nevertheless theological language never had that ontological implication anyway, but has a different kind of function; or you may conclude that it did, and is to that extent discredited, but that nevertheless it still has a particular function which persists despite the illusion of belief; one option here is a kind of crypto-Buddhism, deploying language from the Christian tradition according to a Buddhist principle of selection.

Why not settle for believing the Word of the God who dominates your mind. God's Word has much to do with conduct, with the still, small voice, with the shadow of the valley of death, and so on. But wouldn't someone be deeply disappointed to discover that whereas they thought there was a God, it is 'just' that their mind is dominated by an idea? I think it *would* be 'disappointing', and is likely to lead to a loss of conviction, and the danger is that the *function* of the idea would be lost along with the idea. It would be a matter of coming to see that what one was doing was quite other than what one had thought, in a way that might cause you to desist. Your faith could be that there is a God, but isn't that a waste of faith's energy, better employed in finding the kingdom of heaven within you, and there is not even going to be an eschatological verification, since neither the souls of the just nor those of the unjust are going to be in a better position than we are to know that there is a God, whether they are being rewarded or punished. What we *have* are rational ideas, interpreted to sense by means of pictures, aesthetic ideas. Human experience, at the most radical level, sets the mind in motion towards ideas that are then given expression in the language, and then passed to the next generation. The language may have the vibrant power to set new minds in motion, or they may become gradually inert, and people start to think 'objectively' about religion.

If the *ideas* are in terminal decline, if certain uses of language no longer speak to us, then what we have to return to are *the conditions under which the mind is set in motion*. It is that movement that matters most of all. At least, we can discern two moments in Kant, and separate them out, the one is that of the mind being set in motion, and the other is the formation of ideas. Earlier I referred to Kant's comment that the poet interprets such ideas to sense through representations of the imagination. There is some implication there that the poet thus interprets ideas that are *already* established in the culture. The more radical activity, then, still of the poet, is the establishing the ideas in the first place, coming to them, out of one's experience, and giving them expression. Whether, though, the mind *must* come to any particular idea is, as we saw, questionable. But the implication is profound, if 'the faith' is a dead time's exploded dream, then it is time to wake up to realities, or dream new dreams and have new visions that will lead us to awakenings.

Whatever we may think about the *idea* of a supersensible substrate, it is bound to the experience of nature that occasioned it, the dim and undetermined sense linked to the huge cliff, instinct with voluntary power, which becomes its symbol. But the cliff itself, or its representation, also functions as an *aesthetic* idea. In being the image or representation of the supersensible, it is also an exemplar of nature itself as the semblance of a presentation of what lies beyond it. But this affords us the possibility of thinking nature as such and as a whole, in a way that Kant insists is forced upon us by reason itself at the moment that imaginations fails in comprehending the particular. *But this suspends us from our normal activity*, and is a disturbance, as I said before, of our settled view of ourselves and nature. So, again, whatever we may think about the *idea*, which is anyway 'indemonstrable' for Kant, it brings us to this condition. However, I confess to being dissatisfied with the way Kant continues at this point. For him nothing in nature is after all 'sublime' but is merely the occasion for our discovering the genuine sublimity of our minds, great beyond every standard of sense. The problem is that I am not sure how to read this. It *sounds* too much like a reactive self-assertion in the face of an overwhelming and disturbing experience, displacing the disturbance away from the self to the imagination, so that the mind remains untouched and also therefore unchanged. On the other hand, it also recalls Wittgenstein's sense of being 'absolutely safe', an expression he thought important at the time he wrote about it but also 'strictly nonsensical'. This *could* be a feeling that persists through the deepest disturbances of the self – destroyed, yes, turned upside down, but absolutely safe, even at the front-line . . . But what is thus safe?

The mind's being sprung to the rational idea of God has the function of bringing us to the contemplation of the world as a limited whole and *sub specie aeternitatis*, it becomes the means by which we are able to contemplate the form of our being, its conditionality and that of the world in which we find ourselves. On the other hand it may also represent a fearful response to contingency itself. Nothing *within our experience* is free of contingency, only contingency is non-contingent. We have to ask ourselves whether the idea of God is a recourse to an originating necessity beyond experience because we cannot face it steadily . . . but the idea may help us to face it steadily, and then we can let the idea go.

The announcement that God is dead, the claim that the metaphysical world has no effective power and bestows no life tells us about the ideas, it does not disclose anything about their function, which can survive their demise, only that they can themselves no longer serve that function. And still the vital thing is the mind's being set in motion, in the absence of which the idea of God and a supersensible world is already dead. It may be that God is dead, etc., but the idea of God provided us with the means of attending to contingency, and that possibility is still alive because it depends upon just those kinds of experience that formerly set the human mind in motion towards the idea of God in the first place, which anyway involves a backwards and forwards movement between God and the world. But what is the point of attending to contingency? The answer depends upon whether anything is awakened in us under that condition.

3

Kant seems to me to offer in effect an account of the imagery of limit and threshold vital to the understanding of a religious consciousness. The sense of it could be illustrated by another short passage from Wordsworth, from *Tintern Abbey*:

> . . . once again
> do I behold these steep and lofty cliffs
> *that on a wild secluded scene impress*
> *thoughts of more deep seclusion*. (my italics)

The wild secluded scene sets the mind in motion towards the idea of a corresponding inner state. Imagery that belongs to the very limit of what we *can* imagine stands as an *image* of *ideas*. The point is not that the steep and lofty cliffs should stimulate the idea of more deep seclusion than the greatest that can be imagined: the scenery speaks for, is correspondent with, the possibility of a state of mind and it is *that* which, if it achieves reality, becomes the object of further comparison. Thus 'the mind has mountains' serves still no matter how much we enter into its regions, and serves still *because* of our deeper entry. It beckons towards deeper experience which in turn resonates in the words: indeed we discover the source of the resonance that beckoned. We have to come to see what reality such talk attempts to reveal or express, and we have to come to see what the conditions are under which such a thing might be seen in the first place. In that case the idea is constitutive, not merely regulative, it draws us towards a deepening of experience.

Instruction to the artist: graphically realise a scene to strike terror in human souls, and then place in its midst a serene and unperturbable being. That task is comparatively easy, since it is almost merely the juxtaposition of two images to produce a potent third. Almost, but not quite. What is the difference between superimposing upon an image of the camps a bleeding crucifixion scene, and superimposing a serene and unperturbable being? And how much rhetoric is there in the question, for where would resurrection fit? And yet, isn't it the case that Buddhism contains little, either in its experience or in its literature, of the realities of extreme human affliction, little to correspond with Gethsemane, Golgotha and the Resurrection as dense images structuring the form of a possible experience, and not just possible either. Christ before Pilate is a central image of Western culture: the two 'kingdoms' face each other and take their courses, which now we have to describe, perhaps like good followers of Manichee, as darkness seems to swallow the light entirely, and yet.

A more difficult instruction is to set out in detail what we conceive to be conditions which would destroy a human being's capacity for love (a concentration camp?) and then to set in its midst, and show the effect, one in whom it is not so destroyed. This is more difficult because we have to imagine what they might say or do, their demeanour under particular circumstances, the effect upon others, and our ability to do this would depend upon how far we were familiar with the phenomena of love, the extent and nature of its powers and influence. So maybe we would not know how love might express itself in such circumstances with the same familiarity, perhaps, as we have with the phenomena of hatred. We offer in our prose fine portraits of these, writing about the known. The Kantian idea is very central here. The look of love alarms . . . Maybe we have never been animated by such a potent force and maybe there is no such thing as such a potent force, and so we do not know its operations, if there are any such. And maybe there are those who do. Maybe its actual limits and precarious conditions are those we already know, and it is as we define it, and maybe not. What for some may be a present reality may for us be the remotest possibility that we have not conceived even as that. And how terrible, in its way, to discover that what we had called love was soft deceit and idleness, rejecting which we pass into an interval, is it an interval? . . . of darkness.

According to St Thomas's doctrine of analogy (partly as mediated by Herbert McCabe), if we use the term 'love' to refer both to divine love and to human love, we apply the term analogically in the two cases. What is unexpected and profound is the thought that the primary application is to divine, not to human love. So this allows us to start with the *idea* that the phenomena of love, the forms of its expression in human life, the nature and scope of its influence, are only imperfectly understood or grasped only marginally in our present state: the reality that is

signified stretches beyond us. But such an idea can be appropriated independently of any commitment to belief in God: there is an issue
whether or not we can continue to enter into a reality only imperfectly
appropriated now. Iris Murdoch and Simone Weil write in this vein. For
the latter, a person can act 'in' Christ, they can have the compassion of
Christ in them. But to qualify 'compassion' by reference to Christ in this
way is to signal the possibility of an indefinite trajectory, the permanent
possibility of something beyond the present phenomena. Meanwhile,
love remains marginal because it is conditional, and checked, and
obstructed or overwhelmed in familiar ways in the world of Pilate: it
lacks efficacy: our present state allows in only a pale reflection of the
reality of love. Or rather, more modestly, we can conceive the idea of
the negation of these checks and infirmities: and so the issue is whether
such a conception represents merely wishful thinking. However, one's
judgment about that depends upon the scope of one's own experience,
and the permanent danger is that of taking up a kind of psychological
empiricism which causes one to judge that one's present experience is
decisive (cf. Henry Fielding, *Tom Jones*, bk vi), the measure of what is plausible or implausible. The *way we represent* the reality of love is determined
by its reality as we find it, but it could be that it *transcends* that *modus sig-
nificandi*, that there are constantly aspects of its reality that elude us
because the conditions are absent under which we could apprehend
them. But many contrasts are already available in the community, in the
tradition, transmitted in the language, precise delineations, images and
scenes. Giving substance to these ideas depends upon precise descriptions, and we need stories to explain the presence or absence of love, to
see pathways from the one to the other. But what we want to call the
reality of love, more or less imperfectly expressed, must be testable on
the pulses of experience, as Keats would say, though as I have just said,
not necessarily *present experience*, sometimes we must wait to see the truth
of some remark, until our pulses are stronger and more stable. What I
am trying to say is that it is pointless merely to spin possibilities out of
thin air: we already have contrasts, the language is available and always
growing, things have already been said and done, established in the
memory of the community or forgotten. No, we don't just spin possibilities out of thin air, but they present themselves under the pressure of
circumstances which are proving unsatisfactory. But if we are to talk
about *our* imperfect understanding then there is an implicit contrast with
that of others, who speak or have spoken about their own experience.
But I labour under a methodological difficulty, that there is less human

agreement here than elsewhere. Kantian ideas of reason should always take us just a little further at any time, a little possibility to be tested and tried, in many directions, at the edges of experience, at points of felt weakness and unsatisfactoriness, sometimes with a sudden, though cumulative effect. We can always, on the basis of our present limits of experience, say that this person has only an imperfect grasp of the nature of love, who speaks nevertheless with confidence, but to do so we need to be able to point out its defects and limitations, and say what stands in its way and how it may be removed: otherwise this is wishful thinking, or, at least, we do not know that it is not. But we are aware also that the present limits of our own experience may stand in the same case and we may press on investigating the sources of further dissatisfaction. What I am trying to say is that if there is such a reality available to human life, its form, its grammar, set out in the lives of human beings, in poetry and literature, then it provides a means of comparison for actual lives. If we knew the workings of love then we could trace out in individual lives its distorted and imperfect expressions and recognise them as such and be able to explain them. In the absence of such a contrast, the sense of further and other possibilities beckoning us on, how would we try to define the nature of love except by how we found it and where we recognised it. But if we did so we would not know that we might be wrong: what we might have identified as a distorted and imperfect expression (needing reasons for such a judgment) would be taken for the thing itself.

4

Heidegger's strategic response to Nietzsche's pronouncement is nicely encapsulated in a short work, *Science and Reflection (Wissenschaft und Besinnung)*, where he makes an important distinction between *Bildung* and *Besinnung*:[1]

Besinnung is of a different essence . . . from . . . *Bildung*. The word *bilden* . . . means first: to set up a preformed model and to set forth a preestablished rule. It means, further, to give form to inherent tendencies. *Bildung* brings before man a model in the light of which he shapes and improves all that he does. Cultivating the

---

[1] included in the above collection translated by William Lovitt. He translates *Bildung* as 'intellectual cultivation', but it seems to me that the adjective excessively narrows the scope of the concept. I shall use the German term. He translates *Besinnung* as 'reflection' which, again, does not seem to me to quite capture the scope of Heidegger's word. The word 'mindfulness' may carry some of it. I shall use the German term.

intellect requires a guiding image rendered secure in advance, as well as a stand-
ing-ground fortified on all sides. The putting forward of a common ideal of
culture and the rule of that ideal presupposes a situation and a bearing of man
that is not in question and that is secured in every direction. This presupposition, for its part, must be based on a belief in the invincible power of an immutable reason and its principles. (180)

One may have reservations about the final sentence: about whether the
concept of *Bildung* cannot after all be separated from the idea of a
'belief in the invincible power of an immutable reason and its principles', as opposed more simply to 'the common ideal of a culture', even
though the *actual* background may indeed be a belief in an immutable
reason. Nevertheless, it is clear enough what Heidegger is referring to,
I think. The white, uplifted faces of Arnold's Carthusian monks may
provide an image. The death of ideas is also the death of practice, so
that we are left with nowhere to go. The issue is not so much to do with
an immutable reason as with a self-confident culture which provides
unquestioned models for human cultivation and criteria for what constitutes the proper direction and development of our inherent tendencies. The cultural loss of belief adumbrated by Nietzsche's
pronouncement of the Death of God locates us in a world in which the
foundations for such self-confidence are no longer so secure, or are
even, apparently, entirely destroyed, 'and we are here as on a darkling
plain'. Arnold's two worlds give us two themes, that of the process of
death, and that of the process of gestation, both of which provide apt
imagery. The lived experience is of a world behind, no longer available, and no clear sense of a world before. The dead world allowed a
particular form of life, a particular *Bildung*, whose conditions now are
absent. Heidegger offers *Besinnung* as a way forward, and associates it
with a 'venture after sense and meaning', a notion that fits the account
we have already given of the aesthetic idea and the flickering of sense
it offers our attention.

This means more than a mere making conscious of something. We do not yet
have *Besinnung* when we have only consciousness. *Besinnung* is more. It is calm,
self-possessed surrender to that which is worthy of questioning. (180)

He elaborates the contrast as follows:

Besinnung remains more provisional, more forbearing and poorer in relation to
its age than is the *Bildung* that was fostered earlier. Still, the poverty of *Besinnung*
is the promise of a wealth whose treasures glow in the resplendence of that uselessness which can never be included in any reckoning.

It is 'more provisional' etc. than '*Bildung*' because, presumably, it does not represent the profile of a dominant form of life and thought. When Heidegger refers to 'that uselessness which can never be included in any reckoning' he seems to be referring to the objects of this kind of reflective attention, just those snatches and echoes, of thought and impulse, that we are inclined to marginalise because they do not enter as substantial items into our calculations, on the borderland of the pre-reflective and the fully reflective, like the sense of *mauvaise foi*, half-conscious, half-unconscious unease, half-conscious intimation, on the edges, fugitive, a metaphor for the emergent sensibility that questions established thought. And maybe there is treasure to be found there, and maybe not. But we are to go in search of a possible treasure, because something shines or glints on the margins, in the distance, and that takes us back to possible paths:

The ways of *Besinnung* constantly change, ever according to the distant view that opens along the way into that which is worthy of questioning. (181)

Heidegger's *Besinnung* suggests to me something akin to the Buddhist notion of *sati* or mindfulness. We might put it another way and talk of inwardness. But there is a strand of thinking here that continues to yield the idea of 'a philosophy that is not a philosophy', that seems to say that insight and understanding depend upon the cultivation of a particular state of mind or interiority in the midst of human experience. The notion of *Besinnung* seems to suggest a stance of mindful reflection, a stance that questions and opens up a path with the answers it receives. But what is the distant view a view of, and what is it like to get there? Is there indeed such a place? Such questioning must, of course, be of the essence, and what is at issue is precisely epistemological. We start *again* with an attitude, a questioning stance, without knowing where it might lead, in a world whose horizons press much closer than they formerly did, because previously available self-formations have apparently been closed off, previous bearings, previous identity, lacking. We have to return to the beginning of the formation of ideas formed by the mind in response to its experience. Perhaps Kant's fault was that he merely identified with too great confidence ideas that already existed. The sublime in nature undermines imagination but awakens reason to its own sublimity and independence. We are too undermined for that, we have to look again at the conditions of self-construction.

CHAPTER NINE

Arnold's recast religion

I

Despite myself, in my early twenties, after I had persuaded myself that I was an atheist, or that I ought to be, on logical positivist grounds, I was comforted in adversity by lines from a psalm that I had chanted regularly at Vespers: *manus tuae fecerunt me et plasmaverunt me . . .* the rise and fall in the second verb, the strange sound of it . . . *da mihi intellectum ut discam mandata tua.* It came from my most intimate mind. I still suffered from childhood fears, then, of the dark, of the possibility of ghosts and spirits, about to call me to some reckoning, or simply threatening to manifest themselves out of dreadful air. I would go rigid trying to keep out the insistent awareness of ghosts. I no longer believed 'that there was a God', but I still took comfort from the words, after a long absence: *your hands have made me and shaped me; give me the intelligence to learn your laws.* It advanced and receded, advanced again, so that I noticed it was there in my mind, listened, then took it up, joined in what I was already singing.

The dim perception in *Dover Beach* of an impulse towards connection and away from enchantment and alienation becomes, twenty or so years later, the leading idea of *Literature and Dogma*, where Arnold is able to say that '*God* is . . . really, at bottom, a deeply moved way of saying *conduct* or *righteousness*' (46). This exasperating remark needs, of course, to be set in context before it is dismissed out of hand. It would be premature to *dismiss* Arnold's position on the grounds that he merely offers a routine reduction of religion to ethics, as though we knew already what ethics was, and without first clarifying how *he* conceives it. The real issue is how much space a position like Arnold's allows us, how far it will take us. Unfortunately, our views about that may well depend upon different conceptions of how far there is to go in the first place, though it seems to me that the path should be thought of as remaining open. If we were to cast Arnold's God into the form of a regulative idea of reason, then we should need to point out the rare brilliance of his recognition that the path opened up is an ethical one.

John Mackie (1982, ch. 11) has raised a question about the possibility of a middle position between religious realism and a naturalistic expressivism of the kind associated with Richard Braithwaite. Since Braithwaite has declared that Arnold is the patron saint of his thinking about religion, it is easy to assume that their positions will be very similar, and that Arnold is some such naturalistic expressivist. However, and Braithwaite acknowledges this wryly, Arnold seems to hold on to what I have called a modest non-theistic transcendentalism, and it is worth considering the *possibility* that this gives us the form of the middle position mentioned by Mackie, a position that puts pressure on our conception of nature rather than our conception of God. Arnold gives us more than *Besinnung* and I think, at least, that in Arnold we have the beginnings of the notion that 'conduct' or 'righteousness' increasingly open us to realities that were formerly and otherwise concealed. In other words, changes in the human subject, to be understood as reciprocal ethical changes, understood, that is to say, in terms of *sangha* or spiritual community, alter the initial conditions of possible knowledge. There are, on this view, realities that are concealed from the unregenerate consciousness. This seems to me entirely in line with the position we have already seen Tanabe Hajime take up in his view of philosophy as metanoetics. We shall find, also, in Arnold's notion of the 'not ourselves' something akin to a phenomenological reading of the notion of 'Other-power'.

2

We should not under-estimate the personal devastation wrought by the Victorian loss of faith, the dead time's exploded dream, by the realisation that the existence of God could not be 'verified'. Seeing that this is so, or, more neutrally, concluding that this is so, leads some thinkers to ask themselves, well, what is *really* going on here? I believe that Matthew Arnold's experience led him to see the real nature of the 'game' more clearly than other natural historians of religion, led him to see the real conditions of its construction. Or better, he saw more clearly the *possibilities* enshrined in the language and the practice of religion. Thus, I am sure that much of what Freud says about 'what is really going on' is accurate, but he only sees a particular range of phenomena, he lacks the scope of Arnold's vision.

Arnold also saw shrewdly enough that the hierarchy was hopelessly wrong-headed in trying to restore the fortunes of the church by attempting to defend the personal first cause by argument. In other words, he saw the confusion in their assumption that the reasonableness of religion is demonstrated by showing first the reasonableness of belief in the existence of God.

Arnold's considered response to positivism, to the 'sciolists', is two-sided, reflecting the earlier movement of his thought from the perceived illusoriness of belief to the emergent realities of the ethical life. Although he wholly accepts the positivist critique of theology, he attempts, with striking originality, to ground what he takes to be the 'real' truths of Christianity by deploying the very same experimental method. In other words, he brings an anti-speculative and experimental method to the task of illuminating the spirituality of his tradition. The disenchantment with religious belief is given conceptual expression in the criticism that the 'assumption' that there is a personal first cause of the universe, cannot be *verified*. The reflective turn towards the realities and conditions of the ethical life is given expression in his account of the nature of 'conduct' or 'righteousness' as it is ascertained by *experience*.

Arnold wished to give to the Bible 'a real experimental basis', a basis 'in something which can be verified, instead of something which has to be assumed':

whatever is to stand must rest upon something which is verifiable, not unverifiable. Now, the assumption with which all the churches and sects set out, that there is 'a great Personal First Cause, the moral and intelligent Governor of the universe', and that from him the Bible derives its authority, can never be verified. (*Literature and Dogma*, x)

If, Arnold says, we are asked to *verify* that there rules a great Personal First Cause, 'we *cannot* answer'. He presumably takes this from the critiques of philosophical theology offered by Hume and Kant, which would have led to the positivist *conclusion* (it is not an arbitrary premise) that genuine knowledge depends upon empirical observation. (The rise of science, and the success of its procedures, has to be put side by side with the process of attrition suffered by theology and metaphysics.) When Arnold says that the relevant theological assumption cannot be 'verified', I do not think his complaint is that it is unsatisfactory because it cannot be verified *in experience*, as the logical positivists seem to have thought. I think the point is that it cannot be verified, the matter cannot be *settled*, through metaphysical argument, on the ground that metaphysical argument has been shown to have failed. That leads us to the positivist conclusion that the only reliable knowledge depends upon *empirical* verification. So Arnold then looks at the Bible with a view to seeing what *can* be verified, in experience, appropriating the new conceptual tools of verification and the experimental method to the task of understanding it. This seems to me to be an unusual and important move, though its importance clearly depends on what Arnold then *finds*.

He does not, incidentally, take the Logical Positivist step, of claiming that if theological statements have no means of verification, then they are factually meaningless, do not have any meaning as statements which can be true or false. He leaves open, or does not consider, the possibility that the unverifiable assumption *could* be true (or false): all he is concerned to assert is that we are just not nor could be in a position to *know* whether it is the one or the other. That is hardly the end of the story for the theological realist, but there is a *pragmatic* side to Arnold's dismissal of belief in the personal first cause as an 'assumption'. It is an assumption that has been rejected by the 'lapsed masses', and they are not, he believes, going to return to what is true and vital in religion by being persuaded to accept it again:

[T]his theology is . . . now a hindrance to the Bible rather than a help; nay, to abandon it, to put some other construction on the Bible than this theology puts . . . is indispensable, if we would have the Bible reach the people. (xii)

In order to understand how Arnold arrives at the thought that 'God' is a deeply moved way of saying 'conduct' or 'righteousness' we need to place it in the context of this *alternative* 'construction on the Bible'. That construction depends upon his appropriation of 'the experimental method'.

3

His central claim is very simple, and amounts to something that could be given a Buddhist spin, that what is true and vital in religion is its knowledge of cause and effect as it applies to consciousness and ethics. Thus he talks about the 'method' of Jesus, and his 'secret'. The connection between method and secret depends upon a testable discovery of moral experience. The method, briefly, is *self-renunciation*, and the discovery it yields is the emergence of an ethically higher self in which joy or happiness is found to be connected with 'conduct or 'righteousness', in a more abundant sense of 'life'.[1]

This is a classical theme of spirituality, and it is here that Arnold discovers for himself the 'real meaning' of the Bible. Sometimes one has to remind oneself that it is an enormous claim, and that a person may live their life without ever discovering whether it is true. Indeed, maybe it is the hardest discovery of life, the movement from egocentric self-enclosure to joy in the welfare of another human being (the conversion of Scrooge). But the language of discovery and of the experimental method seems appropriate, even if the means may consume a person's life, to be able to speak at last to another human being, as though one had never spoken before to another human being, to discover that there is something that answers to that description, of a different order from the whole of one's previous experience. On the other hand, though, and to repeat, it would be a mistake to think of *Entsagung* either as an end in itself or as simply a means to a private end of self-gratification, the 'enjoyment' of a 'higher self', for instance. As usual we are surrounded by the possibilities of corruption and self-delusion. Goethe remarked that renunciation is unavoidable in human life, it confronts us at every choice. We already need an ethical context, in this sense, that it is already in the midst of realising the effect of our actions on others to whom we wish no harm that we see the need for self-renunciation. The point is that it is already the act of a higher self even as it brings us closer to embodying it.

In other words, Arnold shows an intuitive grasp of the principle of *pratitya samutpada* or 'dependent arising' as it is instantiated in particular New (and Old) Testament teachings. This is not of course to say that the Bible *teaches pratityasamutpada* as a doctrine, but the teaching Arnold mentions shows a clear recognition of the way one phenomenon arises in dependence upon another. In any event, the more 'abundant life' ('I have come that they may have life, and have it more abundantly') is the critical, spiritual notion, one that links Arnold to his admirer, Tolstoy, and the mainstream connection between 'life' and 'love'. I suggest that it is an essentially 'open' and *epistemological* category by which we are borne into knowledge and insight. (Though one has to distinguish here,

[1] Arnold refers to Goethe's notion of *Entsagung* as an essential aspect of *Bildung*. He makes it clear that he is not advocating any extreme of asceticism for its own sake. He has in mind the moral enterprise of constraining sensual and egoistic impulses as they intrude on the well-being of others, advocating a means to an end, the removing energy from unregenerate impulses, to strengthen and secure the higher form of life he seeks to characterise.

as ever: it is not the fact that a person uses this language, of 'life' and 'love', etc., that matters, but *how* they use it, and that has to be illustrated through the use of examples in the Wittgensteinian manner.)

However, if the connection between virtue and happiness is a matter of experiment, then it needs to be put to the test. It may be objected that Arnold's confidence about 'life from righteousness' is misplaced, even if it does capture a crucial New Testament teaching. He announces, in his emphatic and incautious way, that happiness *undeniably* follows conduct or virtue. But the idealist philosopher F. H. Bradley (1988, 318) denied it with disdain, and with cold, though, I think, misdirected, precision:

> If what is meant be this, that what is ordinarily called virtue does always lead to and go with what is ordinarily called happiness, then so far is this from being 'verifiable' in everyday experience, that its opposite is so; it is not a fact, either that to be virtuous is always to be happy, or that happiness must always come from virtue.

Bradley's dismissal of Arnold is cold, but his counter-claim, despite his scepticism about 'verifiability', is germane and needs an answer, since Arnold's whole enterprise is grounded in a particular application of the experimental method. How are we supposed to adjudicate between Bradley and Arnold, as surely we should be able to if we are in touch with such a method, which can, presumably, be applied by anyone? The ironical difficulty is that Arnold has identified an experimental method in which the experiment is made upon the state of the individual subject. In respect of the connection between righteousness and happiness or the sense of 'life', Arnold rather than Bradley is the one who makes the traditional claim.[2] But it is not to be tested on the basis simply of what any particular person's *present experience* happens to be, as though one were to settle the matter just by seeing how it stood with oneself or others, independently of the implied notion of a *developed or achieved experience*.

Bradley is right to question what we 'ordinarily' mean by virtue or by happiness, and in order to address his criticism on behalf of Arnold, because I do not think Arnold himself is any use to us here, we need to refer again to that crucial ethical distinction between continence and temperance. The distinction is between, on the one hand, a virtue that is achieved through successful control ('continence') and against the

---

[2] The beginning of the *Dhammapada*, for instance, tells us that 'if a man speaks or acts with a pure mind, joy follows him as his own shadow'.

grain of contrary impulses, and, on the other, the achieved effortless virtue that is associated with temperance, that arises out of a transformed inwardness and interior disposition, not over against an unregenerate one. But we need to refer to something else. We should remember that the resolution of *Dover Beach* was the movement towards another person. There is a crucial point here, about what is to constitute the paradigm of virtuous action. It concerns its motivation. Bradley may well have had in mind the Kantian virtue that acted for the sake of duty in the teeth of contrary inclinations, and that seems both joyless and heroic. But this is an alienated virtue. Goodness consists not merely in acting for the sake of someone else's well-being, but in doing it for *them*. Not only does it seem possible that you can do something for the benefit of another without doing it for *them*, but it seems to be what we most often do. I can act for the sake of your well-being, and be indifferent to *you*. I can fail to do it for you, because acting for the sake of your well-being can serve other ends, it is itself only an intermediate end. The joy or happiness traditionally associated with 'virtue' comes from acting *for* another person, for their sake . . . is what they say, and the question is whether it is true. The claim that virtue and happiness are connected is not tested by immediate inner experience (of what remains to be transformed) but by observing the consequences of fulfilling the conditions upon which the truth is claimed to depend. That is the point of Jesus' *method* and his associated *secret*. The claim is very similar to one we have already seen to be implicit in Kierkegaard's writing. Kierkegaard has a view about what constitutes the subjective appropriation, say, of one's own mortality, that implicitly draws on a culture of accumulated experience of determinate changes in determinate circumstances. I remarked that this is a ground of Kierkegaard's sensitivity to the need for 'indirect communication,' which is clearly an issue here, if human beings are divided by the form of their experience.

There is something else in favour of the purported link between virtue and happiness. We might say that Arnold is deploying the same notion as Blake when he refers to 'these virtues of delight'. In other words, the joy or happiness comes from a certain state of the person, that of a flourishing moral sensibility, in which there are no longer any internal impediments to right action. But the condition for the possibility of that flourishing is renunciation of unregenerate desires, the egocentric self-enclosure that is blind to other values, to other reasons for action, to the real presence of others.

4

Perhaps the most striking thing that Arnold does is to highlight the biblical notion of 'life from righteousness'. It is not a vague or free-floating notion, but refers to something determined by the moral regeneration that is claimed to be its ground. To know what the term 'life' refers to requires one to have undergone the transformation that brings it about. The promise of 'life' is the promise of a determinate outcome of a determinate process. To put it another way, this essentially ethical category of 'life', which is parallel in some ways to the Buddhist notion of *Brahmacarya* (often itself translated as 'spiritual life'), is also an *epistemological* category whose progress charts our understanding of the world. The enjoyment of this 'life' is claimed to give us an expanded and expanding sense of our own lives *and* of the world in which we live.

If we return to Mackie's question, whether there is a middle way between theological realism and naturalism, it should be clear that the answer depends crucially upon where such a 'spiritual life', such a faring, leads us. But then we have a problem. What are the grounds for the relevant claims? And who is to test them, and on the basis of what experience, if the experiment is on the form of our experience itself?

It is a matter for individuals to find out for themselves. To find out the answer to Mackie's question, individuals will have to undertake the relevant procedures, since reports from others can only be confirmed or disconfirmed by such an undertaking. So, at the heart of the most crucial issue, one withdraws . . . How are any claims I make one way or the other to be assessed? Is there a path that opens up only under the condition of interior change? Or is there not?

Arnold's unexpected disciple, Richard Braithwaite (1971), is generally taken to represent the 'naturalistic' position, on the grounds that he reduces religion to the '*agapeistic* way of life'. But we are left uninformed by Braithwaite, perhaps ironically, about what that way of life amounts to. We just do not know whether this expression opens up a fissure into something religiously profound. (On the other hand, we do know that his critics make naturalistic assumptions about *agape* as they dismiss him as a reductionist.) However, we know more about Arnold's intentions; we know at least that he has a strong grasp of the practically determined concepts the Buddhists identified as *virya*, *sraddha*, *smrti* and *samadhi*, energy, confidence, recollection and concentration. This kind of analysis already gives us a perspective on what it is to know another person at all, since it determines a set of positive and negative distinctions by which to construct the type 'person'. It shows us what can be known or disclosed through the ethical relation. What becomes crucial is the experimental tracing out of the lineaments of these categories, of what the life Arnold seeks to describe itself discloses. Most crucially the claim is that *ethics* is the epistemological condition of discovery of how things are. But that is too bald and indeterminate a claim: there are truths or realities disclosure of which depends upon entering the 'life of the spirit' or *brahmacarya*. It would be an intellectual mistake to foreclose on what is to count as living such a life and what it might reveal to us, as though one knew in advance what realities were or were not disclosed when the grain of wheat falls into the earth and 'dies'.

But I succumb to the temptation of leaving the expression 'how things are' undetermined, as though the words spoke for themselves, which they clearly do not. The temptation is to an epistemological construct independent of the range of contexts in which a determinate meaning can be given to the thought that things are thus rather than so. And we need to recall the implicit contrast, the state of the person associated with ignorance and delusion, and that associated with overcoming those conditions. The delusion that what we are doing is exercise of virtue, the ignorance of our own tyranny, for instance, these are also contrasts associated with the knowledge of how things are. On the other hand, there was an occasion some time ago, a Buddhist convention, the Sangha assembled in large numbers, much *metta bhavana*, a meditation developing 'loving-kindness', long festive puja, lovely chanting, the air itself becomes charged with palpable and tranquil energy, and invisible beings are moving amongst us, profound presence concentrates space and time. So who is in a position to say what really occurred when it feels like the visitation of angels? In the quiet time afterwards one moves subdued and recollected in a state of wonder, as though one had entered life at last, and in essential communion with others.

It is clear that the kind of discovery Arnold has in mind is not limited to that of the connection between virtue and happiness, even though that is of the first importance to him. His imaginative sense of the modalities of energy or *virya* takes him to unexpected places which are, at the least, on the edge of anything that could come within the scope of the experimental method. In *Immortality* Arnold had already talked of the energy of life being kept on after the grave, but not begun. He draws on and develops such thoughts near the end of *Literature and Dogma*. He has just dismissed there what he considers the 'futilities' of metaphysical defences of the immortality of the soul, and its 'fairy tale' representations that cannot, he tells us, survive the turning of a steady regard upon them. He suggests we begin instead with *certainties*, by which I take it he means 'facts' that can be established:

And a certainty is the sense of *life*, of being truly *alive*, which accompanies righteousness. If this experimental sense does not rise to be stronger in us, does not rise to the sense of being inextinguishable, that is probably because our experience of righteousness is really so very small . . . At any rate, we have in our experience this strong sense of *life from righteousness* to start with; capable of being developed, apparently, by progress in righteousness into something immeasurably stronger. Here is the true basis for all religious aspiration after immortality. And it is an experimental basis. (377)

The fact or 'certainty' Arnold refers to is the 'strong sense of life from righteousness' and this is the form of what he says is hoped for in immortality rather than a ground for belief in its existence. If anything is to count as the life of immortality it is the life from righteousness that we can have the experimental sense of now. He has already made a similar claim in *Culture and Anarchy*:

The whole religious world . . . use now the word *resurrection* . . . in one sense only. They use it to mean a rising again after the physical death of the body. Now it is quite true that St Paul speaks of resurrection in this sense, that he tries to describe and explain it, and that he condemns those who doubt and deny it. But it is true, also, that . . . he thinks and speaks of it in a sense different from this; – in the sense of a rising to a new life before the physical death of the body, and not after it . . . For him, the life after our physical death is really in the main but a consequence and continuation of the inexhaustible energy of the new life thus originated on this side the grave. (153)

The life after our physical death is a consequence and a continuation of a rising to a new life now. Arnold does not defend this claim, since it is surely at the very edge of his experimental method. On the other hand, he talks of it as the basis of a *hope* rather than as the ground of a belief. It is *this* life that is hoped for, not any other, not an undetermined 'survival', or in the form of bourgeois fairy tales.

Far from offering us a 'merely naturalistic' reduction of religion to ethics Arnold has allied himself, through his highlighting of the biblical notion of 'life', with the great experiential spiritual traditions. What we have is a spiritual category that stands, epistemologically, quite independently of the particular theology that Arnold wished to reject. It then provides him with the terms in which to 'recast religion' and offer an alternative theology.

5

The idea of a progressive transformation of individuals through the ethical relation, by means of which reality is gradually revealed or disclosed is consciously identified by Arnold in *Literature and Dogma* through a notion of the 'given' and its quasi-personified form, 'the Eternal not ourselves that makes for righteousness', a notion that may recall us to the discussion of Tanabe's *tariki*. Bradley has some fun at the expense of Arnold's idiosyncratic, carefully non-theistic, turn of phrase, but the notion it expresses is important. Arnold is invoking the idea of a gradually revealed *given* that cannot be traced back to our choice or construction, though we do indeed construct a great deal around it when we reflect upon it theoretically in the form of what he calls *Aberglaube*, the term by which he refers to certain dogmatic beliefs, or rather certain dogmas understood in the terms of the natural theology he has criticised. He refers to this given as 'the not ourselves', in a way which shows his firm sense of the notion of a progressive revelation that depends upon his experimental method:

In the first place, we did not make ourselves, or our nature, or *conduct* as the object of three-fourths of that nature; we did not provide that happiness should follow conduct, as it undeniably does. (*Literature and Dogma*, 27)

Arnold goes on

The *not ourselves*, which is in us and in the world round us, has almost everywhere . . . struck the minds of men as they woke to consciousness, and has inspired them with awe . . . Our very word *God* is a reminiscence of these times, when men invoked 'The Brilliant on high' . . . as the power representing to them that which transcended the limits of their narrow selves, and that by which they lived and moved and had their being. (29)

It is hard not to discern in these remarks the same tendency as we found in Kant's reflections on the sublime in nature, setting the mind in motion towards the idea of God. This formulation suggests a personification of the same perspectival illusion that I claimed earlier might fuel the *jiriki–tariki* distinction. From the perspective of a 'narrow self' the emergence of something 'higher' presents itself as a visitation, a grace. It is as though the compelling *possibilities* of 'righteousness' presented themselves as a given, and are personified as the Brilliant on high. This also fits Kant, as does the following famous Arnoldian comment:

the word 'God' is used in most cases . . . as by no means a term of science or exact knowledge, but a term of poetry and eloquence, a term *thrown out*, so to speak, at a not fully grasped object of the speaker's consciousness. (12)

This is not an alienated projection of human values, or need not be, but rather a reflection back to ourselves in an obscure way of what draws, compels and beckons us, as receding limit quivers into threshold, light and energy beyond the doorway, towards which we move only gropingly.

Having announced the notion of the given, Arnold now says of the Israelites:

> They had dwelt upon the thought of conduct and right and wrong, till the *not ourselves* which is in us, became to them adorable eminently and altogether as *a power which makes for righteousness*; which makes for it unchangeably and eternally, and is therefore called *The Eternal.* (32)

This is a long way from the first recognition of this 'stream of tendency' in *Dover Beach*. It is hard not to apply it to Arnold himself, from that moment in the poem where the notion of conduct is given him as the only place to turn, presented as a 'not himself', not deriving from his choice. He is offering us a projectivist reduction of theological language of a distinctive and impressive kind. He claims that human beings attempted to personify a progressively disclosed *given* or 'not ourselves' of human experience by which reality is made manifest through 'conduct'. It is not any product of our choice or of our construction that things are thus and so, that they follow these laws, it is a given, a 'not ourselves'. Human beings have used theological language to represent to themselves 'that which transcended the limits of their narrow selves'. The 'not ourselves which is in us', our very impulsion towards the expression of the laws of our being referred to in *The Buried Life*, the impulsion to 'find our true, original course', becomes 'a power which makes for righteousness'. Whatever one may want to say about the accuracy or adequacy of this as an historical account of the use of God-language, it shows how Arnold perceives the 'not ourselves' as a graduated opening to us of reality, in a way that depends upon our satisfying in our lives the conditions for the possibility of that opening. His alternative construction on the Bible substitutes a so-called experimental notion of God for that of the personal first cause. On the other hand, that substitution is surely, ultimately, a rejection of the theistic language. What Arnold sees is that it functioned to secure a beckoning *agape* that transcends and summons the unregenerate self. To see this is to see also that it does not need to be thus secured.

One of Arnold's least plausible-seeming suggestions may here present itself in a different light. He had said that religion was 'morality touched by emotion', a typical Arnoldian slogan or war cry, treated contemptuously by Bradley and his later crony Eliot as though it were a formal definition. Whether it is true or not depends on how we understand 'emotion'. If we locate moral sensibility on a trajectory defined by *akolasia, enkrateia* and *sophrosune,* we may think that Arnold has intuited something important. Emotion defines the inner condition of morality, and it deepens and expands the self which is thus opened up to the world, narrow selves see narrow worlds, attention to reality expands and transforms the self. Morality touched by emotion is moral life seen as the deepest expression of our being.

The 'not fully grasped object of the speaker's consciousness' is just this obscurely present given that opens out progressively to conduct, and, of course, *towards* it. The use of God-language is then to be understood in terms of assertions that can be verified in experience:

> Let us announce, not: 'There rules a great Personal First Cause, who thinks and loves, the moral and intelligent Governor of the universe, and *therefore* study your Bible and learn to obey this!' No; but let us announce: 'There rules an enduring Power, not ourselves, which makes for righteousness, and *therefore* study your Bible and learn to obey this. (323)

Arnold's account of theological language makes its use no more than a cultural contingency, a means by which the intimation of a progressive disclosure of reality is articulated. This is not a revisionist voluntarism that makes belief a *commitment* that saves us from futility, as Cupitt seems sometimes to offer. What he puts in the place of 'belief' or faith is the notion of a revelatory *life*. It is not a position that will satisfy the theological realists, but was never intended to. On the contrary, it is the product of a painfully developed process of thinking that arose out of the dismay that followed his loss of Faith. Arnold has contributed to a piece of cartography, to the description of a path that has opened up before us. The verification of the description is not going to be easy, and we may, if we try it, be questioned by Arnold's gaunt and taciturn host, the wind 'shaking his thin white hairs', and have to give the same answer. Or maybe we shall arrive with friends.

6

It would be a mistake, I think, to press too hard the parallels between the thought of Matthew Arnold and Tanabe Hijime's use of the Buddhist distinction between self-power and Other-power. But it seems a useful distinction to *apply* to those phases of Arnold's poetry in which a kind of regeneration, or at least the form of its possibility, presents itself to him, not out of his own efforts, though clearly his own efforts are a condition, but as a sort of grace of nature, something given. In the moment of darkness possibilities arise that it seems would not have come unless the darkness had come first. Aelred Squire has remarked that the *Grande Chartreuse* is a less successful poem than the more famous *Dover Beach*. Whether that is so or not there is an interesting difference between the two poems. The poet in the former is represented as between two worlds, one dead, the other powerless to be born. That is the perceived position upon which the poem dwells and with which it remains. In the latter poem, however, we do see the beginnings of the new world of spiritual life arising as a gift in the place of bleakness, arriving precisely as a given.

Arnold's notion of the 'not ourselves' seems to parallel that of *tariki*, at least as understood phenomenologically. The 'not ourselves', or Other-power, conceptually linked to that of 'life', seems to stand between a naturalistic reductionism and a theological realism, suggesting a world opening to the view of those who have eyes to see. Now the nature of this 'not ourselves' is problematic for the philosopher. I have cheerfully talked of 'realities' that are disclosed progressively, but I have been fairly coy about what they actually are. Perhaps I should make my position clear: I am not making claims, but trying to represent the form of a position which seems to depend upon establishing a relationship between knowledge and the interior condition of the knower. Even that is difficult enough, since whatever we might say about the realities that a transformed subjectivity discloses we are all already constituted by a particular subjectivity and our views about its possible transformations *may* reflect an unrecognised narrowness of vision. Tanabe himself is anything but hubristic. Access to the distinction between *jiriki* and *tariki* depends upon coming up against human *limitation*. In any case the essential point about the 'not ourselves' is that it represents an *open* dimension of being, to adopt a phrase of Herbert Guenther. Its *conditions* are determinate, but it is a progressive opening into what remains so far undetermined. The concept of dependent origination, the idea that things in general arise in dependence upon conditions, is given specific application in the context of knowledge. One of the crucial stages is to be found in the claim that 'knowledge and vision of things as they are' arises in dependence upon 'concentration'. It is enough at the moment to point out that it has at least the form of an empirical, testable claim. It also has an interesting corollary, that to the extent that we are not 'concentrated' we have access only to 'appearance', and then we have to give an account of what it is *not* to be 'concentrated', just as we have to give an account of 'concentration' itself.

It may also be felt that I have left the notion of *life* hopelessly vague. It is certainly true that those who urge us to say 'Yes to life' may have very different conceptions of what this might entail, or have no very clear conception at all. However the concept that I have derived from Arnold is reasonably well determined, though no doubt more needs to be said, since Arnold has hardly *analysed* 'conduct' or 'righteousness'. It is bounded by concepts like 'righteousness', 'happiness' and 'self-renunciation' in Arnold's writing. These concepts need further determination too, of course, but it is clear enough that Arnold was seeking to determine the New Testament promise of 'more abundant life'. In a Buddhist context we should need to say more about the *panca indriyani*, the 'five spiritual faculties', that I have already referred to as intuitively appropriated by Arnold himself. But given these boundaries, it is clear that 'life' is not hopelessly vague so long as we remember its conceptual connections. Those connections are ethical, and yet I want to say that 'life' as thus conceived is also an epistemological category, since it is a medium of disclosure.

7

But what about immortal longings, the energy of life kept on after death, but not begun, what about a soul well-knit? Arnold's views on immortality, or, rather, his *conception*, is intriguing and seems to derive from Goethe. James Simpson (1979, 137) draws our attention to a Goethean remark cited by Allott in his edition of Arnold:

I do not doubt our continued existence, for Nature cannot do without the entelechy. But we are not all immortal in the same way, and to manifest oneself as a great entelechy in the future, one has to be one here.

Some people talk of encoding or information being carried on, in this context, but what we need, conceptually, is an encoded force or energy. Simpson (137) also draws our attention to a letter to Clough of 1848: 'our spirits retain the heights they have succeeded in raising themselves to'. All of this suggests that the form of consciousness is more important than its survival and that the better sort of survival is of a form of conscious being that is not attached to survival. Once out of nature I shall never take / My bodily form from any natural thing, / But such a form as Grecian goldsmiths make / Of hammered gold and gold enamelling. This image of Yeats' suggests those references in the Buddhist tradition to the formation of a 'vajric' or 'diamond' body. Well, recent Buddhist writers have properly emphasised the importance of scepticism and agnosticism about such doctrines as that of rebirth, for instance. It doesn't seem to be a straightforwardly empirical doctrine, and there is a serious question about how far the hope of a future life is motivated by attachment and egotism.

However, I wonder whether the 'soul', unlike 'God', is really after all an empirical concept. If we are to be sceptical, as opposed to agnostic, say, then we need to be sceptical for the right reasons. It seems to me that one form of scepticism in this area depends upon a *conflation* of 'mind' and 'soul' that infects at least the Western tradition, including the work of Aquinas and Descartes.[3] In brief, it does seem genuinely incoherent to talk about a disembodied *mind*, for talk of mind simply refers in summary form to a set of activities, of thought and volition, that belong to a person or a being. In that sense a mind can be 'ensouled' as well as embodied. In other words, talk of soul is quite distinct from that of mind. It makes sense, then, to talk of a *physically* disembodied soul, as a being capable of thought and volition. Indeed, this is how the western tradition has tended to talk of souls, wandering in Hades or wherever. The possibility of a physically disembodied soul does not of course give us immortality; such a being may well have a briefish life span.

But we haven't reached anything empirical yet. All I can say further is that I have been interested in and troubled by an impressive convergence of accounts of disembodiment which I should like, as they say, to share with the reader. I had better distinguish, first, between so-called out of the body experiences and so-called near death experiences. The latter are well known to be important and consoling to those who have had them. However, I am impressed by the evidence of their causal relationship with oxygen deprivation, etc. Out of body experiences seem to require a different account. The idea of the soul as a separable entity seems to be formed as a response by exemplary individuals to the startling experience of *separation from the physical body*. (Of course, the *transmission* of the concept is through the usual social channels.)

First, Plutarch (1992, 339 *et seq.*) at 590B of *On Socrates' Personal Deity* refers in a literary context to the experience of one Timarchus, whose description of what happened to him is reported thus:

---

[3] See my 'The Locations of the Soul' in *Religious Studies*, 32, 1996, some of which I have raided here, for a fuller discussion.

He said that after he had gone down into the place of the oracle, at first he encountered deep darkness, and then, once he had prayed, he lay down for a long time without really knowing whether he was awake or dreaming. What was clear, however, was the impression he had of his head being struck, with an accompanying bang, and of the sutures of his skull opening up and releasing his soul. His soul withdrew from his body and to its delight blended with air that was translucent and pure; it seemed at first, when that happened, as though his soul had recovered after a long illness, and was flexing itself for a while and increasing in size, unfurling like a sail.

There is a similar account in *On God's Slowness to Punish* (*ibid.*, 283). Part of the interest of this circumstantial account is its comparability to descriptions of the Tibetan Buddhist practice of *phowa*, in which the metaphor of the archer shooting an arrow is employed. Herbert Guenther (1986, 201) comments: 'the oozing of blood or lymph at the fontanelle opening is a phenomenon as yet unexplained by the medical sciences, though well attested by all who have performed this practice'. Among whom, I should say, I am not numbered, and have had no such experiences, which for many of us will remain no doubt fugitive or bizarre. Such experiences would only at best yield evidence of separation, not of rebirth or life after death. On the other hand, they might well change someone's view of what is possible, from scepticism, perhaps, to a reasonable agnosticism. On the other hand, I had had a severe headache, I was sitting on a chair, there were two people doing a healing meditation for me, and all at once I was larger than my own body, enclosing it in a state of energy, and then I subsided again. But these are not things to invest hope or belief in, only to observe and be surprised by. But then there is the *Hui Ming Ching* (Wilhelm 1972, 75):

First the spirit must penetrate the breath-energy . . . then the breath-energy envelops the spirit. When spirit and breath-energy are firmly united and the thoughts quiet and immobile, this is described as the embryo. The breath-energy must crystallise; only then will the spirit become effective. Therefore it is said in the *Leng-yen-ching*: 'Take maternal care of the awakening and the answering'. The two energies nourish and strengthen one another. Therefore it is said: 'Daily growth takes place.' When the energy is strong enough and the embryo is round and complete it comes out of the top of the head. This is what is called: the completed appearance which comes forth as embryo and begets itself as the son of the Buddha.

These remarks may appear strange and mysterious, but by that token they are strange and mysterious to *someone*, an individual, and it is only a covert or unconscious empiricism which seeks to measure their sense by reference to present experience when precisely that has become the issue, since what is described is clearly a process of some kind.

Theism, non-theism and Haldane's Fork

I

But this reductive spiritual realism I am trying to articulate is only one response to positivism and the Death of God. It is a response from someone who sees no way back, and is trying to make sense of intimated possibilities that announce themselves to a more or less alert consciousness that has to learn how to attend. But someone of the same attentiveness may want to interrogate the Death of God itself, and return us to a classical theism which it is felt that Nietzsche and other secularisers have wholly failed to understand, a return to the notion of God as that 'great ocean of being' who is 'beyond the order of all beings' and their uncaused cause. And someone who took that direction may well have taken a hint precisely from Heidegger's idea of a 'calm, self-possessed surrender to that which is worthy of questioning'.

The classical form of critical theological realism envisages an uncaused cause of all there is and claims that we can know by the light of reason that it exists, but that we cannot either comprehend or adequately represent it. Given that we are able thus to establish that there *is* an uncaused cause of all there is whose provident nature is revealed independently in scripture, we can know something of its operations by reference to its effects. It is this God that is, according to Nietzsche, 'dead'. Such claims, of course, have always been in contention, and that no doubt was the source of Matthew Arnold's conclusion that they cannot be verified. There is anyway a tradition which denies the efficacy of the proofs as a route to belief, whether they are 'valid' or not. This denial is commonplace among theologians, but their dismissal of them neglects the possibility that the proofs, rather than 'showing' or failing to 'show' that there is a God, provide the focus and form of dawning assent and worship.[1] It seems plausible to take at least the cosmological

---

[1] Dewi Phillips' first book, *The Concept of Prayer* brings this out.

argument as a formalised version of the vision offered of 'creation' in Genesis. On the other hand, that does not mean, *pace* Aquinas, that we *can* 'know by the light of reason' that there is a God, an uncaused cause. It is the intellectual formula for a vision which commands the assent, because it forms the mind, of the 'believer'.

So, then, the existence of God . . . well here I must put my cards on the table like anyone else. I was brought up as a Catholic and 'believed in God' and then I stopped 'believing in God'. Brought up as a Catholic, ah yes. I had 'wanted to be a priest' from an early age, three or four. The church had seemed huge, it is the early fifties, always packed full with 'the people', latecomers 'fulfilling their obligation' try to find a seat before or after the sermon, as the priest makes his way between the sanc- tuary and the pulpit and the congregation is noisily rising or sitting down, and leave ('slip out') straight after the *Ite*. We were not like that, were never late, our large shining family, poor but spotlessly clean, walking together soberly to Sunday Mass. At the consecration there was the priest, perhaps in white or gold, the bells ring, the sanctuary is flooded with light, with flowers and candles, he genuflects and raises the host or the chalice, genuflects again, a tremendous hush in the church, the congregation huddled on their knees, their heads bowed low. Not understanding Latin, they did not follow the mass with a missal, nor were they invited to respond, but we sat or stood or knelt on cue, their rosary beads moving between their fingers, but knowing the holiest parts of the mass, and the parts when they could relax. There used to be crowds in the churchyard afterwards, spilling out into the road, between masses, as one lot came out into the sunlight and another pressed to go in. Then people everywhere were greeting one another, calling each other by name, the men raised their hats, as they paused for a word, the children looking on, or bashfully looking down, as they were spoken about or addressed, hopping from one leg to the other, Irish names, Irish voices all around.

I was brought up on Aquinas's Five Ways, there they were, the proof of God for some, rejected as 'invalid' by others. I suppose eventually I came to the conclusion that they 'failed', though recognising that they were not the only or even a main source of 'faith', so that whether they 'worked' or not hardly mattered that much. They were of interest to logicians, a useful occasion for illustrating an alleged quantifier shift fallacy . . . Meanwhile we lived securely in the 'world' that Matthew Arnold, and Arthur Clough and their contemporaries, like Froude, had already found to have died on them a hundred years earlier. You know where you are in a world, and you need to know what it is like to be *between* 'two worlds', you have to suffer it, to pass from one world to the next. As for me, it is seventy-six years since Arnold has died of a heart attack in Toxteth, and I am despatched at the age of fourteen by the Bishop of Shrewsbury to a small boarding school in the hills of North Staffordshire, alas now a ruin. In the long Victorian dormitory, in a world which had known Newman and Faber rather than Arnold and Clough, fifty boys, fifty beds, fifty white counterpanes, the wild alarm of the morning bell, violent return to unhappy consciousness, conscious of desperate, solitary sleep-inducing sin. Now the roof is open to the rain and there are great holes in the floor, caused by fires lit by vandals. Once or twice I woke to a quiet rustling and whispering coming from a near-by bed, so was he, I was too ignorant then to think it, was he there in the night, crouched by your bed to hold and knead you, to touch your face, stroke your hair, kiss your mouth. If you died in a state of mortal sin you went straight to Hell, and besides . . . it injured Our Blessed Lord and His Holy Mother. So why were you so casual about it, how could you make jokes? And I wondered, in permanent misery, how it was that I could keep on in my sin when I was here to become a priest, just as you were, paid for by the bishop, to offer myself as a pure sacrifice before the Lord, as I was taught by priests, who were perhaps men under their own torture. I would strive vainly to resist the impulse, praying to Our Lady to help me to be pure, desperate, anxious, states to accelerate the outcome, always the same, the point came, struggle ended, when I would turn, shut it all from my mind, and begin, then lie miserable in the drowsy knowledge of my sin. But I was constantly in love with wonderful boys, consoled by their beauty as they passed down the aisle, after mass, and prayers before lunch, and prayers before bed, Brethren, be ye prudent and watch, for the devil, who is your enemy, goes about roaring like a lion to find his prey, *fratres, sobrii estote et vigilate, quia adversarius vester diabolus, tamquam leo rugiens, circuit, quaerens quem devoret: cui resistite fortes in fide*, but you, oh Lord . . . I was unable, strong in what kind of faith, to receive Holy Communion the morning after, since I was in mortal sin, and to receive the sacrament thus was also a mortal sin, more precisely, a *sacrilege*, even worse, if there can be degrees of mortalness, perhaps different circles of Hell. So often I had to be seen, the immediate mortification, not going up to the altar rails to receive upon my tongue the Body of Christ, because my own body, the Temple of the Holy Spirit, was defiled. I hated to be seen staying in my place, highly visible as we went up row by row, since there could only really be one reason, and I knew myself contemplated by others under that description. I used to imagine plausible reasons for staying put, *and half believed them*, kneeling in a casual posture lent by the plausibility. Certainly I did not dare to approach the sacrament. Not only a sacrilege, it would be a gesture of contempt towards my crucified Lord to present myself in such a state. At Grove Park, the senior seminary, on the other hand, it was impossible, in a small group of twenty men dedicated to the Lord, in a tiny chapel, not to join the others every day for Holy Communion, and I never noticed anyone else not going. Here the thought of being seen to remain in my place sustained me better than more obviously spiritual consider-ations through the temptations of the flesh. For a whole year I managed to control myself and remain 'chaste', giving myself wholly to Christ and his Blessed Mother, for to become a priest was to become another Christ. But I would many nights lie there in my bed crying out to him to save me from temptation, and the tall window frames, as I looked out into the darkness, swam into my vision against the sky in the form of crucifixes upon which hung the tormented body of the Son of God.

I arrived at Buddhism, a non-theistic form of spiritual practice. Non-theistic rather than atheistic, if an atheist is one who declares ('in his heart') that there is no God, since a non-theist simply by-passes the issue, making no essential reference to God. This seemed to me a useful fact, a way of starting on an already beckoning spiritual path, when so many delayed the journey until they had sorted out the question of God. That is how it seemed to me, that delay. I had the sense of something beckon-ing, actually the form of the Buddha in calm meditation, but no clarity about what seemed to lie concealed from view – because one can some-times sense, whether rightly or wrongly, that there is something *there*. But many of my friends felt that if they could not establish that there was a God . . . then they could not set out. Maybe the Psalmist is right, to refer to the *fool*. In fact, it seems to me that the theist and the atheist are in the same position, that the issue cannot be settled between them. That does not make the theist a fool, though. The fool is someone who ignores or rejects all the promptings of inwardness. However, those promptings do not in fact need to be secured by theism, do not lead directly or inexor-ably to the uncaused cause of all there is. I was on Caldy Island, I was twenty or twenty one, suborned by logical positivism, so why was I *there*? my own rigorous teachers may well have asked. But there was Cornelius Ernst, ah, he said, as I confidently announced the meaninglessness of theological language, so you have had no sense of something far more deeply interfused? and there was a silence as I remembered. On the other hand, I know believers who find nothing *secured* by theism, that is their faith, the strongest passion of their subjectivity, though they differ on whether it is or is not *unreasonable* in Wittgenstein's sense. Still, I have doubts about locating faith just here. I do offer a diagnosis, though, which may not be very well received. My impression is that many philosophers and theologians are culturally *ignorant* of non-western traditions of the meditational kind. The issues really do present themselves to them as either theism or scientific materialism. They are unaware of other plausible narratives. I have heard one well-known Dominican thinker announce that Christianity is the only serious contender against materialism. The scholarly Buddhist community, which includes many practitioners, has clearly not made much of an impact outside its own circles, and maybe that is unavoidable at this point in the history of Buddhist Studies in the west. The availability of Buddhism among western intellectuals is still largely dependent on the views of people like Schopenhauer, Hegel and Nietzsche.[2] It is still generally assumed that Buddhism is quietistic and negative, that *nirvana* really means some kind of grateful extinction for an unhappy consciousness, as opposed to what it really is, the blowing out of the defiling passions or *klesas*, the conative side of *bodhi* or awakening.

Recently, though, I read a debate between J. J. C. Smart and John Haldane (1996) on Atheism and Theism. Haldane defends Thomistic and similar arguments with a forceful elegance that has made me have to think it through again. We have to confront these questions. It is strange, though, how fashions change. There have been periods when no one has been prepared to consider these arguments: 'it is only with moderate enthusiasm . . .' Strawson once said in his book on Kant as he turned to the critique of philosophical theology . . .

'Doubts' were beginning, creeping into my mind, about the truth of the Real Presence, insidious and repressed, then blatant and mocking, first one doubt, then the next, if this is false, then so is this, and this, and this, where was a where was a place, but I had nothing bold to boast, my soul was without wings. I was frightened too that the harmless cleverness praised at school should turn out to have such a sharp edge and cut into my life, slice through its supports. It was at the beginning of the second year of our 'training', at Oscott, where Newman had announced a Second Spring. I had a room on the same corridor, apparently, as Frederick Rolfe had been on, though his room was now

---

[2] For a view of how Nietzsche appropriated Buddhism see Morrison (1996).

a lavatory . . . I had left by the Christmas, of 1965, in a terrible state before I went: it was remarked that my hands shook, that the end of the billiard cue trembled, my friends in the common room looked askance, and I could only mumble to my confessor. But I had to leave, I could see no alternative, I was being overtaken more and more by doubt even though to leave was quite unthinkable, and I thought that everything would fall about my ears. I could imagine no future for myself, I could not see myself in any scenario, the terms of my identity were going missing. I needed a *world* and I was being unworlded by the process of my own reasoning. Once, at Grove Park, I had become dismayed by the thought of the Beatific Vision, in which the soul is caught up and *lost* in the Godhead, it was a beginning of terror. As I dwelt devoutly on this doctrine I became frightened and started to fear for myself, what would become of *me*? I had spoken about it to one of the priests. He had looked at me with some curiosity and then said that everyone would be known by their name in heaven, a reply from which I drew comfort. If I now were to leave the seminary I would lose all my bearings, but it was a prospect that I had no choice but to contemplate and in my anxiety I fell with self-disgust into the practice of masturbation, finding consolation and despair in hateful and joyous ejaculations, sprawling on my bed hiding my face from the God that I loved, drops of semen straying onto my long black cassock, the token of my calling soiled.

I had this dream when I was a student, in which I was climbing a high tree in a wood, carrying books and dressed in my cassock. There were two men below me on the ground, urging me to come down, but I ignored them. One of them was a priest from my old seminary, the other man I didn't recognise. As I climbed the going got more difficult, so first I threw down my cassock, and then, later, the books I was carrying. When they hit the ground, they burst into flames. I continued to climb, higher and higher.

Many years later I dreamt again about that priest. I was walking by myself, thinking, along the perimeter of a field, when he joined me and engaged me in conversation, asking polite, respectful questions about my position on various philosophical topics, though manoeuvring me all the time towards an area which grew denser and more overgrown until we were in a dark wood and suddenly he turned his face to me and looked at me with an expression of frightful, naked hunger that took me terrified out of sleep. Maybe that was the reason my book has the form it has taken: the undergrowth had also to be confronted.

2

Haldane recalls us to a famous passage from Romans:

What can be known about God is plain to [men] for God has shown it to them. Ever since the creation of the world his invisible nature, namely his eternal power and deity, has been clearly perceived in the things that have been made. (Romans 1: 19–20) (141)

And he remarks that although it is natural 'that the religiously informed think of the question of God's existence in terms of a certain preconceived Divine identity', nevertheless Paul 'is asserting that even those who do not already have an idea of God are in a position to determine that God exists simply by reflecting on the natural order' (141). Well, it is easy for *him* to say, Paul I mean, that God has shown men enough for them to see that he exists, without their having a prior concept of God. Paul is certainly already 'religiously informed' and is hardly innocent of Genesis. It is easy to forget that monotheism took a long time to develop. God's 'eternal power and deity' are not that clearly perceived in the things that have been made, though if you have already *responded* to that natural order by coming to the notion of God, then perhaps it is too clearly perceived. Haldane talks of reflection on the natural order. But there is more than one way of reflecting on the natural order. I may indeed, as I have already said, have a sense of something far more deeply interfused, a sense of streams of *Life* surging below, beyond and within the sensible order of things, I may find myself straining towards something supersensible, but I seriously wonder whether, if I am not already prompted by belief, by a long developed tradition of belief, I would find the azurous hung hills . . . to be . . . his shoulders majestic. But there, surely, you will say, *someone* did . . . Well they found themselves impelled to *refer* to the Spirit of God moving over the waters . . . but that is precisely a *response* to the natural order. It is *not* to determine that God exists, even if we agree that it establishes the necessity to invoke the presence of mind in the otherwise cold universe, invoking it, though, in only one way among others.

3

At one point Haldane comments as follows:

The hypothesis of theism explains the existence of an orderly universe, of rational animals and of the harmony of thought and the world. Scientific materialism explains none of these things. (129)

This is a good example of the culturally narrow sense of the available options. Many of us would agree more readily with the second of these two statements than with the first. Scientific materialism seems to offer an inadequate description of the universe, though not necessarily a false one. There are clearly aspects of reality that scientific concepts 'grasp' or illuminate, but the issue is what they might miss, what might remain unnoticed in their shadow. The concepts it deploys leave out subjectivity, or at the least still have a serious problem explaining it away. Unfortunately Haldane's Fork offers only theism as an alternative. Scientific materialism cannot explain its own fundamental terms. But the existence of God *would* explain the order in the universe, we might suppose, if we are not hostile to the idea of God as an 'hypothesis' in the first place. One reason for being hostile is that this at least is an hypothesis too far for confirmation.

If there is a God, then perhaps the existence of an orderly universe, etc., is indeed 'explained', if that is not a presumption to knowledge of the mind of God. But we don't generally secure a hypothesis solely on the grounds that it would explain what we think needs to be explained. Even as an argument to the best explanation, there is no consensus about this and there are no independent grounds. The conclusion to God seems to rest here entirely on the felt need to 'explain' the existence of an orderly universe. I am not myself against dwelling on that arrival at the world as a limited whole, or even on the felt need to 'explain' it. And then we should need to trace out where such attention actually led us to, not in our reasoning now, but in our interiority. But Haldane and others refer to the '*a priori* improbability' of a universe such as ours, given the highly specific conditions, the 'fine tuning', upon which the emergence of self-conscious beings in an ordered world seems to depend. If the conditions upon which we depend were only slightly altered, it is said, nothing like us or our universe would have emerged. Haldane writes:

The basic laws of nature feature contingent ratios that the laws do not themselves explain, and the fundamental particles whose behaviour they regulate also exhibit apparently contingent numerical properties. If any of these ratios and quantities had been different in the slightest degree then not only we, and our predecessors in the history of life, but orderly matter itself would not have existed . . . any explanation of this fact has to look beyond the framework of natural causation and that leads to a conclusion of purposeful agency.

No doubt it is true that 'any explanation of this fact has to look beyond the framework of natural causation', the question is whether there *is* an explanation. The claim that these ratios and numerical properties are contingent, or 'apparently' contingent (a significant retreat, this qualification), appears to be based on the thought that we can imagine or think them to have been otherwise. But the fact that we can imagine or conceive them to have been otherwise does not imply that they *could* have been otherwise. Generally, establishing that something could have been otherwise requires us to refer to the conditions upon which they are thus contingent. The argument itself depends upon this move: we and orderly matter are dependent upon these initial natural conditions, that is part of what makes *us* so contingent. But these necessary conditions of our own existence do not depend on anything further, at least in the natural order and *ex hypothesi*. We know of no further conditions for them to be contingent upon and so we are in no position to judge that they *are* contingent, even if further research shows that they in fact are, depending on something else that does not itself appear to be contingent. There is no regress here. The judgment that these ratios are after all contingent and that they stand in need of an explanation in fact come together: the contingency is not something established first. *Ex hypothesi* the fundamental structure of our natural laws does not derive from anything else within nature. Hence the perceived need for a theistic explanation in terms of purposeful agency. It seems incredibly unlikely ('*a priori* improbable') that the structure should be thus rather than so, but 'seems' is not 'is' and we have no means of knowing, as though from an original position, what is likely and what is unlikely. (Isn't '*a priori* improbable' just a rather intellectualised expression of wonder, with no very determinate cognitive content?)

Now it is certainly true that the fact that many people do not think there is a need for any further explanation does not entail that there is no need for one, or that there is no explanation. The forms of order are thus and so whether there is an Orderer or no, but they could be the product of his hand even if no one believes this. So there is no denying that Haldane could be right that the order of the universe is the product of purposeful agency. The problem is with the establishing that this is true, and it is clearly not enough to say, if we are going to use this language, that the hypothesis of God explains the order and regularity of the universe.

4

Perhaps the issues become clearer if we move from the question why a highly specific set of determinable conditions have produced a highly specific outcome, to the more general question about the supposed need for an explanation for a world of contingent, dependent entities in general.

We can think of the *totality* of things whose existence depends on something else, of things whose existence is contingent upon particular conditions. In doing so we should remember that our explanations are frequently halted, our spade turned at bedrock, though sometimes 'bedrock' only appears so at first, and we find we can dig deeper after all. So we could make a *further totality* out of those things whose existence depends upon something else *and* the conditions upon which they depend, for which we find no further conditions. For instance we have already referred to the ratios that belong to our basic laws of nature, to the numerical properties of fundamental particles. We reach conditions which do not themselves depend upon anything further that we can ascertain, even if this leaves us feeling that it is all horribly 'contingent'. And we can think of the totality of all these conditions and the entities which depend upon them. We might be inclined to suppose that there it is, we reach the end of particular explanations, and there is a totality which contains a range of such ends of explanation. However, the cosmological argument presses us to reflect on this totality as something that itself needs explanation, as itself dependent upon some condition outside of it. But if this something that the totality of contingent things is now claimed to depend upon is itself no more than a further contingency, dependent on something else again, it would simply extend the totality and not explain it. There remains an issue whether the totality does indeed stand in need of an explanation, but if anything does explain it then it must be non-contingent or necessary. (Necessary being is perhaps best understood in purely negative terms as the denial of contingency, which is to say that a being is necessary if it is not such as to be brought into or maintained in or taken out of existence: it is not the case that it could have been otherwise, though sometimes we are just not in a position to see what could have made something otherwise.)

Philosophers who press this Leibnizian argument insist that the totality of dependent things and the natural conditions upon which they depend, is itself dependent, or better, insist that it *must* be dependent, a judgment that comes in tandem with the belief that it needs to be explained. Others have no such belief, are not dissatisfied by the idea that the totality of things that are explained by conditions that have no further natural explanation needs no explanation itself. This difference is extremely important. But *if* anything explains the totality of contingent things, it must itself be free of contingency and, of course, be capable of the creative act required.

But now in the Smart–Haldane debate Smart suggests that the world itself is a possible candidate for necessary existence. And indeed why should we not claim that the universe is neither brought into existence, nor maintained in existence, nor brought to an end, and that dependent entities arise within it in a way that depends upon the character of fundamental and unchanging conditions? Of course this is simply speculation, that is why I have introduced it here, for reasons that will become apparent. Well, I could say it now, there is no method of *settling* the matter. However, the idea that the world itself has necessary existence does serve to *explain* the emergence of contingent entities, but only in terms of natural conditions for which there is no further natural explanation. The problem with such a speculation is that just as we were in no position to judge that the natural conditions upon which we depend are themselves contingent, we are similarly in no position to judge that they are non-contingent: we cannot establish the one thing or the other.

Perhaps we can do better than this, however, and introduce life into the material universe, say by invoking something like the Spinozistic distinction between *natura naturans* and *natura naturata*, so that nature has within it the creative conditions of contingent things, of the things that are thrown up out of the great ocean of being. Aquinas uses that phrase as a way of referring to God, but it can be deployed differently, as a description of the naturing and natured totality. Mind is conspicuous by its absence in these speculations, and seems to depend for its introduction on Haldane's Fork (theism or scientific materialism). But there is more than one way to introduce Mind. One way is to refer to the Mind of God as responsible for the tremendous creative act that sustains Creation in being (Peter Geach refers us to a lovely metaphor: God makes the world in the way that a musician makes music, which lasts only as long as he makes it). But there are versions of pantheism and idealism that make mind part of the world, and so on. Schopenhauer claimed that our own interior experience of volition gave us insight into the noumenal world of will upon which phenomena depended as their expressions or manifestations to sense. Perhaps there are unchanging causes of change within the world itself, an unchanging tendency towards phenomenal and even conscious expression, from which change emerges and into which it subsides. And maybe these conditions include unknowable forms of conscious being, an aspect of the universe that could be radically unknowable by us, a necessary condition of the possibility of experience that could never be the object of a possible experience. St Paul and Aquinas concur that by reason and reflection we can know *that* there is a God, without thereby knowing *what* he is. The real situation as it seems to me is that these matters are radically incapable of being *settled*. Someone may be dissatisfied with the idea of a totality of dependent entities that are not explained by a necessary being that transcends them. Someone else may not. Perhaps the universe is to be explained by the purposeful agency of a necessary being, an unconditioned, absolute cause of human experience, say, that cannot in principle be the object of such experience. Perhaps there is a God who is '*extra ordinem omnium entium*', beyond the order of all beings. Or perhaps the universe is beyond the order of all the beings which it contains. The point is that the question cannot be *determined*. It is not something that we can settle, whether there is or is not a personal first cause of all there is. As Arnold said in *Literature and Dogma* the 'assumption' of a Personal first cause cannot be *verified*. His point was not, as I said, that it cannot be settled by any experience, which, indeed, it cannot, but that it cannot be verified by reference to the arguments. They are not sufficiently compelling. Someone may be persuaded by the arguments, which are considerations leading in a direction rather than 'proofs' in a strict sense, and it is not unreasonable or mad to be persuaded by them. But nor is it unreasonable or mad *not* to be persuaded by them. There is a moment, if you like, when a person makes an act of faith. But the act of faith is all at once in the cluster, *that* there is a God, *that* there is an explanation, *that* an explanation is needed. A particular picture is already in place.

I am not in the least suggesting that such an act of faith cannot be the vehicle for a profound spiritual life. At this stage it is enough to suggest that there are different versions of what is to constitute a spiritual life in the first place. I happen to know more than one person for whom the possibility of a spiritual or religious life seemed to them destroyed by the undermining of their belief in *God*. Arnold was an intelligent man. Having concluded that the existence of the God of the philosophers could not in principle be settled, he set out on a different course, to establish what, in the religious tradition of Judaeo-Christianity, *could* be settled by reference to experience. Similarly, the Buddhist tradition leaves these ultimate questions to one side, on the grounds that they are indeterminable. It immediately comes to specific contingencies, to what depends upon what in the context of human misery and human ignorance, recognising that even the nature of our reflecting on the natural order is dependent upon conditions.

5

The conditions under which western appropriations of Buddhism have arisen are clearly connected with the Death of God and what some writers refer to as a 'hunger' for spirituality. But Buddhism does seem to provide us with a path to the threshold of Arnold's second world, and even the means of passing into it, the one that, to change the metaphor back to his, had been in the early eighteen fifties, powerless to be born, and which then he had been powerless to *conceive*, a brave new world, at the beginning of things, in which older forms of *Bildung* are no longer available. But *Besinnung*, as we saw, is 'calm, self-possessed surrender to that which is worthy of questioning' and 'in *Besinnung* we gain access to a place from out of which there first opens the space traversed at any given time by all our doing and leaving undone' (ibid.). These remarks suggest movement from unreflective immediacy to some degree of ethical awareness or self-knowledge, to the inwardness of action, and what I suggest is worthy of questioning is, not *that there is a world*, which is in danger of leaving the *questioner* out of the question, but the very forms of our experience and relationship. We have to change the direction of our causal questions, and focus them upon ourselves and *the conditions and possibilities* of the forms of our experience and relationship. It seems to me that an unformulated interrogative attentiveness is not so unusual or uncommon, and is a form of waiting upon what may be seen which has its own causal consequences.

What I want to draw from this, especially in the face of the Nietzschean pronouncement, is the idea of the *naturalistic sources* of meditative states of mind and the exploration of where and to what, *if anything*, they lead. Some exponents of Buddhism may look askance at this qualification, but there is a canonical insistence on testing the word of the Buddha for oneself, and this provides precisely the methodology of those who are testing a path, testing whether it is genuinely leading somewhere worthwhile, questioning the forms of their own experience and relationship in the aftermath of the collapse of 'Platonism'. Such an experimental stance, moreover, with its contemporary western ring and its ancient Buddhist endorsement determines which aspects of the Buddhist traditions will recommend themselves. It is because meditation has naturalistic sources, by the way, that it is not incongruous to say as I did that we can see Buddhistic concepts forming in Arnold's poetry.

What is available in Buddhism are images of causal process and the development of human agency. This requires the imagination to move backwards and forwards between what we would leave and what we would turn towards, between the ugly and repugnant imagery of suffering and entanglement and the imagery of release, with representations also of the *possibilities* such release gives rise to, 'beautiful images of liberation', to use Marcuse's phrase. The figure of the Buddha, teaching or in meditation, may, as it did with me, attract, beckon, catch the imagination, represent, in the form of a 'realised person', an apparent possibility of being, represent the demeanour of a teacher in relation to one who would listen. The demeanour precisely represents a way of being which may lead, through the sharp sense of a contrast, to the interrogation of the *limits* of one's own forms of experience and relationship, which at least *feel* 'unsatisfactory' (*dukkha*) in the light of the represented form. The figure is an image not only of self-possession (*Besonnenheit*) or tranquillity (*samatha*) but also of knowledge or understanding (*prajna*) and a compassion (*karuna*) that seems to belong with the knowledge. The self-possession and knowledge are perceived as beyond the attainment of its observers, the compassion as directed towards them in the readiness to teach. To that extent, what the figure of the Buddha awakens is desire and what the figure represents is the object of desire, the shape of possible attainment and resolution. This is not, again, to say that there *is* such knowledge or such tranquillity or such compassion. Desire is awakened in the inquirer for what may, for all *they* know, be an illusion. It is also a desire for something which cannot be *had* or possessed: one becomes it, if indeed there is anything to become, and so it seems that a condition of so becoming is a releasing of ourselves from grasping. The inquirer may be inclined to *mimesis*, to do what the Buddha is seen to do, and to sit in meditation, in the same posture as the Buddha. Meditation is a natural activity. In its formal aspects it may seem bizarre or exotic, but everyone is aware to some degree or other of meditative states, a calm, questioning awareness of the landscape and its horizon. Just sitting can be pleasing, a pleasure of the body and a relaxed stillness of the mind, so that formal meditation is a development of a natural process of relative harmony and concentration or increased alertness of the whole person, in a way rather similar, perhaps, to Schiller's (1967) description of aesthetic experience as a context in which a person's fragmented and unbalanced faculties come into balance for the period of the experience. What the traditions describe is a purported process of *causal* development in which the coming to be of one stage depends upon the attainment of another: they apply, in other words, the principle of 'dependent origination' (*pratityasamutpada*), perhaps the fundamental principle of Buddhist doctrine, which has, for instance, been formulated as follows:

This being, that becomes, from the arising of this, that arises; this not becoming, that does not become; from the ceasing of this, that ceases.

But the general formula is given particular applications in relation to suffering or unsatisfactoriness (*dukkha*) and the set of causal links leading to the arising of 'enlightenment'. Thus, for instance, the crucial traditional claim is that in dependence upon 'concentration' (*samadhi*) arises 'knowledge and vision of things as they are' (*yathabhutajnanadarsana*). I say 'crucial' for the perhaps obvious reason that we pass here from representations of what we might call subjective states, to a claim about their upshot in a knowledge of what is really the case, where the realisation depends upon some particular such state of the person. The claim is crucial for another reason, viz., that this is the point of departure: we are confronted with the positing of a recalcitrant experience (recalcitrant from the point of view of the settled way we take the world to be) or, better, a *recalcitrant becoming* which opens the inquirer into the knowledge that is represented in the demeanour of the human figure of the Buddha. The central Buddhist *procedure* is to introduce or apply, in particular stages, the principle that everything depends on conditions, an apparent commonplace that only the 'awakened person' is supposed uniquely to know. The crucial Buddhist *claim* is that there arises in dependence upon 'concentration' (*samadhi*) precisely this knowledge of things as they are, which it presents, as I say, almost bathetically, as the knowledge that things depend upon conditions. What (if *anything*) constitutes this realisation *remains to be seen*. Our relationship to it, in other words, is always my or your relationship: we do not *know* that there is any such thing. Or perhaps you do, who are reading this, and then you are as baffling to me as the notion of realisation itself. The implication, of course, is that we are presently in a state of radically conditioned ignorance, are profoundly unaware of *a way of knowing* that things depend on conditions which depends on conditions (of our own possible being) that we do not therefore know. Knowledge of things as they are might just be the interior knowledge of the realities revealed through the forms of consciousness and being that depend on sets of conditions lived through by the progressively changing inquirer, the perspective, in other words, that derives from a consciousness in its fully accomplished or achieved state: a brightly shining mind, if there is such an accomplishment or such luminosity.

This may even be an optimistic view of the epistemology of the situation. But the epistemology nevertheless has implications for the appropriation of Buddhism. The recommendation, in brief, is that it be approached, at those points at which it recommends itself, with a positive scepticism and the spirit of experiment. Post-Christians are not necessarily post-believers, but perhaps post-Christian Buddhists ought to be. At least there is reason to be aware of the difficulties attached to being a 'believer',[3] to the simple and uncritical absorption of the world-view within which the favoured practices are embedded, shedding one set of traditional beliefs and donning another. The case of the critical theological realist is different from this but I speak only for those for whom that project is too perplexing a leap into the possibility of spirituality and too entangled with unfortunate associations. What is available instead is a responsiveness to the possible opening up of a path which may lead to a trans-natural realisation of what was not formerly known. We do not *know* that there is such a thing as 'enlightenment'. For *us* (one has to speak for oneself) it serves as a regulative idea which may lead somewhere, and in which confidence (*sraddha*) grows to the extent that it does. This is not to say that the imagination may not be utterly seized by the beauty and power of representations of the prospect, in the shape of human forms, but it is not unacceptable for there to be a tension of this sort between intellect and imagination, the one hurrying, the other restraining. Imagination may indeed be a form of faith leading to understanding so long as what we count as understanding is not compromised in advance by the faith that seeks it: so faith in a process rather than a prior faith in its end:

The ways of *Besinnung* constantly change, ever according to the place on the way at which a path begins, ever according to the portion of the way that it traverses, ever according to the distant view that opens along the way into that which is worthy of questioning. (Heidegger, 181)

---

[3] And there are still so many 'believers', one is surrounded by them, in my time I have failed again and again to pronounce the shibboleths of various born-again Freudians, Marxists, Wittgensteinians, post-modernists, etc., all characterised by a sainted intolerance, self-conviction and refusal to think anything through.

6

In a recent book the Buddhist writer, Stephen Batchelor (1997), dwells on this issue of 'belief' as he develops the notion of Buddhist agnosticism. The Buddha, he tells us, announces 'four ennobling truths',[4]

those of anguish, its origins, its cessation and the path leading to its cessation . . . Anguish . . . is to be understood, its origins to be let go of, its cessation to be realised, and the path to be cultivated. (4)

Batchelor then laments the process by which 'four ennobling truths to be acted upon are neatly turned into four propositions of fact to be believed'. At this point, he says, 'Buddhism becomes a religion. A Buddhist is someone who *believes* these four propositions' (5). And later he says,

While 'Buddhism' suggests another belief-system, 'dharma practice' suggests a course of action. The four ennobling truths are not propositions to believe; they are challenges to act. (7)

I agree it is proper to resist a certain way of introducing the notion of 'belief' into Buddhism, but one needs to be wary of this rapid and simplistic way of distinguishing Buddhism from the other religious traditions. It seems to assume that we had a clear concept of the 'belief' in which these others are enmired and from which a virtuous Buddhism is free. New Buddhists need to be sure that they are not valorising their Buddhism at the expense of a degenerate or simple-minded version of the other spiritual traditions. What would Kierkegaard, for instance, make of this antithesis between truths to be acted upon and propositions to be believed? A Christian 'believer' is someone who *has confidence in Christ* in a way which informs the existential process of their *metanoia*: there is no salvation in 'merely believing' a set of doctrines or propositions. Believing is not *mere*.

It would be a mistake, too, to lose sight of the propositional presuppositions of Batchelor's 'challenge to act', viz., that human suffering arises in dependence upon craving, aversion and ignorance, and that their overcoming brings about its cessation. There is a clear propositional element to the challenge. But it doesn't follow, and thus I agree with Batchelor if this is what he is saying, that we need to *believe* these propositions in order to take up the 'challenge'. *This is a matter of the first*

[4] This is a slightly eccentric formulation of what is normally referred to as 'the Four Noble Truths'.

importance if we are to introduce a new paradigm into our understanding of the spiritual life. Dwelling upon the experience of suffering or *dukkha* may lead us to *see* its connection with craving, etc., or *start* to see it. In that sense someone may start to form the belief that there is such a connection. A practitioner may try meditation because they have heard it brings benefits. It may lead to a relaxation of various cravings and a temporary cessation of mental anguish, and they may connect the one with the other. On this basis they may begin to explore or put further to the test the 'truths' announced by the Buddha. It is a matter of *testing* the reality of the supposed causal links, rather than believing, merely or otherwise, that such links exist, and such testing doesn't presuppose a belief in what is tested, even if it is compatible with such belief. There is a danger of setting up a *false* opposition between 'propositions to believe' and 'challenges to act'. In his review[5] of Batchelor's book my Buddhist teacher Urgyen Sangharakshita rightly remarks that 'believing in a proposition of fact is not incompatible with acting upon it' (25). This is true, but 'acting upon' a proposition does not entail that one believes it, or should I say, rather, and this is the nub of the thing, that *responding* to a proposition does not entail that one believes it. Sangharakshita's own presupposition seems to be that not only is 'believing in a proposition not incompatible with acting upon it', but that acting upon it *requires* belief, and this leads him into the epistemologically suspect notion of 'provisional belief'. Sometimes, he comments, we cannot be sure that the goal we have set ourselves really exists or that we have adopted the right means for its achievement:

Nevertheless, *believing that it exists and that the means we have adopted are the right ones* (my italics), we go on employing those means until such time as experience confirms both our belief in the existence of the one and our belief in the rightness of the other – or does *not* confirm them. Belief of this kind is relative, not absolute; qualified, not unqualified; provisional, not final; and tentative, not certain. It is on account of this *provisional* belief . . . that we accept the four truths as propositions of fact and act upon them in the particular way each requires and according to the degree of our belief. (26)

What Sangharakshita describes here is in reality the situation of only *one* kind of practitioner, one who is seeking confirmation of what they already believe, but ready also to acknowledge the possibility of disconfirmation. But there is an implicit voluntarism in the notion of provisional belief, which implies that one can *decide* whether and how far to believe a proposition, whereas one's propositional attitudes tend to be determined, to be forced upon one, by the state of the evidence in one's possession. Now I take it that Sangharakshita's thought is that 'the goal we have set ourselves', whose reality we (provisionally) believe in, is that of *bodhi* (or 'awakening'). This brings us to the crux. There is a traditionalist bias in his representation of 'the goal' of dharma-practice. The point is that there is another possibility, another kind of practitioner, and I take it that Batchelor's position turns on it.

The other possibility is that a practitioner of the *dharma* does not have to be someone who 'believes in the possibility of *bodhi*'. In other words, the *idea* of *bodhi* can work upon the imagination, can entirely absorb and reorient us, without our believing that there genuinely *is* such a goal. In that sense, it is true, our goal is not *bodhi*, but is rather that of establishing whether *bodhi* is a *reality* that can enter our lives. I suggest that *this* goal is that of many of us who have been converted to Buddhism.[6] It may be retorted that this is an intermediate enterprise, to be superseded by the goal of *bodhi* itself. But the crucial point is that the practitioner is *situated*, and their situation determines the representations that are available to them. In that case the retort begs the question. It may well be that we come eventually to believe, on the basis of developing experience, that it *is* a reality, but such rational belief does not need to have been preceded by the epistemically dubious state of 'provisional' belief. I was impressed at an early stage in my engagement with Buddhism by the claim that 'in dependence upon concentration arises knowledge and vision of things as they are'. But it was never something that I believed. It was a truth claim that commanded not my assent but initially my astonishment then my attention and imagination, as something whose truth was to be *tried*, as something, indeed, whose trial was of the greatest importance. *What mattered was to find out, not to believe.* It was profoundly *interesting*, but not something of which it could properly be said that I was prepared to believe it (or continue to believe it) until I had achieved a more satisfactory cognitive stance, which I take to be the sense of 'provisional belief'.

7

What raises a person out of their ignorance and unregeneracy depends upon bringing about the conditions under which their attention can be

---

[6] I do not see why this attitude should not be a possibility for a Christian who is intrigued and startled by the claim that 'the kingdom of heaven is within you'.

refocused, so that the content of their imagination is renewed, diverted from the paths of habit. The development of mindfulness brings about such a refocusing and sharpening of the attention in those areas in which it is blurred. What, among other things, the practice of meditation achieves, is a temporary cessation of thought itself, the silencing of the 'usual preoccupations of the conscious mind' in favour of a *listening*, at first, really, only a bare listening to *something*, like the breath, but then to be put to *use*. Schiller, surely correctly, thought that something like this was achieved in aesthetic experience, through listening to music, for example. In aesthetic contexts we are charmed, or sometimes shocked, into a state where our normal trains of thought recede, and we contemplate, e.g., representations of states of affairs which elicit responses that are not normally available to us because of noise. Here we offer a kind of hypothesis about human nature: *that such and such a state of affairs, when properly attended to, elicits such and such a response.*

In the first of Rilke's *Sonnets to Orpheus*, the beasts of the forest fall silent when they hear Orpheus singing:

> their stillness did not come from fear or craft,
> but from having heard: their ordinary noise
> abated in their hearts, so that where before
> there was only a hut to receive it,
>
> a hiding-place for obscurest longings,
> entered between shaky timbers,
> there you made a temple in their hearing.

Feelings on the barest periphery of consciousness come with grandeur to the foreground, for the interlude, until they recede before the returning demands of self-preservation and appetite. The unexpectedness of such feelings (surely partly defined in terms of images, and images, at that, of *forms of relationship*) is an important aspect of our experience of them, and unfortunately, or maybe hilariously, depending on where you stand, this is a possible ground for scepticism about their existence. But they arise under particular conditions. Consider how someone who has never been swept along by the wild wind of jealousy may protest their entire and tranquil innocence of this emotion: until a particular concatenation of circumstances comes together. Similarly in art, we find ourselves confronting representations of the objects of strong and even unfamiliar feelings, because normal activity is *suspended*. In meditation, where thought itself, rather than merely dominant thought, may disappear entirely, the *listening* that art achieves by stealth, is developed systematically. This *opening-up* of the person, achieved through listening and attention, is a process of *education*: the self stumbles upon itself, as it were, through stumbling upon the objects it registers: it rebounds against objects, or, to put it in a less dissociated manner, we rebound against each other, and discover our selves in the discovery of forms of relationship. But what has been *discovered* has then to be *realised*, and given expression in the *creation* of enabling forms.

So, the idea is of a *suspension* of normal activity, of established paths of thought, as a condition for the arising of other forms. But it hardly happens in a vacuum: we already know the background, the general nature of the established paths of thought, and the general nature of the preferred trajectory. 'New feelings' arise in a context of established forms of relationship, which include the expression of an emergent sensibility around . . . *ahimsa* . . . forms of *ahimsa*-relationship that are only yet delicate plants. Movement is between *himsa* and *ahimsa* forms, violent and non-violent, harm and non-harm, delicate plants spreading skilful roots, *kusalamula*, as well as pushing upwards, the interdependence of the upwards and the downwards movement.

I see friends drag themselves around in the straitjackets of their fixed postures, unaware of their own exhaustion or despair, despair whose objects they confuse with its causes, content with the contentment that their condition allows – and see them as they might be, a Blakean form steps lithely out of their stiffening frame. Cramped thoughts are projected onto the world and read back as reality. A gradual shift of focus of an unexpected kind. I am starting episodically *not* to think of these limbs, these hands, this frame, as *me*. I start to see that I *contain* 'my body'. I am in it but separable, perhaps, a column of energy, extended, rising and circulating, sustaining the particles of the flesh. But what am I if I move beyond eyes, ears, nose, this skull, these bones . . . not an *idea*, this, but an experience.

8

It is worth pursuing the relationship between the idea of contingency and that of *pratityasamutpada*, which is precisely a doctrine about 'everything depending on conditions'. This principle could be invoked as a criterion of the 'natural' but it may lead, as we trace out its applications, beyond the horizon of our current natural categories. I guess that Buddhists would say that what 'unchangeably abides' is the fact of contingency or conditioned co-production itself, its unfolding universality, and that there is no basis for personalising the unchanging as something over and above the totality of contingent things. What unchangeably abides is thus not a *cause* of all there is but simply the *profound* totality of causal dependency itself. On the other hand, human beings do have sometimes the experience of their own dependency, and this may further lead them into the idea that we are dependent on God.

However, it is vital to include the *form of our experience* within the scope of *pratityasamutpada*, as indeed I hope I have done. In that case we can perhaps see from a fresh angle the error of personalising what 'unchangeably abides'. The normal form of our experience is of ourselves in relationship with, and in dependence upon, other contingent beings and things. However, in the context of meditation, when we withdraw from such relationships, the form of our experience becomes concentrated within itself in *dhyana*. Now it *may* be that *dhyana* is itself the condition of encounter with other, higher beings (that at least is a traditional claim) but there is also anyway the powerful experience of the concentration and intensity of consciousness itself. We have then a form of experience to which the language of contingency is no longer appropriate, and that experience *may* reinforce the belief that what we are in contact with instead is the presence of God, who unchangeably abides.

CHAPTER ELEVEN

Erotic reformations

I

Although I think that Plato introduces a profound connection in the *Republic* between harmony of soul and ethical disposition (justice is the peculiar excellence of the mind, injustice its defect), I do not think that his account of that harmony is successful. In the first place, Plato does not explain why anyone who enjoys harmony of soul should particularly want to act justly, except in the negative sense of not having insatiable appetites of a kind to make them ride roughshod over the interests of others. In the second place, what he presents as harmony is in reality an unstable inner conflict or tension, a tension which gives point to Nietzsche's accusation of 'tyranny'. Socrates *remains* 'a cave of every evil lust' if we follow the anecdote about Zopyrus, but he is 'master of them all'. This means he is really the victim of an inner division, he both rules himself and he rules the unwilling, an unresolved division of energies. I am not saying that we are not divided, nor that ethics doesn't require us to act sometimes against our inclinations. The point is we are being told a story about harmony that is not being delivered by the text.

On the other hand, something much closer to a genuine harmony with ethical implication, or *rather*, an ethics with implications for harmony, is found in the *Symposium*, in Diotima's description of the progressive states of *eros*, of the stages of the ascent to absolute beauty; in particular, in the implied idea of a decisive conative shift in the direction of someone's habitual attention and affective interest from physical beauty to 'beauty of soul'. These seem to be the proper terms for characterising the development of 'temperance' (which I am now distinguishing from *sophrosune*, seeing it as its outcome). Such a development might plausibly be described as 'spiritualised sensuality', to adopt a phrase of Nietzsche's which underlines the point of calling Socrates 'a great erotic' and a figure who 'exercises fascination', though Nietzsche himself does not make this connection.

I never met Socrates, but I have known one or two, perhaps three, people in my life, who have radiated a strong 'inner beauty' as one might call it, though many people do this episodically. But this notion of 'spiritualised sensuality' is an important one, and, again, it probably operates like the receding horizon of the rational idea, in the sense that it appears to represent a state into which a person can more and more deeply enter, and it stands in sharp contrast to the embattled self that Nietzsche diagnoses, which seems to me to have an entirely different presence. In the Buddhist context of *dhyana*, there is a graduated set of descriptions which seem to me to suggest this sense of a deeper entry:

... and there is nothing in all his body untouched by the pleasure and joy arising out of concentration ...

... and there is nothing in all his body untouched by his mind purified and cleansed ...

In other words, the state of the mind has repercussions for the states of the body, though that is a way of putting it, perhaps, that merely reflects the dualism in our thinking that derives from a settled experience of inner division. *Dhyana* one might say, is an integrated state of the person, of a single being. An image may be the heightened, non-ejaculatory, state of relaxed sexual feeling, not its 'agitation' as Plato puts it, but its state of raised calm. And even now I may be deceiving myself, but maybe it is *years* between the one experience and the other, between the 'pleasure and joy' and the 'mind purified and cleansed' . . . it was thus that they traditionally described the difference between the *dhyanas*, in this case the second and the fourth . . . years in which what is transformed is not just one's power of concentration, which may be episodic, but one's *sense of the enterprise*, and one's freedom from cramps. One begins by being startled and absorbed by the pleasure and the joy, and then, oh so slowly, has a sense of the presence of 'mind' working its way through the 'body'. Astonished by the pleasure and joy you only slowly realise that these are merely an *effect* of the emergence or release of the 'mind' that contains and sustains the 'body'. It is only under such conditions that one can begin to re-evaluate the received ontological categories . . . What is more immediately described is the dhyanised or dhyanic body, the body as it is affected by meditation, another way of talking about spiritualised sensuality which, remember, was offered by Nietzsche as a definition of *love*.

Since the development of temperance is clearly neither easy nor straightforward, it is predictable that we should find the tensions I have indicated in Plato's thinking, and that we should be liable to the same tensions ourselves, because we are writing at the edges of experience. But since, as I believe, there *are* tensions within a possible trajectory beyond them, I think Nietzsche is premature in his dismissal of Socrates as in effect embodying a *life* of what I would call *negative continence*.

Nietzsche's attribution to Plato of this negative conception of *enkrateia* needs to be challenged, but I can imagine people saying, well, what has this got to do with *philosophy*? Am I not moving out of philosophy proper into some kind of religious meditation? – an anxiety raised by Winch in the context of Simone Weil's writing. Well, I think that what is crucial is to remember that although a Wittgensteinian philosophy describes the *possibilities*, offers a general description of the *Lebensraum*, and does so in a sense neutrally, nevertheless one's settled sense of what the *Lebensraum* is in the first place, the position from which one makes judgments about what the possibilities *are*, comes unavoidably into the picture. One's own states may circumscribe one's sense of what there is to be described. I think Winch acknowledged this when we were in India.

2

I was arguing irritably with a colleague about some text I was trying to expound, a couple of others were looking on but not saying anything, which made me uneasy. But I get up and start to walk towards the window, and glancing outside I see an enormous and beautiful blue sea, almost as high, perhaps higher, than our three-storey building, and there are giant sea animals on the surface, fascinating but not alarming, great walruses, as large as whales, riding the waves, rising and falling with the swell of the blue water. Then I realise that the water is about to swamp us all, and I go out. Now I am involved in some sort of rescue work, from another part of the building. Everyone is sitting out in the square in the warm, spring weather – an atavistic pull and I don't have a clear head. I think I'll go for a walk. And as I walk, under the trees, across the meadows and over the drying mud along the edge of the Yare, in the sunshine, out of the many thoughts that come into my head there emerges at last a dominant one, suitable for the spring, that maybe, round the next corner, she'll be there, walking towards me . . . my conscious mind intervenes . . . and what if indeed she were and walking arm in arm with a lover, laughing, what would I feel then? A sharp pain . . .

Yes, but surely it's not so strong. And it's not feeling I want to escape, but the grip of delusion and fantasy. I think of the lightness of the flesh, the swift, light movements, but more now I am alarmed by its heaviness, it warns me off, saying no, no, I don't want it, I don't want to go under into that deadness of perception and of sense that I'm still too weak to avoid. I see it with absolute clarity in another person's bearing, the change to a different and heavier presence. I keep on walking through the familiar routes that my life at present takes, the uneventful passage of time, in the personal domain, and fail to see a wider context because my attention is glued to my private concerns. I do not much consider my moral luck, that I am not looking for work, that I do not need to think of stealing food, that circumstances haven't thrown me yet on the wrong side of the system. Maybe it's an interlude, an oasis, in which it is desperately necessary that I change, and necessarily at leisure, and one thinks that it is life itself, or thinks nothing of that. And then, when the chips are down, how I shall act will already have been decided. How we shall all act. The objects of dormant feelings are already there in front of us, except that they are rendered invisible by the prior commitments of our vision. We have to still such preoccupations in order to see what is there to be seen, need to establish conditions in which it is possible to do that, but our preoccupations are themselves invisible to us and project a final form onto our world. Here is some point to Schopenhauer's emphasis on the domination of perception by the will, and the need to liberate it in order to see what is there.

But really, if mindfulness is a virtue that can make a difference to philosophy itself, what is the nature of the difference that it can make? If I describe it . . . the reader of the description needs to have some acquaintance with the phenomena to measure the accuracy of the description, otherwise they merely hear words they can give no application to. I mean this seriously. Meditation, like poetry, opens up the psyche, provides a produced given that cannot be assessed by the previous given of psychic life, a development unassessable in terms of the undeveloped *status quo ante*. How can that not sound *arrogant*? And yet, what else can one say? It is a way of bringing theory and practice into a manifest unity. That is why I want to stress the importance of Kant's notion of an aesthetic idea, or what I am calling aesthetic perception. Mindfulness produces the conditions under which it is possible to *realise particular truths* and, in realising them, to discover an attitude, a *stance*, which is directed towards the conceiving of relevant action. Motivation occurs within a boundary or horizon of thought. To realise what we had not formerly realised is to see a change in the horizon, a shift in the boundary, and thus a shift or change in what can possibly motivate us, precipitated, I suspect, by the pressure at a less conscious level, of the emergent attitude itself. But mindfulness has a further aspect. It is the capacity to keep the change in view, in other words, to 'protect phronesis', to nurture and sustain the emerging realisation and its pattern of possible action. The horizon . . . there is a perspectival illusion that really it is a wall, that sets a limit on the world, an illusion that depends on not moving much.

But if we talk constantly of a need to change our thoughts . . . we need an account of what is wrong with them, of what from, of what towards . . . and *why*.

It has got to be a movement away from some kind of ignorance or *avidya* (involving a spurious confidence that we *know*), an ignorance, moreover, that relates to *persons*. A movement from ignorance requires the application of *theoretical reason*. There also needs to be a diagnosis of the *causes* of that ignorance in deeply rooted preoccupations (the *klesas*) . . . which more or less gives us a Buddhist perspective unifying ethics and epistemology, if we add the possibility of *liberation* from the *klesas* (sometimes translated as the *defiling passions*).

So the virtue of mindfulness is a condition of realisation (coming to see what one had not formerly seen) and thus a condition of action. I shall talk about my moral realism again, but it is represented constantly by Iris Murdoch. Ethical life is often not a matter of agonising decisions about what to do, though of course it is that as well, but of the shock of recognition – motives late revealed, etc. – where one sees too late and all of a sudden what one had *really* been doing, and there are no ethical diffi-culties about the fact that one would have rejected it if one *had* seen: the sort of tyranny I mentioned earlier, and you see what is staring you in the face for the first time, formerly concealed from view because you were deep in some fantasy, some pleasant dream of yourself, while someone pines unnoticed at the breakfast table.

Just to return, to my effort to distinguish *sophrosune* from temperance, on the ground that Aristotle's etymology ('protecting wisdom') allows a connection with *sati* or mindfulness, or better, with *apramada*, non-intox-ication or vigilance,[1] so that *sophrosune* ideally *issues* in temperance . . . so what does mindfulness issue in? What comes closest to 'temperance' in the sense of letting go without difficulty, not being distressed by the loss of a pleasure? It seems to be non-attachment (*alobha*), though this must,

---

[1] See the Crosby and Skilton translation of Shantideva's *Bodhicaryavatara*, 23

presumably, be understood in conjunction with non-aversion (*advesa*). But isn't that interesting about Buddhism, that its key positive terms, *alobha, apramada, advesa*, and, of course, *ahimsa* or non-violence, are all formed out of negations of what a practitioner is beginning to discern to be unsatisfactory states, such as greed, so we celebrate 'non-greed', for want of a positive term; or negligence and intoxication, we come up against it, it hinders us, we aspire to 'non-intoxication'; or violence, we begin to recoil against it, and embrace 'non-violence', and slowly, over generations, these 'negative' expressions gain independent positive content. A process of re-evaluation, a new mind begins to rise to the surface, and its first intimations are to be found in its unhappiness at the familiar, settled realities.

3

I succumb in my writing to a particular way of thinking about the emotions which masks the presence of the personal. Schiller says that impressions move the soul, and it is natural to expand this in the way I have: impressions are perceived under descriptions, and it is in the light of our discernment of particular realities and their causal connections, represented thus and so, that we are moved to action or restraint, though to what action and by what impressions, depends on the state of the agent, an aspect usually neglected in discussions of emotion. To say this is to make a quite proper gesture towards the intentionality thesis as it relates to sensibility, and it marks the cognitive aspect of feeling: we respond to realities as we take them to be. But we need some strong qualification if we are to characterise the nature of our ethical responses.

The tendency to which I succumb is to swerve away from the personal. If we say that impressions move the soul, it is easy to refer that to facts, to states of affairs, to situations, to the objects of the emotions. There is nothing wrong with this, but there is an essential rubric under which it should fall. We are not just affected by what happens in the world: we are affected, under certain conditions, by how *persons*, and, more generally, fellow-creatures, are affected by what happens in the world. Such natural patterns of response conflict with and may be submerged by egocentric or communal patterns of thinking in which events are related exclusively to oneself or one's own community. But even in our own case we respond to states of affairs *as they affect us* (and they affect us according to how we are then constituted) whether in immediate reaction, or through some conception of ourselves as persons among others, which may or may not be adequate to how we are then constituted. Thus we *act for our own sake*, perhaps to remedy a situation by which we are adversely affected, or see ourselves as adversely affected. This can include apparently ethical action.

What I am really trying to say is that it is not enough to see ethical action as concerned with good and harm: I can seek to eliminate your distress, not for *your* sake, but for my own, because it upsets me, for instance. I act to relieve your suffering, but I am completely indifferent to *you*.

But that is a distortion of ethical action. And I am not merely stipulating what we are to count as 'ethical'. Rather, what I want to do is to locate our sense of ethics, and thus its deviations and distortions, in another kind of response, where the agent's motivation is *not* 'a situation', but *someone-in-a-situation*. Thus I do not respond simply to the distress of others, but to *them-in-their-distress*. I respond to their 'call', to them, that they are in distress. A person, being in distress, becomes the reason for acting, and what is done is done for them. Perceiving you to be in distress, I am moved to act by *you*. Strictly, what moves me to act is you-perceived-as-distressed. We call forth action from one another. It is not the belief, *pace* Kant, that we have a duty, that stays in our minds, but the *image of a person*. To repeat, we do not respond to their distress, but to *them-in-their-distress*, or to them, that they are in distress. I do not think this is a trivial qualification: we respond, or fail to respond, *to one another*. Reference has to be made to good and harm, but characterisations of the object of morality as good or harm *simpliciter* is an alienated deflection from its real object, viz the sentient being whose good we seek, whose harm we try to avoid. That describes a demeanour that is primitive in relation to judgments about what it would be right or wrong to do. To say, for example, that the ethically motivated person is moved by the distress of others, does not show *how* such distress works upon us. It is not this that is primitive, as though justification came to an end just here. Nor, by contrast, is the action to relieve harm something we do for its own sake. It is done for the sake of the one on whose behalf it is done. There is this way we have of responding to one another, and this is what informs what we call ethical action, what we come to commend as such: talk of obligation and requirement is its garbled echo, heard from a long way off.

All this is implicit in the form that ethical appeals actually take. 'Think of the children, what it will do to them'; 'do it, for their sake'. We say 'I must restrain myself, for their sake'. We make direct appeals for an attention to those concerned that we expect to yield characteristic results in behaviour. We do not just ask people to consider the consequences of their behaviour, but to do so in the light of the thought of those upon whom the consequences will fall. However impractically in particular cases these are appeals to the capacity for *love*, which is what thus discloses itself as the heart of ethics.

4

I started to stray into the confusion of assuming that values can be grounded in a proper and independently ascertainable conception of human nature. The truth of the matter, by contrast, is that our values are an *expression* of the nature we form a conception of, and our account of the one cannot be justified by reference to the other (Winch). So I am claiming that the intentional object of an ethical motivation is *someone-in-a-situation*, that one acts for *them*, that they are in distress, for instance. The just act is not done for its own sake, then, or done for the sake of the advantage it might bring. We respond to one another, and we *do not choose to do so*. This lack of choice is built into the account of motivation that I have given. The same phenomena can be viewed with the mildest form of unease or the strongest possible kind of rejection. There is not just one *pitch* of response or recognition of a reason for action, for the motive force of a reason can grow more powerful, so that other motives recede into the background or simply drop away. A person's dissatisfaction with the nature of their work, for example, can grow from vague unease to an urgency that carries all before it. (How the pitch is able to express itself depends upon conditions.) It is not so much, as Nietzsche said, that you choose your motives, as that the strongest motive chooses you. But against Nietzsche it has also to be said that a person can make decisions about what will become the strongest motive . . . but even that is motivated, is the motive strengthening itself. But you cannot make decisions about what will count as a motive at all. Imagine the change from unease about the war to the passionate rejection of it, as something that matters above all else. Something that is sometimes called a lack of proportion. A person can, under certain conditions, sacrifice everything that had previously held them back. So you no longer have anything to lose. Freedom. Moral freedom: one's will the power only to do that which one judges to be necessary, without distraction. There was a small furore in the press when the Minister for Defence had refused to deny that intruders into missile bases might be shot. One of the women had said she was prepared nevertheless to go in. A sort of madness. Of course, one has to distinguish cases. But a person can be in a state in which they have already left the world behind – whether this is good or not depends upon the proposed action. We could call this state a kind of madness. It is frightening, partly because it is attained as an extreme state, say in war, in the midst of crisis, to be sustained for the duration and then perhaps lost forever, rather than a steady state developed over time. But leaving the world behind may well be the condition of moral freedom. And this is just what Tanabe claims, in his talk of acting as though one's death were already behind one.

The real point about our relation to our motivation is this: whether we like it or not, we find that such reasons weigh with us, we find ourselves with this attitude. We are detained, more or less effectively, by these considerations. The datum is *the insistence of such reasons upon the mind or attention*, an insistence that amounts, under certain conditions, to *a formation of the mind itself*. The vitality or vigour of affect as I have interpreted it reduces to a vitality of motivation. This vitality is the source of the 'effortless action' that I take to be one of the fruits of *sophrosune*, the balance of the well-centred body, in which we are able to withdraw attention from the objects of appetite and sense without resistance or sense of loss. The vitality that 'silences' the counter-attractions is constituted by an *animating concentration* or absorption of the attention in which other possible objects recede to the periphery of consciousness. This is the fully realised state of the relevant affects. The 'silencing effect' is an unmysterious dominating of consciousness by a particular set of intentional objects. The experience to be represented is that of a single-pointedness of attention, a state in which 'contrary inclinations' hold no sway when that attention is focused. The development of such a concentration depends upon a systematic *ascesis* in which the balance of temperance begins to emerge. But the affective states that I am trying to describe themselves reinforce that balance. It seems reasonable to say that for such an agent there is 'no alternative' to the proposed action, in the sense that possible alternatives do not beckon. There is no energy behind them. Thus temperance is the mirror-image of *akolasia* ('licentiousness'), except that the state is one of Spinozistic action rather than passion.

Someone who is motivated by 'moral' considerations, one for whom they constitute reasons for actions, is not 'bound' by them in the way in which someone might be bound by the rules of a club. And nor is it a matter of 'caring' about such reasons, either. They provide, rather, the form of one's activating perceptions, the terms in which one regards (and intervenes in) the passing scene, as a changing agent whose trans-formations are reflected in the changes that take place within the terms themselves. There is no 'moral' ought: rather there is the peculiar anguish in certain contexts -'moral' contexts – of realising what we have done or failed to do. 'I ought not to have done that' is at once to say that there were reasons against it and that, in consequence, it is what one would have refrained from doing in the absence of whatever lack of control it may be which has made one responsible for the mess that follows. If I have not said it already elsewhere, I agree with Tanabe that this remorse is the beginning of *metanoia*. It is a form of *dukkha* or unsatis-factoriness which may be the first signal to oneself of an awakening or emerging state of mind as it begins to operate, weak though its initial signals may be against the noise of dominant desires. Attention to the *remorse* releases the attitudes from which it springs, changes the person of the one who thus attends.

At the point of action it is the released strength of motivation itself which 'silences' counter-attractions. This is because the *appetites* become silent, and that they do so is a function of the concentration of energy else-where. On the other hand, it ought to be said that the absence of temp-tation is not always a function of concentration in another direction. Although it is true that the quality or level of concentration itself deter-mines what could or could not be a possible object of serious attention, there are cases where the object of '*temptation*' is itself internally related to the object of *attention*. I have referred already to the spiritual demeanour of the Bodhisattva figure, but, since it has been discussed lately with great trenchancy by Peter Winch (1987, ch. 11), let us take the example of the Good Samaritan. Suppose, as Winch does, that some companion urges him to hurry away from possible danger. But he is sufficiently moved by the victim, we might say, for the danger not to occupy him. (Here temper-ance is clearly not enough, and courage needs to be invoked, as intelli-gence, or presence of mind, in the face of danger.) But there is more involved. Hurrying away would, in any case, bring it about that the victim went unrelieved, and *that* description attracts the original concern for the victim in his plight. Thus any temptation to hurry away is not only dimin-ished by the Samaritan's strong affective state in relation to the victim, but also, coming within its scope, and coloured by it, turns to ashes. A certain concentratedness of affective attention, which in reality spans and unifies perception and action, brings it about that *the agent cannot be turned*, even if they can be prevented by forces outside of them.

Thus the Good Samaritan becomes absolute in his concern for the victim. Reaching what is absolute in a person's endeavours, we discover *a particular kind of being*. Attention to the predicaments and sufferings of others, compassion, is part of a spiritual demeanour or orientation in the world. The profile of the Bodhisattva that emerges is not drawn along the lines of a set of ultimate ends, but along lines yielded by the focus of an attention to particular realities and particular kinds of response. So impressions move the soul, but it is our sense of what is happening as it affects one another for good or ill that moves us to *ethical* action. And we cannot avoid the issue that our sense of what is harmful or beneficial is dependent upon what we take ourselves to be, upon our sense of the nature of our own reality. To put it another way, with an obvious Kantian resonance, in the ethical life we become for each other *ends of action*, though much turns on the scope of that 'each other'. What I mean by this is that we come to want to sustain each other in our own being. But our conception of what we are may or may not coincide with the *realities* of personhood. For instance, our view of what it is to be a person may fail to acknowledge the truth of the claim, if it is a truth (and that has to be grounded in experience) that unless a grain of wheat fall into the earth and die, it shall not bear fruit. Such a claim is about the realities of transformation, it is something we know or fail to know. But if we seek to sustain each other in our own being then we need to know whether it is true or not, and, if it is true, in what *way* it is true. We stand in different relations to such a purported truth, and this makes moral realism difficult in unexpected ways.

5

What is called reason in Plato is that part of the soul that is able to contemplate the eternal forms, a contemplation which constitutes our greatest good. Since it is the supreme good for human life, and it is reason which knows it, presumably reason is the *best* judge, the best-informed judge, of what constitutes good and harm by reference to what enhances and what undermines the possibility of the trajectory to the ultimate good, which is 'good' in virtue of being what is ultimately *sought* or desired. Reason is that part of the soul which is capable of knowledge of the real world, and which knows, in consequence, that this world is merely a shadow of reality. The contemporary verdict is that there is no such knowledge. Nevertheless, given that there is such knowledge, the basis of reason's claim to rule, is that it really does know what is best for the whole. The judgment is not merely arbitrary. But once we remove reason from the throne, once we remove the grounding in a knowledge of a higher reality which reveals our true nature, reason becomes an arbiter of morality that lacks authority. Instrumental rationality may be said to relate means to ends, but what happens to judgments about our best or real or true interests? We have lost the criterion. If reason once knew too much, it now knows too little. Rousseau gives us a reason that appears to relate action to its consequences for others, but it cannot deliver judgments about the consequences *for their best interests*, since it is not well enough informed.

We respond to someone-in-a-situation, according to a conception of their personal being. And we have the idea of someone who is absolute in their endeavour or striving in this direction. And we become for each other *ends of action*. The background motivation here is not an intellectual or so-called 'ethical' commitment to the flourishing of persons. The motivation arises from the *finding*, and the finding satisfaction in, possibilities of mutual response, solidarity, and other notions constructing the arrival of an 'existence for one another'. All these notions could be summarised under that of *appreciation of persons*. But the arrival of these possibilities *determines the self that comes to be constructed out of them, and which did not previously exist*.

To put it another way, the terms in which we become for one another 'ends of action' depend crucially upon the realities associated with 'appreciation'. Under certain conditions, of *meeting* and *union* and *begetting*, which bring about this 'existence for one another', we come to appreciate *beauty of soul*, and are thereby regenerated in a way which should, rationally, be reflected in our conception of personhood. This appreciation provides a background sense of what persons are that can become the ground not only of delight, in the presence of another's flourishing (*mudita*) but of compassion, in its absence (*karuna*). It can become such a ground for an important reason. Our *sense* of what is harmful or beneficial, of what we can rejoice in or feel compassion for, is dependent on what we take ourselves to be. Well, I keep saying that, but isn't it actually the reverse? That our conception of 'what we are' is built up *by* our sense of what is harmful, what is beneficial. In other words, these judgments are the medium of (changes in) our conception of what we are. The point is that there is no fixed nature on the basis of which we form judgments about what our interests are, given that nature, say. Our responses are part of our nature, and they change.

But if we are constituted by the trajectory I am trying to describe, then what diminishes its possibility we shall treat as harm and what enhances it as benefit. I refer to a trajectory, and that allows us to say that there is a time before and a time after we come to appreciate beauty of soul and to treat persons as ends, as the objects of an *eros* whose quality is determined by the nature of its object, a time before and a time after, that is to say, the emergence of *ethics*. And since, as Diotima insists, we desire to beget in the beautiful, it is out of the reciprocal appreciation of the beauty of personhood, and hence of its possibility within one another, that forms of life are constructed in which persons are let be and enabled to become. The trajectory is one of *eros* and its transformations are initially faint and then unstable and finally dominant.

Since I am making central to my account this Platonic notion of appreciation of beauty of soul and the associated desire to procreate in beauty, I had better rehearse how I think such beauty can be the object of desire, or rather, how certain states of persons can be considered 'beautiful'. Someone who *exemplifies* such beauty embodies or mediates a certain concentration of energy, that by which a certain demeanour and perspective is sustained, a perspective and demeanour that become the *form* of that energy (spiritualised sensuality, the dhyanic body). By perspective here I simply mean the being moved in a determinate direction by particular kinds of reason, the being of persons in particular situations. Coming to treat persons as ends is a matter of coming to be established in the corresponding ethical sensibility focused on well-being. As I have just said, the sustaining of such a perspective, such a sensibility, depends upon a concentration of energy around the relevant forms of attention and action. But such energy *radiates* and attracts, is an object of *eros*, a form of beauty. That is what the figure of Socrates or the Bodhisattva must do, radiate and attract. But what radiates and attracts is a concentration of energy around the perceiving others as ends of action, so it is an achieved form of *eros* as well as its object. It is the accomplished form of that sensibility. In its very attractiveness it is an image of the trajectory it completes, an image of what it is to appreciate beauty of soul and of what beauty of soul is.

One reason such forms attract, are the object of *eros*, is that they represent the direction of our own *Bildung*, our own future: the energy radiates in demeanour and disposition, which provide the criteria of identity for forms of energy. However, the *conjunction* of such energies, between persons, produces new forms, a new spirit, and these *discoveries of contact* produce transformations that rationally determine changes in our conception of personhood and hence of what we take to be harmful or beneficial. I'm not confident that talk of 'beauty of soul' will go down well in this day and age: but it is the kind of reality the expression applies to that is important. It is a radically different picture of human virtue from those traditionally offered in philosophy. But how are we going to spell out the conception of humanity under which we judge the distinction between good and harm? I have offered something reflexive: that what counts to the preservation of someone's good is the preservation of that very orientation towards good itself. If we are constituted in part by the orientation towards treating one another as ends, then it is part of our treating one another as ends that we preserve in one another that very tendency itself. Once we establish the primitiveness of certain forms of motivation the task that follows is representing the nature of the world they focus on. So we recognise the implication of the human subject from the beginning in history and politics, in a world of masters and slaves, in the emergence from that condition, an emergence which has no inevitability about it all.

So I am talking about a condition in which we treat each other as ends of action. Well, that is not quite Kant. For him the categorical imperative in its later formulation does not turn on the distinction between treating others as ends or merely as means: it is a matter of treating *humanity*, whether in our own person or in that of any other, as an end, or merely as a means. I prefer to conceive the issue as one of treating a person-in-their-humanity as an end. One *comes* to treat them that way under certain conditions: the imperative is intended for the *akratic*, there is nothing primitive about it, it merely marks the precariousness of what *is* primitive, viz., the coming to an appreciation of persons.

A nasty experience when I am marking the script of a beautiful girl: before I realise, I am exercising sexual power, sexual pleasure in the twists and turns of the prose she is doing her best with, giving out the best she can. She is in my power as I read what she is struggling to say, I imagine her body, I am flirting with her words, which cost me nothing, an ugly mental act. For the world is, after all, constituted for one in part by the range of one's desires: one conceives the rational idea of a co-incidence between the real world and the world of one's desires. One starts to blab about the real world at every new direction of attention. Meanwhile you dwell within the space provided between yourself as subject and the objects of your desires. You have a sense of yourself in the interaction between the self and the intentional object, while all around you wars may rage and you not notice, may? *may*? Reality waits for its moment. Reflection is still possible for a person locked within their appetites: you see your self-made impotence on other fronts, you see yourself rendered powerless where you have reason to act.

6

So we have the ancient claim that Reason should rule. In one way its claim has now been disallowed, since reason has moved down to lower case. It is not that Reason knows best any more, but that reason was a word we once used for representing our disposition to make judgments about what is good for us and what harms us. Our mistake was to assume a definitive answer, whereas judgment alters along with our self-understanding. I think it is reasonable to say that we are in part constituted by an erotic trajectory that centres on beauty of soul, but that still leaves us with questions about what is good for us in the situations in which we find ourselves. It may be that we are disposed to see each other flourish, and that that disposition must flourish if we are to flourish at all, but there is still the question of what it is to flourish beyond the concern to see, as it were, flourishing flourish.

But here is a problem of a radical kind about our self-understanding. We find ourselves with a sense of, a judgment about, *what preserves the integrity of our being*, and thus we seem to have a criterion for allowing or disallowing particular feelings into consciousness, whether they enhance or diminish the conditions for that integrity. It may be that there is a known range of feelings that cannot be allowed expression, on these terms, as well as a range of those which must be (precisely those which support and obey reason). But what we judge cannot be allowed expression depends upon a *particular* conception of what constitutes integrity or well-being, and the resident danger is that the impulse to change be stifled, with dangerous or unfamiliar feelings strangled at birth, but it was the birth of a possible transformation of our being, whose old integrity we desperately seek to preserve.

If an emotion is judged to be 'inappropriate' on the grounds that it is incompatible with the demands of reason, then that must be because of the connection of our emotions with *action* (and inaction): it is these that are inappropriate or not, in relation to a 'rational agenda'. But in that case we can drive a wedge between an emotion and its natural expression in action: or better, we can distinguish the moments of an emotion between conception and act. It may not be inappropriate to *feel* an emotion, even if it is 'inappropriate' to act on it. But many people will have been formed in such a way that they will not allow themselves even to *feel* what is thus judged to be inappropriate. They won't even acknowledge its presence, because they are 'rational' and it is not. They are so slavishly submissive to 'reason' that they will not acknowledge *themselves*, even when they return in the form of the repressed. Throw out nature with a pitchfork, it will still finally come back, *usque tamen recurrit*. (But they *must* know it is there: you can only refuse to acknowledge someone if you are aware of their presence.) And so 'bad faith' is not an embarrassing piece of continental psychologising with little to do with philosophy, it is a comment about the nature of the philosophers' unacknowledged starting-point: Nietzsche's 'daylight at any cost'. And it strengthens the point about the onesidedness of phallocentrism. We have to proceed case by case. I may have murderous thoughts, but observing these feelings is not the same as indulging them, and by observing them we may come to make a distinction between wishes and wants, and see a function for murderous wishes which is remote from the desire to *kill*.

There is one thing wrong with this account however, the Platonic account, I mean. It talks about preserving our own being in the abstract. But the whole point is that we are always *situated*. The nature of what confronts us in the dangerous world is always changing, though our conception of what endangers us perhaps follows more slowly. Nietzsche, of course, sees the perceived danger of excess among the Athenians as evidence of decline, but whether we agree with him or not, he at least sees that a reference to our situation has to be made if we are going to talk about what preserves the integrity of our being. So when Socrates says that reason should rule, that spirit should obey and support reason and that both should keep the 'insatiable' appetites under control, he is drawing on an image of a State which needs to maintain internal discipline in order to counter its enemies, and the nature of the internal discipline is a function of what is required in order to defend oneself. In such a state of alert there is no *leisure* for internal reorganisation, one defends oneself as one is, and so there are sections whose interest lies in *maintaining the state of alert* against external enemies, for they thus maintain the *status quo* of their advantage.

So, part of the claim of reason to rule, on the Platonic account, is that it can reflect about good and bad and has the ability and foresight to act for the whole. However, if reason is to act for the whole it can only do so on the basis of some *conception* of the whole, how it is constituted, the proper relations of the 'parts'. In the Zopyrus incident, as Nietzsche presents it, there is no conception of a larger context in which 'containment' might be conceived as a *temporary* expedient in the development of the concentration of the psyche associated with temperance, in the formation of a *dhyanised* or *dhyanic* body. Admittedly, although the larger context is available in Plato, it is not clear whether he is always able to see continence as a temporary expedient rather than a permanent necessity, but at least he is strongly aware of the larger context. By making use of the Zopyrus incident Nietzsche presents us with a much diminished Socrates for whom the rational options are also much diminished. This is what I mean by 'negative continence'. In the absence of any grasp of other possibilities the expedient of containment would simply become *the* way, seized on by reason, for avoiding vice and assuring ethical action, *the* way, even, for preserving the unity of the whole as reason conceives it. But the strategy of containment, even in Plato, derives from the use of political force and depends upon a conception of the soul that derives from the political analogy that Plato is concerned to draw. Nietzsche effectively charges Socrates with the 'invention' of internalised repression. But what he calls the tyranny of reason is in reality the tyranny only of a particular *application* of reason. If reason acts for the whole, then it acts in the light of particular *conceptions* of the whole, particular conceptions it is capable of transcending in the light of further information and reflective attention. The resident danger is that a particular expedient of reason has consigned the further information to darkness, and relies effectively upon repression of the possible evidence. A 'rational expedient' premised upon a particular understanding (the real determinant) might impede the development of understanding itself. But then the tyranny would not be of reason but the failure of reason. For example, the development of 'spirit' is threatened if our conception of it leads us to repress those of its impulses that stray from the role we think proper to it (viz to obey and support reason). The transformation of sensuality towards a *dhyanised* body might be endangered if our hostility to our libidinal impulses becomes too mortal on apparently rational grounds. The problem with the view of Socrates that Nietzsche presents us with by means of the anecdote is that it gives us only a negative containment or control, with no sense of the possibility of transformation that is available in Plato. On this view Socrates *remains* 'a cave of every evil lust'. He is master of them all, and is thus divided within himself, and there is no notion of the possibility of sensuality wedded to the spirit in such a picture. Nevertheless the picture determines our sense of what would be a rational strategy, and as far as tyranny goes, it is the picture that holds us captive. The other thing to say here is that though Nietzsche fingers a real fear of excess he attributes it falsely to a state of *decline*. What he fails to see is that it is a symptom of a struggle to attain a marvellous *development*. Nevertheless it represents a strategy that might undermine that development.

7

I buy a new philosophy book and instead of looking with interest to see what people are contributing to the field I look with incipient envy and resentment at possible intrusions into areas that I consider my own private property. Nor am I a credit to my teacher, the key to what I am saying I almost always miss out: there is something specific before my mind as I write in general terms, some incident that I remember, some scene. The scene is an essential part of the text, because it shows the *application* of my general description, and yet I constantly leave it out. I don't mean that the description applies exclusively to that particular scene, but that the particular scene shows the *sort* of application that the description has, and the point is that in the absence of any such indicators significantly different applications are left undetermined. And now my teacher *ist tot*, and unexpectedly. He is not *there* . . . That means it is *our* responsibility now, to continue the tradition, to pass it on, we are hardly clever enough . . .

Simply lying back and watching the progress of one's own thoughts, the usual preoccupations of the conscious mind, their structure, their repetition: they are limitations, one's prison, forms in which one's energies are locked, strangled, the domestication of the libido, bromide in the tea, in the drinking water. All this would fill me with despair if I hadn't often just sat and watched the progress of my thoughts, and seen them quieten down, and felt the intensity of my own being where they have no place, and that of others, just sitting, draped in their blankets, eyes closed, faces relaxed and inward, candles flickering and the wind outside murmuring against the walls.

One must go quietly and not force the pace, be vigorous without being violent, but there is a great beauty and happiness in my meditation at the moment, as I breathe quietly and feel the centre of my awareness moving down my body and spreading out, the breath coming from below the navel and seeming almost to die away, and sometimes, looking quietly ahead of me, my eyes close of their own accord and I become taken up into the greatest intensity, swimming suddenly right up to me, into which I seem partially to disappear and almost entirely dissolve into the earth's own elements. But it only touches me, glances against me for a moment or two, something that seems like eternity itself, and waking up slowly and wonderfully I see the dearest freshness in the familiar shapes and objects that surround me in my room.

Oh reader, please beware of me.

The trouble with me is that I write my lines jealously with my elbow covering my text, viewing others with suspicion, as though it were my own property, which it is not, seeing the activities of others as incursions into my private space. And it is like that with my spiritual state. I want it to be exclusively mine, so that it becomes a weapon with which to beat other people and keep them in their place . . . casually looking at others across a room I suddenly wake up to the fact that my look is *baleful* . . .

'I wander through each charter'd street . . .' But actually to see 'marks of weakness, marks of woe' is to notice something that can become invisible again. I was beginning to stir, it was slow, there was no focus to my weak attention, the dark tunnel I moved along pressed downwards against me and on all sides, the air was thick and sooty, and my heart was heavy as I travelled. What is this place I have come to, where there is no light, but only lurching shadows? The narcotics are wearing off, I see, and I see that I am in an evil place. My heart is heavy and I am afraid. I thought that to open my heart I should receive light and grace. I did. I saw the truth.

8

The notion of being 'master of them all' implies that one is also a slave. In the *Republic* Plato ironically notices this. Remarkably, Agathon in the *Symposium* is also made to talk of 'mastery', though the application is rather different:

> In addition Love [*Eros*] is richly endowed with temperance. Everyone admits that temperance is mastery over pleasures and desires, and that no pleasure is stronger than Love. If, then, all pleasures are weaker than Love, love must be the master and they his subjects. So Love, being master over pleasure and desires, will be in a pre-eminent degree temperate. (196c)

This is a joke that happens to say the truth about *Eros*. It is *Eros* that dominates consciousness, and the stages of its affective development dominate consciousness in their turn. And that is the real secret of 'temperance' (as opposed to *enkrateia*). The idea is of an affective consciousness dominated by a particular state of *eros*, a particular focus of the attention, so that other impulses and interests recede quite naturally, as when someone quite beautiful comes in to the room.

The ascent of *eros* to *moral beauty* then takes on a special significance. It represents a quickened interest in the well-being of others. It is developed by the *sight* of moral beauty, and then it searches for it and seeks to establish it, becoming a form of interest in others, becoming, by this means, *itself* an example of moral beauty. In other words, the ascent of *eros* to seek moral beauty in others is already a formation of moral beauty in the *erastes*. And since we are highlighting a person's relation to truth and delusion, that becomes the environment in which one seeks to serve their well-being. (The phrase, though, is ambiguous. An *erastes*, an older person, can rise to a *moral* interest in the progress of their younger *eromenos*. But the irony of the Alcibiades incident in the *Symposium* is that Alcibiades is the *erastes* attracted by the moral beauty of Socrates. So we have to think in terms of the attractive dynamism of mature virtue, which is also tough, and its burgeoning 'in the young'.) On Plato's view the quickened interest in the other's well-being depends at first on their physical attractiveness. Or rather, the physical attraction and relationship that starts the ascent of *eros* is one of the conditions under which an interest in the well-being of another starts to emerge (in 'noble sentiments' but really 'words of beauty', *logous kalous*, 'beautiful words'). On the other hand, the sexual relationship is one of the great sites of delusion. As far, though, as the ascent to *moral* beauty or, really, the beauty in souls (*to en tais psuchais kallos*) is concerned, it is vital to realise and I am not expounding Plato here, that its natural expression will include *compassion* for human misery as well as rejoicing in human good:

> And mark in every face I meet
> Marks of weakness, marks of woe

which lines I always hear as set by Vaughan Williams. But the *natural responsiveness* in the words to the 'mind-forg'd manacles' *gives* us the motivating power of 'moral reasons'. We start with such reactions, or come to them naturally. Moral reasons are essentially 'reasons of the heart', a matter of what the human heart is touched by, or can be touched by if it opens itself: in every cry of every man. Otherwise, heartlessness and villainy. What *hardens* the hearts of men and women? This is not to deny that there may be conflicts between 'heart and head'. But we are talking now about the foundations of 'morality', the conditions of its possibility.

There are two general forms of reaction to others, more or less quickened, more or less deadened, in our consciousness, compassion for human misery and rejoicing in their well-being. These are *sources* of 'morality' and are not themselves the product of any kind of imperative, though they may give rise to them, but imperatives which express and reflect a natural and prior human motivation. Kant's misanthrope is too hard-hearted yet to be a moral agent, whatever else he is. Well, come on, of course he is a moral agent, but duty for its own sake is the only kind of reason he can bring himself to acknowledge, it's the story he tells himself! 'Morality' is a more or less distorted recognition of impulses of the heart, contaminated by fear and other negative and communal emotions, and, of course, has always in its most distorted versions attempted to stifle these very impulses.

9

Here now is a crucial section that is essential to my whole enterprise. The harmony of soul that Plato takes, in the *Republic*, to be a condition of the disposition to justice, is possible only with the dominance in the psyche of love, or *Eros*, at a particular stage of its development, as described in the *Symposium*. In the *Republic* this just seems mysterious, *why* there should be this relation between a disposition for justice and a harmonious soul. The point is not that the two dialogues cannot be reconciled, but that there is a significant tension between them. They can be reconciled, presumably, because the justice of reason's claim to know what is best for the whole is grounded in its own erotic impulse towards reality. Diotima describes the stages on the path to the perfect revelation of absolute beauty

beginning with examples of beauty in this world, and using them as steps to ascend continually with that absolute beauty as one's aim, from one instance of physical beauty to two and from two to all, then from physical beauty to moral beauty, and from moral beauty to the beauty of knowledge (211c)

And so on until one knows at last what absolute beauty is. Once you have seen that, she says, addressing Socrates,

you will not value it in terms of gold or rich clothing or the beauty of boys or young men, the sight of whom at present throws you . . . into such an ecstasy (211d)

This provides a suitable image of the decisive shift of attention that I think is also involved in the transition from a desire for physical beauty to a desire for moral beauty or beauty of soul. What is described is a change in what or whom a person is absorbed by, a shift in their real inclinations or preferences, that is to say, a re-ordering, not of what they think they ought to prefer, but of what they really prefer (or prefer in their heart). There is a parallel here with John Stuart Mill's 'competent judge'. The criterion for what makes one pleasure or way of life more 'worthwhile' than another is that it *is* preferred, by someone who has experience of both, without any sense of moral obligation to prefer it. On this expressivist view of value, a re-ordering of a person's real preferences constitutes a re-ordering of their scale of values. Someone who has become acquainted with absolute beauty will not set it in the same scale as the beauty of boys and young men. But it is not as easy as that:

> With a groan I crashed into inferior things. This weight was my sexual habit. But with me there remained a memory of you. *I was in no kind of doubt to whom I should attach myself, but was not yet in a state to be able to do that.*

There is still a necessary transition from the continence/incontinence polarity to the temperance which increases the power of action. What Alcibiades is shown to fail to understand is that in offering his body for what Socrates knows, he is proposing to exchange dross for gold: that is what the bargain will look like from where Socrates is. Since in that encounter Alcibiades is scarcely exhibiting beauty of soul, Socrates will not be attracted but repelled, an affective response which kills physical desire. The joke is that, *pace* Alcibiades, Socrates is *not* exercising massive self-control under the shared blanket. Well, I say that. Presumably it is contestable. And the problem with the contest is that people will refer to their own experience, as the measure of its plausibility. And Plato is positing a progressive development of experience, which itself becomes a standard of judgment of what people find plausible. Moreover, since I am making a person's relation to truth and delusion a measure of their well-being or their suffering, I ought to mention that these remarks of Diotima about the ascent of *eros* are *truth-claiming*. And if they are true, they are a measure by which we may judge our lived experience. *Is* there a natural affective response to moral ugliness which kills physical desire? Poor Alcibiades/Plato, but a genuine point is surely being made, that desire *can* be killed, that a morally 'ugly' person really isn't attractive . . . Someone may say tell that to the birds . . . but we are talking about states of the person . . .

Diotima's description of the stages of the ascent is one of the most brilliant things in philosophy. Notice that the next stage of the ascent, after the desire for moral beauty, is that of the beauty of *knowledge*, a claim which, again, I can connect with the internal relation between well-being and knowledge and ignorance. There is a clear connection between the stages. A quickened interest in the well-being of others is the condition for a desire for knowledge just because a person's relation to truth, delusion and ignorance, to what they know and what they fail to know, is a feature of their moral attractiveness. And one of the criteria, as I keep saying, of their *eudaemonia*. And then the *next* stage is that of love of *to en tois epitedeumasi kai tois nomois kalou*, love of the beauty to be found in institutions and laws, again internally related to the love of beauty of soul. Institutions *secure* well-being, provide structures within which the well-being of 'young people' can be developed and protected. Moral beauty, knowledge, education. That we are indeed talking about an effective re-ordering of desires is underlined by Diotima's remark that someone who reckons beauty of soul more valuable than beauty of body will be *content* to love and cherish a virtuous soul 'even in a body which has little of the bloom of beauty' (209e). What is described here, I believe, is a determinate physical and affective state, a determinate state of *Eros*, of preference, which expresses itself evaluatively. It is not the description of someone who has the notion that they *ought* to be content, but of someone who is. And so, what are the conditions under which we can determine whether or not such descriptions are *true*? The distinction between the virtue of continence and temperance marks the stages by which the re-ordering of *Eros* becomes effective, it is a description of our lived experience of that re-ordering.

It may be objected that the *enkrates* (someone who is continent) – or even the akratic Alcibiades – shares the same values as the *sophron* (someone who is temperate), but has different inclinations, and so it is a mistake to try to establish too close a connection between inclinations and values. Certainly my position privileges the developed inclinations of the *sophron* over the *enkrates*, but it does so because, I think, the *enkrates* (or even the *akrates*) has an *evanescent* experience of the re-ordered preferences of the *sophron*. The *enkrates* has, incipiently, or with less vital power, some of the inclinations and preferences of the *sophron*, but is less free of contrary inclinations. The switch of attention quickens less readily. Continent and incontinent persons (we) will have had experiences which are decisive for their conviction (i.e. for their finding) that beauty of soul is more worthwhile, more attractive, more interesting, than mere physical beauty (which is never, of course, encountered 'merely'), and this glimpse will provide the perspective from which they will view the passion they are yet unable to let go of as 'beneath them and of small account'. What is decisive, both for the *sophron* and for the *enkrates*, is that *they experience the comparison in these terms*, and this perspective is more or less successfully embodied in their behaviour, visible in their demeanour.

The shift in a person's inclinations needs to be connected with a changed *conception* of the previous object of their passion and of the passion itself. Such a person has entered a larger world in which comparisons can be made that were not formerly available. In the light of one's appreciation of beauty of soul what had previously seemed of vital importance does not count for so much; one might not even understand how one had come to attach so much importance to it. One may begin to see, for instance, the condition upon which the intensity of one's previous desire depended (e.g., the felt absence of the liberating sensibility within whose world one now finds oneself). The person who has come to appreciate beauty of soul 'will be led to consider physical beauty taken as a whole to be a poor thing in comparison' (209e–211a). I do not think such a position entails any failure to appreciate physical beauty: it is only a poor thing in comparison, and taken by itself. But the real point, surely, is that the desire for it can be quenched by moral ugliness. This is a matter of affect, a natural loosening of attachment because of a greater affective energy elsewhere.

I have overdone this, because in Diotima's speech the crucial shift is towards *absolute* beauty. It is by comparison with *that* . . . but essentially the same point is to be made about a re-ordering of preference. Maybe the point is that it is only the experience of 'beauty itself' that can finally free us from the pull of contrary inclinations, only at a pitch beyond appreciation of beauty of soul can beauty of soul be secure and not in conflict with physical beauty. In that case, what is this desire for beauty itself, unadulterated, as Wittgenstein once wryly remarked, by anything that is beautiful . . . ?

What I need to do now is draw out in more detail what an appreciation or love of beauty of soul might consist in, and try to render plausible the idea that someone could come to value beauty of soul more than physical beauty, in such a way that this is an expression of their real preferences, in such a way that they are physically engaged in that appreciation, and in such a way that they could be described as possessing the virtue of *sophrosune*. The shifts of attention and preference, reflected in changes in a person's scale of values, actually provides the *infrastructure* of morality. The transition from the love of physical beauty to love of beauty of soul is the transition from a state in which Glaucon's remark that no one is just save under compulsion is true, to a state in which there is a natural disposition to be just. The shifts of *Eros* in the *Symposium*, indeed, are an essential counterbalance to the *Republic* account, where harmony of soul unaccountably brings about just actions. There is no explanation there about *how* it might be an 'excellence of the mind'. The *Symposium* gives it. *The disposition to be just in a harmonious soul is a matter of a quickened and lively interest in the welfare of others* (for *their* sake). Catherine Osborne (1994) has made the claim that *philia* is better translated as 'alliance' than as 'friendship', on the grounds that *philia* can exist between parties who are not merely 'friends', but who have various reasons for being concerned with the furtherance of each others' interests. In that case we need to highlight a distinction between an *interest* in the well-being of another, and a concern for the well-being of another that is for *them*. Plato has sometimes been criticised for an egoistic conception of love, understood as *Eros*. The desire for possession or enjoyment or whatever. But I think he has the idea of *metta*, of an *agapeistic* sensibility, as a feature of a particular stage of the development of *eros*. The desire for 'knowledge' and for 'institutions that benefit the young' are expressions of a quickened interest in the well-being of others, for *their* sake. However, it depends upon a claimed pitch of concentration of the soul which *contents* and absorbs the body. It is effective in a *dhyanic* body. Thus I do not agree with Plato's comment in the *Phaedo* that

Purification . . . consists in separating the soul as much as possible from the body, and accustoming it to withdraw from all contact with the body and concentrate itself by itself; and to have its dwelling, so far as it can, both now and in the future, alone by itself, freed from the shackles of the body. (66E)

This leaves out the possibility that the physical body can become a spiritual body (a *soma psychikon*) even in this life, or at least be diffused with its energies through *dhyana*.

I have already noted Diotima's comment that someone who reckons beauty of soul more valuable than beauty of body will *love and cherish* 'a virtuous soul even in a body which has little of the bloom of beauty'. And surely it is true that we can love someone who has a beautiful demeanour, that we love the beauty of their presence, an old man (Dhardo Rinpoche), or an old woman. But the comment hints at an *explanation* for someone's preference turning in this direction. It grows out of the emergence of a sensibility they become resident in, and of corresponding forms of *relating*. (Friends who met Dhardo have reported a completely focused *interest* in them.) The condition for that emergence is already present at an earlier stage of the ascent. It begins with someone falling in love on account of the *eromenos*'s physical beauty. What Diotima

says is *begotten* out of this form of relationship, and what I suggest determines the possibility of progress towards love of beauty of soul, is 'noble
logoi' or 'noble conversation'. The ethical life starts as pillow talk. There
are *many* starting-points, but pillow-talk is one of them. Beauty of soul,
and love for it, develops out of this kind of talk. And, as someone earlier
in the dialogue remarks, the lover does not want to be ashamed in front
of the beloved. It seems reasonable to suggest that the natural term, the
perfection, or full development, of these 'noble *logoi*' is to be found in the
person of confirmed virtue, though 'at a later, very much later time'.

   I am reading the ascent to absolute beauty as a particular application
of *pratityasamutpada* or 'dependent arising'. Diotima has already pointed
out that there are persons

whose creative desire is of the soul, and who long to beget spiritually, not physically, the progeny which it is the nature of the soul to create and bring to birth.
(208c)

This progeny is wisdom and virtue. To be attracted to beauty of soul,
then, is to come to cherish *someone* whose presence embodies these qualities, or seems ripe to do so (so that a youth, Charmides, and Socrates,
can be understood to represent different stages of the development of
this beauty). If we take seriously Nietzsche's notion of sensuality wedded
to the spirit, then we need seriously to *imagine* the distinctive presence
and demeanour, the freedom of movement, of such a person. What we
are looking for is not someone dissociated from unregenerate impulses,
but someone in whom the body is itself transformed, with a distinctive
aura and attractiveness. Plato clearly envisages two different scenarios.
One is addressed to the older *erastes* and is clearly intended to ennoble
his desire for youths. But the other is one in which Socrates, the very
figure of *Eros*, has become in a sense the beloved. In either case the *con-
tented* love of beauty of soul must already itself participate in that beauty.
What a person begins to appreciate in beauty of soul is *someone*, who
manifests the developed expression of the noble *logoi* of an earlier stage.
The person who is attracted to Socrates (the figure of *Eros* is also the
object of *Eros*) is attracted both to his person and to what he represents
(which indeed determines the state of his person), the *natural development
of their own emergent sensibility*, and thus of themselves. This sensibility
determines the direction of their preferences, which will be expressed in
their scale of values, in how they are with one another. Thus Socrates
represents the progress of their own *Bildung*, and the direction, therefore,
of what they will conceive to be their own true interests, which will be

manifest in a way of being human. In that case they might be said to be in the region of harmony of soul that is looked for somewhat vainly in the *Republic*. Since reason judges of good and evil and has the foresight to act for the whole, it should not demur at this venture of spirit towards its own perfection, and since the affective life that emerges engages and contents the body, the harmony will be one in which sensuality is wedded to a rational spirit.

Now here is the crucial point. The natural connection between harmony of soul and justice is established for us in the *discovery* of a relation to others in which we are absorbed and whole. When that inevitably dissolves we may find ourselves wondering how we can return to that happy state of harmony . . . *rather than wondering how we can find our way back to that relation to others*. The point about 'harmony of soul' is to think of it as an experiential notion, which functions as a state remembered, that remains in the *memory* even when it is lost. In trying to find it again, we neglect to seek what brought it about. Having found such a harmony, such a state of energy, a person may find the unruly passions which undermine it more difficult to bear and may seek the remedy of repression. *Pace* Nietzsche, this would not be evidence of degeneration, but a failure fully to understand the realities of a necessary transition.

10

There is a connection I have neglected to make – though Kant and Plato would be uneasy bedfellows for more than one reason. Diotima had taught Socrates that the ascent to absolute beauty began with the desire for a beautiful body, and that one had to learn along the way the striking lesson of non-attachment that 'the beauty on any body is the brother [or sister?] of that on another body'. However, the love of physical beauty 'begets' noble or beautiful words, as we have seen (Christopher Williams suggested 'noble conversation') and we move thence to the beauty of soul, of knowledge, of institutions that 'improve the young', and beyond, an internally related list as I have indicated. But the relationship between the begetting of noble conversation and the desire for the beauty to be found in souls can maybe be mediated by the notions of aesthetic ideas and indirect communication. In other words, talk, poetry, perhaps, and poetry is also a form of pillow-talk, begets its kind in the receptive mind of the *eromenos*, so that what is there conceived are *ideas*, of the productive Kantian kind, which form the mind itself, giving it the shape of sense.

But such conceptions need to be gestated and brought to birth, nursed through infancy and brought to mature life and expression, then begetting their kind, and so on. What is being described is the inception and progress of energies, their procreative exchanges. And we have noticed Diotima's powerful remark that there are persons whose 'creative desire is of the soul, and who long to beget spiritually, etc.'. A common feminist criticism of the *Symposium* is that Plato seeks to annexe even female sexuality, and appropriate it for men. But something more profound is going on, I think. Sexual language is unavoidable because it reflects our general experience of nature, and what is thus reflected is manifested even in our inner lives. The basic given is *erotic relationship* and reproduction, it surrounds us and informs us. Physical sexuality is only a particular manifestation or instance of something more general. The use of sexual language to explicate the life of the soul is not metaphor but metonymy, the part for the whole. The discovery of the possibilities of wisdom and virtue (and *their* impulse to reproduce their kind) is a further manifestation of the sexuality of nature, is another manifestation, rather, of the nature of *eros*.

I confess that I have always been sceptical of the general form of an idealist argument which moves inductively from our human inner life of volition to the conclusion that volition of some kind or other is present throughout nature. It always seemed to me to be too frail a generalisation. Perhaps it is because I had too inadequate a conception of the will. *Eros*, however, seems more likely, we are surrounded by swelling and arousal, copulation and conception, fecundity and reproduction is all around us, is part of our physical lives and is present in the life of the spirit, birth pangs as well. It is not so much that there is reason to think that the rest of the world is like us as that we are like the rest of the world – because we are a manifestation of it. *Eros* informs nature, and the path to wisdom and virtue are a further manifestation of it. The ethical relationship, in other words, and what it begets, is the condition of knowledge of the world, it is itself a further manifestation of the world. Life in the biblical sense is an epistemological category. And one of the things we may discover is that, to use a Buddhist term, we are 'non-different' from our surrounding environment, we participate in it, we discover the non-duality of subject and object by discovering the same processes within ourselves as we see around us.

Whilst Aristophanes holds his breath, the physician Eryximachus, in a speech tedious enough to have cured his hiccups by itself (*Symposium*, 186aff), nevertheless says the crucial thing of *Eros*, 'it is a great and wonderful god whose influence extends everywhere'.

James Mackey (1992) has reflected, in a slightly different sense, on the possibility that 'a defensible and meaningful use of the term "God"' could be derived from a notion of an *eros* which arises *within* us but not noticeably *from* us, and refers to 'a kind of pervasive force in the universe out with our human agency' (158). He refers to 'an originating, but not originated eros-type impulse' (159), and raises the question whether we are 'incarnations' of this 'universal and original divine force'. I suppose I hesitate on principle to go so far. These are indeterminable matters. On the other hand, to return to my thoughts about Haldane, it may well be that we cannot find any *origination* of the *eros* we find in the world, we do not discover its presence to be contingent upon anything else, though it seems clear that its *forms* depend upon conditions. But that hardly makes it divine: we just know its presence in the forms that we know about. Mackey thus projects a perfected *eros* into the heavens. I should rather say, that we find these manifestations of *eros* within us and outside of us, we are witness to its manifestations in the life of the spirit, in the development of wisdom and virtue, we find ourselves formed and still forming . . . and can say no more. What we discover are forms we seem to have created and yet also embody, in ways, remember, that depend upon *renunciation*.

CHAPTER TWELVE

A language of grasping and non-grasping

I

The landscape as we climbed up to Pune was not entirely strange, even though I was at last, for the first time in my life, *unter einem anderen Himmel,* under a different sky, a means of inner change, it looked the same, so far . . . but there were rice paddies, multitudes of egrets, then lovely hills, cascading waterfalls down sheer rock, everything, rock and vegetation, drenched or dripping. I had seen the silhouettes against the horizon of bare-legged boys, standing by their goats or cows, holding up an umbrella or with a piece of plastic sheeting round their heads. I was surprised to be ill at ease at the country stations, a wildness about some of the people, a fierceness about their posture, one old woman, small and straight, glaring at everything, up and down the track, and I did not want to meet her eyes, and then she is squatting down on her haunches, mild, nodding, a lovely child whispering in her ear.

Before I came to India my imagination was already beginning to suffer from a kind of vertigo. I am reading the paper, I glance at some snatch of foreign news, about a train crash, say, in Peru, and I reel away from the information, from the image that formed in my mind, because not only would I have to summon up pain and injury and death and people bereaved and having to be told, and rescue workers, and ambulances and hospitals, but also an elaborate railway system, with trains and timetables, and a socio-economic system that had been established long ago and which had developed with the rise and fall of whole generations, millions of people, who lived out their lives, had been born and died – and none of it bore any relation to *me*, or to my world: there were worlds well established that had no dependence on or connection with me. My imagination could not cope with it, could not grasp this utter sameness and utter difference, as now I see an entirely different daily scene from what I am accustomed to, so that I can sense its ordinariness, its alltäglichkeit, even though it is not an everydayness for me. So my imagination found itself at the edge of an abyss in which it feared to lose itself. It was adapted to, and ranged within, my individual and local world, the searchlight swung in an arc and what was beyond its reach and was invisible, did not exist. Except, that on such stray occasions, reality let itself in and undermined me briefly. Or I would read about the treatment of political prisoners in some barbarous regime. It seemed an objection that so many died *in complete obscurity*, intolerable that the world should not know, and at the same time I knew that the obscurity of their fate was beside the point. I felt nervous about my trip to India. As I walked through the streets of Norwich, or moved about the house, I would get the illusion that I could smell incense. Later it was shit, everywhere. I started to imagine what it would be like in Bombay, I thought that I would be overpowered, be drenched, in the odours of shit and incense, intensified in the heat, these powers of Bodies, ideas of secondary qualities, and I felt myself epiphenomenal, the by-product of a deeper reality, some profound process out of which we had been briefly thrown up, foam and scattered spray. It came upon me as a kind of giddying vertigo, as a dawning truth beyond my powers. I was buying a kerosene stove in a crowded little side street, open-fronted shops, the usual scene. Suddenly I had lost the fat, amiable Muslim's attention and he was staring hard up the road, speaking to his assistants, who also started to stare, very hard. There seemed to be a dispute between two young men, maybe one of them had been pushed off his bike or had run into the other. The whole little street was alert, but then the scene somehow subsided, everyone relaxed. But a riot could have taken place within seconds.

2

Professor K. J. Shah, a pupil of Wittgenstein in the late forties, is a visitor at the Poona philosophy department. He said that one has to train oneself in order to know how to act, one has to discipline one's relation to oneself and discipline one's relation to others. It might be very easy for me to overwhelm you as a person and so it is my duty not to overwhelm you. Similarly, I must not overwhelm myself, in the sense of not allowing one part of me arbitrarily to dominate the rest. (Sounds like Schiller.) He's a good Wittgensteinian, wanting me to be more specific all the time, to give him concrete, particular examples, so that we could see the truth to be found there and then pass on. He thought this demand was one of Wittgenstein's contributions. He was critical of what he called the spiritual obsessiveness of men like Kafka and Kierkegaard, whom he thought were unable to *act*. He thought that one ought not to change one's religion, that one had a duty to stay within it. Gandhiji had considered converting to Christianity, but he had been told to re-examine his own tradition. I thought that that might have been because his own tradition was particularly rich, rather than because of an *a priori* assumption that one ought to remain, but he disagreed and said that one had a duty to one's own religion. He spoke movingly and humbly about Wittgenstein's fierce rebuke when, as a young man, he had spoken slightingly to him of his own Jain tradition. He was sceptical about the interest that westerners were showing in Buddhism, etc. The idea of a westerner becoming a Hindu or a Tibetan Buddhist was unintelligible to him. He said that Ramana Maharshi had had many disciples who were not Hindus, including Muslims. You did not need to become a Hindu to be a disciple of Ramana. It was the presence in India of men of such great spirituality, even in the twentieth century, that made the difference between western and Indian attitudes to religion: the presence of such spirituality was something that Indians were confronted with and had to take some account of. We could not be 'brothers' for structural reasons to do with the relations between our countries, i.e. capitalism made fraternity impossible between us. Fraternal feelings are not a substitute for fraternal relations, of which, however, they may be both the cause and the consequence. Fraternal relations are rooted in specific conditions, an image of which might be our eating at the same table, from the same cooking pot. But within societies and between them, this is not how things stand. The absence of fraternal relations is a form of estrangement. Not only are there gross inequalities, but there are causal relations between the presence of wealth and the presence of poverty. *Those* are the structural conditions which estrange us.

Flushed and overheated, dancing wildly in the hot sun, as at a disco, boys and young men, to the beat and roll of the drums, before their Ganapati shrine.

If Gandhi had converted to Christianity, there would have been political consequences, of course, not least bearing on his authority as an emblem of his own tradition. What would have made it in some way *wrong* is his doing it to the *neglect* of his own tradition, already more or less consciously, unconsciously working within him, and so setting up dangerous internal conflicts. To speak for oneself, it is not so straightforward a matter to talk of remaining within Christianity as a sort of duty.

There is an equivalent bizarreness about people from the west converting to Hinduism or Buddhism, there has to be a meeting or rapprochement of some kind, not a wholesale crossing over without comparison or criticism or proper discrimination of elements. The western tradition, any living tradition, is constituted by a series of acts of self-transcendence, a constant moving on through new discovery and self-criticism. And that is hardly *not* the case with the other major traditions. It is not so clear what 'remaining within Christianity' would amount to. In other words, against what Shah said, there seems to me a middle position between wholesale 'conversion' and 'loyalty'. But even as a Buddhist practitioner my mind constantly returns to the *language* of Christianity, I remain, as with Braithwaite, nourished by the stories, or some of them at least. I suppose I could be described as a Catholic Buddhist, but not as a Buddhist Catholic.

Beyond the trees, mostly now in shade, a young Englishwoman in a pale sari walks through the shadows, looking reflectively down at the ground ahead of her, and passes through a band of speckled light cast by a few rays of sun which illuminate the green leaves in their path . . . The wind has risen, the trees in the garden sway, dead leaves rattle along the marble floor, the dog barks as the thunder starts. In the west there are low clouds billowing, close and sulphurous as the sun sets. In the east it is much darker: above the tree tops it is uniformly grey. There is a wind again, the whole sky lights up and flickers; it thunders, but not loud. There is also the traffic noise, the usual sounds, horns, a train, changes of gear; the sky flickers again, the wind bangs shut a door, scatters dead leaves across the marble; it has started to rain. The sky lightens, then the burden of thunder. It lights up nearly orange, reflecting the west. The rain gets harder, noisy on the leaves and foliage, a sound like frying. Now there are thuds of thunder, close and loud. It is the last days of the monsoon.

3

Writers about Buddhism and other oriental traditions constantly allude to a particular crux about the subject–object poles of experience. We are variously told that the Buddhist tradition invites us to 'overcome' or 'transcend' or 'go beyond' the 'subject–object distinction' or the 'subject–object dichotomy' or the 'subject–object duality', or informs us that we must 'realise' the 'non-difference' between 'self and other' or the 'non-duality' of 'self and other'. So many mystical students have talked like this, and I never understood them, and now the French. But these are slippery phrases and it seems to me that there is much conflation and confusion.

Buddhism offers us a pivotal application of the principle of dependent arising, in the tantalising formula that 'knowledge and vision of things as they are' arises in dependence on 'concentration' or *samadhi*. If such knowledge is available only under the condition of concentration, then the absence of concentration implies the absence of knowledge of how things really are. And since concentration is represented as a state to be achieved, then clearly the formula addresses our condition and informs us that we are deluded and ignorant. So at least we know that, one might say, though that depends on what counts as knowing, as opposed, say, to belief. The same principle is expressed negatively in the claim that suffering arises in dependence on craving (*lobha*), aversion (*dvesa*) and ignorance (*moha*) or delusion (*avidya*). Craving and aversion at least reinforce if they do not determine our ignorance and delusion.

What we are talking about is the domination of consciousness by particular states that obscure reality from us. We could say, if we wanted to make the Greek connection, that we are talking about states of *eros* that prevent us from seeing what is there to be seen, let us not prematurely metaphysicalise the expression 'how things really are'.

Now traditional Buddhist thinkers have made use of the doctrine of 'the three natures', a version of which I want to introduce into the discussion and connect with these polar notions of concentration and knowledge and craving aversion and ignorance. But exposition of the doctrine is not straightforward.

4

Vasubandhu's *trisvabhava-nirdesa* – the Treatise on the Three Natures[1] – opens as follows:

The imagined (*parikalpita*), the other-dependent (*paratantra*) and the absolutely accomplished (*parinispanna*): these are the three natures, which should be thoroughly known by the wise. (Kochumuttom's translation)

So, the doctrine of the three natures, which should be thoroughly known by the wise, the 'imagined' nature, the 'other dependent' nature and the 'absolutely accomplished' nature: – Aspirants to wisdom may well start

[1] I am using the text as translated by Thomas Kochumuttom (1982).

by asking, the three natures of *what?* since otherwise it remains unclear what the doctrine is about.

Kochumuttom comments that 'the entire doctrine of the three natures hinges on the subject–object *duality*' (my italics) and he goes on to gloss his definitions as follows:

every individual in his absolutely accomplished state of existence . . . is neither a subject nor an object of experience, but is reality as such (*tathata*); then he slips into the unfortunate situation called *samsara*, where he is led to find himself as the subject enjoying all else as objects of experience: this state of existence being conditioned by the forces of one's own past deeds and habits, is called the other-dependent . . .; the forms of subjectivity and objectivity that are projected on to the things by the individual in the other-dependent state of existence, are the imagined nature.

Kochumuttom refers, then, to three 'states of existence' in seeking to expound the three *svabhavas* (or three natures) and he relates them, as he says, to what he calls 'the subject–object duality', doing so with an unblushing metaphysical resonance: we are, in our 'absolutely accomplished' nature, 'reality as such'. However, just as 'states of existence' is a vague phrase, we should not be too ready to assume that we know what the phrase 'subject–object duality' means, either. It appears to me that Kochumuttom conflates a subject–object *duality* with a subject–object *distinction*. So I need to make good the claim that there are distinct ideas here. He passes from the claim that the doctrine 'hinges on the subject–object duality' to talk of being 'neither a subject nor an object of experience' and thus seems to imply that to recognise the error of thinking in terms of a subject–object duality is to recognise that there is 'neither a subject nor an object of experience'.

In his fine book, *Mahayana Buddhism*, Paul Williams (1989) refers, not to the Three Natures, but to the three 'Aspects', and he too offers an exposition linked, properly enough, to 'subject–object duality'. His answer to our question, the three aspects of *what?* is that 'All things which can be known can be subsumed under these Three aspects' (83), which again suggests an objectivist reading, though one ought to say that subjects of experience are presumably included among 'all things which can be known'. Thus in explaining the *paratantrasvabhava* (or other-dependent nature) Williams tells us that

According to the *Trisvabhava-nirdesa* it is that *which* appears, in opposition to the *way* in which it appears, which is the first Aspect, the conceptualised aspect . . . In other words, it is the substratum for the *erroneous partition into inherently existing subjects and objects* which marks the conceptualised aspect. (83, my italics)

Williams has 'conceptualised aspect' instead of Kochumuttom's 'imagined nature'. (I shall return later to his claim that the *paratantrasvabhava* is a 'substratum'.) Notice how he refers to 'an erroneous partition (of the substratum) into inherently existing subjects and objects' as what marks the 'conceptualised aspect' (the *parikalpitasvabhava*). But is the 'erroneous partition' a matter of drawing a *distinction* between subject and object, or is it a matter of drawing a distinction between an *inherently existing* subject and object? There are clearly two possibilities, since one can have the notion of a distinction between subject of experience and object of experience without taking the step of assuming that these 'inherently exist' or *stand* as such independently of experience. Is the mistake the reference to inherent existence or to a subject–object distinction?

In fact Williams seems to offer us a double conflation. On the one hand is the conflation I have just mentioned of 'subject' with 'enduring subject', but he also makes the same move as Kochumuttom and assimilates talk of a subject–object *duality* to that of a subject–object *distinction*. Now it may be that he is merely being faithful to the texts, and I am not the scholar: my concern is to discuss a possible case of conflation, whoever its authors may be. Williams explains the *parinispannasvabhava* ('fully accomplished nature' or 'perfected aspect') as follows:

The final Aspect is called the perfected Aspect . . . According to the *Samdhinirmocana Sutra* it is the 'Suchness' or 'Thusness' (*tathata*), the true nature of things, which is discovered in meditation . . . It is said to be the complete absence, in the dependent Aspect, of objects – that is, the objects of the conceptualised aspect.

I find this account puzzling. Something important is being said about the notion of things as they really are (*tathata*, the suchness of things) and the conditions under which we discover it. In translating *parinispannasvabhava* Williams refers to the 'perfected aspect', Kochumuttom to the 'fully accomplished nature', basing themselves on the *Samdhinirmocana Sutra*. Williams makes 'the perfected aspect' refer to the 'suchness' of things, as it is discovered in meditation; and Kochumuttom says of the *individual in his 'fully accomplished state of existence'* that *he* is reality as such, not to be characterised as either subject or object of experience. They both, then, make use of the notion of 'suchness' to explain the 'perfected aspect' or the 'fully accomplished nature'. One of them refers this to 'things' as they really are, the other to the individual, though presumably these are simply differences of emphasis.

What is puzzling is that 'perfected' or 'fully accomplished' should be used to qualify *either* things *or* the individual's 'state of existence', since *parinispanna* so clearly refers us to the outcome of a process: 'perfected', 'fully accomplished'. It seems more reasonable to refer the *parinispannasvabhava* to something that we could sensibly identify as capable of perfection or full accomplishment. Admittedly, 'individual' seems a better candidate than 'thing' here, but I suggest that the best candidate is *consciousness* or experience, or *form* of consciousness or experience. It makes sense to refer to a particular, *developed* state of consciousness, since consciousness is the sort of thing which could become 'fully accomplished' or 'perfected'.

Doing so seems to me to give an indication of how to answer the question, the three natures of *what?* We are talking about the three natures of *consciousness* or experience, *one* of which discloses the *suchness* of things, and is able to do so because the 'complete absence' that Williams refers to as characteristic of the *parinispannasvabhava* is really the complete absence, not of 'the *objects* of the conceptualised aspect', as he translates *parikalpitasvabhava*, but of the distorting form of the conceptualised aspect of consciousness itself, which precisely *fails* to disclose the suchness of things for reasons we shall come to. If we think of the 'three natures' as a doctrine about experience then we shall see that it implies that different *forms* of experience are more or less apt for disclosing how things are.

5

Paul Williams glosses his brief exposition of the *parinispannasvabhava* or 'perfected aspect' as follows:

What it amounts to is that through meditation we come to know that our flow of perceptions, of experiences, really lacks the fixed, enduring subjects and objects which we have constructed out of it. There is only the flow of experiences. The perfected aspect is, therefore, the fact of non-duality, there is neither subject nor object but only a single flow. It is also emptiness, explained for this tradition as meaning that one thing is empty of another. That is, the flow of perceptions – the dependent aspect – is empty of enduring entities – the conceptualised aspect.

Williams is surely right to point to the mistake of our thinking in terms of 'fixed, enduring subjects and objects' as an important part of the Buddhist critique of human experience, as though either subject or object existed as such and independently of the forms of experience within which they arise. But this is an intriguing passage, and it contains some difficulties, of a kind to be found in Kochumuttom too. Through meditation we come to realise that '*our* flow of perceptions . . . lacks the *fixed, enduring* subjects and objects which *we* have constructed out of it' (my italics). There are two issues here. Firstly, Williams is forced into a reference to a subject ('our', 'we') in order to explain that doing so is some kind of delusion, though he does this because he uses the phrase 'enduring subject' interchangeably with 'subject' in this passage. Kochumuttom does the same: he refers to 'the forms of subjectivity and objectivity that are projected on to the things *by the individual*' (my italics). But maybe the point is that to do so is unavoidable, not because we are in a state of delusion, but because the accounts are confused. Secondly, Paul Williams says that through meditation we realise that 'our flow of perceptions . . . lacks the fixed, enduring subjects and objects which we have constructed out of it'. This takes us back to my earlier point about the difference between inherently existing subjects and objects and *non*-inherently existing subjects and objects of experience. Is it the case that through meditation we realise the lack of subjects and objects of experience or is it rather that we realise the lack of *fixed, enduring* subjects and objects of experience? Realising the latter is compatible with retaining a *distinction* between subject and object, suitably non-fixed and non-enduring. However, it would seem that Williams (and I only mean Williams in his role of Yogacara expositor) disagrees, since the passage continues:

There is only the flow of experiences. The perfected aspect is, therefore, the fact of non-duality, there is neither subject nor object but only a single flow.

In this passage there seem to be two philosophical mistakes. There is a conflation of the idea of fixed, enduring subjects and objects with that of subjects and objects *simpliciter*, but also 'the fact of non-duality' is glossed in terms of the absence of subject and object, as with Kochumuttom, who claims, as we have seen, that the *trisvabhava* doctrine 'hinges on the subject–object duality' and tells us that to recognise their non-duality is to see the mistake of *distinguishing* between subject and object at all, a mistake only realised by means of the fully accomplished nature.

It seems to me, though, that the doctrine of the non-duality of subject and object *depends upon* a recognition of their bi-polarity or *distinction*. (I am not denying that there can be powerful states of non-intentional consciousness, forms of awareness in which there is no experience of subject and object. What I do deny is that we can infer from such experiences that the distinction is unreal, or that the non-intentional state is a disclosure of *tathata*.)

It is inevitable that Williams, in his role as Yogacarin, should go on to make the move that he does now make, which is a Humean one, because he has deprived himself of any subject or object of experience. He says 'There is only the flow of experiences', 'a single flow of perceptions' *rather than* a subject–object distinction. But part of the problem with the Humean position is that it is vulnerable to Kant's criticism about the transcendental unity of apperception. It just is not the case that there is a single flow of perceptions *rather than* a subject–object distinction. Perceptions need perceivers as well as perceived. In negotiating between Kant and Hume, we may want to say on Hume's behalf that there is no experience of a *self* (no empirical self) over and above the perception itself; and on behalf of Kant we may want to say that there *is* a self which unifies the flow of perceptions into a single, coherent experience: this self, however, is transcendental in the sense that it cannot be an object of experience. That is not, however, to deny that it changes in dependence upon conditions, even if we can only determine those changes by reference to the felt form of experience. To use Wittgenstein's *Tractatus* metaphor, 'the eye is not part of the visual field', but it doesn't follow that we have no access to the shifting qualities of the eye through the shifts in the visual field. Or better, and with Hegel, the Self is known through its operations. There can be a happy as well as an unhappy consciousness, there is something that it is like to be the one or the other. The prereflective *cogito* has a distinctive *quale*, not to say *suchness*.

6

So, then, let us retrace our steps and look again, in the light of my own suggestion that the 'three natures' refer us to forms of conscious experience:

That which appears is the other-dependent, for it depends on causal conditions; the form in which it appears is the imagined, for it is merely an imagination.

The perpetual absence of the form in which the other-dependent appears, is to be understood as the absolutely accomplished nature, for it is never otherwise.

So what 'appears'? Presumably we surge up into consciousness, and to a 'form' of consciousness, and it is that which appears, our own conscious experience, in the form in which we find it, conditioned as we are by the *klesas* or defilements of craving and aversion and the like. If we think of the other-dependent or the 'paratantric' nature as qualifying consciousness, we could say that what 'appears' is a consciousness, both in its subjective and objective aspect, *whose form depends upon conditions*, that the form in which it initially appears is its imagined or constructed nature, and that 'the perpetual absence' of that form is what characterises the 'fully accomplished' nature of consciousness.

But that clearly needs further explanation. To refer to the *parikalpita* or 'imagined' nature of consciousness is to refer to something that it doesn't have, to the nature that we *imagine* it to have, that we project upon it. We precisely project onto consciousness as its very *nature* the only form of it that is available to us, even in our reflection upon it (an unnoticed empiricism). It is here that Williams and Kochumuttom have introduced the thought that what we thus imagine is that experience is constituted by a subject–object *duality* (sound Buddhist doctrine), which is then taken to be equivalent to a subject–object *distinction*. The *parikalpitasvabhava* thus becomes experience constructed in terms of the subject–object distinction, and the *parinispannasvabhava* becomes a form of experience not so constructed, in which there is no subject or object.

7

However, it may be possible to see this all somewhat differently, by drawing away for a while from the talk of *subjects and objects*, and introducing a new pair of terms, relying on the fact that Vasubandhu actually makes a distinction between grasper (*grahaka*) and grasped (*grahya*) rather than the more neutral sounding subject and object.[2]

Kochumuttom (31) refers us to *Madhyanta-vibhaga-karika* 1,2;

There exists the imagination of the unreal, namely the discrimination between the graspable and the grasper. However, there is no pair, such as the graspable and the grasper.

Although I say that the subject–object language is more neutral than that of grasper and grasped, I do not intend to imply that the latter terms cannot be used neutrally in a similar manner. But it is important that we can put an ethical gloss on the idea of a grasper–grasped relation, since

[2] I am immensely grateful to my old graduate student Dr Robert Morrison for persistently drawing my attention to the significance of this usage.

Vasubandhu wants to refer the determination of the imagined nature (*par-ikalpitasvabhava*) to the *alaya-vijnana* or 'store-consciousness' and its various defilements. More to the point, it is the grasper–grasped distinction, rather than that between subject and object, that is said here to be unreal.

Andrew Skilton (1994) describes the *alaya-vijnana* in the following terms:

In its defiled state it is the subconscious collectivity of *bija* or 'seeds', which are 'sown' by previous moments of consciousness, and which 'perfume' future moments of consciousness with perceptions of duality, and thereby constitute the means by which *karman* operates . . . This function of the impure *alaya-vijnana* is also alluded to in its name, which also means 'clinging consciousness'. (127)

Given that this is so, I suggest that we can construe the error of the 'imagined nature' of experience not as the view that there is a subject–object distinction, but as the view that experience is *essentially* constructed in terms of the distinction between *grasper and grasped*: the false view is *not* that experience is essentially constructed around the *subject–object* distinction. It is one thing to say that a particular, conditioned state of consciousness leads us into the error of supposing experience to be constructed in terms of a grasper–grasped relation, and quite another to say that it leads us into the error of constructing it around a subject–object relation. *Grasping* is a determinate state of consciousness that arises out of the defilements, it is an unwholesome way of filling the subject position that systematically distorts what occupies the object position.

Correspondingly, the characteristic feature of the 'fully accomplished' form of experience is that there is neither grasper nor grasped, *pace* Williams's 'there is neither subject nor object'. It is characterised by the 'complete absence' of grasping, *not* the complete absence of subject and object. The construction of experience around the *grahaka–grahya* distinction merely reflects a particular, conditioned form of experience, which we then mistakenly take to be the thing itself, even though we have no warrant for doing this, since we have no standard of comparison, because our conscious experience is precisely limited by the *klesas*.

However, if someone were to realise another form of experience (which is surely the point of the *parinispannasvabhava*, the fully accomplished nature, whose possibility surely depends upon the conditioned or 'paratantric' nature of consciousness) then they clearly *would* have a standard of comparison by which to judge that the grasper–grasped relation was *not* an essential feature of experience as such.

8

But now let us turn our attention to the notion of non-duality, 'realising' which is claimed to be the crux. Retaining a *distinction* between subject and object (which is itself now to be distinguished from its own special case, that between grasper and grasped) does not at all commit us to denying the *non-duality* of subject and object (or that of grasper and grasped: if subject and object are 'non-dual', and grasper and grasped is a special case of subject and object, then grasper and grasped are also 'non-dual'). We must recall that according to my interpretation of Vasubandhu the conditioned form in which experience or consciousness *appears* is that of a duality of grasper and grasped, and that we have to come, through the process of purification (*asraya-paravrti*, 'a turning around in the basis' (i.e. in the *alaya-vijnana*)),[3] to realise their non-duality.

We are dealing with obscure claims here, which some readers will be impatient with, but I believe that commentators have misconstrued the claim that 'there is no pair, such as the graspable and the grasper' and rendered it as a thesis about the subject–object poles of experience. But the point is that the discussion really has nothing to do with the latter. The idea of the 'non-duality' of grasper and grasped involves the doctrine of emptiness or dependence upon conditions and really entails that *under certain conditions* the grasper–grasped distinction is *not to be found*. (To put it another way, the absence of the *distinction*, under certain conditions, is not equivalent to the non-duality of its terms, but one of its consequences.)

We start with the false conception that the very form of conscious experience is constituted by the way it initially appears to us, in the conditioned form of grasper and grasped. But how are we to realise that this conception is *false*, if we have no standard of comparison? The coming to have such a standard depends upon realising that grasper and grasped are 'non-dual' or *advaya*. They are 'not two'. But how can what appear to be two distinct items be really 'not two'?

I have already expressed scepticism about the reduction by Williams and Kochumuttom of non-duality to non-distinction in the context of the terms subject and object. The claim that subject and object are non-dual is not the same claim as that there is no distinction between subject and object. It is my impression that confounding this point is liable to lead a person too precipitately towards some form of

---

[3] Skilton, 1994, 126

unearned philosophical monism or idealism, the 'suchness of things' becoming Reality known when the subject–object distinction is 'transcended'.

By contrast, there is a way of making sense of the non-duality claim that makes it *require* the bi-polarity or distinction claim. Thus to say of two apparently distinct items that they are 'non-dual' is not to say in a peculiarly non-committal way that they are *the same* in the sense of numerical identity, but to say that they are the same *in some respect*, that they share a common characteristic, are qualitatively identical in some way. They are 'not two' *in some respect*, and that is why the claim that two items are 'not two' does not imply that 'there is no such pair'. In the present context, then, what is the common characteristic shared by grasper and grasped, or indeed subject and object? The obvious answer, I suggest, is that they are 'not two' in respect of their common *dependence on conditions*, in respect of 'emptiness'. They do not have any *unconditioned* reality or 'inherent existence'.

Realising that grasper and grasped, which together *constitute* the 'imagined nature' of experience, share this dependence upon conditions, provides us with the route out of the false conception that we start with, since to realise that they are conditioned is to see that grasper and grasped are not inherent factors in experience. Realising that they are thus conditioned is not, however, a matter of giving one's assent to an abstract idea, but a matter of a transformation in our experience which *shows* the dependence upon conditions by exemplifying it. In other words, the transformation in our experience *gives* us the standard of comparison by means of which we can realise that our initial conception is false, because we have found another form of experience in which the grasper–grasped relation is not to be found, where indeed there is no such pair. The form of experience constituted by a grasper–grasped relation is simply a conditioned form of experience, and the promise held out by Buddhism is that a form of experience is achievable in which that relation is 'perpetually absent'. And moreover, we are released from the delusion that there is a duality of grasper and grasped – which just means we are released from the delusion of believing that grasper and grasped are *two* in respect of dependence upon conditions: we think *we* are separate from the changing flux we seek to grasp and fix for the sake of our grasping ends. Our settled illusion is that we stand separate and apart over against the flux of our environment; whereas we are part of the scene we thus witness and act in, in flux ourselves, a particular manifestation of nature.

So the non-duality thesis does not say that there is no genuine distinction between subject and object, grasper and grasped. On the contrary, it *requires* there to be such a distinction and it says that its terms share the characteristic of dependence upon conditions. This brings out the significance of the second of the three natures, namely the *paratantrasvabhava* (the other-dependent nature), that essentially consciousness is conditioned, that we can move from *parikalpita* to *parinispanna*. The thrust of the Three Natures doctrine is that it is possible to realise that conscious experience contains the possibility of a development from the imagined nature to the perfected or fully accomplished nature. That form of experience which is constituted by the distinction between grasper and grasped is only a particular form of consciousness, determined by the *alaya-vijñana*. To bring home the difference between 'subject-talk' and 'grasper-talk', we could say that in dependence upon conditions grasper and grasped could *disappear*, without the disappearance of subject and object. To put it another way, if the subject of experience is not present in the form of *grasper* then neither is there anything *grasped*, which is not to say that there is no object of experience. The conditions determine the *form* of the subject–object relation. This is one reason for agreeing with Williams's point that one should not think of subject and object as fixed and enduring (though who thinks that 'objects' are fixed and enduring? Our problem is that we wish that they were: it is enough for the duality delusion that we think that the subject (as opposed to the object) is fixed and enduring – if in fact we thought that they were *both* fixed and enduring we would be committed to a *non*-duality thesis). Grasper and grasped are just two possible substitution instances in the subject–object positions. This gives us the possibility of ascribing a second sense to *advaya* in this context. Grasper and grasped, or indeed subject and object, are 'not two' in the further sense that they necessarily co-exist. It doesn't just happen that they share the feature of conditionality: they are mutually dependent. To deny the one is logically to deny the other, to affirm the one is to affirm the other. They constitute a *relation*, if there is no grasper there is no grasped, if there is no subject there is no object (the truth in Berkeley), if there is no object there is no subject, etc.

9

Now the *trisvabhava-nirdesa* says of the *parinispannasvabhava* or fully accomplished nature:

the perpetual absence of the form in which the other-dependent appears, is to be understood as the absolutely accomplished nature, for it is never otherwise.

We now have a way of interpreting this. The *parikalpitasvabhava* represents a triple illusion: we surge up into a grasping consciousness in which our self-image is that of fixed subjects of experience in the midst of a maddening flux, which we are not; and our grasping is futile because it cannot deliver what we want; and we come to believe that this is the very form of conscious experience as such. But we can move away from this, so it is claimed. If we think of 'fully accomplished' or 'perfected' as qualifying the form of a possible experience, we can say that in its fully accomplished and developed nature our experience has wholly transcended this grasper–grasped relation, the grasping consciousness simply disappears. It is wholly overcome and we have thoroughly realised the non-duality of its terms, the characteristic they share of dependence upon conditions, *by eliminating the conditions upon which they depend.* The *parinispanna* nature and the *parikalpita* natures are simply *poles* of the paratantric or conditioned nature of experience, the *terminus a quo* and the *terminus ad quem.* A 'fully accomplished' form of experience entails the *knowledge*, as opposed to the *ignorance*, of non-duality. But the gulf between ignorance and knowledge here is that between the unawakened and the awakened mind. The fully accomplished experience entails the 'perpetual absence' of grasping and its associated delusions. But that is not to say that we cannot have an *intermittent* or evanescent enjoyment of its absence, on the basis of which we might posit a *parinispannasvabhava* of conscious experience in which what is evanescent becomes settled and assured.

But now, the fully accomplished form of experience, which is the developed manifestation of its essentially paratantric or conditioned nature, is said to allow us to see things as they are. How, then, *are* they? The answer is that they are *thus (tatha)*: they are just as they appear to this consciousness, which, if you possess it, you do not need to be told, and if you don't, you cannot. However, presumably the triple delusion of the *parikalpitasvabhava* is unravelled: we will not be grasping, and in that case there will be nothing grasped; we will not believe that we are separate from the change by which we are surrounded, because we have knowingly undergone a change out of grasping ourselves; and we will not believe that the essential nature of consciousness is constituted by grasping, because grasping is not what we do, and grasping will not set limits on what we are able to see and acknowledge.

But there is something curiously impersonal about these dense little verses of Vasubandhu, and it may be helpful to conclude with some reflections on grasping that place it into an ethical context. In the first place, we must presume that the disappearance of grasping, through the overcoming of the *klesas* or defilements that determine it, doesn't simply leave a vacuum. On the contrary, it is displaced by the development of *metta* or 'appreciation' and its modifications of *mudita* or sympathetic joy and *karuna* or compassion as determined by the condition of those who receive it. Thus we restore the human and sentient landscape that seemed to be in abeyance in the midst of talk of objects and graspables. In his own terms Heidegger has relevant things to say here about how the masterful enframing of reality by a technological mind-set does indeed find out true things about reality, but also leaves things concealed, precisely those things that do not yield to this kind of grasping. The point about grasping is not that it does not see what is there (it sees, after all, just what can be grasped), but that there are things that it fails to see, and as far as human relations are concerned it *conditions* what is there: there are aspects of our being that are not available to coercion. It is a project of the attention that is indifferent to what falls outside its own habitual focus. It is perception dominated by egocentric and deluded self-enclosure. The primary point about being a grasper, though, must be that it is an ethical criticism that one 'grasps', and that it signifies the form of one's relations to others at least as much as to the objects of perception. Heidegger talks of 'eine Gelassenheit zur Dinge', 'a releasement towards things', but we should not focus on that to the exclusion of a profound change in our relation to *others* which is constituted by allowing the grasper–grasped relation to disappear from among the constituents of our human relationships.

Finally, the commentators I have discussed have tended to objectify the three natures, perceiving them as a doctrine about reality rather than about the forms of consciousness in their subjective and objective poles. One consequence of this is that the *paratantrasvabhava* or 'other-dependent nature' becomes itself the way things really are, its 'thusness', and so 'beyond language'. I have denied this, claiming simply that the *paratantrasvabhava* of consciousness represents its essential nature as dependent upon conditions, taking a *parikalpita* or a *parinispanna* form, as conditions may determine. But I want to draw attention to this notion of being 'beyond language'. Paul Williams says of the dependent aspect, the *paratantrasvabhava*, that it 'is, of course, beyond language, since language is the realm of the conceptualised aspect – language necessarily falsifies, constructs inherently existing entities' (84).

But surely it is not the case that language falsifies. Language *generalises* in its descriptive function, it proceeds by locating kinds. We might be misled by this, but there is no falsification. One would be misled, for instance, if one thought that one could be given a description of the way things are present to a 'fully accomplished' consciousness and thus know how things are. By the same token concepts do not 'falsify' either. It is not so much the deployment of concepts that stands in the way of our seeing things as they are, but rather what we might call *conceptual habituation*, a habit of mind in which conceptual reflection and abstract thinking *dominate* consciousness, so that we are hardly aware of our surroundings, or of others or ourselves. Or we are preoccupied by the ends and expectations (*akanksa*)[4] associated with grasping so that our interest in things is restricted to bringing them under relevant concepts. Or as we talk you point to the open field, whose harvested, sun-lit beauty delights you, but I just register a 'field' and carry on talking, and later, when we enter the woods, circumvent the green things that stand in the way. It is in the particular ways in which we *use* language, and in our assumptions about what language gives us that we express our ignorance or delusion, conditions which such language then reinforces. In other words, the way we talk about ourselves and about the objects of our perception gives expression to our false conceptions, if our conceptions are false. It is true enough that descriptive language generalises, and that it would be a sad mistake if one thought that one knew the tree because one knew that it was a tree, but the way Williams talks of language here neglects its *expressive* capacities. So, to return to the notion of *tathata*, I can express my delight in the thusness of things by giving you the sense of the dare gale skylark in the rhythms of my speech, as well as the thusness of the dull cage and the bone house, mean house . . .

It is not so much that there is an ultimate Reality that eludes the grasping consciousness, as that such a consciousness only tends to see what it seeks to possess, it is a defiled *eros*. The 'thusness' of things, how they are, is simply what appears when ignorance and delusion retreat as we overcome craving and aversion. We are ourselves precisely in the grip of a grasping consciousness, and as the grip relaxes we enter a larger world, both inner and outer.

---

[4] I am grateful to Dr Satya Gautam for introducing this term to me.

II

Diotima tells us that one stage of the ascent to absolute beauty is an *eros* directed towards the beauty in customs and institutions that 'improve the young'. I think we may properly assume that these are to be distinguished from other customs and institutions, also already in place, into which the young are initiated, towards which they gravitate, that do not tend towards their improvement, but rather provide forms of expression for the *alaya-vijnana*, in which beauty of soul is unable to flourish, and can be undermined. We can include *language* among these customs and institutions, damaging or liberating the soul, according to what is expressed in the forms we are initiated into. Human unregeneracy, as well as its regenerate possibilities, are given expression in the forms of the language.

This is the context for reflecting on the idea of a private language of the kind Wittgenstein said was impossible: the idea of a language that only I can understand. The idea of a language that no one else can in principle understand has I think to falter ultimately for *ethical* reasons, because it would have to lie outside this Buddhist trajectory out of the *alaya-vijnana* from *parikalpita* to *parinispanna* states of consciousness. Wittgenstein's comment that 'the common behaviour of mankind is the system of reference by means of which we interpret an unknown language' is deployed in the philosophy of the social sciences to good effect. But what we have here is a particular *gloss* on the 'common behaviour of mankind': it is regenerate or unregenerate. These are the terms of our common understanding – we understand each other only too well: the private language user would need to be someone we *couldn't* understand in these terms, someone who couldn't be understood in terms of the struggle against grasping, etc. The real issue with such a person is whether there is anything left to understand.

Language is *not* a form of rule-governed behaviour. It is rather the case that *like* the practice of obeying or following a rule, the use of language depends upon doing the same thing, going on in the same way, etc., where deviation from a certain *regularity* of practice issues in unintelligibility . . . or another sense. And the point is that we very much *do* 'go on in the same way' and in the same way as each other, we understand each other. 'If language is to be a means of communication there must be agreement not only in definitions but also (queer as this may sound) in judgments' . . . remarked Wittgenstein. And some commentators have commended an appropriately vertiginous astonishment that this should be so. But judgment, remember, takes place in the midst of activity, we make judgments about what is or is not the case as we pursue our ends. The judgments upon which communication depends have a background of shared activity and common forms of behaviour. The point is that we are already communicating with each other from infancy, from infancy we know how to communicate our desires, to make them clear to one another, and, almost from infancy, we respond or fail to respond. What I am trying to say is that our common forms of behaviour already have a morally identifiable status: we come out grasping, our behaviour is already an uneasy expression of an *alaya-vijnana* dominated by clinging. We *share the condition*, for instance, in which forms of grasping determine the nature of our discriminations, what we notice, what we overlook, what we are ignorant of. As Winch pointed out, citing Goethe's *Faust*, in the beginning was the deed. The deed, we might add, was unregenerate, but *uneasily* so. We come to use language under the condition of original sin, under the condition of the *alaya-vijnana* or store-house consciousness. It is thus that we understand each other. We are initiated into what we already gravitate towards. It is thus a mistake to suppose that it is just the language that limits us. Forms of *eros* are already in place. As Simone Weil points out, discrimination and classification are already written into the body itself, the infant refuses the dummy and seeks the nipple, knows what to suck and what not to suck; we salivate in the presence of this kind of object but not in the presence of that.

Collingwood remarked that Dance is the mother of all language, insisting thereby, I think, that *expression* is fundamental to language. We are able from the beginning to communicate our desires to one another, and from *very* early on to *use* expression as a means of communication. But expression and desire come together, we may say, desire, discrimination, communication constitute our primitive formation or entelechy. The presence of *eros* already implies discrimination, in a form internally related to the erotic form that implies it. In Buddhist terms the forms of *sanna* or conceptual discrimination depend on *sanskharas* or forms of motivation. *Eros* already implies the ability to tell the difference between one thing and another, in a context in which it matters. Concept *acquisition* is a refinement of this. That is to say, conceptual discrimination in a form relative to the formation of desire is an innate feature of our lives, our evolved entelechy, and the acquisition of particular concepts is a development, dependent on initiation into relevant practices and procedures.

The point of these latter remarks is to raise doubts about John Haldane's (1996, 114–17) ingenious construction of a cosmological argument to a Prime Thinker who is supposed to stop the regress of concept acquisition. His point is that, as it were, 'Adam and Eve' cannot serve to stop the regress in virtue of their concepts being innate while for the rest of us they are acquired. While I think he is right that there is a potential regress of concept-acquisition if concept-formation depends solely on acquisition, I believe the regress is halted by the forms of primitive discrimination that are an innate feature of our earliest desires. To put it another way, and without neglecting the expressive dimension of language, whereas our development depends upon learning or acquiring concepts in the context of learning language, it depends also upon learning the terms for and the evaluations (those perhaps of the dominant male) of what we *already discriminate* in the context of primitive desire.

However there is still the issue of accounting for the 'natural transition from the non-conceptual to the conceptual' (117), which is clearly a particular form of the question about how we are to explain the emergence of life (on the planet). Haldane's Fork again gives us no choice between scientific materialism and theism, so that those of us who doubt that the present structure of science has the concepts to 'explain life' are herded towards theism. Perhaps we should never suppose an inventing mind as source. There is life in the universe, perhaps we shall be able to ascertain the natural conditions upon which its emergence depends, perhaps we shall not. But what are the forms of life, is it appropriate to talk about the conditions for the *emergence* of life, or the conditions for particular formations? Who, if I cried, would hear me among the angelic orders? I may be a non-theistic pan-psychist, but only because there are sometimes intimations of higher forms of life, and no perceived necessity for invoking God, as opposed to Buddhas and Bodhisattvas.

12

Language is constituted by a multiplicity of uses or customs set in a multiplicity of contexts and activities, and it is in the midst of the latter that we are taught the names of things, learn what things are called, *learn what it is to call something by a name at all*, and come to have something to say, referring and predicating, distinguishing what is true and what is false, getting things right and getting them wrong. Getting things right and getting things wrong is fundamental to our initiation into customs, uses, institutions. When we learn a new descriptive term, for instance, we do not learn to restrict it to this object here, but immediately pick up that we are learning the term for a *kind* of thing, and onlookers are not satisfied that we have learnt the kind until they see what we call the same and what we distinguish it from. These jejune remarks are intended to indicate how language is something that we learn against a background or in the midst of a determinate condition of the soul expressed in the behaviours we are initiated into and gravitate towards. This condition, and the possibilities of transformation as they emerge, are also expressed in the language. Buddhism talks of the purification of body, speech and mind, and it is important to recall that speech is an area of behaviour in which we can conduct ourselves well or badly.

Part of the significance of Wittgenstein's subtle reflections was to show how deeply infected we were by the incoherent assumption of privacy, which we might connect with the assumption of separateness that in Buddhism is said to reflect our failure to realise non-duality. It is a failure fully to enter into the world in which we find ourselves.

It is true that we can come to acknowledge that we learn mental predicates in a public context, learn to discern resentment and friendliness in the behaviour and demeanour of others, recognise that we come to know our own mental states in just the same way. But actually, we are often invisible to ourselves. It is much more difficult to *see* our own resentment, say, than it is to see someone else's. Our own behaviour can be invisible to us, so we assume it is invisible to others, and we come to think that we have this private space in which no one can see us or follow us. But not even language could enter such an abstract and decontextualised space.

13

In *Spreading the Word* Simon Blackburn (1984) offers a discussion of Wittgenstein's anti-private language argument in which he comes to the following conclusion:

there is no compelling reason why there cannot be a practice of judging that our own private sensations are thus-and-so. And the intention with which we apply the classification may, so far as the argument goes, be identified by private ostension. (107)

In a moment I shall examine the considerations which lead Blackburn to this conclusion. But first I want to point out that this is an unexpected way of expressing disagreement with the anti-private language argument, and it reveals Blackburn's inability to take its real nature seriously. It is unexpected because, standing as it does, without qualification, the first sentence says nothing against which Wittgenstein need disagree (if we leave out of account Blackburn's use of the term 'judging' in this context). For example, at 256 where he explicitly mentions 'the language which describes my inner experiences and which only I myself can understand' Wittgenstein says

How do I use words to stand for my sensations? – As we ordinarily do? Then are my words for sensations tied up with my natural expressions of sensation? In that case my language is not a 'private' one. Someone else might understand it as well as I.

As he points out elsewhere, the sense in which my sensations are private is that in which they can be said to be experienced only by me. The issue is not whether there can be a practice of 'judging' whether our own private sensations are thus and so, but whether there can be a language which describes my inner experience *which only I can understand*. Otherwise, of course, talking about our sensations is an everyday occurrence, popular with hypochondriacs, and the possibility of the enterprise is not what is at issue:

'. . . "sensation" is a word of our common language, not of one intelligible to me alone'. The richness of the language we have at our disposal for talking about sensation does not need to be elaborated: it is a vehicle for conveying the nature of sensation to others: we do it by means of analogy, by reference to causal conditions, and by reference to natural expression.

Blackburn essentially objects to what he takes to be the sceptical nature of Wittgenstein's challenge, by the claim that if scepticism works against a private language it will work against a public one as well. According to what he takes to be Wittgenstein's challenge, a form of verificationism, we cannot tell in the private linguist's case either what the difference is or what constitutes the difference, between his really following a rule, his following it incompetently or his being under the illusion that he is following any rule at all. Against this Blackburn simply argues that the public language is in the same case:

if the moral of the rule-following considerations is that we, the public, cannot meet this challenge except by insisting that we do know what we mean and that we mean the same, and know this by knowing our intentions, then the would-be private linguist can avail himself of the same liberty. (99)

But this hardly meets Wittgenstein's point, which relies neither on verificationism nor on memory scepticism: in the public language we take part in a practice, in the private case we cut ourselves off from the particular practice within which *the use of terms* is embedded and the consequence is that we have nothing left but illusion. As Blackburn himself says, it is like driving an imaginary motor car or playing an imaginary piano. As far as memory is concerned, the point is *not* that an unaided individual memory is unreliable, or may for all we know be unreliable, but that *there is nothing determinate for it to remember*, because the familiar publicly devised activity, of obeying a rule, or naming a sensation, or giving an ostensive definition, has become that activity in name only: the private linguist is no longer doing what we *call* 'obeying a rule', 'naming a sensation', etc. He is doing something that is disconnected from the technique of these activities. That is why he is deluded. It has nothing to do with verificationism at all. The use, the custom, the institution of ostensive definition, in the absence of its public construction, becomes nothing at all. There is nothing that one is supposed to remember either rightly or wrongly. In the absence of any criteria for what constitutes the right or the wrong procedure, whatever is going to seem right is right. The misunderstanding is to suppose that we are really talking about someone settling down to offer an ostensive definition all by themselves, in a private interlude, and to suppose that the challenge is to the effect that the guy will get it wrong without a little help from his friends. But that scenario already presupposes a public use, an activity called ostensive definition, which is public and in principle intelligible. This linguist could tell us what he was up to, could communicate the sensation he is referring to. Wittgenstein's point is an essentially anti-Cartesian or anti-Lockean manoeuvre, as Blackburn makes clear, attempting to overthrow a whole model of language. The inner pointing move just forgets that pointing is an intelligible convention with an already complex linguistic background. You don't tend to point for your own benefit anyway, and the issue is what would constitute *inventing* such a practice in private: what would make it 'pointing'? You point because you are explaining to someone else, and pointing is something understood, a practice with a learnt significance, not merely a motion of the hand.

Blackburn does consider the point that in the public language there is a technique or practice within which terms are embedded, and that such a technique is absent in the private case, but he deals with it in a way that shows he misses its significance. He deals with it on the general rather than the particular level. The point is not that there happen to be techniques in the public language and no techniques in the private language: it is easy enough to remedy that in the way that Blackburn actually does, which is by saying, well, OK, let us *imagine* techniques in the private language. But the point, rather, is that there are *particular* techniques in the public language already for the use of the most fundamental linguistic acts, which make those acts the acts that they are, which make the relevant terms the terms that they are, from which the use of those terms is *divorced* in the purported private case. Blackburn says

> But suppose on the contrary that the private linguist's performance *is* part of a technique which he is forming, testing, trying to render reliable. The technique is to bring order into his life. By correlating the recurrence of one experience with the recurrence of others of related kinds . . . the private linguist can begin to find order in his subjective world . . . (100)

Blackburn is talking about an enterprise rather than a technique. But let us look at the plausible phrases constructed in the language that no one else is supposed to be able to understand: 'to bring order into his life', 'the enterprise to which the classification of private experience belongs . . .'. These phrases are plausible because they are the names of possible activities, historically developed, which we can readily render intelligible to ourselves: we know what this 'private linguist' is doing because Blackburn is giving it deft public expression. There is no hint, in the contexts in which we could more or less readily place them, of an engagement in a so-called private language. But Blackburn is drawing tacitly on the publicly intelligible interpretations we are likely to make of these phrases, in order to render plausible his claim about the private zone. There is already something we understand by the procedures of 'bringing order into our subjective life', 'classifying our feelings/sensations'. These are identifiable procedures. But the private linguist must be supposed *not* to be doing the things that we understand by these expressions. If he were it would not be the disputed private act whose possibility Blackburn seeks to defend. The trouble is that the public has been here already. The private linguist is deluded if he thinks he is doing so. He is doing something else, under the same rubric: but it is at the level of the rubric that the identity ends. He must now justify the use of that rubric by reference to the publicly intelligible activity with which it is associated. But *ex hypothesi* he cannot do this, either to others or to himself. It is as though in imagination we were looking at the contents of a screen in front of us but which depend, in real life, upon projection from behind. But there is no projector, we are trying to imagine the presence of the phenomenon in the absence of its necessary conditions. 'It is not a matter of course that a person is making a note of something when he makes a mark.' A private language which no one else could in principle understand would have to be, not one in which there were secret codes for the fundamental activities of language, but one in which the fundamental activities of language that we are familiar with were absent too, in which expression were given to something entirely other.

To use one of Wittgenstein's metaphors, the intended rule provides a measure or yardstick to lay along a new sensation, which will then conform with it or not as the case may be. Let us say that a man is *faithful* to the original christening if there was an original episode of ostensive definition of this kind, which gave him a definite intention to call only sensations of a certain kind or quality 'S', and if the man later uses that intention as a rule which allows some sensations to *be* 'S', and disallows others. (95)

One can see why Blackburn should be puzzled by the anti-private language argument, because once our original ostensive definition is off the ground then the 'problems do not look very convincing'. But the problems actually start with the original and, it seems, entirely unsuspected, ostensive definition:

'But I can (inwardly) undertake to call THIS "pain" in the future' – But is it certain that you have undertaken it? *Are you sure that it was enough for this purpose to concentrate your attention on your feeling?* (my italics)

This says nothing about unreliable memories, but rather something about the conditions under which someone can be said to have 'undertaken to call' something by such and such a name, with the implication that that is not done by concentrating one's attention on the feeling. A person can only be faithful to the original christening if indeed there was an original christening. But what has to be justified and has not been is the claim that we have here a genuine case of ostensive definition rather than a bare pointing. 'Bare pointing' does not quite capture it, either: pointing is a conventional act, a gesture with an understood meaning. Let us suppose then that our private linguist is actually the solitary inventor of language. Not only would he be providing himself with ostensive definitions, he would be inventing ostensive definition. The rejoinder is likely to be that it is not an act of bare pointing but an ostension with a definite intention that sensations of this kind should be called 'S'. But the rejoinder fails as it stands because the intention to call something 'S' can only succeed if there is a genuine action of this kind, around which an intention can be formed. In other words, it is not enough to say to oneself that one intends to call this 'S' in the future. What makes it true that my uttering the word 'pain' in the presence of a certain sensation constitutes the act of *calling it pain*? What distinguishes it from a cry of joy, a groan of dismay, a grunt of surprise, a post-hypnotic reflex, a warning, a mantra, a . . . But one doesn't, anyway, just call something something. One uses a name in the context of a proposition or, better, in the context of an illocutionary act with a determinate content. Because we have agreement about what things are called, we can draw each other's attention to things – 'look, there's a big fat pheasant in the field over there' . . . 'S' could hardly be used to draw my own attention to a sensation whose presence I should already need to know about to be in a position to draw my own attention to it by the use of a name.

It is tedious nowadays to relate, but we know well enough that people are not taught the meaning of terms *simply* by ostensive definition. There is already a great deal of linguistic stage-setting implied: it's hardly the aboriginal act. (The act of pointing, upon which ostension depends could be based upon the act of reaching out, anticipated by others.) The way that one is being invited to direct one's attention already depends upon an assumed background of knowledge and training. The trainee is already supposed to have realised that we are concerned with the colour, or the length, or whatever. Ostensive definition is a relatively sophisticated practice, and in teaching someone what something is called, we also show the trainee the place of the term in the discourse: at the same time they are learning something about the world, they learn what kind of thing something is, its place, for example, in practical life. This goes quite against the unWittgensteinian protestor: '"Once you know *what* the word stands for, you understand it, you know its whole use"'. The point, rather, is that 'when we speak of someone's having given a name to pain, what is presupposed is the existence of the grammar of the word "pain": it shows the post where the new word is stationed'. In the case of the private linguist the new word is posted nowhere: it is a determination to insist on calling the disputed act an act of calling a sensation 'S' in the absence of the conditions which make the act of calling something something the act that it is. In the absence of these surroundings it is less than a bare pointing. To call something by its name is to show its position in discourse: it is a learnt, public use: when we imagine someone calling the sensation 'S' we take all that quietly for granted, import secretly what we ourselves have put an embargo on.

the rule fixes the connection between the term and the private sensation, lying solely in my mind. (93)

This is confused. I do not need rules here at all. It may be that applying a term is a *case* of obeying a rule, or that obeying a rule is a *case* of applying a term: the two activities are analogous, light is shone on the nature of the one by reflection on the other. But we hardly use rules *in order* to apply terms, because that would require expertise in a certain kind of activity as an explanation of our ability to perform the same kind of activity. I learn to call a certain kind of thing by a certain name. So I am already disposed to think of what lies before me as an example, a token. When I come across a new case I already know what it is called. The introduction of a rule to fix the connection is entirely otiose. In order to apply the rule I must already know what it is supposed to tell me. It requires me to recognise that it is this sensation rather than any other, that it is this name rather than any other. I already *know* the conditions under which the rule is to be applied. I already know what the rule is supposed to show me. Here is another 'S'. I have a rule to call only sensations of a certain kind 'S' . . . Which kind? Why, the kind I call 'S'.

End of September. It is four o'clock in the afternoon, the clouds have gathered, the thunder grumbled, the rustle of the wind through the trees, the thunder nearer, the wind stronger, the sky darker. I took a cold shower and then the lights went out, the rain swept down in the gusts of the wind, the green trees, the grey sky. Out on the verandah later I looked down at the clean leaves, smelt the wet, metallic earth. The lights came on, but only with a charming yellow dimness of no practical use. The rain is heavy and hard now, the sort you might dance naked in, and the thunder rolls, the wind dies: on the drive the ruts from the rickshaws in yesterday's rain have now filled with water: streams pour from holes in the gutter, a few crows call. The thunder just growls lazily around the sky, the rain just falls, the storm takes its leisure.

In the last few days I have felt myself on the edge of the presence of a reality which seems set to extinguish me in some way: to be frank it is humanly frightening. The self-preoccupations of the conscious mind, the chatter and the calculations, seem absurd and yet expected. I must go on and make myself wise.

31st October. 12 o'clock, an assassination attempt on Mrs Gandhi.

A revision of the Cosmological Argument: suppose we start to *investigate* the possibility of an unconditioned reality, suppose we realise the contingency of this world, and then wait: for a dawning. But when the

Buddhists talk of unconditioned they imply a not being conditioned by greed, hatred and delusion.

1st November. We huddled over the World Service, eager for news. All India Radio was less forthcoming. Then we thought we would go to the restaurant for something to eat, though it was unnaturally quiet outside. We walked down the street, there were a few people out, but the silence was marked. There was no traffic, a stray bicycle, and, as it soon became apparent, the whole place was deserted of rickshaws: the restaurant was closed, and so was everything else, the ground-floor of all the buildings dark, the shutters down, lights on only in the flats above: there was hardly anyone about, and we walked quietly back: the people we saw had a numb, subdued look, attention as usual caught by the sight of foreign faces, but in a way almost unseeing. We cooked a meal together, which we would not normally have done.

This morning there was the usual bustle on the streets, scores of cyclists, but few buses or trucks, a few rickshaws, small groups of men standing near the news vendor, an air of helplessness. There were also youths, with an excited look in their eyes – though this is Pune you could feel it, their sense that during this hiatus we could do what we want: you felt the presence of half-formed speculation as they looked at you, vaguely casting you in some scenario. But this was far from Delhi where there was danger for Americans. I saw no Sikhs for several days.

14

What we get a purchase on, or apprehend, or *grasp*, through the senses or through instruments of observation, is what is there available to just these forms of cognition. But what we thus grasp in the midst of our given projects becomes the immediate focus of habitual attention, and we normally do not attend to *that*. For us there is nothing beyond the periphery, we are scarcely aware *of* the periphery, though we are in no position to make that judgment. We do not look back over our own shoulder . . . unless we have already been seized from behind. So we cannot say that there are no modes of being outside the reference of the senses. But can we say that there *are*? All we can do is begin to track the effects of meditation, trace the pattern of what begins to unfold. It may be that first we learn of a richer pattern to be discerned through the senses, as one enters a field of wonderful energy, light dancing through the branches of the beeches in late October, enters it willingly and allows it to work upon one's being. You return to normal consciousness, to its cramps and crises, and you see that grasping is a kind of avoidance of the unknown, a fearful holding on to what we know, inhibiting the flows of energy that surround us, except along the channels of our settled and established desires. So grasping goes with avoidance and ignorance. We are *tensed*, more or less rigidly, around particular projects and habits of perception, and refuse to relax.

CHAPTER THIRTEEN

'. . . *sinne / like clouds ecclips'd my mind*'

I

I have a recurring image, the elders of some city overlooking a plain gathered at the walls, gravely. It is night and someone is holding up a torch. The gates remain open. They are calm, but know they will probably be put to the sword. One of them says quietly, I can hear them coming . . .

Evagrius Ponticus (Simon Tugwell, 1984, 25ff) described the trains of thought (*logismoi*) which distract us during prayer and daily life. They need to be overcome, like the Buddhist 'hindrances', for the sake of entering the mind's 'native light'. Sadly Evagrius' nice taxonomy grew into the Seven Deadly Sins, a description which belongs to a different mind-set. In fact they are the natural expression of the present state of our energies at this point in our evolution. They are 'passions':

Evagrius, rather mysteriously, says that once we have reached a certain degree of passionlessness, the mind becomes aware of its own native light.

One should respond to the premises of the philosophers with the diagnostic intent of the spiritual writer, which is really what a philosopher should be. We should be concerned to liberate each other. It turns out, I am pleased to notice, that the 'fruit of passionlessness is love'. Such a statement is essentially empirical, but it can hardly be tested immediately by reference to one's own present experience, since it is the forms of our experience that are being *interrogated* by such claims, as I keep saying. You would have to wait until you had become 'passionless': which is not the same as 'emotionless', far from it. You have to follow the *procedures* by which you are carried from the unregenerate to the regenerate state. In the Buddhist tradition you have to free yourself from the 'defiling passions' or *klesas*. They are what have to be 'snuffed out', as a candle, the extinguishing of *nibbana*, not an 'extinction of the self', whatever that is supposed to be. The relations between states of mind and behaviour is obvious when we think of Evagrius's list of *logismoi*. The 'passions' are not merely trains of thought which distract a person in prayer, but manifest themselves in behaviour. Overcoming, or transforming the passions, is done on the street and in the house rather than simply on the meditation mat. The goal is the establishment of a passionless, a '*klesa-less*', state of mind through and in behaviour, where the battle is lost or won. And it has to be motivated, this struggle, by the ethical perception that otherwise one *continues to cause harm*, which one cares about for the sake of those who are thus harmed. The insistence on kindness or charity, on the part of spiritual writers, rather than on the winning of 'mystical states', simply reflects the realisation that states of mind find their natural expression in behaviour – behaviour has its interior in 'states of mind', it might be better to say. One needs consciously to control the expression of the passions, not as an end in itself but as the means of their growing elimination in favour of 'higher states' (Arnold and Mill again), which can come through the more strongly as the passions lose their grip, come through in the form of *love*. You can only see what is wrong with these forms of self-preoccupation and distraction through *contrast*. I say that, but maybe I should be more careful. We may be able to see *that* something is 'wrong' through reflection on our own behaviour, without attaining the awareness of the contrast, before, I suppose, we are reduced again by sin and feel, as Tugwell says, its bitterness. We may have the *idea* of an alternative without achieving or realising it. But it seems to me that already the bitterness or unsatisfactoriness that we feel when we see the damage we are doing, or reflect upon the damage that we have done, is the first probing intimation of a higher state of mind, Arnold's 'ethically higher self', Tanabe's *tariki*.

We do not, by the way, recoil from an action because we think it is 'wrong', or feel impelled towards doing it because we think it is 'right'; we call it 'wrong' to express our felt recoil, 'right' to express our impulsion towards it . . .

But the talk of a contrast, and of a state that is 'higher', forces us surely to state the terms in which it comes out *as* 'higher'. I do not think there is anywhere to go, from that point of view, except to invoke Mill's competent judge who *prefers* the life dominated by the higher pleasures to the one dominated by the lower, who feels the *bitterness* and constriction of its loss, until, that is, it fades from memory. That is why 'memory' is so vital in Plato and Augustine. Remember that the higher pleasures are not just the pleasure of intellect, but of *imagination and the moral sentiments*. The use of 'preferable' over 'preferred' is an expression of recommendation, I suggest, grounded in an *epistemic* judgment that under appropriate circumstances others *would* come to the same preference. In other words, the competent judge (Mill) speaks with a universal voice (Kant). 'Preferable' may well imply 'ought to be preferred' but we shouldn't assume so rapidly that the ought implies some kind of moral obligation to prefer. It simply implies an expectation of agreement, though with attitude, it must be said, since we are likely to look askance at those who do not meet this expectation. But *that* doesn't imply that the expectation is a 'moral' one.

Tugwell said that the reference to the 'native light' was mysterious, and treats it as a metaphor. I am not so sure. There are Chinese references to the 'circulation of the light'. Love is the natural outcome of a concentration of the person which supersedes the natural preoccupations of a lower level of energy. This is something about which one cannot pretend. One may only speak out of the awareness of that contrast, make a report. I do not think I am a very reliable informant. *And anyway I am wrong to put it like that, that love is the outcome of a particular concentration of energy of a person.* It is quite the other way around. There is a certain concentration of our vital forces that we call 'love', a concentration that begins with a weak attention that cannot much sustain itself, to the well-being of another. It is the idea of that disinterested relation to others that does the work, not the talk of a concentration of energy, though it is not effective until it reaches the level of concentration that allows action. That is what I am calling 'temperance', 'mindfulness', *sophrosune*. Meanwhile people need 'continence', once we have chosen our goal, or better, once our goal has chosen us, once we have discovered where we want to go:

by continence we are collected together and brought to the unity from which we disintegrated into multiplicity.

But here Augustine was talking specifically about *sexual* continence. In any event, our lives constitute a movement between incontinence, continence and temperance. We don't reflect much about the latter because it is so little part of our experience, but that doesn't mean that no reality corresponds to it amongst the possibilities of the human psyche. We come back to the tyranny of reason and the claim of reason to rule. In Cicero's more relaxed version of the Zopyrus incident Socrates comments that the vices he had at birth had been 'overpowered by reason'. Brought up, as we might be, in the belief that reason is the slave of the passions, we might ask, how *could* reason be a stronger force than the passions, a question tellingly asked of Kant by Schiller. But the seeds of Schiller's own solution – that the natural force of impulse and inclination must come to flow in the same direction as reason – is already partly there in Plato's view that in the harmonious soul 'spirit will obey and support' reason – e.g., in the form of indignation in the face of recalcitrant impulses. But Socrates' remedy depends upon an unconscious *cunning* of reason: spirit is *duped* into obedience.

What I mean is that reason alone cannot hold out against the passions. The power of judgment about good and evil that Socrates attributes to reason *essentially needs* the support of 'spirit'. Its judgments have to *motivate* us to act in its light and to constrain unruly impulses, and to motivate us it has to represent (and thus not misrepresent) to us the world as it moves us. But, as I have already said, reason's *conception* of the well-being of the whole person it supposes itself to speak for can be a repressive and distorted one, and the repression comes from *us*, for believing it. Matthew Arnold (1932) has something similar to say, correcting a one-sided view of culture as 'making reason and the will of God prevail':

Only, whereas the passion for doing good is apt to be overhasty in determining what reason and the will of God say, because its turn is for acting rather than thinking, and it wants to be beginning to act; and whereas *it is apt to take its own conceptions, which proceed from its own state of development and share in all the imperfections and immaturities of this, for a basis of action*; what distinguishes culture is, that it is possessed by the scientific passion as well as by the passion of doing good; that it demands worthy notions of reason and the will of God, and does not readily suffer its own crude conceptions to substitute themselves for them. And knowing that no action or institution can be salutary and stable which is not based on reason and the will of God, it is not so bent on acting and instituting, even with the great aim of diminishing human error and misery ever before its thoughts, but that it can remember that acting and instituting are of little use, unless we know how and what we ought to act and to institute. (*Culture and Anarchy*, 45, my italics)

Institutions to improve the young, one assumes, with 'reason and the will of God' the ciphers for moral discernment: and Arnold highlights the problem that we keep on refusing to face, keep on deferring. So what is going to count as human flourishing?

2

And so to something important, there are many ways of 'flourishing', there is a multiplicity of ultimate ends and so we need a commitment to pluralism without a descent into relativism. Okay, then, there are rational limits on human ends. No, it's not that there are 'rational ends', even if this notion is interpreted as 'expressive rationality' as the late Martin Hollis concluded. This is partly because there are also rational limits on self-expression, and self-expression, anyway, needs to be tempered by *Entsagung*, by renunciation, a closure which opens up the self against the odds, it is claimed. I have to insert the fact of my debt to Martin Hollis, formerly a senior colleague, who simultaneously encouraged and baffled me and forced me by his brilliant, kind shafts to think harder than I had thought I could, thus bringing me into a space I might not otherwise have entered.

The way to present the relation between Reason and Action is by way of the idea of *sensitivity to particular truths*. (Notice that I did not write 'Truth' here.) We have knowledge on the one side, ignorance and delusion on the other, and in between is action and the pursuit of goals. We act, we deliberate, in the light of our knowledge of particular truths. Sometimes we lose sight of them, and go for long periods without the *memory* of them, and then we discover them again, and then we cannot act in their light but they remain in our memory. A rational being acts in ways that are sensitive to many truths, or perceived truths or beliefs. The realisation that *'love is the power that moves the human heart by consent'* is one of them. Our actions reveal our knowledge or ignorance of this. Sometimes we realise we are acting in a way that runs counter to our acknowledgment of this fact. So we are not wholly converted to this truth in our actions. It then becomes a measure or standard by which we judge the sense or foolishness of our own actions or those of others. And maybe that realisation gives point to the claim that love is an outcome of 'passionlessness', since it is our passions that remain unconverted to what we acknowledge to be true. *You cannot have by force what can only be given by consent.* And you need to learn what you can only have through consent. Macbeth became aware of this at the point when he wanted what he knew he was now incapable of asking for. He no longer knew how to win anything other than by force. But he still knew what he now could not look to have. Sometimes we can mark and trace the slow dawning of such truths in a person's conduct, in their maturation. I am going to have to say that the concept of 'human flourishing' is *already* a moral notion, and so cannot *ground* morality, and it is constituted by what we *know* and what we can act in the light of. Perhaps instead of Mill's 'higher and lower pleasures' we should have what a person knows and what they *don't* know.

And if we turn the coin, we find ourselves acting in the *false light* of particular delusions: 'a little water clears us of this deed'. Or more mundanely, the persistent delusions about what will make us happy, what we *find* does not in fact make us happy, which we then forget, and go through the process again, and then again.

We could follow Kierkegaard, with some caution, and refer to 'subjective truths' and to the distinctive nature of their appropriation. What, after all, are the conditions under which one learns the distinction between what depends upon consent and what can be had through the use of force. Maybe there are people who only know what can be had by force. What kind of conversation can be had with them about the things that depend upon consent? What a person knows and what they are ignorant of or deluded about provides the moral framework of their actions, and the criteria for whether they are 'flourishing'. There is a myriad of such truths, or contested truths, that people know or fail to know. Arnold's claim was that *'happiness follows virtue'*, essentially a biblical claim, though one found also in other traditions. If this is true then people pursue their happiness in the knowledge of its truth or in ignorance of it. Or, *he who would find his life must lose it, unless a grain of wheat . . .* And similarly, and perhaps more crucially 'the Four Noble Truths'. People act in the knowledge of, or in ignorance of, the 'truth' that human suffering is caused by craving, aversion and ignorance, and that it is overcome by the eradication of these mental states . . . And so forth. These are 'truths' that can be discovered, tested, confirmed or disconfirmed. The point of all this is that moral philosophy becomes the analysis of the forms of *moral intelligence*. 'Harm' or 'well-being' are then partly defined by reference to people's relation to truth and delusion. 'Human flourishing' becomes a matter of *learning from experience*, of moral change. We then have space for talk of the conditions for the possibility of action, for talk of the conditions for receptivity to truth. We live in the knowledge or ignorance of the laws of *karma*, of cause and effect as it impinges on human life, and its operations are independent of our knowledge or ignorance, we burn our fingers, we burn those of others, in a myriad ways. Most of us don't *want* to harm others, and it is painful to discover that we had been ignorant of the ways in which we do, our unconscious tyranny, or whatever it might be. Moral realism is simply a matter of moral intelligence about the truths that affect us. There is no question of a *moral imperative* here, that we ought to act according to the truth, avoid delusion, etc. The point is that we rebound against delusion and ignorance when we find out the truth, we simply seek to take account of how things are in our deliberations, it is what we do, not what we are morally obliged to do, whatever that means. And clearly, it is just because we feel the force of the truth and its impact on our life that we also seek to avoid it, under the counter pressure of what we wish to be we avert our gaze from the truth, and we do this because we *know* that if we pay attention to it we shall be forced to change. The truth of my situation comes to me as I stroll over to the bookshop, and then I greet a friend as I walk in, but the thought comes back and I uneasily attend, but here is a new translation of the Elegies, I wonder how it compares with the old one, oh this is *terrible*, I glance up and catch sight of that pretty girl again, chastely cast my eye down once more to the page, then remember I have a class, notice as I hurry off that the thought had left me, but there is no time for that now . . .

Wisdom and virtue here get their sense. We are wise to the extent that we are undeluded and our virtue consists in our ability to act in the light of what we have learnt.

The question of how we should live is answered by reference to, cannot be answered independently of, our ascertaining of the truths we act in the light of, our dispelling the false light of delusion. The traditional problem with trying to secure the criterion of morality by reference to 'happiness' or *eudaemonia* or 'human flourishing' has always been the contestability of different accounts of 'flourishing'. It is easy to succumb at that point to an easy relativism or subjectivism. But the account I am offering here undercuts such different conceptions and to some extent provides a standard of judgment between them. It is not the whole story, but it presents a human life in the light of moral intelligence. Our actions and our speech reveal us as knowing or failing to know the common truths of human experience, or as victims of common human delusions. And this is a criterion of our well-being, the richness or the poverty of our life. Knowledge comes close to acknowledgement here, and ignorance and delusion to self-deception. For there is an issue also of bad faith or *mauvaise foi*, what we don't want to allow ourselves to acknowledge. There is certainly a pluralism of ultimate ends that cannot be adjudicated between, but what I am referring to are the *horizons of thought* within which these ultimate ends are pursued, and *they* are a matter of knowledge and ignorance: even if it is only that heroin has these effects . . .

3

I still have to tackle the ascent to absolute beauty, still have to write about it, I also mean. The atmosphere is different as you go higher, and, frankly, I cannot cope with it for very long, I have to turn away. But although I have made use of some of the stages of the ascent, I have not attempted to respond to Diotima's talk of 'beauty itself', which is clearly problematic to anyone who does not buy into the Forms. On the other hand, the language Plato uses is clearly compelling, and it does seem to me to reflect very strong meditational experience.

What one has to isolate here is the idea of a calm, a serene, concentration of consciousness – a powerful self-translucency let us call it – an experience the recognisable approaches to which are already felt in the love of physical beauty, the love of moral beauty, and so on . . . but in meditational states the experience is concentrated and heightened to a pitch no longer to be associated with any 'object' of attention, but is the beautiful intensity of consciousness in advance of the return to the extensity of knowledge and action . . . What Diotima says is important. Once you have seen beauty itself, she says,

you will not value it in terms of gold or rich clothing or the beauty of boys and young men . . .

Let us say that there *is* a kind of experience that corresponds to the knowledge of absolute beauty, but let us not call it absolute beauty except for poetic reasons . . . because we are just not so well informed as Plato, nor could be . . . We also know that Augustine has been here, but he is, as usual, more realistic, or, better, he is more aware of *failure* than Plato seems to be, there are more 'groans' in Augustine. We can also move over into an analogous Buddhist context, and savour the wit and wisdom of the Buddha. There is a famous passage which is translated like this:

Ananda: Half of the spiritual life is spiritual friendship, spiritual association, spiritual intimacy!

The Buddha: Say not so, Ananda, say not so. It is the whole of the spiritual life.

What is interesting about this is that the word for 'spiritual friendship', *kalyanamitrata*, is actually an ambiguous one[1] that can be translated as

---

[1] I am grateful to Robert Morrison for pointing this out in discussion.

'association with the beautiful' *and* as 'beautiful friendship', a translation that makes the Platonic parallel more explicit. Now 'association with the beautiful' can be related to meditational experience in just the way I tried to relate Diotima's talk of knowing 'absolute beauty', to delight in the beautiful and the wonder of it, going progressively deeper. And the *fruit* of this profound experience is a *return* to the dawn of the world, to the joyful sight of its beauty and the pity of its cruelty. Generations have trod, have trod, have trod . . . It is *kalyanamitrata* that is the whole of the spiritual life, and the two terms of the ambiguity stand in a causal relation to one another.

4

They have just freed the latest victims of a miscarriage of justice, who had languished in prison for years. There is talk, naturally enough, of bitterness and anger, about ruined and broken lives. All this is said with justice and cannot be gainsaid, people have been destroyed. But it's the sort of thing Tolstoy might have written about, and with an impossible-to-be received message, that it is *conceivable* that one of them could say, in a long retrospect, . . . that he became a better man for having been sent to prison for a murder he did not commit.

One could even imagine someone finally being *glad* that it happened. This is not a claim that seeks to justify anything. And the life of someone else in the same position may well have been destroyed. What does this possibility tell us about the nature of morality? We can only speak with humility and with trepidation about what constitutes the good and what are the means to the good. Any moral philosophy has to be able to encompass the possibility that someone could legitimately be glad that they went to prison for a crime they did not commit, even though it is the grossest injustice. 'Flourishing' or 'well-being' are themselves already moral categories. The man who undergoes a moral change through affliction may regard his *past* self with compassion, which is a form of love. There is no Archimedean point by reference to which we can say who is right. The unregenerate criminal would be dismissive and possibly bemused. The regenerate one does, in fact, see both sides of the question. Someone may say, but how much affliction can one be 'glad' about? We approach the territory of the theodicist here, who invokes the notion of 'soul-making' as a justification for God-permitted evil. But we do not enter it. The thuggish policeman who fakes a confession does something we condemn, we do not allow him to justify his actions by saying, look at the good outcome. And one can only be ready to accept

affliction for *oneself*. I can say, perhaps, I am finally glad that this evil
befell me because of the good it produced. But it would be dreadful to
say that one was glad that evil befell someone else, even if that was the
instrument of one's own moral change. There was also something on
television about a Nazi woman falling in love with a Jewish woman. This
is comparable with the Lady Windermere point, about how radical re-
assessment depends upon the accidents of experience. She could never,
perhaps, have had the sense of a Jew as a fellow human being unless she
had fallen in love with one unknowingly.

Aesthetics. 'I was frightened'; 'it was frightening'; 'I was bored'; 'it was
boring'; 'it gave me pleasure'; 'it was beautiful'. (Kant grounds the judgment that something is beautiful in pleasure.) 'I was frightened' simply
says something about me. 'It was frightening' seems to say more, in particular it seems to imply that a person *ought* to be frightened, reading this
as an expression of the expectation that anyone *would* be frightened by
such and such. But we are often dismissive of such claims, 'come on, it's
just you, you're neurotic, it's not *really* frightening'. Sometimes we are a
little more accommodating. We might say, I can see how a *certain sort* of
person would be frightened, how it would be frightening for *them*. So
there is still a kind of universalisability here. Something is frightening if
a class of persons had reason to be frightened, would perceive a danger.
But the expectation is empirical. And similarly for beauty. The expectation that others will agree is just that, an empirical expectation. In thinking it is beautiful I expect others to take pleasure in it as well, that is to
say, I believe they ought to in the sense that there is reason to think that
they will. It was beautiful implies that anyone *ought* to take pleasure in it,
implying the belief that they will do so. Of course this empirical expectation is often disappointed. But there is still a middle position as with
'frightening'. I can see how a certain sort of person would take pleasure
in that, though I do not myself. Something is preserved of Kant's 'universal voice'. Notice that the issue is more complicated than one of
simple disagreement of the form 'it is beautiful', 'it is not beautiful'. To
say that it is 'not beautiful' is actually to deny that anyone would take the
relevant kind of pleasure in it. There is an intermediate position: I do
not take that pleasure in it myself, but I can see how a person *could*. So
Kant's universal voice is not denied simply because someone says 'I do
not find it beautiful'. It is consistent with people not being able to appreciate the same things. But there is still something very important here,
which may well connect Kant with Plato. 'I can see how someone *like
you*, or someone *in your position* would find it frightening' acknowledges a
relationship between a state of the person and what would frighten

anyone in that state. Similarly with beauty. There is a relationship between a state of the person and what anyone in that state would take aesthetic pleasure in. And now map that on to the ascent to absolute beauty. At different stages of the ascent there are things one can and things one cannot take such pleasure in. There is a tension, though, it might be thought, between Kant's claim about disinterestedness and Plato's that 'beauty' is the object of *eros*. They are, however, compatible. The desire for beauty does not guarantee that one will take the relevant kind of pleasure in it when it is there. It may even be a desire for just that sort of pleasure, but the pleasure is not the satisfaction of the desire, but something else, namely the enjoyment of the state of mind of one who is engaged with the beautiful object. When we think of beauty of soul in the youth rather than in Socrates, what do we have in mind? It is the possibility of virtue that we take pleasure in. They have courage, say, or they reflect on things, they are not conceited, they show signs of compassion, they have an eagerness for life, a generosity of spirit, and so on.

5

I made a distinction between *innocence* and *experience* as part of an attempt to draw attention to the way in which ought-judgments can have an epistemic function in moral contexts, not just a practical and not at all a 'moral' one. The *Judgment of Innocence* is represented by the belief that someone ought to care about the terms of a moral appeal . . . when that implies that there is reason to think that they *will*, because people generally *do*. This is a naive epistemic or inductive expectation, because, of course, the belief is *false*. The innocent person who utters the claim gives expression to their sense of the presence of an anomaly. And the whole point is that it is a dangerous and frightening one. Perhaps I am being a little unfair. In Hume's terms, the expected sentiments, if not the actions, are 'natural' as opposed to 'rare and unusual'. Unfortunately the moral derelict is not that rare or unusual, though maybe a psychopathic absence of the sentiments of morality *is*.

But I did not develop the 'ought of experience'. A person can know very well that someone does not care about 'moral' considerations, and nevertheless form the judgment that they *ought* to, again in an epistemic sense, giving expression to their belief that anyone *would* care, if . . .

But I had problems filling in that 'if' . . . I toyed with the idea that it might be completed by some such phrase as . . . 'if they were properly in possession of their humanity'. In other words, experience might lead someone to make a judgment to the effect that the presence or absence of certain attitudes manifested a *defect*. Taking that line actually allies me with Plato's psychology: justice is the peculiar excellence of the mind, injustice its defect. To be in full possession of one's humanity would be a matter of achieving harmony of soul. Though I should repeat that really, harmony of soul is a result not an end in itself: a certain passionate relation to others, love, brings the state of harmony. Also, such a view implies a developmental view of human nature. However, the really serious question is going to be about the *measurement* of that development. Well, there is certainly going to be disagreement about it. On the other hand, I have already had the thought that one measure is that of the development of *understanding* and *knowledge*. As far as 'well-being' is concerned, we often have to acknowledge a diversity of human ends and aspirations, avocations, talents, gifts, desires, ambitions . . . ways in which people might be said to flourish or fail to flourish. But cutting across all that is the idea of what they understand or fail to understand, in particular about the specific applications of *pratityasamutpada*, 'dependent arising', as it relates to *them*, as it relates to them as *constituted* by it. We do not stand determinately over against the laws of cause and effect, they are part of our very being, the forms of our consciousness depend upon conditions. *That* is the *anatta* doctrine of Buddhism, rather than Hume's 'bundle of perceptions', which are precisely *mine*, though I am subject to radical alteration and holding on will not help because I shall alter anyway, you cannot face it steadily, but this thing is sure . . .

For David Hume reason is the discovery of truth and falsehood, and morality is 'more properly felt than judg'd of'. But we are moral agents within a *world*, and so our assessment of a person's sympathy depends upon an assessment also of their knowledge of cause and effect as they bear on those to whom they show their sympathy, acting within the limits, most like, of 'limited generosity'. The Buddhist path seems to be about the undermining of the limit. And, indeed, morality is not *grounded* in sympathy, sympathy is not its source. As I say, we take it seriously or not depending on the account given of the nature of its object. We must not forget Nietzsche's gibe against Schopenhauer's sympathetic morality, his *laede neminem*, a morality for old women: the point of willing no one harm depends absolutely on what we are going to call *harm*. We need *knowledge* of what is going to cause or remove the pleasure or pain we seek or avoid. It is possible to reconcile Plato's claim that 'reason should rule' with Hume's 'reason is, and ought only to be the slave of the passions'. They do not exactly refer to the same thing when they talk of 'reason', which moves as it were from upper down to lower case when we come to Hume. Hume says that we confound two things, the calm passions and the mental activity of reason, and that is why we make exaggerated claims for its capacity to determine action. But Plato in fact incorporates Hume's distinction in his concept of Reason, because it is part of the soul whose desire is to contemplate the Forms, it is *interested* in the Good and seeks to return to its contemplation. That is why it is in a position to judge what is best for the whole (an instrumental judgment in the light of a prior end). This still leaves us with the need to find a place for Plato's Spirit. Maybe they are 'violent passions' that protest our errancy. In any event, we should not think of the tyranny nor of the slavery of reason in relation to the other parts of the soul or to the passions in the Humean sense. They all need to work together as partners. Democracy within the soul.

We are not going to develop an account of the ethical life which will show how *anyone* might be motivated by 'moral considerations'. But that does not imply that we have failed to show how such reasons *motivate*. What we are motivated by reflects our state. You have to become a certain sort of person. But the concept of human nature is already a 'moral' one and cannot be used to *ground* 'morality'. So there is not going to be a generally accepted answer to the question, 'how should we *live*?' But that does not imply a retreat to relativism. There is no moral relativism because really there is no 'morality'. The reason I have put 'morality' in quotes is that I hope to have dispensed with the conception that identifies the phenomena *as* 'morality' (and which also thereby distorts them). I have, in contrast, simply tried to sketch out natural sources of motivation of the kind that mediates the experienced passage from the condition of Rousseau's 'narrow stupid animal' to that of the 'creature of intelligence'. It is the easiest thing in the world to be ignorant of the fact that our very being is contingent upon conditions, the very form of our consciousness and experience. And so it is easy, too, to suppose that we have a fixed and stable identity. But we do not. You cannot face it steadily . . . But the most important thing is that what you *understand*, or what you have not yet *grasped*, is not a matter of your choice.

Once we focus on understanding and knowledge, we introduce Platonic thoughts about the connection between knowledge and virtue. What is wrong with the idea that a criterion of 'knowledge' here is behaviour and *demeanour*? It depends upon whether you accept the idea that there is such a thing as knowing with one's whole being. That may sound like an easy way to save Plato, but there *are* lesser forms of knowledge or understanding – as well as one in which you are *constituted* by the knowledge, without conflict. This is the point of distinguishing between continence and temperance. The virtue of temperance is to do with the ability to give a matter sustained and undistracted attention. Thus we are talking about the knowledge or understanding of an *undivided* being. Plato is vindicated *via* the question, *who* understands? Elizabeth Anscombe used to cite the adulterer who can correctly be said to 'know' that adultery is wrong but who commits it anyway. Doing so does not show that, after all, they did not know it was wrong . . . And this is surely right. You may baulk at the idea of degrees of knowing. Maybe we should talk rather of degrees of integration of what one knows. Again, though, the issue is that of what constitutes the being of the one who knows, and one of the possibilities is that one can be constituted by the knowledge itself: nothing works against it in contention. 'No one willingly does bad things': if you have a view about harmony of soul as a condition of just action, then clearly you will think this is true: parts of the soul will make their protest, even if the protest is hardly heard. But then, continence implies a condition in which we are unable to do *good* things entirely willingly either. What Plato offers us here is a view about what human beings are like really. His position makes sense of the epistemic 'ought' of experience: there is reason to believe that you would care about these things if you were in full possession of your humanity, if you had achieved the harmony of soul that you inwardly strive for, whether you realise it or not. But it is a large claim when set in the perceived Platonic context, which we cannot anyway allow ourselves. To go back, I have made 'morality' a matter of natural and historically developing motivations – a widening human sympathy goes with an increased expansion of consciousness. Someone who comes, through the connection between virtue and happiness, to Arnold's sense of 'inextinguishable life', knows something that they did not know before and that others who have not followed them also do not know. It would be reasonable for them to see this 'life from righteousness' as the inherent tendency of human beings. And it would give them a perspective from which they could explain why people acted badly, a perspective from which they could say, but you should not be like this, with the implication that you would not be if you had found your own humanity. There is no external point of assessment of this claim. There is, though, an internal one. We *start* with dirty hands, with 'egocentric self-enclosure', and there is a sensed *mounting* to a more abundant life (love is the unfamiliar name . . .) We do not choose where we stand on this trajectory, but describing it takes in the sense of an inner necessity. And now we have to describe its terms, again through the setting out of truths we know or fail to know. A person starts to come round from an anaesthetic and they are in a kind of hell in which they need to protect themselves from *everyone*, a profound distrust and suspicion of the motives of others which they perceive as hostile to themselves. They see everyone as an enemy, or the dupes of their enemy. Everything is given this deluded, sinister, paranoid interpretation, *everything* is sinister. This is deluded, egocentric self-enclosure, this is where we start from, trailing clouds of glory.

He betrayed his friends and it led to their death and his life became thereafter itself a sort of death . . . or are there such casual consequences, as traced out in great literature? Is it true, or is it not, that we commend the ingredients of our poisoned chalice to our own lips? These are the real issues of 'moral realism'.

Another way of putting the point about the epistemic 'ought' of experience is to express the idea in terms of being 'prevented'. This makes a connection with Mill's talk of necessity in terms of 'nothing prevents'. Experience may lead someone to the conclusion that human beings are moved by 'ethical' considerations, *unless they are prevented*. The Kantian version of the Platonic thought, then, is that we are prevented from acting in the light of pure practical reason 'by the sway of contrary inclinations'. When you address the moral derelict, saying, 'but you *should* be moved' (by their distress, say), knowing full well that they won't be, we should understand you to imply that there is reason to believe that the derelict *would* be moved by such things, if they were not prevented. In other words, you expect the relevant attitude to be missing, and you have an explanation: you have traced the cause of the anomaly. (Well, the azaleas *should* be flourishing by now, but they were planted in the wrong kind of soil.)

6

Kant writes plausibly enough about the need of imperfectly rational beings to address imperatives to themselves, but it seems to me he becomes confused when he associates prescription with 'ought'. He claims that 'all imperatives are expressed by an "ought"', and this because they are addressed to a will which is determined by other considerations than the good, and so has to be *necessitated* (hence the imperative). In the case of the holy will, on the other hand,

there are no imperatives: '*I ought*' is here out of place, because '*I will*' is already itself necessarily in harmony with the law. Imperatives are in consequence only formulae for expressing the relation of objective laws of willing to the subjective imperfections of this or that rational being – for example, of the human will. (Paton, 78)

But there is only a contingent relation between the presence of 'ought' and the need for self-addressed imperatives. 'Ought' as the modal auxiliary for a practical judgment applies as much to the holy will as to the imperfectly rational will: it simply implies the presence of a reason for action. Once a reason has been established or has become apparent, the holy will is no doubt determined appropriately, says 'I will' and acts. This is not the case with most of us, but this fact simply reveals the imperfect human context in which ought judgments are uttered, as it were, through clenched teeth. In any case it seems plausible to offer an epistemic reading of the so-called imperative. To claim that as rational beings we *ought* to act in such a way that we always treat humanity, whether in our own person or in that of any other, never simply as a means, but always at the same time as an end, is in effect to claim that there is evidence that this is what rational beings *would* do, by their nature, if they were not prevented by the sway of contrary inclinations, which is precisely experienced as an obstacle to what we feel compelled to do. We *are* moved to treat humanity as an end – unless we are in some way prevented – and to that extent, of course, our actions are in conformity with universal law, in conformity, that is to say, with a conception of what any human being is. And Kant does says elsewhere that human beings are good by nature and evil by nature, good to the extent that we are rational beings, evil to the extent that we have those awful bodies. Again, though, we are not in a position to be so confident about human nature. All we have is the felt experience of *dukkha* and remorse when we act 'badly', and the expansive impulsion towards a greater generosity of spirit, from which we look back at our former selves and its counterparts with compassion. And we are aware of realities formerly concealed from us. Our becoming is traced along the trajectory of moral insight. 'I'm glad now that I went to prison' is one of its baffling, almost impossible statements: we are talking *crucibles* here, not do-gooding, about things whose possibility is humanly frightening.

So what I am really saying about the *Judgment of Experience* is that it makes its judgments on the basis of a learnt and developed human nature, seen as something that is awakened to life, and that it knows the conditions under which this life emerges and those in which its possibility may seem to be destroyed. So it claims to know what a human being would do in particular circumstances unless they are overcome by the passions, or whatever, or are not allowed entry into the conditions of ethical action. It claims to know what human beings have become under historical conditions, what can be created and what can be destroyed.

7

What may tempt a philosopher to think that moral statements possess some sort of 'mind-independence' is the fact that there is sometimes a determinate answer to the question, about some proposed action, 'what *makes* it wrong?' Furthermore, a child seeking reassurance, who exclaims, 'it's *true* that it's wrong, isn't it?' may reasonably be given the same determinate answer. But this reference to some action judged to be 'wrong' is hopelessly under-determined. So let us look at an example. Simon Blackburn (1984) offers an apparently promising one – 'it is wrong to kick the dog' – and he says,

it is not because of the way we form sentiments that kicking dogs is wrong. It would be wrong whatever we thought about it. Fluctuations in our sentiments only make us better or worse able to appreciate how wrong it is. (217)

So far as fluctuations in our sentiments go, the intentionality thesis allows space for the *rooting* of them in specific kinds of situation, their objective correlative, which is also a criterion of their identity. If our emotions are unstable, the criteria of identity are not, for they represent the cognitive element which a person may hang on to despite the ebb and flow of affect. Though the thought that such and such an action would be *wrong* may be fairly drained of affect, it is nevertheless the channel along which feeling flows, and even the heroic, willed refusal to commit the act draws strength from the motivating description, and represents a modification of feeling, feeling as it is under certain conditions. The idea that our sentiments are subject to *fluctuation* reflects, of course, a particular, contingent experience of them, and the philosopher's distrust of the sentiments reflects too thin a view of their nature. However unstable what we call our feelings are, their counterparts in the language, the evaluative *foregrounding* or *isolating* of specific phenomena, by which we give them expression, is itself relatively stable, even in the midst of affective instability. The relationship between evaluation and description reflects the intentionality of motivation.

But Blackburn's comment seemed to provide some grounds for a 'quasi-realist' position on moral statements: it seems to be true that the action is wrong whatever we think – or feel – about it. It also helpfully provided a *caveat* against a too simple view of the implications of asserting a 'subjective source' for ethics. He goes on to give the obvious answer to the question, 'what makes it wrong?' and it is the answer one might well give to the child who wants to be reassured that it is *true* that it is wrong to kick the dog: 'what makes it wrong to kick the dog is the cruelty or pain to the animal'. If we wanted to reassure the child we may well say that it is *true* that it is wrong to kick the dog because doing so causes it pain. But is this really such a satisfactory example of a moral statement whose candidature for truth or falsity we can now go on to discuss? The example seems to imply that there is something in virtue of which an action is wrong, something, moreover, that makes it wrong whatever any particular individual may think or feel. In fact it is completely unilluminating. It does no more than show the relation between one description of an action and another, one that presents it precisely as the focus, the intentional object, of a particular sentiment. Kicking dogs is wrong because it causes them pain, and causing an animal pain is something there is some reason to expect that anyone will recoil from, though as we know very well the expectation may be disappointed. Presumably, though, we should want to say, not only that it is 'wrong' to kick the dog, but that it is 'wrong' to cause animals pain, or needless pain, which is, after all, what is 'wrong' with kicking the dog. But if it is 'wrong' to cause unnecessary suffering, or, to use an example of Timothy Sprigge's, 'wrong' to cause pain to others for one's own enjoyment, then *what makes it 'wrong'*? I present that as a rhetorical question, since I do not think the case is parallel with asking what makes it wrong to kick the dog. That question, I suggest, demands to know what the relevantly motivating description is, a motivation whose general direction is *expressed* in the use of the word 'wrong' in connection with causing unnecessary pain.

But if what I presented was merely a rhetorical question, can we not ask, nevertheless, whether it is *true* that causing unnecessary suffering is 'wrong'? Some philosophers would simply treat it as an emotive utterance, not to be taken as a genuine statement at all. Others may see it as a truth to be discerned by rational insight. Others again may see it as the expression of a principle we simply have to choose or commit ourselves to. My own position is closest to emotivism, insofar as I agree that the statement draws a kind of exclamatory attention to the intentional object of an emotion. But it is to an emotion, as it were, that we expect to find. And here we must return to the discussion of the epistemic ought, so that I can offer at the same time a naturalistic reduction of so-called ethical statements *and* an emotivist reading of such terms as 'wrong'. What qualifies my genuflection to emotivism is that while I think that 'wrong' gives expression to a response, it is to a response that *anyone ought to have*. What I mean by this is, a response there is reason to believe anyone *will* have. Let us leave on one side for the moment the necessary qualification 'unless they are prevented'. We are initiated into these expectations, learning profiles of personhood in the acquisition of language. It might help to make this plausible if I point out that when a speaker says something like 'you shouldn't kick the dog' and offers as a reason 'because it will cause it pain' they do so to remind, or bring to the attention or understanding of the hearer, a *fact* which they expect to move them, a fact, that is to say, that they think *will* move them, and this thought is grounded in the background belief that people *are* moved by such considerations, a belief which gives point to the attempt to draw attention to the relevant fact, an attempt premised on the assumption that anyone will be moved, or, with experience, may be moved, or may just possibly still be moved. To exclaim that it is *wrong* expresses, as do tones of voice, etc., the nature of that motivation, but it is essentially a motivation that it is believed anyone ought to have in the sense I have indicated.

I think the implication of this is that to claim that some form of conduct is 'wrong' implies the belief that it is a form of conduct that anyone ought to avoid, and this is to be construed as: a form of conduct there is reason to believe anyone *will* be moved to avoid. The advantage of this analysis, incidentally, is that it allows for non-expressive uses of 'wrong', including its use in non-asserted contexts. Thus when I say that x is 'wrong' I may or may not *express* the attitude I thereby imply that anyone ought to have. In non-asserted contexts, where I say, 'if x is wrong, then . . .' I am implying 'if x is such that anyone ought to avoid it, then . . .', which is to say, 'if x is such that there is reason to believe that anyone will avoid it, then . . .'.

If what I say is more or less on the right lines then we need to part company with the simple emotivist analysis of 'it is wrong to cause unnecessary suffering'. What I offer instead is 'causing unnecessary pain is something anyone ought to be moved to avoid', which is to say, 'causing unnecessary pain is something there is reason to believe that anyone will be moved to avoid, unless they are prevented'. And often I shall be giving *expression* to the attitude I believe anyone ought to have. Part of the interest of a quasi-realist view of moral statements was to yield statements which, though subjectively derived, nevertheless made a claim to truth independent of what any individual happened to think. But I have already drawn attention to possible truths which are stronger and more interesting candidates for realism. Thus, maybe there is a truth about the conditions under which *forgiveness* is possible, which holds firm quite independently of what anyone happens to think of the matter, as is the case, say, with the truth of 'fire burns'. If we ignore either we are likely to be hurt. The sort of truth I have in mind enters into our conception of good and harm, and is significant for the moral realism I have tried to develop, which is to be distinguished from this present talk of 'quasi-realism'. I have tried to sketch a conception of ethics which shows our moral dispositions to be expressions of determinate states of our spiritual life. The proposition that there is a determinate state in which we would naturally recoil from cruelty, for instance, is certainly truth-claiming, and obviously underpins the evaluations which give expression to it: '*cruelty*'. To the extent that it is an expression of our being, we are harmed if the emergence of that state is suppressed. Such states of the spiritual life are a matter of the *sustaining* or holding together of the relevant sensibility, the holding in focus of the objects of awareness upon which action depends, and the maintaining of the possibility of action itself. The transformation of personhood is thus a matter of the concentration of energy within the relevant forms, forms that construct the person out of an ethical sensibility. The ethical sensibility becomes the form of the person, and the travails of its emergence are the travails of personhood.

8

It is a common experience that when someone finds the ethical sensibility – love as a form of belief in the existence of other persons, one which *constructs* the nature of that existence – when someone finds this perspective and form of contact and loses it again, they experience the loss as a darkening and oppression of the spirit, in a way analogous perhaps to the expense of spirit that occurs in sexual excess. We should associate this darkening of the spirit, not merely with the sense of energies scattered and concentration and focus lost, but with its corollary, what I would call a loss of *world*, a closing in of the horizons, depletion, isolation, envy, hatred, which again is imaged in the sexual life by the experience of lust as 'a drug against imagination of all but carnal forms' (Charles Morgan); and we may contrast this with the sense of energies returned and gathering, increase in intensity answered in extensity of scope, enlargement of sympathy, responsive to a touch, a glance. The ebb and flow of spirit is the epistemological ground of rational expectation in regard to conduct. The ebb and flow is between what Blake calls 'the two contrary states of the human soul', between what Rousseau calls the state of nature and the just society. Blake talks about *the* two contrary states, not about two among a number. He gives us the poles of the natural possibilities. What is crucial is the experience of *oscillation* between them, between the two contrary states of the human soul, between the conditions upon which depend Cruelty, Jealousy, Secrecy, Terror, on the one hand, and Mercy, Pity, Peace and Love, as Blake represented it, on the other. We do not choose between these states, we are *hung* between them, more or less poised in an upward or downward direction. Well, whether there is such a trajectory from one state to the other is something that has to be personally appropriated from experience, the culture and the tradition. What has to be a matter of personal appropriation, a truth that can only be established subjectively, as Kierkegaard would put it, is the experience of an oscillation away from and in the direction of a *determinate orientation*, a tendency away from one form of life and towards another, so that our estimation of the poles is already stacked in favour of the *terminus ad quem*.

It is significant that the negative phases of this movement may be felt as a diminishing of the power of action, and a loss of world, because it entails the loss of the concentration of energy upon which such action depends, and the dismemberment of a formation of the self. Indeed, one of the extreme points of oscillation involves the total eclipse of the perspective by which the contrary pole is constituted. Perhaps the eclipse is usually only partial, manifested in the experience of *incontinence*, which is an important clue. It represents an inability to act in the light of ethical considerations, even though one *is* moved in that direction. Incontinence represents a kind of partial eclipse, a moment between total eclipse and unimpeded vision. It is a state of mind which *prevents* someone from *acting* in the light of acknowledged good. I suggest there are analogous states of mind which can prevent a person, not only from acting but also from being moved by the relevant impressions in the first place. So the claim is that the derelict *would* respond if their vision were not obscured – except that that will not quite do, a person can look and look and not be disturbed or moved . . . We need already from the beginning a *way* of looking, you need to be responsive to respond, to escape the grip of the *Gestell* in which you are held even as you thus hold others, perception under the domination of a will that does not pause in the presence of others.

9

I know that philosophers are not going to take it seriously, because they do not in general take aesthetics seriously, except as a place to find more 'central' issues, but responsiveness can come from what I have called *aes-*

thetic perception and from the experience of art. These are what break it, appetency, on its metalled ways, for a moment or two, meditation for longer . . . Paul Valéry (1980) puts it nicely when he talks about the 'poetic emotion' as the dawning sense of a *universe*. In talking like this he seems to me to draw on the Kantian notion of an aesthetic idea:

> I said: *sense of a universe.* I wanted to say that the poetic state or emotion seems to me to consist of a dawning perception, of a tendency to perceive a *world*, or a complete system of relations, in which people, things, events and acts, though they resemble, *each to each*, those which live in and make up the tangible world . . . stand, however, in an indefinable though marvellously precise relationship to the modes and laws of our general sensibility. (44)

Except that I should want to say that such a dawning perception is also at the same time an alteration in our sensibility itself, it is the dawning perception of a world that is a world for that sensibility. But we need to add that it needs to be an *ethical revelation*, the realised sense of one's own humanity and that of others. Or let us call it just the dawning of a 'moral vision', the ability to see these relations. We have to *break through* into the space of the ethical life. One day we can not know it is there, the next we can be in the midst of moral beauty. It is the obscuration of vision that prevents the possibility of ethical action, that is to say, the *finding* of those forms of contact that determine our treating one another as ends of action. I make that qualification because the image of obscured vision could be misleading: it might suggest that a sort of ethical vision is there all the time, if only the clouds were not in the way. In reality the obscurations prevent the *formation* of that vision.

So the claim that the moral derelict *would* respond ethically if they were not prevented amounts to saying that a certain formation of the person *would* develop if they were not entrenched in the states of mind that prevent it, not an arbitrarily privileged formation, but *the only one we have found* to take us out of *dukkha*, out of the egocentric self-enclosure that we do not know encloses us until we have already begun to escape. The derelict is entrenched, we should have to say, in the known states of mind that prevent the insisting tendency that belongs to them as persons, a development by which we are constituted. It is appropriate, I think, to draw attention to the precariousness of this claim. I have already said that whether we are constituted by this trajectory is a matter to be subjectively established, a truth to be ascertained between persons, and within oneself. It is hardly *well* established, there are too many instances where, if not disconfirmed, it is certainly not confirmed. On the other hand, people do change, and the presence of goodness has had observed effects. So we rely on a view, to be subjectively established – and the philosophers won't like that – about how we are constituted, a view about how anyone is constituted, to the effect that we are progressively constituted around the two contrary states of the human soul, around the trajectory I have described, around the emergence of an ethical awareness, and around the travails of its emergence. And it can start to fade away again. And there are only *two* states of the human soul, it is either Cruelty, Terror, Secrecy . . . or it is the other thing.

If someone's *conception* of a person is derived from the experience of that transformation, a transformation that represents their *Bildung*, then their judgment that the delinquent *ought* to be moved by ethical considerations can reasonably be thought of as epistemic, even if it is compounded by consequential evaluations. The delinquent ought to be thus and so because that is how people are, and how people are is a matter of the embodiment of the natural history of an ethical sensibility. In addressing the derelict in these terms – you should not be like that – the speaker attempts to recall them to themselves. The corollary is that our sense of what is harmful or beneficial is dependent on what we take ourselves to be. If we are constituted by the trajectory towards the ethical life that I have described, then what prevents its possibility is felt as harm, and what furthers it is felt as benefit. We thus have a rational conception of the good that undercuts much moral relativism while being compatible with wide cultural divergences in the expression of determinate spiritual states. This is a point worth highlighting because it is a common enough problem in moral philosophy that while morality is focused on the avoidance of harm or the furtherance of well-being, we have radical disagreements about what is to count as good, what is to count as harm. While there are wide cultural differences in the matter of what will bring about harm, or what will *be* harm, it seems to me that a rational limit is set on such conceptions by the fact, if it is a fact, that we are formed out of a sensibility associated with treating people as ends, seeking to sustain them in their being. But such a progression of *eros is* their being, and if it is undermined they are harmed. *Treating people as ends becomes a matter of sustaining them as beings who have precisely that aim and the sensibility, and its modifications, that such an aim entails*, sustaining each other in the relationships that thus unfold.

I am tempted to talk here in terms of our real constitution, but I think it is a temptation to be avoided. The implication would be that we are thereby fully formed and that there is some independent standard by which we could confirm as much. But maybe we are still forming. The experience of a progressive concentration around the emergence of an ethical sensibility must already to some extent undermine the idea of a fixed self we need to hold on to, and perhaps a doctrine of *anatta* could be developed from the idea that the flourishing of that sensibility is dependent upon conditions. Among those conditions is the steady retrieval of energy from forms of conduct and patterns of reaction and thought that are already *unsatisfactory* (or *dukkha*) from the point of view of the emergent sensibility which already announces itself in pre-reflective unease and '*post-mortem*' remorse.

So, let me say it again, because I find it difficult and it is crucial. I am relying on the notion of an emergent human nature, of a nature that emerges from one state to another under certain conditions. The transition can be expressed in different ways, we move from being a 'narrow stupid animal' to being a 'creature of intelligence', for instance, if we think of Rousseau, for whom this is importantly also a transition from the state of nature, where our lives are dominated by the rule of arbitrary power, to the just society, whose laws are framed to release us from such domination. Although there is an indefinite variety of possibilities of human *expression*, from the point of view of our conduct towards one another there are only, as William Blake put it, *two* (contrary) states of the human soul to be thus expressed, though we are each poised at different points on the trajectory and for most of us our behaviour is the conflicted product of contrary impulses, as though we were balanced precariously, our feet straddling the two sides of the fulcrum of a see-saw, now swaying this way, now that, until we have reached a point of stability, on one side or the other, negative or positive. However, this picture of *anatta*, of a self that changes under certain conditions, needs to be modified. We do not exist independently of the world or of particular forms of relationship to others. Kierkegaard perhaps goes too far in defining the self *as* a relation (that relates itself to its own self) but it does seem that we are constituted by our orientation to the world and by our actions. So the conditions upon which our changing selves depend for their constitution must include our manner of thinking and acting, the alteration in these being an alteration within us. I have suggested that silence, or some form of suspension from normal activity, is one of the conditions under which the possibilities of transformation make themselves manifest, silence or *dukkha*. I have tried to articulate the possible transition as one between a kind of egocentric or communal self-enclosure, partly determined by forms of ignorance and delusion (and we cling to what we think we know and hate what seems to undermine it, because we believe, falsely, that *we* are thus undermined) – and, on the other, an opening up to others which also depends upon allowing ourselves to be worked upon by particular *realities*. Now, we are each the residents or inhabitants of particular states, from which we venture forth with our judgments. I have strongly emphasised the notion of an epistemic or inductive expectation as reflecting the real or at least dominant function of 'ought' in moral discourse, and have suggested that our judgments are naive or tempered by experience. They are essentially judgments about how a person ought to be, grounded in judgments about how people generally are. They essentially reflect the condition of the person who makes them, and the expectation of how people generally are is, as I say, naive or qualified. As people emerge from the darkness of ignorance and delusion and discover responses and forms of relationship that reflect a motivating knowledge that was formerly obscured or impeded, then they will regard the failure of the moral derelict precisely in terms of what their condition prevents them from seeing and doing. There is no archimedean point here that allows us to say that these judgments are *right*. But nor do we choose where we stand.

I wake up in the early hours, and I am conscious, yes, but my consciousness is not distinct from my surroundings, how is one supposed to say this, but I am part of a conscious stream of life in which I am not distinct from the swirling currents all around me, below the level of the surface appearance of things, the primary and secondary qualities of Bodies, which I also know I shall be in the midst of later. And then I find myself with the urgent thought that it is *humanity* that is to be redeemed, not knowing quite what I am thus telling myself. Well, it goes against individualism, the idea of private redemption, of course, and so there is the sense of individuals in their relations – we have to redeem human life itself, we have to become *sangha*. Then, strangely, the 'store-house consciousness', the *alaya-vijnana* – I have a picture of it as a person, a being, of which we are the expressions or the members, *that* has to be transformed and utterly, and is so *pari passu* with our individual exertions. We are the parts of a universal person, restlessly asleep, dreaming of the need to wake up.

It began quietly, almost sombrely, with dimly discerned fantastic images carved in dark wood, men and monsters, gargoyle faces formed in the contours of the sheets and bedspread, then the walls and curtains, gaining slowly as time passed in clarity and verisimilitude, vendors called outside, children played, workmen shovelled gravel, the sun burned through the windows in the afternoon . . . then there were heaving, lumbering, clumsy shapes of humanoid beings among rocks in underground caverns, the air gloomy and red from flames, shadows swaying to the slow action, a lurching group, in dumb concentration, had joined to tear another of their kind to death, limb from limb, without either haste or energy, the torn flesh parted and gave way, meat and bone, pulsing blood spilling down the charnel, down the channelled floor, the flames flickered, red jelly wobbled under skin torn from a breast, a tug at the nipple, accomplished in silence . . . there is complete silence and a charming man in a tailored overcoat climbs from a limousine and waves to the cheering crowds behind the barriers, who then drift away, into small, separate groups, leaving for home, the talk excited, the eyes bright, a boy in a cockney cap walks with his father and his inquisitive eyes are darting everywhere, he comes up close to peer at a monument, unaware of my presence is how it seemed, he looms up before me as though I were not there, invisible to his clear eyes, and others drift towards me, through me and past, I can see their faces clearly as they lean across each other, laughing or smiling, nodding in agreement, recalling the event. I open and close my eyes but all I see are the scenes of human life, panning up close to people's faces, to their eyes, always their eyes, which never meet mine. Troops of cavalry gallop across the plain, soldiers shouting in silence, calling to each other for the courage of brothers, their eyes bright with the hope of valour . . . and a man of power looms, reins in to approve the scene, an oriental general on his horse, the light of success in merciless eyes, the soul in his eyes, in all their eyes . . . a girl sits quietly in her room, in a long gown, her head bent, I come up close to her face, her eyes dream, but not of births, or loss, or estrangement . . . an old woman grieving, her face close up to me, her eyes open, wide and inward, kneels in a chapel and prays, but the soldiers gallop in abandon, leaning forward over their horses' necks, looking across at one another, calling out . . . a party of naked men and women sway in a sombre orgy, a pair of lovers lie quiescently in bed, moonlight through a casement window illumines the disarray of sheets, touches their soft bodies . . . and now a beautiful male head appears above the evening horizon and slowly moves towards me, comes up close, the eyes full of life, the skin luminous and real, but one eye splinters and then splits, a hole takes its place, revealing the light of day and drifting clouds, another head appears, and cracks open at cheeks and temple, it spins slowly round, to show itself only a perfect surface without interior . . .

CHAPTER FOURTEEN

Concentration, continence and arousal

I

My reason for attempting to reintroduce meditational practice into philosophy is that it has the capacity to transform its subject-matter. To attempt to do philosophy in this way depends upon developing degrees of concentration or absorption which are themselves modifications of the consciousness whose structure one is concerned to investigate, and which are also supposed to determine disclosures of reality not otherwise available. An analogy may be found in the activity of attending to or becoming aware of the breath in meditation. This has a tendency to alter the pattern of breathing that is attended to, and makes a difference to the quality of the attention.

Meditational thinking is a concentrated activity of reflection which itself thereby emerges as part of what is there to reflect upon and understand. This is not the claim that reflection must also reflect upon itself, but that meditational thinking brings about a transformation of the phenomena to be reflected upon. The processes of concentration involved in such thinking determine the self, and its access to reality, that are, in general, the subject-matter of philosophy.

Augustine (1991) writes that

by continence we are collected together and brought to the unity from which we disintegrated into multiplicity. (202 [x xxix (40)])

If this were read empirically we should have to ask what grounds there are for the claim that we are thus *restored* to an original unity we have *lost*, and from which we fell. But, on the other hand, it may be true that different degrees of the contrast suggested can be encountered in the process of concentration, a contrast between energies gathered into a unity, and energies scattered and dispersed. In any event, Augustine's point seems to be that sexual continence reinforces the gathering of energies that is demanded by contemplative stability, and that incontinence subverts it. In other words, he represents his own inability to attain a state of continence as an impediment to his spiritual quest. It is an impediment to the process of self-inquiry that constitutes meditative philosophy, since the processes of absorption or concentration, of being 'collected together', determine transformations which become part of the subject-matter of meditative thought, and condition access to reality:

By the Platonic books I was admonished to return into myself. With you as my guide I entered into my innermost citadel, and was given power to do so because you had become my helper . . . I entered and with my soul's eye, such as it was, saw above that same eye of my soul the immutable light higher than my mind – not the light of every day, obvious to anyone, nor a larger version of the same kind which would, as it were, have given out a brighter light and filled everything with its magnitude. It was not that light, but a different thing, utterly different from all our kinds of light. It transcended my mind, not in the way that oil floats on water, nor as heaven is above earth. It was superior because it made me, and I was inferior because I was made by it. The person who knows the truth knows it and he who knows it knows eternity. Love knows it. (123 [vii x (16)])

The translator, Henry Chadwick, here refers in a note to a remark of Plotinus; 'one who has seen the good, the desire of every soul, knows what I mean when I say it is beautiful', and tells us that Plotinus adds that it is known with the passion of love, a reminder of the Platonic thought that the object of *eros*, and what it lacks, is 'beautiful'. Plotinus' remark is of some importance for the epistemology of the spiritual life, both because it indicates a procedure for understanding the nature of communication and because it highlights its difficulties, since the presence or absence of 'realisation' is a *condition* of understanding. There is, by contrast, a covert, almost inevitable, empiricism that tests the claims of others, their 'ideas', we might say, by reference to its *own* 'impressions', without realising that the latter may be too narrow in their scope. This is not to say, however, that we are obliged to rehearse Platonic or neo-Platonic categories about the real and the apparent world. In fact we obviously have to reconsider, in our own terms, precisely what Augustine is here trying to describe, without drawing precipitate conclusions about what it 'must' be, a temptation which confronts Augustine as much as it confronts us. In reflecting on what can and what cannot be said about his experience we face the danger of presuming that we have identified it when we have manifestly not. One is not positing, incidentally, a 'bare' or 'pure' experience below the level of description. The kind of experience that Augustine seeks to describe is conditioned by a set of determinate procedures, and he seeks a metaphorical purchase on it: it is his *philosophical* description that is at issue.

But the immediate question concerns the epistemological status of Augustine's reflections: they imply a discovery about 'what is' which is supposed to depend upon certain transformations of the self. It is only under the condition of a particular withdrawal and concentration of the self that the real nature of things becomes manifest. Augustine describes his entry into the 'innermost citadel' in greater detail a little later, in a way that makes this clear. What it also makes clear, by implication, is something of the nature of the concentration of forces, the *samadhi*, that is involved, and why, in consequence, sexual continence is taken to be a necessity. What is involved is an arduous gathering of forces and focusing of *attention*. Thus he writes:

And so step by step I ascended from bodies to the soul which perceives things through the body, and from here to its inward force, to which bodily senses report external sensations, this being as high as the beasts go. From there again I ascended to the power of reasoning to which is to be attributed the power of judging the deliverances of the bodily senses. This power, which in myself I found mutable, raised itself to the level of its own intelligence, and led my thinking out of the ruts of habit. It withdrew itself from the contradictory swarms of imaginative fantasies, so as to discover the light by which it was flooded. (127 [vii xvii (23)])

Thus seeing the 'immutable light' with the eye of his soul depends upon a progressive withdrawal from the objects of sense, from fantasy and discursive thought. And Augustine diagnoses the extreme transience of his experience of 'the light' as a consequence of his sexual incontinence. Now his remarks about entering into his innermost citadel is reminiscent of language used later by David Hume in his famous discussion of personal identity near the end of the first book of the *Treatise*:

when I enter most intimately into what I call *myself*, I always stumble on some particular perception or other . . . I never can catch *myself* at any time without a perception, and never can observe anything but the perception.

It will be instructive to make a comparison in order to highlight the claim that meditational thinking, entering one's innermost citadel, transforms the subject-matter. It will help to show how the presence or absence of *contemplation* makes a difference to what is there to be reflected upon. What Hume claims to observe, the perceptions he stumbles upon, are impressions and ideas. In seeking to establish that there is no impression of the self, against those who claim that we are at every moment intimately conscious of it, his introspection *as a matter of fact* turns in upon what we might call 'normal consciousness', upon precisely those activities Augustine describes himself as withdrawing from. Hume reflects on what he insightfully describes as a sort of republic or commonwealth of different perceptions linked together, among other things, by the relation of cause and effect. It is not my intention to criticise his procedure, and nor am I trying to show that he ought after all to have found a self. What *is* worth pointing out, though, is that a Buddhist psychology, or a Platonic and Augustinian one, would have shown that what determines a person's mental contents are states of mind that are 'skilful' or 'unskilful', amenable or inimical to ethical and spiritual development, a republic divided against itself or one in internal harmony, states of mind, in other words, that determine *what* thoughts are present, and *what* passions are associated with what impressions and ideas. The *parameters* of Hume's philosophical psychology are constituted by his descriptions of a determinate terrain that remains undisturbed by his procedures. I am not endorsing or rejecting Hume's 'findings'. The point is that as philosophers we are confident that we have the same access as he has to the structures of consciousness he seeks to describe. The real question is whether we have any right to be equally confident about our access to the terrain that Augustine describes, since, it seems to me, Augustine does what Hume fails to do, and what he attempts to describe is partly determined by the changes wrought by his contemplative activity itself, the effects of his withdrawal into his innermost citadel. He describes *vertical* changes that determine the general ethical character of what could and what could not appear on the *horizon*. 'In the flash of a trembling glance' his mind attains to 'that which is', an experience which brings about a re-ordering, or at least the possibility of a re-ordering, of his real preferences. Thus he writes:

I was astonished to find that already I loved you . . . But I was not stable in the enjoyment of my God. I was caught up to you by your beauty and quickly torn away from you by my weight. With a groan I crashed into inferior things. This weight was my sexual habit. But with me there remained a memory of you. I was in no kind of doubt to whom I should attach myself, but was not yet in a state to be able to do that. (127 [vii xvii (23)])

As we have already seen, 'by continence we are collected together and brought to the unity from which we disintegrated into multiplicity'. By contrast Augustine's sexual habit is seen to be the cause of his being torn away. It is hard not to see the general form of his sexual activity entering the very terms in which he describes enjoyment, climax and depletion. His sexual incontinence not only renders his experience of 'what is' transient, but it colours its form and the terms of its description. St Augustine has described a kind of ascent and withdrawal, a gathering of 'force', which brings about a *discovery*. He uses a perceptual metaphor to describe it, which may seem strange, at first, when we consider how he has removed himself from perceptual and discursive contexts. Our ability to judge whether the metaphor of a light seen with the eye of the soul is appropriate depends upon our being able to make a comparison, upon being privy to *both terms* of the comparison, though one can presumably be drawn by the language even when one has no such access: indeed it precisely draws one *towards* such access. Augustine goes to some trouble to *stress* that he is speaking metaphorically when he refers to the light, and yet the word 'immutable' is introduced without comment. Having introduced it, he goes on to say, as we have seen, that the immutable light is *above* him because he was *made* by it, an assertion he makes more general a little later, when he introduces the idea of degrees of being:

And I considered the other things below you and I saw that neither can they be said absolutely to be or absolutely not to be. They are because they come from you. But they are not because they are not what you are. That which truly is is that which unchangeably abides. (124 [vii xi (17)])

This passage shows the mistake of philosophers who take the notion of 'necessary being' to be simply a philosophical device for limiting and explaining contingency. It is clearly a spiritually derived notion, related to a felt experience of 'unchangeable abiding' which is then taken to define what is truly real, by contrast to which our own existence appears imperfect and less real. But Augustine already appears to know too much. We have seen how he carefully qualifies the use of the word 'light'. Even so, he seems to know that it is a light which is both immutable and *creative*. Our own existence, and that of the circumambient world, is taken to be contingent upon it. *How could he know this?* The point, of course, is that he doesn't. He is interpreting the nature of 'what is' and his mind's attaining to it in the light of the theistic tradition to which he already subscribes. He cannot derive immutability from the experience itself. We draw the conclusion that things are mutable on the grounds that we see them or things of their kind in process of change. We can hardly draw the conclusion that something is immutable on the grounds that we have not seen it change, especially in a case where we are about to acknowledge that our experience itself was fleeting and unstable. The issue of continence and the practice of ejaculation are not irrelevant here. The language of ardour, enjoyment and depletion, which derives from the experience of ejaculatory sex, from a particular *organisation* of male sexuality, is simply projected, even under conditions of abstinence, onto the profile of 'what is'. A reorganisation of the form of sexual experience, even of what one abstains from, might have brought about a quite different relation to the 'light'.

To describe oneself as being *made* by the light might be *a* means of representing an experience, representing what it is like. That is to say, a person trained in the relevant practices may find themselves at a certain point as it were suspended in a medium of tremendous power and energy which presents itself as equally without them as within them, and see *why*, under such conditions, Augustine might gesture towards the image of a light by which he was made, a light beyond the order of phenomenal and reflective experience, upon which his existence depended, and from which he was by no means separate. But that is a way of intimating what it is *like*. If you are culturally predisposed to think in terms of a Creator such experiential language might seem to authenticate the tradition and (prematurely) announce the nature of what is experienced, foreclosing further exploration. If God is Creator, he is above his creation, he is extra-mundane, he is non-contingent and non-mutable. The experience under the description of being made *by* the light reinforces the judgment that the light is immutable, and seems to me to be the spiritual ground out of which talk of contingency and necessary being arises. But if the tradition itself depends upon and grows out of such experiences, then we can easily imagine how it might have gone differently. The current Dalai Lama, for instance, refers to *merging* with the light. It is an essential part of Augustine's claim that he has come to see 'what is', that he is not merely undergoing a kind of surge of subjectivity. But instead of saying that he was as it were made *by* the light, he might have said that he was made *of* the light. Someone may acknowledge that they had 'attained to what is' but deny that they were in the presence of God, or, better, deny that they yet had good reason to assert that they were. They might say they have attained to reality in the sense that they have come into the inner radiance of phenomena, to their effulgent interior, to what they themselves and their circumambient world really and truly are, in a region in which there course beings yet to be named.

The point I am trying to get at is that the talk of immutability is premature, even if we want to say that Augustine has gained access to 'how things really are', has made a discovery about what the one and only world is really like. The experience is too light, the theory too heavy. None of this, I should say, is intended as a conclusive discussion of the issues. It is meant as a sketch of what might be called philosophical meditation, and an attempt to show that it is compatible with *disagreement*. I have dwelt on this at length precisely in order to insist that we need radically to re-examine in our own idiom the phenomena associated with concentration of the person, and to find a way of coming to philosophical terms with the possibility of an associated disclosure of reality without uncritically or piously rehearsing how the tradition has sometimes made sense of it. Discovering the conditions which give rise to such language is not by any means to endorse it. Rational experiment and the processes of transformation may provide a better basis for a future philosophy of religion than the pillars of Faith and Reason as traditionally conceived.

I say that there is that blessed realm in which the most general features of contingent being appear to be absent, except that the arrival there was itself contingent upon conditions. There is no space for talk of *things*, of their coming into or going out of existence. Perhaps we have to leave it at that. It is not that there isn't anything we are referring to when we start to talk of necessary being, or of the eternal or the infinite, it is just that we say too much. It is not that we find what is *im*perishable or *in*finite, but that there is nothing upon which the *language of contingency* can gain a foothold, and so we turn that nothing into a something and find God too soon and know too much, reifying the inapplicability of the language of mundaneity.

Isn't what is really happening in this kind of meditation that we have reached a state of consciousness that is 'beyond the world' in the sense that it has withdrawn from it in intensity, from objects, from discursive thinking, into silence, into the mind's 'natural light'. We shouldn't make our own most intense consciousness into God, and nor, if we meet anyone there, should we assume that it is God. God is not met, in any case, but is a condition of experience beyond experience. And isn't the point of such withdrawal into intensity a refreshed return into extensity, a seeing the world again for the first time and under the aspect of beauty, which arouses compassion as well as joy, and is the impetus for action.

2

Caught up to God by his beauty, Augustine was torn away by his own weight, the weight of his sexual habit, and though he crashes with a groan into inferior things, he declares: 'but with me there remained a memory of you'. Augustine's previous enjoyment (of God) conditions the direction of his erotic quest. His desires are re-ordered around his *remembered* experience, which functions as a representation of the goal, in a manner reminiscent of Plato's ascent in the *Symposium*. But Augustine implicitly qualifies Diotima's account by showing us that the erotic ascent to absolute beauty is also an erotic *return*.

This qualification, indeed, makes sense of the Platonic account, since the enjoyment of 'absolute beauty' or 'beauty itself' becomes a *given*, even if only as remembered and fleetingly known. Now Augustine's 'seeing the light' is presented as an experience in which he also discovers what *he* is, that is to say, it includes a discovery of what it is to be a human being at all. If his experience is one of a disclosure of 'what is' it is at the same time a disclosure of what *we* are in relation to it: 'our hearts are restless till they rest in thee' defines us, gives us the trajectory which constitutes us, albeit in theistic terms we may not all want to follow. Implicit in the account is a conception of personhood which shows it to be oriented towards, and re-ordered by, the attainment to what is, the attainment of wisdom. To put it crudely, contemplation, tracked by meditational thought, is supposed to lead us to the attainment of wisdom, to knowledge of how things really are, and into what we are in relation to that. The danger of meditation is that we should come to think that the withdrawal of consciousness from the world brings about union with the one or realisation of *Brahman-Atman* or the Godhead, reifying the absence of the world, finding out 'how things really are' *there* and not in the world. Whereas really it helps us to see the world *not* under the domination of the obscuring passions, if only evanescently, and wisdom lies in an essential alliance with virtue, as the obscuring passions are gradually cleared away. And this leads us to the conversational, inter-personal axis of philosophy, where we need to start balancing the need for sexual continence against the need for sexual arousal.

The absence of wisdom is constituted by ignorance of 'what is' and by attachment to other things, a disordered hierarchy of preference. Philosophical thought, in a contemplative context, leads to insight, to wisdom and virtue, and philosophical *conversation* will therefore be *essentially* a matter of what Kierkegaard calls 'indirect communication', a relationship between a teacher and a pupil in which the pupil is initiated into the processes which lead to the independent discovery of what really is and the consequent re-ordering of desire through the skilful intervention of the one who knows. But what is the motivation of the teacher, or, indeed, the pupil? The answer in the *Phaedrus* (1973) is that it is essentially *erotic*. But that is by no means a straightforward answer. The erotic object, the object of desire, relates to the attainment of wisdom, to a conception of personhood as completed in wisdom. The teacher is attracted to the person of the pupil in their aptness for wisdom, the pupil by that of the teacher in their perceived wisdom. The context is clearly a perilous locus of illusion and betrayal, as Kierkegaard recognised, and there is little in 'the Platonic books' about such matters, or the misery of failure, a point well made by Augustine. But the form of the mutual attraction which constitutes the philosophical dialogue, the philosophical flirtation, has both an immediate and a reflective aspect. That is to say, the immediate focus of *eros* is determined by the reflective conception of what constitutes the person to whom one is attracted. The attraction is mediated by the conception of personhood, established in experience, under which the exchange occurs. In that case, *physical* attraction becomes a merely contingent aspect of the philosophical relationship, and where it is present, the nature of the physical arousal is determined by how much of the *person* is capable of arousal.

Suddenly you start to see what is there and what is really happening. In dependence upon concentration or *samadhi* arises knowledge and vision of things as they are. *Samadhi* brings about a condition in which consciousness is not dominated by the *klesas*, and so you can see what was there all the time but obscured from view, not what was 'metaphysically' there, but what surrounds you, what we are doing to each other, and so on. And then the state of *samadhi* is lost, the *klesas* return, and what we had seen cannot be retrieved, except that we have the memory of life perceived under the aspect of beauty, even though we cannot thus perceive it now, we have the sense of a contrast, which is a motivation to return to *samadhi*, not as an end in itself but as a means of vision.

I am starting to see that I am *arguing* with Plato and Augustine, at the moment of a false turn. The beauty of consciousness in its greatest concentration is not the ultimate, transcendental aim of the soul, but it *is* the soul, under the condition upon which depends a return to the world with a ripening wisdom and virtue. And maybe the 'world' is expanded under this condition in another way, psychic realities emerge, perhaps, the angelic orders waiting. I talk of the 'soul itself', but the point is that we cannot *say* that it is or is not in union with God or *Brahman*. But this is the whole burden of Buddhism, that thinking in terms of *union* we look the wrong way, not seeing that the concentration of our being is an orientation towards *action*, our spirituality is to be found in the nature of our attitude to temporal things (Simone Weil), now seen from a place not previously available. I used to think that *samadhi* was the condition of final revelation. Now I see, I think, that it is a picture of a gradual attainment, a task, something to be consolidated, something to become perfected or fully accomplished, *parinispanna*.

Concentration or *samadhi* is the condition under which the human person is awakened or aroused: the standard by which we measure that degree is determined by the extent of our appropriation of the erotic ascent itself. In order to explain what I am trying to say here about the relation between concentration and sexual arousal we need to go by an indirect route, moving between Augustine and Plato, through a partial re-telling of Plato along Augustinian lines, reconstructing the scenes of the *Phaedrus* by returning the memory of absolute beauty to this world. In Plato it is in the midst of sexual activity, in the course of a person's sexual life, that the processes come about by which the vision of absolute beauty is attained. It is not an accident that in the allegory 'she' is seen on her throne attended by chastity. Sexual emission and chastity represent the beginning and the end of a single road in which a person is aroused by the sight of beauty. Plato and Augustine both acknowledge a correlation between the degree of *sexual continence* and the ability to sustain the enjoyment of absolute beauty, the ability to attain to what they then take to be 'what is'. But what they also implicitly acknowledge is some relationship between *sexual arousal* and the experience of contacting reality, made explicit in Augustine's case by the sexual language projected onto his experience. When Socrates connects the allegory of the charioteer and the pair of horses to the relationship between the lover and the beloved, the *erastes* and the *eromenos*, he makes much of the necessity for brutal treatment of the 'lustful horse': he talks of a violent tugging on the reins, the charioteer

jerks the bit from between the teeth of the lustful horse, drenches his abusive tongue and jaws with blood, and forcing his legs and haunches against the ground reduces him to torment. Finally, after several repetitions of this treatment, the wicked horse abandons his lustful ways: meekly now he executes the wishes of his driver, and when he catches sight of the loved one is ready to die of fear. So at last it comes about that the soul of the lover waits upon his beloved in reverence and awe. (1973, 62 [254])

As a result of this calamitous remedy 'the wicked horse abandons his lustful ways' so that the soul of the lover, implausibly in such circumstances, 'waits upon his beloved in reverence and awe'. This description already gives us two phases of sexual desire and enjoyment, which explain the purpose of Plato's remedy, the impulse towards ejaculation, and the experience of 'reverence and awe'. The two phases are clearly in tension, in the sense that the urge towards ejaculation brings the encounter to an end in its own terms, and the experience of reverence and awe are affective states that determine, according to their relative strength, their own *non-ejaculatory* bodily condition, though the power of this condition of body and sensibility is weakened by the practice of ejaculation.

I say 'calamitous remedy', but I believe I have taken Plato the wrong way, just as the tradition always has. Of course there is a hatred of the flesh here, but our view of it can be tempered by the thought that the account *expresses anguish*, wishes, not an actual remedy, anguish at something vital being undermined.

For the situation as Plato represents it is clearly one in which the lustful horse will dominate the situation unless it is inhibited by some form of forcible intervention. Plato does not seek to establish the possibility of non-ejaculatory sexual activity as a phase in the integration of sexual energy. He does not have the idea of *integrating* the sexual arousal into what we might call the affective arousal. On the contrary, the sexual impulse must, on his view, be *forcibly subdued*. This may be contrasted with the *forceful redirection* presented by the Taoists. Needless to say, Plato's strategy would considerably reduce the sexuality and the affective vitality of the encounter. Even so, it is noteworthy that in Socrates' story the very possibility of 'waiting upon the beloved' is made to depend upon the prior activity of the lustful horse. His arousal is already a response to the beauty of the beloved, and *he* brings about the encounter:

so they draw near, and the vision of the beloved dazzles their eyes. When the driver beholds it the sight awakens in him the memory of absolute beauty; he sees her again enthroned in her holy place attended by chastity. (ibid.)

But why does the dazzling sight of the beloved awaken in the driver of the chariot *the memory of absolute beauty*? The obvious answer, if we retrieve the vision of the Goddess from the pre-existent life of the soul in a higher world, is that the lover is reminded by the sight of the boy of the vision of absolute beauty because the vision of absolute beauty *reminds him of the love of boys*, reminds him, that is to say, of the heightened state that belongs to the encounter with the beloved. The sight of the boy reminds him of absolute beauty 'enthroned in her holy place *attended by chastity*' because the vision of absolute beauty reminds him of that phase of sexual love and admiration whose continuance depends upon *continence*, the holding back from ejaculation. If we place the experience, and the *memory*, of absolute beauty in this life, what is yielded is, on the one hand, a powerful motivation towards an *erotic return* to what we now lack, and miss, represented in memory, and, on the other, a *reminder* of what we thus remember in the person of the beloved, the vision of whom dazzles our eyes. This brings us to an aspect of Plato's thinking which seems to merit criticism on the ground that the beloved is simply *used*, as a means of achieving this erotic return. The criticism will be well made if it cannot be shown that the erotic return is also an advance, in friendship, towards the gaining of wisdom and virtue.

But what we have to ask here is, *how is it* that we are reminded, by the sight of the beloved, of absolute beauty: or, the other way around, of the beloved, by absolute beauty? One of the connections between them is that they are both *objects of desire*, in the sense that arousal is involved in each case. This is not to equivocate over the term 'arousal', however. The concentration upon which the disclosure of being depends is precisely a form of arousal, a gathering into a unity out of multiplicity of vital forces, in which sexual arousal is included and integrated. The person who enters their innermost citadel, etc., and attains a certain degree of concentration is to that extent in a state of arousal of a kind that is continuous with a stable sexual arousal that can be integrated into and empower the affective centres. So the vision of the beloved, and contact with them, arouses both sexual and affective centres in a way that is similar to and continuous with the development of meditational concentration, whose *form* remains thus interpersonal. But I move ahead too rapidly with the suggestion that sexual arousal is integrated into and empowers the affective centres, since I referred earlier to a *tension* between the urge for consummation and the affective relation to the beloved, an affective relation, though, which is at least *enhanced* by the very urge with which it is initially in tension (the point of the lustful horse's importunity).

Plato's two pairs of lovers become relevant here, since we can locate them within the problem of this sexual-affective tension. They represent two possible responses. The second pair compromise with the lustful horse, and, as it were, give him his head from time to time. They are said to settle for honour rather than wisdom. However, their sexual activity 'does not carry with it the consent of their whole minds' (65 [256]). And the question we have to ask is, why not? In one way the answer is obvious, since Plato is operating already with a notion of what constitutes their whole mind (made manifest in the ascent to absolute beauty) that is precisely threatened by their sexual indulgence. On the other hand, one might say, *they* don't know that, unless we can say that their own emergent sense of themselves is made evanescent and elusive by their sexual practice.

As for the first pair of lovers, who prefer wisdom and virtue to the lesser goal of honour, the *erastes* at least, on our revised view, must be presumed already to be aware of a connection between the ascent and the need for continence, since the beauty of the *eromenos* is supposed to remind him of absolute beauty, and thus aware already also of a preference for the enhanced affective relation over the impulse towards sexual consummation. The enhanced affective relation is a reminder of the vision of absolute beauty because it involves some initial participation in the experience of concentration or *samadhi*. This felt preference gives point to the reiterated Platonic complaints against the agitation and frenzy of sex, which is taken to undermine the charged, and thus creative, encounter between lovers. But his first pair of lovers are nevertheless precisely lovers and Plato describes the bedding of the *eromenos* with an obviously experienced eye. Even in one another's arms they manage to oppose to the ejaculatory impulse 'the moderating influence of modesty and reason'. Thus

they will pass their time on earth in happiness and harmony; by subduing the part of the soul that contained the seed of vice and setting free that in which virtue had its birth they will become masters of themselves and their souls will be at peace. (65–6 [255–6])

But what is the secret of their rather implausible success? Martha Nussbaum (1987, 219) points out that the view is that

The best lovers are said to deny themselves sexual intercourse . . . because they feel that in intercourse they risk forfeiting other valuable non-intellectual elements of their relationship: the feelings of tenderness, respect and awe.

But the question, to put it bluntly, is how are they supposed to manage it, especially since, as she rightly says, 'sexual arousal seems to be an enabling part of the experience of growth'? It is surely right that they would take sexual intercourse to be a risk to other elements of their relationship, and these are surely elements, discovered in the sexual scene, which modify, as Martha Nussbaum says, their sense of how we are constituted as persons. That is to say, they discover reaches of their own minds available only in such relationship, and this must be part of the reason that the second pair of lovers cannot give their sexual activity their full consent. The risk of forfeiture, though, is not the only reason the first pair would want to avoid sexual consummation. The feelings of tenderness, respect and awe are reactions to the personal beauty of their partner, and the enhancement of these feelings in the state of arousal, the feeling of concentration and creativity, is an echo of the wisdom to which at least one of them wishes beyond all else to return, bringing the other with him. His avoidance of sexual consummation, as opposed to sexual arousal, is motivated by his desire not to subvert the possibility of return. This wisdom, the erotic relationship to it, and the virtue that proceeds therefrom are, as we have already seen, the real determinants for Plato of what constitutes us persons. They are thus a standard to measure benefit and harm. In waiting upon the beloved, we are told, the lover treats him with admiration, kindness and affection. The forces of the soul are focused and concentrated in, given form by, these attitudes and demeanours. They are concentrated in a state apt for the begetting of spiritual progeny, as Plato puts it in the *Symposium*. But this is a begetting which in its own right reveals possibilities of interpersonality that modifies still further the sense of what a person is that has already been changed by experience of the affective states conceived in relation to the beloved. This defining interpersonality, and its creativity, is an integral part of the *direction* of the ascent ideally completed in the contemplation of absolute beauty, which is itself further associated with creativity. The solicitousness of the *erastes* towards the *eromenos* will manifest itself in the attempt to bring wisdom and virtue to birth, since that will constitute the form of their well-being, the form of *anyone's* well-being. So philosophy in both its contemplative and interpersonal aspect is born out of a meeting of persons at a junction between sexual arousal and sexual continence.

But we have delayed confronting our sexual curiosity about our chaste pair of lovers. Strictly speaking, of course, they are not chaste, if we define chastity as the natural condition of a state of *eros* that transcends sexuality. Their sexual behaviour, then, is at least non-ejaculatory. But Plato's recipe seems radically implausible, not a recipe at all. As far as he is concerned they achieve this balance by 'subduing the part of the soul that contained the seeds of vice'. The implication is that in doing so they *liberate* the part of the soul in which virtue had its birth. This seems to misunderstand the relationship between the two, and it is precisely this that Nietzsche so unerringly fastens upon.

What is actually required is a situation in which sexual arousal *subsides*, without frustration, *in favour* of a more general arousal of the person, lends its energies to an arousal which it has itself engendered to some extent, and which focuses itself around the heart. Manifestly, there is a tension between the charged and creative atmosphere surrounding the pair of lovers, and their sexual arousal, even though the latter empowers the former. The tension remains unless the sexual arousal is integrated into the affective relation rather than discharged. The possibility of such integration is *reinforced* if there are *techniques* of integration, techniques for the drawing up of so-called sexual energy into the gathering concentration of the whole circuit upon which insight into reality is claimed to depend. The point, I think, is that the tension is capable of *resolving itself* in the sense that the concentration around the erotic return, which is already an intensification of the affective concentration charging the lovers, is capable of reaching a natural pitch of dominance which physically overrides the ejaculatory impulse. But this is not, as it were, the work of a night. In the absence of the methods of integration available in the Taoist tradition, for example, Plato's violent talk is perhaps inevitable. For someone in his position the stakes are high, though it is a calamitous inheritance if we receive it without even knowing what the stakes were supposed to be. We make our accommodations with the vital forces that run violently or fitfully through practical life, and maybe achieve a homeostasis that defines for us the possibilities of self-knowledge and experience. But our own experience is always prematurely the measure:

Thus the average man through mental sluggishness and the desire to conform can conceive of no other goal for his desire than ejaculation. (Sartre)

CHAPTER FIFTEEN

Uneasily, he retraces his steps . . .

I

I have tried to understand the issue of the strength of our moral responses by reference to the Greek virtues of *enkrateia* and *sophrosune* reflecting different modifications of sensibility: *akolasia, akrasia, enkrateia, sophrosune,* represent different moments in the development of the moral sentiments, from unschooled and narrow in scope, through the painful oscillations between control and lack of control, towards a dominant sensibility. The vacillation we experience between control and lack of control, *enkrateia* and *akrasia*, reflects an instability in our emotional life, in our capacity to respond, so that, to quote T. S. Eliot, 'Between the emotion and the response / Falls the shadow'. *Sophrosune* reflects, by contrast, a flourishing sensibility, the directions of whose attention dominate consciousness, so that there is no longer any inner conflict with the contrary inclinations that the enkratic individual defeats, and the akratic succumbs to.

My response to Hume's remark that 'morality is more properly felt than judged of' is that of course it is both judged of and felt. Critical judgment is implicit in the very idea of feeling – 'a tear is an intellectual thing'. As Hume himself (1978, 416) somewhat optimistically asserts, 'the moment we perceive the falsehood of any supposition . . . our passions yield to our reason without any opposition'. But *practical* judgment is also an element in the responsiveness of feeling to the situation that engages it. I have attempted to analyse the modal language of morality in a way which grounds it in our forms of motivation, rather than our forms of motivation in an unexplained modal language. Part of the problem with the early versions of emotivism was their promiscuous readiness to translate *all* 'ethical symbols' in terms of emotive meaning. They failed to see the functional diversity of such terms, and misidentified what made a purported moral statement a *moral* statement in the first place, looking to the form rather than the use. Modal auxiliaries like 'ought' and 'should' have a different use from those of necessity and impossibility, though the two sets of terms are related and overlap. We do not identify a moral judgment by its form alone, by the presence of an 'ought' or 'should' or even of a 'right' or 'wrong', but need to see its grounds and its context. Practical judgments about what we ought to do imply reasons for action, and these refer us to the intentional objects of emotions, which constitute the considerations which move us to act, and that, unsurprisingly, is how moral reasons motivate. The language of moral necessity and impossibility, by contrast, refers us to the 'compulsions of the soul', to the positive and negative impulses of our responses and to their vitality.

2

There is an issue about the *scope* of our moral sentiments, about the selectivity or partiality of their engagement in action, about the bias to the near. Morality is supposed to be not so biased, and that has seemed a further reason for denying that morality has much to do with feeling. The supposition though denies the possibility of the *education* or *correction* of feeling. This development occurs culturally and individually. The development of sensibility in the culture provides the measure of what needs to be corrected in the individual, as we shall see. Correction does not occur in the light of something *external* to feeling, say Reason, but in the light of the historical movement of feeling and judgment. But that the issue of scope is an issue at all is itself an interesting fact. Contemporary gestures of a somewhat wooden kind to universality as an intrinsic feature of 'the concept of morality' may distract us from seeing that the demand for it is an expression of an extraordinary *moral ideal* that has constituted a particular historical and political development, intimated in our spiritual traditions, and frequently received with incredulity. The universality of morality here is the ideal demand that *anyone's* well-being should count in our moral deliberations if our actions may affect it. We should distinguish this sense from the universalisation of Kant's imperative which requires us to ask whether we can coherently or rationally will that the maxim of our action become a universal law of nature. We may conclude that this demand of universalisation is a particular product of the universality thesis, since it seems to provide a test for what we are in principle prepared to will for rational beings. We should also distinguish the universality feature from the uni-

versalisability of moral judgment, which is a logical feature of the relationship between practical judgments and reasons for action. But
making universality a criterion of 'morality' requires us to regard cul-
tures that lack it as 'pre-moral'. It seems more reasonable to acknowledge their moralities and to see universality as a development *within*
morality.

3

There is, incidentally, an extraordinary relationship between the bias to
the near or partiality and the available descriptions under which the
moral sentiments may become engaged. Thus I may have an *immediate*
sympathy for a relative who struggles to face her approaching death, a
feeling for her as my family member. However, something else can dawn
at such moments, so that the immediate becomes *reflective*. This is the
real, and astonishing point that makes *aesthetic perception* the heart of
moral sensibility. Thus I may come to *understand* her struggle as *exemplifying* our common human condition. In referring to exemplification here
I intend it in the aesthetic sense of a vivid reverberation of the universal around the particular. I thus see her not just as my family member,
but as a fellow human being, and to that extent I discover the possibility
of feeling for *anyone* under that description, including myself. The point
is that the transition to universality here is a matter of a *revelation* which
broadens the descriptions under which my sentiments become engaged.
Thus even the plight of an enemy, which I may normally rejoice in, can
suddenly reveal itself as the plight of a fellow human being. This is
important, because I already know abstractly and with indifference that
this enemy is also a fellow human being: the revelation amounts to a leap
of the sentiment to seize on that description, whether I like it or not.
What is revealed is that their *human* plight is an object of feeling. It is in
this sense, then, that humanity becomes an end. In that sense, though,
so can other sentient beings become an 'end', so that we become *engaged*
by their status as 'fellow creatures' or 'fellow beings', and cannot continue to eat them, perhaps, with the same relish . . .

Now think of the love of moral beauty in the same way. An *eros* for
moral beauty, for the beauty to be found in souls, is already expressed in
universal terms; it articulates the transition from the desire for one particular body, to the perception of beauty, and the response to it, where it
is to be *found*. I can come to regard any body in the light of these new
terms of appreciation.

4

The historical specificity of this tendency towards universality, and its tension with the bias to the near, may be illuminated by reflecting on the terms in which Rousseau describes the transition from the State of Nature to the Civil Society in his *Social Contract*.

In effect the nascent citizen obliges himself (and alas the masculine pronoun is gender specific in this case) to temper his actions according to how they might affect the well-being of *any* other citizen, and not just that of himself or his own kith and kin. He obliges himself to be impartial. Thus we see how the notion of 'citizen' stretches us *towards* universality and away from narrow communalism, even though it does not carry us all the way, since citizens are state-specific. The issue about the *scope* of our moral sentiments turns on the development of the idea of a civil society and that of being a fellow citizen, and the issue about their *strength* on the distinction between citizen and subject. The two come together well in Rousseau's description of the 'remarkable change' that the transition from the state of nature to the civil society brings about.

One is at once a citizen and a subject just because the developing self as citizen has to make the resistant self as unwilling subject do what the citizen recognises to be just. Here we can see how the human oscillation between *akrasia* and *enkrateia* has become politically acknowledged and institutionalised, so that 'necessitation' becomes the political reality of justice backed by the force of law. Thus just when the scope of the moral sentiments is broadened and stretched we also see them weaken and falter.

But the point is not to look for the sources of a motivation to act morally, as though morality were to be understood independently of what might motivate us to take it seriously, but to see how what we call morality can itself be understood as a set of motivations, a matter of the primeval distribution by the gods of *aidos* and *dike*, 'shame' and 'justice'. If we see these primitive reactions as embedded in human nature, then we move decisively away from a conception of morality as depending upon an independent picture of human nature, as a device for counteracting limited sympathies, say, and towards a conception of morality in which these reactions can be seen as capable of a development which is also a development of human nature itself.

This is in fact Rousseau's conception, since the 'remarkable change in man' that the transition from the state of nature to the civil society is supposed to bring about is a change from being a 'stupid limited animal' to becoming 'a creature of intelligence':

> it puts justice as a rule of conduct in the place of instinct, and gives his actions the moral quality they previously lacked. It is only then, when the voice of duty has taken the place of physical impulse, and right that of desire, that man, who has hitherto thought only of himself, finds himself compelled to act on other principles, and to consult his reason rather than study his inclinations. (Bk 1, 8)

What we are supposed to gain from the transition is interesting: our faculties are exercised and developed, our minds are enlarged and *our sentiments ennobled*. In other words, the transition is also towards an alteration of sensibility. The contrast is no doubt too stark, but its proto-Kantian ring is clear enough. On the one hand instinct, physical impulse, desire, inclination, on the other justice as a rule of conduct, morality, duty, right and reason. The introduction of reason on the favoured side of this dichotomy, and it is a dichotomy that needs to be interrogated, need not imply that Rousseau failed to see a place for instrumental rationality in the pursuit of desires. Presumably the point is that the satisfaction of desires previously taken for granted becomes itself a subject of rational reflection in the light of one's commitment to justice.

This might just be interpreted as an instrumental rationality in pursuit of larger ends, but it is worth saying on Rousseau's behalf that these are larger ends that depend upon a *theoretical* realisation of one's social identity as a member of the Body Politic.

This is connected to the idea of aesthetic perception, revelation and the training of sensibility. One realises that one has a social and not merely private identity, not just in an abstract way, which is compatible with indifference and resentment, but through a switch of emotional engagement. Here, though, realisation amounts to a (rational) *conversion*, to a dominant way of seeing oneself, a finding one's social identity to be the locus of an emergent sensibility.

What, so I eagerly sign up to the local *armée révolutionnaire*? All right, no, you don't, because everything turns on the *terms* of the identity to which you are converted, on the nature of the emergent sensibility. That is not to be understood in terms of 'temperance' but in terms of *appreciation* as I have tried to elucidate it. It is the domination of consciousness of that attitude to persons that renders one 'temperate'. I need to say that again, because I am sure that Robespierre was 'temperate' in the relevant sense, his mind dominated by ideological forces of a kind that swept other impulses from his mind. I need to recall that Schiller wrote his *Aesthetic Education* as a response to the Terror, and sought to show that the danger of political change was that the new formation would simply reduplicate the one-sidedness of the psyche that initiated it, so that we need to overcome the fragmentation of the personality first.

5

What I wish to try to do is show how morality may be understood as the product of powerful feelings in the face of social experience, as grounded in historical forms of relationship with others and the world. We need to acknowledge the totality of these feelings and experiences, since otherwise we shall end up emasculated or blind. Moral language arises out of our responses to these experiences. If I may deploy the key term for Rousseau's State of Nature, what we have to deal with are the vicissitudes of our collective experience of the arbitrary rule of the strongest, whether on the one side or the other, with our need for mastery and control, and with our contrasting enjoyment of relationships founded not on force but consent and appreciation.

What we call 'morality' has at least a twofold aspect, which corresponds to conditions that human beings have sought emancipation from, and the forms of independent and participatory action that emancipation may enhance. It comprises a defensive, reactive (and exclusive) mode on the one hand, and a constructive, creative (and integrative) mode, on the other. Both modes need to be understood historically and, historically, they need themselves to be integrated.

I want to highlight *sources* of motivation and the *formation* of sensibility and relationship at a collective as well as individual level. But the essential preliminary point will turn on the idea of formative collective *experience and memory*, which generates an evaluative language constituted by a set of practical judgments governed by the motivational necessities of response. These responses are to two different kinds of experience, that of an 'oppressive' coercion or domination, on the one hand, and that of a 'liberating' participation in collaborative creative endeavour on the other. *Both of these forms of experience have a distinctive and memorable 'taste' to which we react*, on the one hand recoiling, on the other seeking to cherish and preserve.

I hope it is clear that I am not simply making a 'moral' move here, deploring oppression and exploitation. I am seeking the sources of 'morality' *in* such experience and the reaction to it at a collective level. So I am not saying that oppression and exploitation are wrong and therefore we should act against them, but rather that our calling them 'wrong' is an expression of a primal struggle against them, an expression, indeed, which some groups and individuals still do not dare even to voice to themselves. This primal struggle depends in part for its identity on what is also at stake when we come under the rule of arbitrary power. It is not a matter of an 'imperative' belonging to some prior and unexplained conception of morality, but of a necessity of recoil. The *content* of the Kantian imperative, however, *is* relevant to this historical condition, since it makes the master–slave relation the pivotal category of moral criticism, or better, that relation is the paradigm of what the imperative excludes. In summary form, we could characterise the hostile reaction to domination by others, to what it makes us suffer and the possibilities it denies us, as a passion for *justice* (a different notion, as Simone Weil pointed out, from that of a passion for one's rights). Such a reaction is essentially collective, the response of one group to oppression by another.

To use Timothy Sprigge's expression, but in an ethical context, *there is something that it is like* to be at the receiving end of the law of the strongest. I should emphasise the sustained *brutality* of this kind of regime. One is not concerned simply with the 'clinical precision' of the use of force in the pursuit of group or national or individual interests, but the use also as an instrument of war or policy, of terror, atrocity, massacre, 'ethnic cleansing', the unleashing of dreadful forces onto the streets, entering each domestic dwelling, wreaking havoc wantonly, revelling in the horror of the victims, and so on. The point about such wanton and such calculated brutality is that, like famine and natural disaster, *it is experienced with horror, remembered with grief, and anticipated with dread*. That, no doubt, has always been part of its point. There is something that it is like to be at the receiving end, and the victims are *strongly motivated* to avoid its repetition, either through slavish submission and progressive demoralisation in which the power of independent action is gradually lost, or, by the action of resentment and indignation, through rebellion and concerted self-assertion. The pendulum swings between assertion and demoralisation, in complex ways which depend upon local conditions. Resentment in the face of the forced submission or obedience to the will of *another* reflects a commonly endured adversity and the denial of expression and *Bildung* for oneself and one's own people. It also breeds the desire for revenge, for answering atrocity with atrocity.

6

My talk of motivational necessity, to reiterate the point, is related to the modal utterances that express these attitudes. Our judgments express recoil and revulsion as well as, sometimes, a natural bonding and solidarity. Thus they include attitudinal judgments about what we *must* avoid or prevent, fused with practical, strategic and tactical judgments about what in particular *ought* to be done. But this form of bonding and mutual sympathy is the solidarity only of a class and is thus only partially integrative. Members of the oppressed class identify themselves in an implicitly communal and conflictual way, over against the hostile other and around the interests and passions by which they have been formed in the crucible of social life. This tends to limit human sympathies to within the group thus defined – the group with the emancipatory common interest, for example. It is not that members of such a community cannot recognise in an abstract way that they are also human beings, nor that they cannot be stirred at all by sympathy for the plight of a fellow creature. The point is that their *dominant* emotional engagement is with the interest that defines them over against the perceived or real hostility of their enemies. And there is a powerful atavistic satisfaction in the destruction of those enemies, a deep pleasure in their slaughter.

Memory and experience play a central determining role in the emergence and the maintenance of the motivations I have mentioned. We respond in determinate ways to 'oppressive' experience (we precisely *find* it 'oppressive') and remembering it, as a group, say, in songs and stories, is an important part of the way the realities, and our responses to them, as well as the possibilities of response, and their various consequences, are kept before the mind of the community, and transmitted to a new generation. These songs and stories also, of course, provide what Marcuse calls 'beautiful images of liberation' and can encode emergent attitudes that extend people's sympathies across classes. People are motivated strongly to do what will prevent repetition of experiences that have caused horror, and that motivation has been expressed in the arising of practices and institutions, the winning of rights, checks and balances, as well as in the inherited language, which expresses, in its evaluations, the attitudes I have mentioned. No doubt this will work at an unconscious as well as at a conscious level. Evaluative terms or special resonances isolate and identify the significant phenomena, the realities we want to avoid and the realities we wish to preserve. Such language is both descriptive and expressive, determining a class of phenomena and marking a collective attitude to them.

The irony of the role that memory and experience play in the development of a culture is that the new generation, for whom the relevant forms of experience have become relatively remote, and the memory dim, is still initiated from childhood into the attitudes, the language and the practices that express or arise out of earlier communal responses to such experience. They are initiated into the forms and practices of motivational necessities, but the primal motivating experience is not *theirs*, the language is not expressive of *their* response to a reality they have not had to endure, and do not remember ('Irish need not Apply'). The initiation process has to be supplemented by sanctions. It is easy to see, then, how they will fail to see the point of particular forms of vigilance, or be unmoved by the initial urgent impulse of their class towards cohesion, bonding or solidarity. *The value discourse will pass them by because the conditions of that discourse are no longer present or remembered*, and their initiation into it is an onerous, even harmful imposition, especially when the form of their own experience is taking them in a different direction. Disintegration follows unless there is an alternative, constructive morality of *Bildung*, which generates its own forms of solidarity and commitment.

7

What I am calling a constructive and integrative morality of *Bildung* and expression is generated by a quite different range of experiences from the one that determines the reactive and defensive mode. The key contrasting *motifs* are the teacher–pupil relation rather than that of the master–slave, and the idea of treating humanity as an end. The latter should, I think, be understood as partly constituted by the willingness to enter into sets of relationships that depend upon mutual consent rather than *force majeure*. We may think of it as a 'respect for persons', but only so long as we construe that as a function of sensibility allied to appreciation, rather than as the object of an imperative. Resentment and sympathy may well be the dominant emotions of the defensive mode of morality, and we need to remember Nietzsche's criticisms of an overvalued sympathy. There is some reason to think of sympathy as essentially a reciprocal attitude of mutual support belonging to partners in adversity or affliction, and this makes sense of his remark that sympathy is not a major value in the lives of the masters, who are more concerned with the disciplines of *techne* than with a freedom they have always had. Sympathy may thus be distinguished from compassion (or *karuna*) which is a feeling that may be aroused by the plight of the less fortunate, though presumably mixed with remorse, in the case of those whose class is responsible for the oppression. Perhaps the dominant moral sentiments of the constructive mode are benevolence, appreciation and the kind of 'sympathy' marked by the Sanskrit *mudita*, an attitude of sympathetic joy in the flourishing of another. Again experience and memory are involved and the impulse is to preserve and protect the relationships that arise around *Bildung, techne* and *poiesis*, their constitutive and emergent disciplines, virtues and values. There is something that it is like to be thus engaged. If people are excluded from these disciplines, and thus become truly *akolastoi*, then they are denied access to the conditions for this essentially integrative dimension of moral life. It is integrative just because it is non-divisive, since it is generated out of irenic activities that at least do not inhibit the scope of the moral sentiments. The reactive mode, on the other hand, depends upon and reinforces a hostile and wounded consciousness. The domination of consciousness by the categories of exclusion, their angry rhetoric and hostile emotions, *does* inhibit the scope of the moral sentiments, and already entails an embattled and divided psyche.

Such domination is sometimes suspended through the work of *poiesis*, the spell of artistic representations, as Schiller pointed out. Sometimes it drops its guard through the spell of *eros* and the pillow talk of noble *logoi*. Experience shows that successful education depends upon an attitude of appreciative expectancy rather than coercive expectation, a distinction which may recall Heidegger's (1977) discussion of the different stances that are possible towards nature. The preoccupation with mastery and control, with 'challenging-forth', leaves aspects of reality concealed from view, real aspects whose appearance or non-concealment depends upon a more 'receptive' attitude. A similar preoccupation in the context of human relationships negates or refuses the expressive reality of those who are made mere instruments, and endangers the same reality in those who make them so, because such an expressive reality is revealed in an interaction, a 'conversation'.

The constructive mode of morality belongs to a culture of reflection and creative collaboration and participation and it gives rise to its own set of natural attitudes and related practical necessities. Forms of activity have arisen which depend on co-operation and the recognition of mutual dependence. The relationships here are not of master and slave, of arbitrary command and enforced obedience, but of partners, fellow participants, masters and apprentices or pupils in the transmission and development of a tradition. Here forms of human relationship are set up and established around education and common endeavour, the transmission of skills, learning and adapting to the ways of nature and animals, the acquisition of knowledge and understanding, the passing on of experience, the teaching of wisdom, and so forth. There are certain real features of such activities and processes, to which the human person has to give ground. A predisposition, in practical contexts, to the use of force to gain what one wants has to give way to patient observation and awareness of cause and effect, the processes by which things are brought forth. The rhythms of process have to be learnt and taught, and human relationships themselves are discovered to be of the same kind, as friendships form and develop according to processes that it is not for any individual to invent but only to discover. Spiritual traditions arise around the discovery of the conditions upon which particular states of mind and their expression in action and demeanour depend, in which the same need for patient observation and attention to real processes has to be learnt. The acquisition of wisdom is a matter of the acquisition of forms of knowledge that depend upon the states of being of the postulant, a fact, if it is one, that has itself to be discovered.

8

What we are looking for now, after the taste and experience of oppression and domination, is a contrasting taste of partnership in the context of human growth and development around education and the transmission of knowledge, and the relationships that are thus engendered. These relationships also have a determinate 'taste', as do the relationships founded in force, and whereas we are motivated, at least as victims, to avoid, to protect ourselves from, the rule of mere force, in the present case we are motivated to hold onto the relations of creative and reflective participation; they are forms whose loss we mourn if we have become established in them, because they precisely form *us*.

But such historical formation determines our conception of the humanity we might be expected to treat as an end, whether in our own person or in that of any other. It needs to be emphasised that people who seek to preserve humanity are to be welcomed or held at bay according to the conception of humanity they carry around with them. Someone who suffers from the kind of imbalance or onesidedness Schiller and Nietzsche describe so well *will seek to inscribe it in those to whom they offer aid.*

9

But there is a shocking corollary to this, which is that the attitudes, the motivational stances, the practical necessities, depend upon experience of and participation in the relevant activities themselves. In the absence of the relevant experience, the value discourse loses its grip because of the *absence* of what it *expresses*. Better, it is seen never to have had a grip in the absence of these conditions. The forms of relationship that I have attempted to describe, and the motivational necessities that belong to them and are expressed in the language, *cannot be sustained* in isolation from the activities from which they spring. Thus an appeal to these necessities and imperatives will inevitably *fail* if they are made to people who have been *deprived* of the possibility of personal development in the context of these activities, if they have been deprived of formation around participation in creative work and reflection. Participation in these forms of activity is a *condition* of much of what we call morality, though we have forgotten this condition and think that 'morality' stands by itself, an imperative, a 'requirement', for all. It is pointless to address people deprived of apprenticeship and a non-oppressive 'education', or even stable and affectionate nurture, in the value language that derives from these, and to decry the rents in the moral fabric of society as though this can be repaired by 'teaching people the difference between right and wrong'. It misunderstands real connections, though people can be forced or conditioned into a kind of submission; 'the use of force alone', however, as Edmund Burke remarked, 'is but *temporary*'. If people stand outside the participating conditions of the motivational necessities I have referred to, then moral appeals in that language will simply mock them, because it is embedded in a form of life rendered unavailable to them. Those who are thus appealed to, moreover, will have no reason to take such appeals seriously, since they cannot recall them to the sense of what they have been deprived of. The reasons are not reasons for *them* because the reasons relate to motivations that depend upon a form of life they have no experience of.

It does not follow from my account that participation in educative formation makes people *good*. Such participation is simply a condition for minimal engagement with the value discourse it generates. There is no question here, either, that this perspective of what Mill would have called the moral sentiments is the *right* perspective, as though some independent standard of measurement were available. In that case it may be thought that what I have said here leaves us with an arbitrary choice of values. But where we stand in this regard is not a matter of choice, but depends upon the formative experience and *praxis* which grounds the values. The 'moral fabric of society' can only be repaired by restoring the infrastructure upon which moral concepts depend, by restoring the possibilities of participation in creative and educative work. Whether that is still possible is another question.

10

We have seen the traditional argument that the totality of contingent things is itself contingent and requires for its explanation the existence of a non-contingent or necessary being, God. The problem with this formulation is that we are talking about the wrong totality, since we identify contingency by reference to its conditions. The totality of contingent things is of course a totality of things that are contingent upon something else, but there is no implication that what they are contingent upon must themselves be contingent on something else again: the criterion of contingency is that there is a condition. The true totality is that of contingent things and the natural conditions upon which they depend.

It begs the question to assert that *this* totality, of what is contingent, and the conditions upon which they are contingent, is or must be contingent on something else that lies beyond it. On the other hand, it begs the question to deny it. The issue is indeterminable. What we can say, however, is that the only thing we can *ascertain* to be *not* dependent upon conditions, to be unconditioned, is that things arise in dependence upon conditions. This is true whether there is a God or whether there is not, since if there is a God then he is *the* condition of contingent things, and if there is not, then there are conditions anyway. But whether there is a God cannot be determined whereas the realities of conditionality can be.

It is interesting that the traditional formulation of *pratityasamutpada* or dependent arising is the unquantified 'things arise in dependence on conditions'. This leaves space for conditions that are not themselves dependent upon anything else (that do not themselves 'arise') so they have the same status as the non-contingent natural conditions we have deployed against the cosmological argument. What is unconditioned is the reality of conditioned co-production.

And what is the point of saying *that*, except that it pushes us away from the question of whether there is a God, and turns the question of the unconditioned, and the attention of the questioner, back to what is *conditioned*, to the intimate realities of conditionality as it bears upon human being, afflicted by craving, aversion and ignorance, or graced by wisdom and virtue.

I I

Akshobhya, rampant, wrathful, perfectly still, mirroring wisdom, dark blue Buddha, out of the east, in meditation my body calmly, strongly, arranges itself into kingly, rampant, wrathful form, and his consort, the dakini, I am her, and I am him, becoming the dakini, becoming Akshobhya, their sexual union, but I am painfully surpassed, the human body too weak, the force of their energies, marriage to the Dakini, the natural spouse of this figure of terror, *Akshobhya* my perfection, my future, enormity of thought, a blasphemy, my reflection in this mirror, held up by a wrathful figure, myself then the object of wrathful compassion, myself then the wrathful figure. Is this my beginning and my end, a picture of the stages of the ascent to beauty itself, of the *nidanas*, the spiral of causal links towards *bodhi* and *nirvana*, an awakening beyond the dark passions.

There are images, words, remembered scenes, that beckon or attract, in advance of one's understanding what they mean. Perhaps this attraction, this being beckoned, is essential to the spiritual life, the real function of symbols, which have started their work before one knows how or why. There is something that calls, one doesn't know what, but one is still compelled and drawn. I am susceptible and also sceptical. I remain with my practice, altered by it in palpable ways, but with no guarantee that I shall act *well*, and when I sit I still have to ask, who, if I called out . . . ? So the form of my meditation is partly still that of a great question, whether like calls to like, and I know too well what I am like myself.

Dukkha or unsatisfactoriness, the grating roar of pebbles, appears to be news from the future, a kind of pressure of growth, the world impinging on us, moving our souls, causing us to start to respond, before we yet know what world is there or that we are responding to it. Remorse, uneasiness, notice of *neuer Anfang, Wink und Wandlung*, first pangs of transformation, towards wisdom and virtue, a trajectory by which we are constituted.

So what accommodation have I made with the thought that has held me from the beginning, that in dependence on *samadhi* arises knowledge and vision of things as they are? There is no point in being *told* how things are if knowledge alters or depends on alteration, if it depends on a certain state and that state is absent. Nevertheless the so-called con-

ceptual answer is simply that things arise in dependence upon conditions. And seeing how things are is one among those things that thus
arise. We live in the midst of contingency, it is in our very selves, that is
all we know on earth . . . except that the claim is that we *don't* know it,
because we have not lived through its reality, not travelled the path of
change from one condition to the next that our dependence on conditions shows us. So to know dependent arising is to know what arises in
dependence upon what, to have realised its possibilities and to have
changed. Meanwhile, we have intimations, evanescent understanding,
pictures of the possibilities that depend on conditions, pictures that are
to draw us along the path of the self's conditionality from a grasping to
a perfected consciousness. We have the picture of a concentrated pitch
of being, that draws us towards the reality it depicts, and towards the
beauty of that reality, of that pitch of being, which alters the ordering
of all our desires. But this is not wisdom, nor is it virtue, it is their source,
a condition of their possibility, which gives us work to do. We cannot say
that there we have fused with Beauty itself, or with the Godhead or the
One, nor can we say that we have not, but the point of turning our gaze
there and drawing towards it, is that we might travel far enough to turn
our gaze back, upon the world we had to leave behind, in order thus to
see it clearly, with feeling intellect, to return to it and then act as our
occasions demand, with *metta* or love, in the form of *mudita* or *karuna*, the
latter, compassion, the former, sympathetic joy. We are unworlded first
and then reworlded.

And yet, although I say we have no grounds for talk of *union*, maybe
I am still not seeing the real point of 'non-duality' and am too resistant
to talk that goes beyond the intensest pitch of concentration. The application or *emergence* of a distinction between subject and object depends
upon conditions that we do not discover until the end. Meditational
experience leads us into the unfamiliar, but perhaps also to a position
from which the familiar becomes strange. We have the intuition of a
state of the world in which we are aware of its unity rather than its
differentiation, from a position within that unity. So, the experience of
what there is in its unity, but *not*, however, of a union with something else
beyond it. It is not just that we reach the highest pitch of consciousness,
in which we are no longer aware of subject and object, but that there is
also an experience of entering into the silent interior of the world and
disappearing as a separate, independent being, and yet remaining
conscious, and *then* we return. I saw the formation of the world and its
demise, the beginning and the end of all contingent things, thrown out

of the depths of reality, to begin and end, to form and re-form, according to laws they had not fathomed, the pounding waves of high seas that dashed against rocks, the rearing of the mountains out of the oceans, the screams of enormous winds, which cease in a sudden silence, before the outbreak of consuming fires: and spread across the dark skies, filling the heavens, there reposed the silvered head of a glorious Bodhisattva, his eyelids delicately closed in an inward smile, his head encrusted with pearls, which, in time, broke free and floated into nothingness: then, at last, the face also broke up, the parts floating, drifting, melting away.

References

Allott, K. (ed.) 1979. *Arnold: The Complete Poems*, London, Longman (Second Edition edited by Miriam Allott)

Aristotle, *Nicomachean Ethics*, 1955. Harmondsworth, Penguin

Arnold, Matthew, 1932, *Culture and Anarchy* (ed. Dover Wilson), Cambridge, Cambridge University Press

   1873, *Literature and Dogma: An Essay Towards a Better Apprehension of the Bible*, London, Smith, Elder and Co

Augustine, 1991, *Confessions* (trans. Chadwick, Henry, 1991), Oxford, Oxford University Press

Batchelor, Stephen, 1997, *Buddhism Without Beliefs*, New York, Riverhead Books

Benn, Gottfried, 'Ein Wort' in Bridgewater, Patrick (ed.) 1963, *Twentieth Century German Verse*, Harmondsworth, Penguin

Blackburn, Simon, 1984, *Spreading the Word*, Oxford, Clarendon Press

Bradley, F. H. 1988, *Ethical Studies*, Oxford, Clarendon Press

Braithwaite, Richard, 1971, 'An Empiricist's View of the Nature of Religious Belief' in Mitchell, B. (ed.) *The Philosophy of Religion*, Oxford, Oxford University Press

Cupitt, Don, 1984, *The Sea of Faith*, London, BBC Publications

Elliott, R. K. 1973, 'Imagination in the Experience of Art' in Vesey, Godfrey (ed.) *Philosophy and the Arts, Royal Institute of Philosophy Lectures, Volume Six*, London, Macmillan

Guenther, Herbert, 1986, *The Life and Teaching of Naropa*, London and Boston, Shambhala

Haldane, J. J. (see Smart, J. J. C.)

Harrison, Andrew, 1973, 'Representation and Conceptual Change' in Vesey, Godfrey (ed.) *Philosophy and the Arts, Royal Institute of Philosophy Lectures, Volume Six*, London, Macmillan

Heidegger, Martin, 1971, 'The Origin of the Work of Art' in *Poetry, Language, Thought*, New York, Harper and Row

   1977, 'The Word of Nietzsche' in *The Question Concerning Technology and other essays* (trans. William Lovitt), New York, Harper and Row

Hume, David, 1978, *A Treatise of Human Nature*, Oxford, Oxford University Press

James, William, 1929, *The Varieties of Religious Experience*, London, Longmans, Green and Co.

Kant, Immanuel, 1952, *Critique of Judgment*, Oxford, Clarendon Press

Kenny, A. 1988, *God and Two Poets: Arthur Clough & Gerard Manley Hopkins*, London, Sidgwick and Jackson

Kierkegaard, Soren, 1968, *Concluding Unscientific Postscript*, trans. David F. Swenson and Walter Lowrie, Princeton, Princeton University Press

Kochumuttom, Thomas, 1982, *A Buddhist Doctrine of Experience*, Delhi, Motilal Banarsidass

Lawrence, D. H. 1950, *Selected Essays*, Harmondsworth, Penguin

Mackey, James, 1992, 'Moral Values as Religious Absolutes' in McGhee (ed.) *Philosophy, Religion and the Spiritual Life*, Royal Institute of Philosophy Supplement: 32, Cambridge, Cambridge University Press

Mackie, J. L. 1982, *The Miracle of Theism*, Oxford, Clarendon Press

Morrison, Robert, 1996, *Nietzsche and Buddhism*, Oxford, Oxford University Press

Nietzsche, Friedrich, 1968, *Twilight of the Idols* (trans. Hollingdale), Harmondsworth, Penguin

Nussbaum, Martha, 1987, *The Fragility of Goodness*, Cambridge, Cambridge University Press

Osborne, Catherine, 1994, *Eros Unveiled: Plato and the God of Love*, Oxford, Clarendon Press

Paton, H. 1948, *The Moral Law: Kant's Groundwork of the Metaphysic of Morals*, London, Hutchinson

Phillips, D. Z. 1966, *The Concept of Prayer*, London, Routledge

Plato, *The Republic* (trans. Lee, 1955), Harmondsworth, Penguin
   The Symposium (trans. Hamilton, 1951), Harmondsworth, Penguin
   Phaedrus (trans. Hamilton, 1973), Harmondsworth, Penguin

Plutarch, *Essays* (trans. Waterfield, ed. Kidd, 1992), Harmondsworth, Penguin

Rousseau, *Social Contract* (trans. Cranston, Maurice, 1968), Harmondsworth, Penguin

Sangharakshita, 1997, 'Buddhism Without Beliefs?' in *The Western Buddhist Review*, no. 2, Birmingham

Schiller, Friedrich, 1967, *On the Aesthetic Education of Man* (trans. Wilkinson and Willoughby), Oxford, Oxford University Press

Scruton, Roger, 1990, *The Philosopher on Dover Beach*, Manchester, Carcanet Press

Shantideva, *Bodhicaryavatara* (trans. Kate Crosby and Andrew Skilton, 1995), Oxford, Oxford University Press

Simpson, James, 1979, *Matthew Arnold and Goethe*, London, MHRA Texts and Dissertations Volume 11

Skilton, Andrew, 1994, *A Concise History of Buddhism*, Birmingham, Windhorse Publications

Smart, J. J. C. and Haldane, J. J. 1996, *Atheism and Theism*, Oxford, Blackwell

Squire, Aelred, 1973, *Asking the Fathers*, London, SPCK

Tanabe Hajime, 1986, *Philosophy as Metanoetics*, Berkeley, University of California Press

Tolstoy, Leo, 1987, *A Confession*, Harmondsworth, Penguin

Tugwell, Simon, 1984, *Ways of Imperfection: An Exploration of Christian Spirituality*, London, Darton, Longman and Todd

Valéry, Paul, 1980, 'Remarks on Poetry' in West, T. G. (ed. and trans.), *Symbolism: An Anthology*, London, Methuen

Wilhelm, Richard, 1972, *The Secret of the Golden Flower*, London, Routledge

Williams, Paul, 1989, *Mahayana Buddhism*, London, Routledge

Winch, Peter, 1987, *Trying to Make Sense*, Oxford, Basil Blackwell

Wollheim, Richard, 1973, *Art and the Mind*, London, Allen Lane

Index

rational ideas 102, 117, 118–19, 121–2, 124, 129
reason 72, 88, 89, 181, 185, 233, 241
   'tyranny of' 73, 75, 88, 187, 232
reasons 29, 76
renunciation (see self-renunciation)
Republic 73, 75, 88, 89, 171, 189, 191, 195, 197
Rilke 19n, 40, 113, 168
'righteousness' 97, 132–6, 141, 146
Robespierre 275
Romans, Epistle to 155
Rousseau 242, 249, 274, 275
Rugby Chapel 97, 99

samadhi 90, 98, 139, 163, 204, 258, 264, 268
samatha 35, 114, 162
Samdhinirmocana Sutra 206
sangha 38, 115, 133, 140
Sangharakshita 166–7
sanskharas, the 80, 219
Sartre 32
Schiller 72, 83, 86, 162, 168, 176, 233, 276, 281
Scholar Gypsy 97, 98, 99
The Scholar Gypsy 98
Schopenhauer 4, 81
Scrooge 136
Scruton, Roger 46
Sea of Faith, The 39–40
self-renunciation 135, 136, 146, 234
Shah, K. J. 201
Shantideva 175n
shibboleths 164n
Simpson, James 146
skandhas, the five 80
Skilton, Andrew 175n, 211, 212n
Smart, J. J. C. 159
smrti samprajanya 3, 52, 98, 99, 111, 114, 139
'self-power' (see also *jiriki*) 12, 13, 24, 52, 115, 144
Social Contract 274
Socrates 73–4, 75, 76, 78–80, 85–8, 98n, 171, 172, 183, 186–7, 192, 197, 232, 265
Sonnets to Orpheus 168
'Son of Man' 94
Sophocles 43
sophrosune 3, 51, 52, 72–75, 78, 79, 80, 98, 111, 114, 144, 171, 175, 179, 194, 232, 271
Spinoza 49, 66, 91
spirit 72, 88, 89
Sprigge, Timothy 247, 277
Squire, Aelred 44n, 145
sraddha 13, 100, 139, 164
Stanzas from the Grande Chartreuse 45, 93
State of Nature 274, 276
Steiner, Rudolf 118
Stevenson, R. L. 75n

'store-(house)-consciousness' (see *alaya-vijnana*)
'subject' 275
subject–object duality 205, 206, 210–17
   distinction 205, 206, 208, 210–17
sublime, the 119–20, 122, 125
Sun Tzu 77
Symposium 73–4, 171, 189–91, 194, 198, 263, 269

Tanabe Hajime 4, 10–14, 17, 18, 21, 24, 25, 39, 45, 52, 53, 78, 82, 99, 114, 133, 142, 144, 145, 179, 180, 231
tariki 12, 13, 14, 18, 39, 44, 94, 142, 145, 231
tathata 205, 206, 209, 217
teacher–pupil relation 279
techne 280
temperance 3, 52, 74, 78, 84, 90, 111, 114, 137, 171, 173, 175, 179, 187, 189, 192, 232
theism 156
Thomas, St (*see* Aquinas)
three natures, the 204–17
thumos 48, 52, 72
Timarchus 147
Tintern Abbey 126
Tolstoy 14–17, 20, 23, 24, 136, 238
Tom Jones 128
trisvabhav-nirdesa 204–17
Tugwell, Simon 4, 230, 231, 232
Twilight of the Idols 73, 87–8

Valéry 46, 105, 251
'values' 28–9, 50, 75
Vasubandhu 204, 210, 212, 216
van Gogh 105
'vajric body' 147
vipassana 35, 114
virya 26, 96, 100, 140

Weeping Woman 103
Weil, Simone 67, 128, 173, 219, 265, 277
Williams, C. J. F. 197
Williams, Paul 205, 206, 207, 209, 210–12, 214, 216
Winch 2, 173, 178, 180, 219
Wittgenstein 9, 82–3, 105, 122, 125, 137, 153, 194, 209, 218, 221–6
Wollheim, Richard 41n
Wordsworth 121, 126
Woyzeck 49

yathabhutajnanadarsana 163

zange 12, 13, 21
zange-do 12, 114
Zopyrus 171, 186, 232